ILLINOIS CLASSICAL STUDIES, VOLUME IV

ILLINOIS CLASSICAL STUDIES

VOLUME IV

1979

Miroslav Marcovich, *Editor*

UNIVERSITY OF ILLINOIS PRESS
Urbana   Chicago   London

Preface

Volume IV (1979) of *Illinois Classical Studies* comprises seven Greek and eight Latin studies. The typescript of No. 7 was found on the desk of the late Professor Mark Naoumides, in a form almost ready to print. Nos. 8, 10, 11, 12, and 15 are expanded versions of papers presented during the 108th Annual Meeting of the American Philological Association (held in New York, December 28–30, 1976), at the session dedicated to Post-Augustan Satire, as organized and chaired by Professor Mark O. Morford, of the Ohio State University.

The publication of this volume was possible thanks to generous grants by Dean Robert W. Rogers, Director Nina Baym, and the Greek Government. My gratitude to them is sincere and immense.

Urbana, 4 July 1978   Miroslav Marcovich, *Editor*

Contents

1

ΚΑΙ ΚΕ ΤΙΣ ΩΔ' ΕΡΕΕΙ:
An Homeric Device in Greek Literature

JOHN R. WILSON

Nothing is more characteristic of the Homeric respect for public opinion than those speeches within speeches that project what people might say after a given turn of events. So Hector in the *Iliad* addresses his spirit as he awaits the onrush of Achilles. If he retreats now, Poulydamas will be the first to reproach him for not having ordered a withdrawal earlier. But the reproach will also be general (22.105–108):

> ... αἰδέομαι Τρῶας καὶ Τρῳάδας ἑλκεσιπέπλους,
> μή ποτέ τις εἴπῃσι κακώτερος ἄλλος ἐμεῖο·
> "Ἕκτωρ ἧφι βίηφι πιθήσας ὤλεσε λαόν.'
> ὣς ἐρέουσιν ...

In Homer this procedure of projecting future opinion is a conspicuous part of the hero's armory, and its formal characteristics are a suitable object of parody. Thus Hegemon, the fifth century epic parodist, vows never again to venture abroad in search of lucre, but will scoop up money at home in Thasos. Never again will anyone be indignant when his wife bakes a holi-day loaf of meagre dimensions,

> καί ποτέ τις εἴπῃ σμικρὸν τυροῦντ' ἐσιδοῦσα·
> 'ὦ φίλη, ὡνὴρ μὲν παρ' Ἀθηναίοισιν ἀείσας
> πεντήκοντ' ἔλαβε δραχμάς, σὺ δὲ μικρὸν ἐπέψω.'

(P. Brandt, *Corpusculum poesis epicae ludibundae*, p. 44, 15–17 = Athenaeus 15.698 f.). The history of a device that is so recognizably Homeric and so linked to the values of a shame culture is of ethical as well as stylistic interest. In each case the approach to an Homeric pattern, or the deviation from it, to some extent defines the moral attitude of the speaker as well as the stylistic affinity of the writer.

Since in Homer these speeches express public opinion, as voiced by an anonymous *tis* or "someone," they belong to the general category of what Anton Fingerle has called *tis*-Reden.[1] As potential *tis*-Reden (expressions of what people might say), they are to be distinguished from actual *tis*-Reden (expressions of what people actually said). Formally the difference is reflected in introductory and capping formulas. Actual *tis*-Reden are introduced in the past tense directly from the narrative, by the phrase ὧδε δέ τις εἴπεσκε(ν),[2] and are capped by the phrase ὣς ἄρα τις εἴπεσκε(ν),[3] ὣς ἄρ' ἔφαν,[4] or the like.[5] Potential *tis*-Reden, on the other hand, in their capacity as speeches within speeches that refer to the future, have an introductory formula that is either purposive[6] or predictive,[7] and a capping formula that is invariably future.[8] The content of a potential *tis*-Rede is either shameful or glorious and reflects the psychology of the speaker who projects it. This is in contrast to actual *tis*-Reden, which are more often than not morally neutral.

In Homer the opinion expressed in a potential *tis*-Rede is usually negative, and the speaker projecting this negative opinion is often attempting to dissuade himself or others from a certain course of action. Hector's soliloquy before the onrush of Achilles is an example. Similarly, in the funeral games of Patroclus, Menelaus urges impartial adjudication of his dispute with Antilochus so that no Achaean can accuse him of pressure tactics. The anonymous Achaean's potential accusation is fully quoted, giving Menelaus ample cause to settle his dispute peaceably (*Il.* 23.575–578). In the *Odyssey*, Eurymachus fears the consequences to the suitors' reputation if the beggar in the palace is given a chance of joining the contest with the bow. Here, as in Hector's soliloquy, the imagined speaker

---

[1] *Typik der homerischen Reden*, unpublished dissertation, Munich, 1944, 283–294 (I wish to thank the Institut für klassische Philologie of Munich University for supplying me with a copy of these pages). See also C. Hentze, "Die Chorreden in den homerischen Epen," *Philologus* 64 (1905), 254–268.

[2] *Il.* 2.271; 3.297, 319; 4.81; 7.178, 201; 17.414; 22.372. *Od.* 2.324; 4.769; 8.328; 10.37; 13.167; 17.482; 18.72, 111a, 400; 20.375; 21.361, 396; 23.148.

[3] *Il.* 4.85; 17.423; 22.375. *Od.* 4.772; 13.170; 23.152.

[4] *Il.* 3.324; 7.181, 206. *Od.* 17.488; 18.75; 21.404.

[5] ὣς ἔφασαν: *Od.* 10.46; 20.384. ὣς φάσαν: *Il.* 2.278. *Od.* 21.366. ὣς ἔφαν: *Il.* 3.302. ὣς φάν: *Od.* 2.337.

[6] ὄφρα τις ὧδ' εἴπῃ(σιν): *Il.* 7.300; 12.317. μή ποτέ τις εἴπῃσι(ν): *Il.* 22.106; 23.575. *Od.* 21.324.

[7] καί ποτέ τις εἴπῃσι(ν): *Il.* 6.459; 7.87. καί κέ τις ὧδ' ἐρέει: *Il.* 4.176. Cf. also the wish καί ποτέ τις εἴποι in the incomplete *tis*-Rede at *Il.* 6.479.

[8] ὣς ἐρέουσι(ν): *Il.* 22.108. *Od.* 6.285; 21.329. ὣς ποτέ τις ἐρέει: *Il.* 4.182; 6.462; 7.91. There is no capping formula at 7.302; 12.321; 23.578. The ring form of these capping formulas reflects in miniature a major structural principle of the speeches in Homer (see Dieter Lohmann, *Die Komposition der Reden in der Ilias*, Berlin, 1970).

is baser than they (*Od.* 21.324). Nausikaa, too, takes seriously the potential reproaches of her inferiors, should she be seen entering the town with a strange man (*Od.* 6.275–285). She admits that she herself would feel the same way about another girl in the same circumstances.[9] The truth is that in Homer there is no such thing as non-valid public opinion.[10]

But *tis*-Reden are not always negative, and their function can at times be to encourage and to persuade. For example, in the *Iliad* Sarpedon encourages Glaukos to fight in the front rank (12.317–321):

> . . . ὄφρα τις ὧδ' εἴπῃ Λυκίων πύκα θωρηκτάων·
> 'οὐ μὰν ἀκλεέες Λυκίην κάτα κοιρανέουσιν
> ἡμέτεροι βασιλῆες, ἔδουσί τε πίονα μῆλα
> οἶνόν τ' ἔξαιτον μελιηδέα· ἀλλ' ἄρα καὶ ἲς
> ἐσθλή, ἐπεὶ Λυκίοισι μέτα πρώτοισι μάχονται.'

The third function of *tis*-Reden in Homer is predictive. An anonymous speech can bring fame or shame in the future without demanding an immediate response. So in a mood of fatalism Hector imagines what will be said about his wife Andromache after the fall of Troy (*Il.* 6.459–462):

> καί ποτέ τις εἴπῃσιν ἰδὼν κατὰ δάκρυ χέουσαν·
> '"Εκτορος ἥδε γυνή, ὃς ἀριστεύεσκε μάχεσθαι
> Τρώων ἱπποδάμων, ὅτε "Ιλιον ἀμφιμάχοντο.'
> ὥς ποτέ τις ἐρέει . . .

But, he continues, may I be dead and buried by then.[11] More optimistic is Hector's idea of an epitaph for one of his own prospective victims (*Il.* 7.87–91):

> καί ποτέ τις εἴπῃσι καὶ ὀψιγόνων ἀνθρώπων,
> νηΐ πολυκληΐδι πλέων ἐπὶ οἴνοπα πόντον·
> 'ἀνδρὸς μὲν τόδε σῆμα πάλαι κατατεθνηῶτος,
> ὅν ποτ' ἀριστεύοντα κατέκτανε φαίδιμος "Εκτωρ.'
> ὥς ποτέ τις ἐρέει· τὸ δ' ἐμὸν κλέος οὔ ποτ' ὀλεῖται.[12]

---

9 Nausikaa's *tis*-Rede is the longest in Homer and serves to depict her ambiguous attitude to the local suitors. See Norman Austin, *Archery at the Dark of the Moon*, Berkeley, 1975, 194.

10 C. E. F. von Erffa, *Aidos und verwandte Begriffe* (*Philologus* Suppl. 30, Heft 2), Leipzig, 1937, 41, contrasts this with the Stoic distinction of ὀρθὸς ψόγος ([Plato] *Def.* 412 C 10 = Andronicus in J. von Arnim, *Stoic. Vet. Fr.* 3.432); cf. Arist. *Rhet.* 1384 a 21–33. Hesiod *Op.* 763 f. represents an intermediate position.

11 Hector's despair about Andromache is matched by Andromache's own despair about Astyanax. At *Il.* 22.496–498, she imagines what more fortunate boys will say to her orphaned child (the gnomic aorist at 496 is applied in the future to Astyanax, as 499 ff. show).

12 There is perhaps an element of persuasion here, in that Hector's prospective victim will become famous by association. Conversely, there is an element of dissuasion at *Il.* 4.176–182, where Agamemnon encourages Menelaus not to die.

After Homer this contemplation of posthumous fame is applied by the writer of personal poetry to his own poetic achievement. So Theognis (22 f.), enlarging the Homeric τις to πᾶς τις,[13] looks forward to his own fame as a poet:

ὧδε δὲ πᾶς τις ἐρεῖ· 'Θεύγνιδός ἐστιν ἔπη
τοῦ Μεγαρέως· πάντας δὲ κατ' ἀνθρώπους ὀνομαστός.'[14]

In the same tradition is a fragment falsely attributed to Epicharmus.[15]

But even in Homer not every projection of opinion is a tis-Rede. When, in Iliad 8.145 ff., Diomedes considers retreating before the thunderbolt of Zeus, he imagines not what "someone" will say but what Hector in particular will say if he draws back.[16] One might add that the "someone" of tis-Reden is usually further qualified as an Achaean, a Trojan, a suitor, or the like. So in Semonides (7.29–31 West), who provides the earliest example of projected future opinion after Homer, it is the ignorant visitor, and not just anyone, who praises a woman whom he has only seen on one of her good days:

ἐπαινέσει μιν ξεῖνος ἐν δόμοις ἰδών·
'οὐκ ἔστιν ἄλλη τῆσδε λωΐων γυνὴ
ἐν πᾶσιν ἀνθρώποισιν οὐδὲ καλλίων.'

Closer to the dramatic context of Homer is the use of projected opinion by Solon in his Salamis poem. This work of about 100 lines is conceived as a messenger speech delivered to the Athenians by a herald fresh from Salamis, which the Athenians are in danger of abandoning to the Megarians. According to Diogenes Laertius, the poem reaches a climax of scorn when the herald wishes he were the citizen of the obscurest island rather than of Athens (Solon 2.3 f. West):

αἶψα γὰρ ἂν φάτις ἥδε μετ' ἀνθρώποισι γένοιτο·
'Ἀττικὸς οὗτος ἀνήρ, τῶν Σαλαμιναφετέων.'

By projecting the scorn that will be heaped upon them, the herald attempts to dissuade the Athenians from letting go of the island.[17]

---

13 See Rudolf Führer, *Formproblem-Untersuchungen zu den Reden in der frühgriechischen Lyrik* (*Zetemata* 44), Munich, 1967, 54.

14 For this punctuation see Felix Jacoby, "Theognis," *SBBA* 1931, 115 f.

15 Fr. 86.12 ff. in Colin Austin, *Comicorum Graecorum fragmenta in papyris reperta* (= *CGFPap.*).

16 At 152 ff. Nestor argues that even if Hector should call him a coward, the Trojan men and women he has widowed would disagree. The authority of their collective judgement would naturally be expressed by a *tis*-Rede, and this general judgement would outweigh any individual judgement.

17 Even more interesting is Solon's projection of actual public opinion, in fr. 33 West. The vulgar crowd consider him a fool for not having abused his powers as arbitrator to

Chronologically, the next example of projected future opinion is an oracle in Herodotus, which is dated by Parke to around 494 B.C.[18]

ὥς ποτέ τις ἐρέει καὶ ἐπεσσομένων ἀνθρώπων·
'δεινὸς ὄφις τριέλικτος ἀπώλετο δουρὶ δαμασθείς.'

(Parke–Wormell 84.4 = Hdt. 6.77). The predictive function of the *tis*-Rede follows naturally from Homer, though the author of the oracle mistakenly applies an Homeric capping formula to introduce it.

It is, however, the dramatic use of the device in Solon that points the way to Greek tragedy.[19] Proportionally, tragedy contains as many instances of projected opinion as Homeric epic itself. This is partly due to the inherently dramatic nature of the device, which is always thought of as a speech within a speech. In drama, though, we must distinguish between non-argumentative projections of opinion developed from Homer, and the argumentative projections of opinion known in rhetoric as *prokatalepsis*, where an opinion is set up for the purpose of being demolished. *Prokatalepsis* is the rule in oratory, whereas poetic examples occur for the first time in Euripides.[20]

In Aeschylus the power of public opinion is typically very different than in Homer. In Homer it has a quasi-objective force because every one subscribes to it. In Aeschylus there is an element of religious compulsion (*Agamemnon* 456 f.) :

βαρεῖα δ' ἀστῶν φάτις σὺν κότῳ,
δημοκράντου δ' ἀρᾶς τίνει χρέος.

---

become tyrant. But elsewhere (fr. 32 West), in a hitherto unparalleled defiance of public opinion, Solon defends his own position.

[18] H. W. Parke and D. E. W. Wormell, *The Delphic Oracle*, Oxford, 1946, I, 158–161.

[19] For Solon as a precursor of tragedy see Gerald F. Else, *The Origin and Early Form of Greek Tragedy*, Cambridge, Mass., 1965, 32–50.

[20] For Euripidean examples see Christopher Collard's edition of Euripides' *Suppliants*, ad v. 184 (but the pre-Euripidean examples he cites are all *tis*-Reden and are not procataleptic). The earliest dated example of *prokatalepsis* in Old Comedy is Ar. *Ach.* 540 (425 B.C.), but this is itself a parody of Eur. *Telephus* 708 N. A possibly earlier example is Pherecrates fr. 154 Edmonds = Athen. 3.122 e. For Middle Comedy cf. Philiscus in Austin, *CGFPap.*, fr. 215.1.—Usually there is no danger of confusing the two types of projection, but at *Ba.* 204 ff., where the opinion to be rejected is a shaming judgement, the first two lines by themselves could pass as an indirect *tis*-Rede:

ἐρεῖ τις ὡς τὸ γῆρας οὐκ αἰσχύνομαι,
μέλλων χορεύειν κρᾶτα κισσώσας ἐμόν.

The very next line, however, shows that the opinion was presented for instant rebuttal (hence, as in Murray's text, one should read 204 f. with an interrogative intonation: "will someone say . . . ?").

Whether their rulers listen or not, what the people say can be effective. It is perhaps the fear of a divinely backed curse that helps Pelasgus in the *Suppliants* to his decision of consulting the people before granting asylum to the Danaids (398–401):

εἶπον δὲ καὶ πρίν, οὐκ ἄνευ δήμου τάδε
πράξαιμ' ἄν, οὐδέ περ κρατῶν, μὴ καί ποτε
εἴπῃ λεώς, εἴ πού τι μὴ τοῖον τύχοι,
'ἐπήλυδας τιμῶν ἀπώλεσας πόλιν.'

The projected accusation, epigrammatic in its assonanċe and its evenly split line, is an enhancement of Homer's (*Il.* 22.107)

'"Εκτωρ ἧφι βίηφι πιθήσας ὤλεσε λαόν.'

Note, however, that it is the people as a group, and not a generalized "someone" who speaks.

Closer both in form and feeling to an Homeric *tis*-Rede is Orestes' tribute to Athena after his acquittal in the *Eumenides*. In that play honour is a matter for the gods, whether Olympian or chthonic. Orestes, the only human being in the play other than the priestess at the beginning and the silent citizens of Athens, is preoccupied with survival. But now that for him at least the storm has cleared and he can return into society, he expresses his thanks by an imagined tribute to the Olympian triad (*Eumenides* 756–760):

καί τις 'Ελλήνων ἐρεῖ·
'Ἀργεῖος ἀνὴρ αὖθις, ἔν τε χρήμασιν
οἰκεῖ πατρῴοις, Παλλάδος καὶ Λοξίου
ἔκατι καὶ τοῦ πάντα κραίνοντος τρίτου
Σωτῆρος.'

Equally Homeric and specifically Odyssean is the passage in the *Libation Bearers* where Orestes seeks to manipulate public opinion in order to assure his admittance to the palace (567–570):

μενοῦμεν οὕτως ὥστ' ἐπεικάζειν τινὰ
δόμους παραστείχοντα καὶ τάδ' ἐννέπειν·
'τί δὴ πύλῃσι τὸν ἱκέτην ἀπείργεται
Αἴγισθος, εἴπερ οἶδεν ἔνδημος παρών;'[21]

In fact, Orestes gains admission with ease and is at once faced with his mother—a moral, not a technical problem. In the *Odyssey*, Odysseus also

[21] Alexander Sideras, *Aeschylus Homericus* (*Hypomnemata* 31), Göttingen, 1972, 228, notes that the *nemesis* that would be aroused in such a situation is actually felt by Telemachus at *Od.* 1.119 f.

thinks of manipulating public opinion to achieve his ends. After the killing
of the suitors he orders the household to engage in song and dance
(23.135 f.):

> . . . ὥς κέν τις φαίη γάμον ἔμμεναι ἐκτὸς ἀκούων,
> ἢ ἀν' ὁδὸν στείχων ἢ οἳ περιναιετάουσι.

But Odysseus' potential *tis*-Rede (given in reported speech) is soon con-
verted into an actual *tis*-Rede (*Od.* 23.148–151), thus confirming the hero's
mastery of the plot.[22]

In a frankly imitative context, Sophocles provides an even more direct
reflection of an Homeric *tis*-Rede. Just as, in Book Six of the *Iliad*, in the
final scene between Hector and Andromache, Hector imagines the words
that will be spoken about Andromache after her captivity, so in *Ajax*, in
the final scene between the hero and Tecmessa, Tecmessa imagines what
her husband's enemies will say about her to his own discredit (505)
once she gets into their power (500–504):[23]

> καί τις πικρὸν πρόσφθεγμα δεσποτῶν ἐρεῖ
> λόγοις ἰάπτων· 'ἴδετε τὴν ὁμευνέτιν
> Αἴαντος, ὃς μέγιστον ἴσχυσε στρατοῦ,
> οἵας λατρείας ἀνθ' ὅσου ζήλου τρέφει.'
> τοιαῦτ' ἐρεῖ τις . . .

Sophocles even imitates the ring form of the Homeric framing formulas,
by repeating the verb of speaking. But the difference in speaker and
intention is also important. In Sophocles the *tis*-Rede is spoken by the
woman as an instrument of persuasion, while in Homer it is spoken by
the man in a vision of despair.[24]

Characteristically, Ajax rejects Tecmessa's premiss out of hand (560 ff.).
The situation she envisages simply will not arise. As for his own future, any
further humiliating possibilities will be forestalled by suicide. One of the
rejected possibilities is a reunion with his father Telamon. It is this same
possibility that his half-brother, Teukros, envisages in detail, as he laments

---

[22] Among Aeschylean examples we should also note *Ag.* 575 ff. However we interpret
575 f., 577–579 project a boast that is recapitulated in Homeric style by τοιαῦτα, at 580.

[23] For an excellent comparison of both scenes as a whole, see Gordon M. Kirkwood,
"Homer and Sophocles' *Ajax*," in J. M. Anderson, ed., *Classical Drama and Its Influence:
Essays Presented to H. D. F. Kitto*, London, 1965, 53–70.

[24] For the exaggerated masculinity of Ajax compared to Hector see Michael Shaw,
"The female intruder," *CPh* 70 (1975), 257 f.

over the hero's corpse. If Teukros returns home without Ajax he will get a grim reception indeed (1012–1018):

> οὗτος τί κρύψει; ποῖον οὐκ ἐρεῖ κακόν,
> τὸν ἐκ δορὸς γεγῶτα πολεμίου²⁵ νόθον,
> τὸν δειλίᾳ προδόντα καὶ κακανδρίᾳ
> σέ, φίλτατ' Αἴας, ἢ δόλοισιν, ὡς τὰ σὰ
> κράτη θανόντος καὶ δόμους νέμοιμι σούς.
> τοιαῦτ' ἀνὴρ δύσοργος, ἐν γήρᾳ βαρύς,
> ἐρεῖ . . .

As with Tecmessa's *tis*-Rede, this indirect projection of Telamon's opinion is capped by a return to the verb of speaking. The formality of the frame contrasts with the supple modulation into a direct address of Ajax (1015), who thus remains the centre of attention.²⁶

It is not accidental that there are two projected speeches in *Ajax*, since the whole plot revolves around reputation, and in this respect is the most Homeric of Sophocles' plays. The only other speech of projected opinion in Sophocles is in the much later *Electra*. There the heroine evokes the glory that she and her sister will gain if (now that their brother is dead) they take it on themselves to avenge their father (975–985):

> τίς γάρ ποτ' ἀστῶν ἢ ξένων²⁷ ἡμᾶς ἰδὼν
> τοιοῖσδ' ἐπαίνοις οὐχὶ δεξιώσεται·
> 'ἴδεσθε τώδε τὼ κασιγνήτω, φίλοι,
> ὣ τὸν πατρῷον οἶκον ἐξεσωσάτην,
> ὣ τοῖσιν ἐχθροῖς εὖ βεβηκόσιν ποτὲ
> ψυχῆς ἀφειδήσαντε προυστήτην φόνου.
> τούτω φιλεῖν χρή, τώδε χρὴ πάντας σέβειν·
> τώδ' ἔν θ' ἑορταῖς ἔν τε πανδήμῳ πόλει
> τιμᾶν ἅπαντας οὕνεκ' ἀνδρείας χρεών.'
> τοιαῦτά τοι νὼ πᾶς τις ἐξερεῖ βροτῶν,
> ζώσαιν θανούσαιν θ' ὥστε μὴ 'κλιπεῖν κλέος.

But this heady vision does not sway Chrysothemis. What good is reputation if one has to face an infamous and protracted death (1005 ff.)?

Interestingly enough, the praise that Electra imagines is actually given to Antigone (though she never knows it). At *Antigone* 692 ff., Haemon, in the hope of swaying his father, tells Creon what the city is surreptitiously saying in praise of Antigone. But Creon is unmoved, and this report of

---

²⁵ To stress the alienation of Teukros, I interpret πολέμιος as *hostilis* (its normal sense) rather than as *bellicus*.

²⁶ Note at 1015 f. the expressively repeated pronominal forms σέ . . . τὰ σά . . . σούς.

²⁷ The polar expression here is equivalent in its inclusiveness to Theognis' πᾶς τις, which duly appears in the capping line (984).

actual public opinion has no effect. We may note that in Sophocles projections of future opinion are equally ineffective.[28]

In Euripides there are twelve examples of projected future opinion,[29] proportionately more than the number in Aeschylus or Sophocles. Half of these are *tis*-Reden of the Homeric type, except that in Euripides the hypothetical speaker is usually a completely generalized *tis* or "someone," and is not even a member of such a broad group as "the Greeks." The imitation of Homer produces an archaizing effect, but at the same time the extreme anonymity of the speaker gives the broadest possible currency to what he says. The remaining half dozen projections of opinion are not *tis*-Reden and show little or no Homeric influence.

The most simplistic examples of *tis*-Reden in Euripides are to be found in the two patriotic plays, the *Heracleidae* and the *Suppliants*. In the prologue to the *Heracleidae* Iolaos, the nephew of Herakles, gives his reasons for sharing in the misery and exile of the children of Herakles as follows (28–30):

> ... ὀκνῶν προδοῦναι, μή τις ὧδ' εἴπῃ βροτῶν·
> 'ἴδεσθ', ἐπειδὴ παισὶν οὐκ ἔστιν πατήρ,
> 'Ιόλαος οὐκ ἤμυνε συγγενὴς γεγώς.'

The ostentatious rectitude of his position, somewhat old-fashioned in its Homeric dress, contrasts with the confident modernism of the Argive herald, whose system of morality is quite different.

Later in the same play, one of the children, Makaria, argues for sacrificing herself to save Athens. Part of her argument consists in envisaging what would happen should she survive the fall of the city that had offered her protection (516–519):

> κοὐκ αἰσχυνοῦμαι δῆτ', ἐὰν δή τις λέγῃ·
> 'τί δεῦρ' ἀφίκεσθ' ἱκεσίοισι σὺν κλάδοις
> αὐτοὶ φιλοψυχοῦντες; ἔξιτε χθονός·
> κακοὺς γὰρ ἡμεῖς οὐ προσωφελήσομεν.'

The feeling anticipated is of shame, yet the thought behind it is practical and quite in accordance with the overall rationality of her speech. If she fails to assist her benefactor now, she can expect no help in the future.

In the *Suppliants* Theseus is shamed by his mother Aethra into helping the Argives gain permission from the Thebans to bury their dead. If he

---

28 To the Sophoclean examples we might add *O.R.* 1496–1500, where a catalogue of family woes is transformed into a speech of projected opinion by the capping τοιαῦτ' ὀνειδιεῖσθε (1500, cf. 1494).

29 The *tis*-Reden are *Heracl.* 28–30; 516–519; *Supp.* 314–319; *Ph.* 580–582; *Alc.* 954–960; 1000–1005. Formally distinct are *HF* 1289 f.; 1378–1381; *Tr.* 1188–1191; *IA* 462–466; 790–800; 1177–1179.

does help, he will be supporting a principle of international law, while if
he doesn't (314–319):

> ἐρεῖ δὲ δή τις ὡς ἀνανδρίᾳ χερῶν,
> πόλει παρόν σοι στέφανον εὐκλείας λαβεῖν,
> δείσας ἀπέστης, καὶ συὸς μὲν ἀγρίου
> ἀγῶνος ἥψω φαῦλον ἀθλήσας πόνον,
> οὗ δ' ἐς κράνος βλέψαντα καὶ λόγχης ἀκμὴν
> χρῆν ἐκπονῆσαι, δειλὸς ὢν ἐφηυρέθης.

Theseus only needs a mild prod to agree. He is, after all, the representative
of Athens and as such he is, in all extant Greek tragedy, beyond reproach
and sure to succeed.

In these morality plays Honour is unproblematic. This is very different
from the tragic world of *Hippolytus*, where the two major characters,
Phaedra and Hippolytus, both passionately espouse honour and the re-
nown it brings, but are victims of their internal enemies or of circumstance.
It is very different, too, from those plays, particularly in the later period,
where the claims of honour, if they are made at all, are not heeded. So in
the *Phoenissae* Jocasta suggests to her son Polynices that he is in a moral
dilemma. If he succeeds in capturing his native city, how will he inscribe
the dedicatory shields (575 f.)?

> 'Θήβας πυρώσας τάσδε Πολυνείκης θεοῖς
> ἀσπίδας ἔθηκε.'

If, on the other hand, he fails and returns to Argos (580–582):

> ἐρεῖ δὲ δή τις· 'ὦ κακὰ μνηστεύματα
> Ἄδραστε προσθείς, διὰ μιᾶς νύμφης γάμον
> ἀπωλόμεσθα.'

But her plea is not even considered, for Eteocles cuts short the debate by
threatening to withdraw Polynices' safe conduct (for he is only in Thebes
on sufferance). In the discussion between the brothers, as in the more
desperate parts of Thucydides, Fear and Ambition are the motivations,
and Honour is expendable.

Alcestis provides a more sophisticated use of projected opinion. In that
play there is a conspiracy of silence between Admetus, Alcestis and the
chorus about the seamy side of Admetus' transaction with his wife, in
which he had allowed her to give him a new lease on life by dying for him.
After her death, this silence is broken by Pheres, the father of Admetus,
who under provocation goes so far as to call Admetus his wife's murderer.
The chorus remains unaffected by this outburst, and does not really comment on it. After the funeral, though, Admetus does change his attitude,
but this is only because he realizes that the bargain he had made with

death was not such a good one after all, and that Alcestis in death is actually better off than he is in life. For Alcestis had a noble death and is now free of pain, while life without her, as he has just discovered, is no pleasure, and on top of that his reputation has suffered. What Pheres has already said to Admetus reappears as the projection of what his enemies will soon be saying (954–960):

> ἐρεῖ δέ μ᾽ ὅστις ἐχθρὸς ὢν κυρεῖ τάδε·
> 'ἰδοῦ τὸν αἰσχρῶς ζῶνθ᾽, ὃς οὐκ ἔτλη θανεῖν,
> ἀλλ᾽ ἣν ἔγημεν ἀντιδοὺς ἀψυχίᾳ
> πέφευγεν Ἅιδην· εἶτ᾽ ἀνὴρ εἶναι δοκεῖ;
> στογεῖ δὲ τοὺς τεκόντας, αὐτὸς οὐ θέλων
> θανεῖν.' τοιάνδε πρὸς κακοῖσι κληδόνα
> ἕξω.

But in imagining what people will say, Admetus by no means subscribes to their views. The key difference from the Homeric model is that it is not just any one who will speak out against him, but rather his enemies, his *echthroi*, whose opinion can be at least partially discounted. His public image may be damaged (a regrettable occurrence), but his self image is relatively unscathed.[30]

In the chorus that follows this episode, the bad reputation of Admetus is implicitly contrasted with the good reputation of Alcestis. Impromptu tributes at the tomb are already familiar from Homer, and just as in the *Iliad* Hector imagines what will be said at the tomb of one of his prospective victims, so the chorus imagine a visit to the tomb of Alcestis (1000–1005):

> καί τις δοχμίαν κέλευθον
> ἐκβαίνων τόδ᾽ ἐρεῖ·
> 'αὕτα ποτὲ προύθαν᾽ ἀνδρός,
> νῦν δ᾽ ἐστὶ μάκαιρα δαίμων·
> χαῖρ᾽, ὦ πότνι᾽, εὖ δὲ δοίης.' τοῖαί νιν προσεροῦσι φῆμαι.

As in Sophocles, the tribute to Alcestis follows the Homeric pattern down to the ring form repetition of the verb of speaking. But though the chorus is supposed to be consolatory, the projected speech of praise for the wife, coming on the heels of a projected speech of blame for the husband, has an ironic effect.

Of the six remaining examples of projected opinion in Euripides, three occur in *Iphigeneia in Aulis*, two in *Herakles*, and one in the *Trojan Women*. At *I.A.* 462–464, Agamemnon contributes to his dilemma by imagining

---

[30] By contrast, in Homer even an enemy's opinion is fully respected (as Diomedes' respects Hector's opinion at *Il.* 8.147–150).

the speech of supplication that his daughter will make. At *I.A.* 1177–1179, Clytemnestra tries to influence Agamemnon by projecting what she will keep on saying to herself back in Argos, if Iphigeneia is killed. At *I.A.* 790–800, the chorus imagine what the Trojan women will say at the prospect of slavery. At *Troades* 1189 ff., as a variation on what people will say, Hekabe imagines what a poet will write on the tomb of Astyanax.[31]

More remarkable is the sequence in *Herakles.* In the pathetic aftermath to his madness, during which he has killed his wife and his children, the hero at first resolves to kill himself too. Like Makaria in the *Heracleidae*, he wonders how he could honourably survive as an exile. He will be bitterly goaded as follows (1289 f.):

'οὐχ οὗτος ὁ Διός, ὃς τέκν' ἔκτεινέν ποτε
δάμαρτά τ'; οὐ γῆς τῆσδ' ἀποφθαρήσεται;'

What distinguishes this from conventional projections of shame (apart from the lack of a formal introduction), is the horrible gravity of the charge. If the charge is true, as it incontrovertibly is, the shame before others is almost forgotten before the horror of the fact itself. That Herakles is not just thinking of what people will say, is shown by the succeeding lines (immediately succeeding, if we follow Wilamowitz). The very elements, so he imagines, will reject him (*Herakles* 1295–1298):

φωνὴν γὰρ ἥσει χθὼν ἀπεννέπουσά με
μὴ θιγγάνειν γῆς καὶ θάλασσα μὴ περᾶν
πηγαί τε ποταμῶν, καὶ τὸν ἁρματήλατον
Ἰξίον' ἐν δεσμοῖσιν ἐκμιμήσομαι.

And yet this blend of shame and guilt is not intellectually assented to, for, as he says at the end of this very speech, it is the goddess Hera and not himself who is to blame.

In the end, under the influence of Theseus, Herakles decides to steel himself to live rather than to die, perhaps in part as a testimony of innocence. In tears he laments his shattered past, and as he prepares to leave the scene of the killings he hesitates to take up his weapons (1378–1381):

ἀμηχανῶ γὰρ πότερ' ἔχω τάδ' ἢ μεθῶ,
ἃ πλευρὰ τἀμὰ προσπίτνοντ' ἐρεῖ τάδε·
'ἡμῖν τέκν' εἷλες καὶ δάμαρθ'· ἡμᾶς ἔχεις
παιδοκτόνους σούς.'

---

[31] For shameful writing, as opposed to shameful speech, cf. E. *Ph.* 573 f.

The surreal picture fits his fevered condition. Here a device that properly expresses the values of a shame culture is adapted to express feelings of guilt, by having the weapons rather then the public speak.[32]

These last passages from *Herakles* boldly realize such hypotheses as that of the watchman in the prologue of *Agamemnon*, who imagines what the house would say "if it could give voice."[33] Yet another possibility is to imagine what the dead would say if *they* could give voice. So in *Orestes* (408 B.C.), the hero asks his uncle Menelaus to imagine that his dead father Agamemnon is speaking through him (674–677).[34] Nine years later we find a similar conceit in Andocides (1.148), and thereafter it becomes a commonplace.

In rhetorical theory, the non-real projection of opinion from the past is a form of *prosopopoeia*, which in principle could also include projections of future opinion such as the Homeric *tis*-Reden. But, as we have noticed, in Greek oratory projections of future opinion are usually argumentative and procataleptic in nature. The one exception is a passage in Hyperides' *Defence of the sons of Lycurgus* (ca. 324 B.C.): τίνα φήσουσιν οἱ παριόντες αὐτοῦ τὸν τάφον; 'οὗτος ἐβίω μὲν σωφρόνως, ταχθεὶς δὲ ἐπὶ τῇ διοικήσει τῶν χρημάτων εὗρε πόρους, ᾠκοδόμησε τὸ θέατρον, τὸ ᾠδεῖον, τὰ νεώρια, τριήρεις ἐποιήσατο, λιμένας· τοῦτον ἡ πόλις ἡμῶν ἠτίμωσε καὶ τοὺς παῖδας ἔδησεν αὐτοῦ.' (Hyperides fr. 118 Kenyon). The passerby at the tomb in Hyperides' projection of opinion harks back to Hector's *tis*-Rede for his prospective victim in the *Iliad*, and the chorus' *tis*-Rede for the heroine in *Alcestis*. The projection of an epitaph as a shaming device is paralleled by Hekabe's epitaph for Astyanax in the *Trojan Women*.

The passage from Hyperides is unusual in other ways. Down to the end of the Hellenistic period, there are only two other instances of a moralizing use of projected future opinion.[35] One occurs in Apollonius Rhodius' *Argonautica*, in a passage where Medea considers the possibility of first aiding Jason and then killing herself.[36] She is dissuaded by the reflection that even suicide would not help her posthumous reputation. Even after death

---

[32] Reproachful weapons also speak in an epitaph by Antipater of Sidon for the tomb of Ajax (Page 7 = *A.P.* 7.146):

τεύχεα δ' ἂν λέξειεν Ἀχιλλέος· 'ἄρσενος ἀλκᾶς,
οὐ σκολιῶν μύθων ἄμμες ἐφιέμεθα.'

[33] Aesch. *Ag.* 37; cf. Eur. *Hipp.* 418; *Andr.* 924.

[34] Compare also the virtuosity of Menelaus at *Hel.* 962 ff., where he attempts to influence Theonoe by invoking her dead father.

[35] Post-Euripidean tragedy, had it survived, might have provided further examples.

[36] This is the only example of projected opinion in Appollonius Rhodius. His epic, however, contains several actual *tis*-Reden, e.g., at 2.144–154; 4.1457–1461.

she will be mocked and become the talk of the town (3.793–797):

καί κέν με διὰ στόματος φορέουσαι
Κολχίδες ἄλλυδις ἄλλαι ἀεικέα μωμήσονται·
'ἥτις κηδομένη τόσον ἀνέρος ἀλλοδαποῖο
κάτθανεν, ἥτις δῶμα καὶ οὓς ᾔσχυνε τοκῆας,
μαργοσύνῃ εἴξασα.'—τί δ' οὐκ ἐμὸν ἔσσεται αἶσχος;

The other occurs in an anonymous papyrus fragment attributable to Cercidas. A modest and virtuous existence is preferable to excessive meddling, which can expose one to shipwreck and to the gibes of one's enemies (Powell, *Coll. Alex.*, p. 218, 37–40):

ἐγὼ μὲν οὖν, ὦ Πάρνε, βουλοίμην εἶναι
τἀρκεῦντ' ἐμαυτῷ καὶ νομίζεσθαι χρηστός,
ἢ πολλὰ πρήσσειν, καί ποτ' εἰπεῖν τοὺς ἐχθρούς·
'ἁλῶν δὲ φόρτος ἔνθεν ἦλθεν ἔνθ' ἦλθεν.'

The remaining instances of projected opinion in Hellenistic literature are confined to predictions of or wishes for praise. Wishes find their Homeric exemplar in Hector's hopes for Astyanax (*Il.* 6.479 f.):

καί ποτέ τις εἴποι 'πατρός γ' ὅδε πολλὸν ἀμείνων'
ἐκ πολέμου ἀνιόντα.

So Hegemon wishes that the passerby of the tomb of the Spartans at Thermopylae will praise them (Hegemon 1 page = *A.P.* 7.436):[37]

Εἴποι τις παρὰ τύμβον ἰὼν ἀγέλαστος ὁδίτας
τοῦτ' ἔπος· 'ὀγδώκοντ' ἐνθάδε μυριάδας
Σπάρτας χίλιοι ἄνδρες †ἐπέσχον αἷμα τὸ† Περσῶν
καὶ θάνον ἀστρεπτεί· Δώριος ἁ μελέτα.'

Similarly, Eratosthenes wishes that people will respond to his dedication at the temple of Ptolemy (fr. 35, 17 f. Powell):

. . . λέγοι δέ τις ἄνθεμα λεύσσων·
'τοῦ Κυρηναίου τοῦτ' Ἐρατοσθένεος.'

Also a wish, though different in form, is Theocritus 12.10–16. But the other examples of projected opinion in Theocritus are flat predictions. So, at 15.126 f., the sources of wool for the blankets of Adonis will proclaim themselves:

ἁ Μίλατος ἐρεῖ χὠ τὰν Σαμίαν καταβόσκων,
'ἔστρωται κλίνα τὠδώνιδι τῷ καλῷ ἄμμιν.'

---

[37] Because of the parallel with Homer, Gow–Page are probably wrong to interpret the optative here as potential. Their reference to the speeches of legendary characters introduced by the lemma τί ἂν λέγοι; or τίνας ἂν εἴποι λόγους; (as at *A.P.*9. 449–480), is misleading. Aside from the fact that the lemma is not part of the poem, the speaker is a particular "historical" character, not a generalized *tis*, and he speaks on a particular historical occasion in the past, not some hypothetical occasion in the future.

More decidedly Homeric is the conclusion of the idyll to the distaff (28.24 f.), where the introductory formula is modelled on *Il.* 6.459, and the comment on a gift is perhaps suggested by the *tis*-Rede at *Il.* 7.299 ff.:

> κῆνο γάρ τις ἔρει τῶπος ἴδων σ'· 'ἦ μεγάλα χάρις
> δώρῳ σὺν ὀλίγῳ· πάντα δὲ τίματα τὰ πὰρ φίλων.'

From the examples I have been able to collect we can draw the following conclusions. In the literary tradition, the most durable of the Homeric *tis*-Reden are those that predict praise. On the other hand, persuasive and dissuasive *tis*-Reden are not found beyond the fifth century. Later projections of opinion with these functions are rare and are non-Homeric in form. Even in tragedy, where projections of opinion are as frequent as in Homer, dissuasive or persuasive *tis*-Reden of the Homeric type are: associated with Homeric situations (A. *Ch.* 567–570; S. *Ajax* 500–504), are romanticizing (S. *El.* 975 ff.), or are deliberately archaic (Eur., passim). This progressive restriction in the scope of an Homeric device is most probably due to the development of a private ethic that rejects the appeal to a generalized *tis*.

University of Alberta

2

The Two Worlds of the *Antigone*

VINCENT J. ROSIVACH

The chorus of Theban elders begins the parodos of the *Antigone* by welcoming the rising sun[1] which looks down upon the fleeing remnants of the Argive army defeated the night before (100–109). The chorus then describes the battle itself, which took place at the gates of the city,[2] between Polyneices and his foreign allies on the one hand, and Eteocles and the forces of Thebes on the other (110 ff.). As prototype of the Argive army the chorus chooses Capaneus, who scaled the wall torch in hand, but was struck down at the very moment he reached the top (βαλβίδων ἐπ' ἄκρων), just as he was about to shout his cry of victory (131–133). Capaneus never crossed the wall but was thrust outward[3] and downward to the earth below (134 f.). The other Argive leaders were killed in their own unspecified ways at the other gates of the city (141–143), Polyneices and Eteocles slew each other (144–147), and the forces of Thebes were victorious (148 f.). The fact that Capaneus' case is the only one specifically described by the chorus strongly suggests that it was meant to be typical of the Argive attack as a whole. If this is so, then the picture which we get of the battle is one of a besieged city, the enemy on one side of the city walls, unable to cross in, and the defenders on the other side, on top of the walls,

---

[1] We are to imagine that the chorus sings the parodos as day is breaking and the sun is beginning to rise (E. Coughanawr, *CQ* NS 23 [1973], 22 f.). The prologue between Antigone and Ismene took place in the dark of night (ἐν νυκτὶ τῇ νῦν, 16); see A. T. von S. Bradshaw, *CQ* NS 12 (1962), 203 f.

[2] The seven gates of the city are mentioned three times in the parodos (101, 119, 141). This particular detail immediately evokes the traditional accounts of the battle (notably Aeschylus' *Septem*). It also reminds us that the city was besieged (cf. also ἀμφιχανὼν κύκλῳ, 118), and that the battle was fought at the walls and gates of the city, not on the open field (see also below, note 4).

[3] τανταλωθεὶς (134). See R. Jebb, *Sophocles: The Plays and Fragments*, Part III: *The Antigone*[3] (Cambridge, 1900), *ad loc.*

and hence unable to cross out.[4] I would suggest that Sophocles had more in mind here than simply presenting a particularly vivid scene to his audience's imagination, for the wall on which the battle was fought can also be seen as a dividing line which separates two radically different worlds, the world within the city and the world without.

Within the walls is the *polis* of Thebes, the city which Creon now rules. It is a city of light in the new day which the chorus had welcomed (100–109), a day which they hope will bring forgetfulness of the wars of the past (150 f.). Within the city, and specifically on the stage, the part of the city seen by the audience, Creon is in control, securing the acquiescence of the Theban elders to his rule, ordering about the guard, and determining the death of Antigone. Like the chorus, Creon looks to the future. In his opening speech he tells the chorus what he will and will not do as ruler (175 ff.), and his decree to bury Eteocles and not to bury Polyneices is the first step in his implementation of this policy for the future (cf. 192). Indeed, for the greater part of our play Creon seems to be a man with no past. There is no mention of anything which he did before the play began except for the decree, and the decree is repeated in the course of the play (194 ff.) and is thus incorporated into present time. As far as the play is concerned, Creon could just as easily have come into existence when he came into power, at the death of Eteocles and Polyneices. Only as the play is about to end do we learn that Creon has a past, when we are told that he was in some way responsible for the death of his son Megareus (1303–1313).[5] We shall return to this point below.

Creon forms his judgement in terms of the city, or more precisely in terms of *this* city. As he sets forth his policies to the chorus, for example, Creon repeatedly uses the demonstrative ἥδε when talking of the city.[6] For Creon it is not simply a matter of abstract principle, that one should be loyal to one's own city; his commitment is concrete and specific, to the Thebes which the audience sees on the stage before them. Eventually, of course, in the Haemon scene, Creon identifies the good of the city with his own will rather than vice versa (cf. 734–738); but it is doubtful that he has already done so at the beginning of the play. In his first address to

[4] Thus there is no mention of a Theban sally to complete the defeat of the Argives (as there is in Euripides' vivid account of the battle, *Phoen.* 1189 ff.), and we are left with the impression that the Argive army abandoned the fight once its leaders were killed.

[5] Teiresias does mention some earlier assistance which he gave to Creon, (993–995, cf. 1058), but this probably also refers to the sacrifice of Megareus, and not to some other event in Creon's past (see below, note 24).

[6] 189, 191, 195, 203, 209; cf. ταύτης (189) and the chorus' use of τῆδε . . . πόλει (212) in immediate reply to Creon's initial statement.

the chorus Creon speaks only of the city: its friends are his friends, its enemies his enemies (187 f., 209 f.), and none more so than the traitor Polyneices, who now suffers the fate he deserves, his corpse exposed outside the city as carrion for dogs and vultures (198–206).

The Greeks buried their dead outside the city walls. Within the walls is the world of the living, outside is the world of the dead. Polyneices lies exposed outside the city, and the dead Eteocles must be buried there also (cf. 23–25), as must Oedipus, Iocasta and Laius, the whole clan of Labdacids, all now dead except Antigone and Ismene. Of these two, Ismene chooses to yield to Creon (63–67) and remains within his control in the city. Antigone, however, refuses to obey (47 f.), and so goes to bury her brother, out of the city and into the world of the dead (99).

In the theater this world of the dead lies offstage to the audience's left, the direction which convention assigns to the countryside outside the city. When Antigone leaves to bury Polyneices, for example, she exits in this direction[7] (by contrast, Ismene's submission to Creon is visibly reflected in her simultaneous exit into the palace). Throughout the play this left side exit is used only as a means of passage to and from the world of the dead, viz. to Polyneices' corpse and Antigone's tomb.[8] The demonstratives ἐκεῖ and (ἐ)κεῖνος used to describe this outer world and its inhabitants[9] also emphasize that world's remoteness and its association with death.[10]

---

[7] Antigone must leave by the left (at 99), also to avoid becoming entangled with the chorus which is entering at the same moment from the right (as old men the chorus would be shut up in the city during the siege, and would not be off to the left out in the countryside).

[8] Polyneices' corpse and Antigone's tomb must be fairly close to each other (and therefore offstage in the same direction), since the burying of Polyneices and the freeing of Antigone are both part of the same expedition out of the city (cf. 1198–1205). At 162, Creon comes from offstage (cf. δεῦρο νεῖσθαι [33] and the chorus' somewhat lengthy anapestic greeting to Creon [155–161], on which see W. M. Calder, III, GRBS 9 [1968] 393, n. 24), but most probably from the right. There is no reason why Creon would be returning from outside the city (i.e., from the left) if there had been no battle beyond the walls (see above, note 4). Creon's κήρυγμα is an "emergency decree announced by the voice of a herald, the normal means adopted by a general . . . to announce his will to the population in conditions resembling what we would call martial law" (B. M. W. Knox, The Heroic Temper: Studies in Sophoclean Tragedy [Berkeley and Los Angeles, 1966], 95). It seems more likely that this sort of decree would be promulgated in the agora (offstage to the right) and that Creon would enter from this direction at 162.

[9] ἐκεῖ: 76, 249, 777; (ἐ)κεῖνος: 71 (= Polyneices), 525 (= Polyneices and Eteocles), 1039 (= Polyneices), 1043 (= Polyneices); in terms of the following note compare also 168 (= Laius and Oedipus), 170 (= Eteocles and Polyneices), 468 (the more remote obligations to the dead contrasted with the closer threat of death at Creon's hand), and perhaps 514 (= Eteocles).

[10] ἐκεῖ is sometimes used as a euphemism for the underworld (LSJ, s.v. ἐκεῖ, 2), and

While the inner world of the city is concrete and visible on the stage, we never see the outer world of the dead. Instead, our knowledge of that world is indirect, through the reports of others, and as a consequence the outer world seems even more distant, less concrete, and so more mysterious. Creon attempts to intervene in the outer world of the dead by prohibiting the burial of Polyneices. Although this prohibition was initially proclaimed offstage, Creon himself repeats the proclamation onstage (198–206). In this way the proclamation is dramatically associated with the onstage world of the city and is seen as an attempt by Creon to project his power, which is identified with the city, out into the world of the dead beyond.[11] The attempt fails repeatedly as Antigone twice buries Polyneices' body[12] and Creon himself finally completes the task.

As Creon dominates the action within the city, Antigone determines the evolution of events which take place in the outer world of the dead, by her burial of Polyneices and by her self-determined suicide, which leads in turn to the death of Haemon. As Creon functions in the light of the new day proclaimed by the chorus (100–109), Antigone functions in darkness: in the darkness of the night before the dawn of the parodos when, in the prologue, she determines to bury Polyneices (42 ff.), in the strange darkness of the duststorm when she performs the burial (417 ff.),[13] and in the darkness of the tomb where she dies and causes Haemon's death.[14] As Creon is the man with no past, Antigone is a girl without a future. The only future act which she contemplates is the burial of Polyneices, and this act has been dictated by events in the past. Beyond the burial she foresees nothing but death, and the sooner death comes the more grateful she will be (460–464). Antigone does not even mention her own suicide,

ἐκεῖνος may be similarly used in reference to the dead (H. Ebeling, *Griechisch-deutsches Wörterbuch zu Sophokles* [Leipzig, 1869], *s.v.* ἐκεῖνος, 1).

[11] Another example of Creon's projecting the world of the city into the world of the dead is his assumption that the first burial of Polyneices was the result of sedition within the *polis* (289 ff.).

[12] I assume here that both burials reported by the guard were performed by Antigone. For our purposes, only the second burial is significant in terms of the evolution of the play's action, and this burial at least, it is generally agreed, was performed by Antigone.

[13] Since the first burial was discovered by the day's first watch (πρῶτος ... ἡμεροσκόπος, 253) it too must have been performed in the dark. The motif of lightlessness continues in κοὐδεὶς ἐναργής (263), Creon's ἐκφανεῖτ' (307) and φανεῖτε (325), and the guard's ἔνδηλα καὶ σαφῆ (405).

[14] At 808 f. Antigone describes herself as νέατον ... φέγγος λεύσσουσαν ἀελίου, recalling the ἀκτὶς ἀελίου greeted by the chorus in the opening words of the parodos (100); cf. also οὐκέτι μοι τόδε λαμπάδος ἱερὸν ὄμμα θέμις ὁρᾶν (879 f.), where the sun-eye recalls ἁμέρας βλέφαρον (104). The curse of the Labdacids is itself described by the chorus as a form of darkness, like black sand stirred up from the sea's dark depths (586–592).

but the actual suicide is itself secondary, for Antigone had already decided upon her own death when she comes to bury Polyneices (cf. 555). Indeed, in a very real sense she died at that moment, as she says, in order that she might benefit the dead (559 f.), and her suicide is simply the consummation of this predetermined death.[15]

Antigone looks only to the past, and that past is her family which dictates her present actions. As Creon's commitment to the city was concrete and specific, to the *polis* of Thebes, Antigone's commitment to family is also specific, to the royal clan of Labdacids. Antigone repeatedly identifies herself and is identified by others as the child of this family, whose ill-starred history is repeatedly recalled (2 ff., 49 ff., 858 ff.) like a genealogy of misfortunes, suggesting that Antigone too must come to grief (cf. 593 ff.,[16] 856, 893 ff.). These earlier Labdacids are now all dead, buried and unburied outside the city, and Antigone's own death will be but a reunion, as she says, with 'my own' (τοὺς ἐμαυτῆς, 893; cf. 867 f.).

As Creon defines his friends and enemies in terms of the city, Antigone defines hers in terms of her family: he who attacks the family attacks her (31 f.), he who is the family's enemy is her enemy too (10, 93 f.). The enemy now is Creon, who has refused to allow the burial of Polyneices and so has intruded himself into the affairs of a family where he had no right to enter (48, 1072). Ismene too is an enemy. She does not agree with Creon, but she recognizes his power (58 ff.), and so refuses to share in the burial. By denying what Antigone considers the legitimate demands of the family upon her (cf. 45 f.) Ismene alienates herself from the family and so becomes an enemy of Polyneices and Antigone (93 f.).

By acquiescing to Creon's proclamation Ismene concedes his right to rule. This Antigone will never do. While Ismene speaks of νόμου and of ψῆφον τυράννων (59 f.), implying some legitimacy in Creon's decree,[17] Antigone speaks only of τὸν στρατηγὸν and his κήρυγμα (8). Generals are not kings, and Thebes is not Creon's. For Antigone legitimacy is only in the past, in the ancestral line of Labdacids, of which she, not Creon, is the sole survivor (τὴν βασιλειδᾶν μούνην λοιπήν, 941).[18] Antigone and Creon

---

15 Even though Antigone has been sentenced by Creon, the chorus recognizes that her death is her own choice (821 f., and Jebb [above, note 3], *ad loc.*). We are thus reminded that in the world of the dead Antigone, not Creon, decides what will happen.

16 The notion of the dead influencing the present is clear in these lines when we realize that the Λαβδακιδᾶν of 593 are the dead members of the clan, not Antigone and Ismene; see H. Lloyd-Jones, *CQ* NS 7 (1957), 16 f.

17 Cf. also Ismene's βίᾳ πολιτῶν (79), echoing her νόμου βίᾳ (59). Similarly the chorus accepts Creon's legitimacy and the legitimacy of his decree; cf. βασιλεὺς χώρας (155), βασιλείοισιν . . . νόμοις (382), etc.

18 Ismene is no longer counted among the βασιλεῖδαι, since she has accepted Creon's rule, thereby failing the test of εὐγένεια (cf. 37 f.).

have two very different views of the relationship between Thebes and
her rulers. Creon, at least in his public pronouncements, sees that relationship in what we might call "modern" terms: that rule depends on the
consent of the governed (cf. 666 f.)[19] and should be directed to the good
of the city as a whole (cf. 178 ff.). Antigone speaks of Thebes in a much
more "primitive" way, almost as if the city were an ancestral possession
(γᾶς πατρίας, 806; ἄστυ πατρῷον, 937) to be passed on from generation to
generation of Labdacids (cf. 941).[20]

In summary then, we find in our play a series of dichotomies which
underscore the basic dramatic conflict between Antigone and Creon:

World outside the city	World inside the city
unseen by audience	seen onstage
ἐκεῖνοι, ἐκεῖ	ἥδε πόλις
dominated by Antigone	dominated by Creon
darkness	light
death	life
family	city
looks to the past	looks to the future
Thebes ruled by old royal line	Thebes ruled by Creon

The separateness of these two worlds, however, is more apparent than
real. In the course of the play Creon may twice reject the bonds of family
as secondary to the stability of his own rule over Thebes (484 ff., 655 ff.),
but in his first address to the chorus he himself invokes the previous rulers
of Thebes, viz. Laius, Oedipus and the slain brothers (165 ff.), and justifies
his rule precisely on the grounds of his own closeness of kinship with those
who had gone before him (γένους κατ᾽ ἀγχιστεῖα τῶν ὀλωλότων, 173 f.).
This ill-omened claim of kinship with the dead is hardly an act of familial
piety, as are Antigone's invocations of kinship, but only a political ploy
used by Creon to help in consolidating his power in Thebes. In effect,
Creon declares himself a Labdacid in order to share that family's right
to rule. In the prologue, however, Antigone (2 ff.) and Ismene (49 ff.)
had accounted for their own sorry state as the consequence of the ills of
their family, and Ismene had mentioned Oedipus, his wife, and the two

[19] In his opening speech to the chorus of elders Creon speaks of the support which
the elders had provided for the previous rulers (165 ff.); and, although he does not
specifically say so, it is clear that his purpose in addressing the elders is to secure the
same support for himself.

[20] When Creon speaks of Polyneices attacking γῆν πατρῷαν καὶ θεοὺς τοὺς ἐγγενεῖς
(199; cf. Antigone at 937 f.), he means πατρῷαν from Polyneices' point of view, not his
own (i.e., Polyneices' ancestral land, not Creon's). Creon's use of πατρῴαν here is
accurate, since Polyneices was a legitimate member of the Theban royal line.

slain brothers (49 ff.). Creon's invocation of the Labdacids here recalls
these earlier "geneaologies of misfortune" and suggests that if Creon will
share in the rights of the family he will also share in the family's curse
which has brought grief to all the Labdacids before him.

The curse is worked through Haemon. Haemon pleads with his father
to release Antigone, arguing that to do so would benefit Creon (701 ff.).
The argument is a good one for Haemon to make: by identifying the
interests of Creon with those of Antigone Haemon avoids the necessity of
making a choice between the two (cf. 748 f.). Creon, however, will not
accept the argument, and by repeatedly charging that Haemon's loyalties
lie only with Antigone (740, 746, 748) he finally forces Haemon to choose
between himself and the girl. Creon justifies his sentence of Antigone in
terms of his own rule over Thebes (730 ff.), but Haemon cannot accept
this Thebes ruled as it now is by his father (734–745). Forced to choose,
Haemon rejects his father (763 f.) and leaves the city (765). His exit is to
the left,[21] to the world outside the city walls. This outer world is the world
of the dead and, as events will show, it will be the setting of Haemon's
death as well.

At the end of this scene between Haemon and Creon, Creon may still
seem to be dominant, but his encounter with Haemon has forced him to
make an important retreat. Creon at first justified his intended punishment
of Antigone as necessary for stability within the city (655 ff.); but the
punishment has become itself a source of civil discord. Creon claimed the
universal support of the city for his decree forbidding Polyneices' burial
(655 f., cf. 508); but Haemon told how he himself had observed the people
of the city secretly lamenting that Antigone is to be punished for the burial,
but fearing Creon too much to make their objections known (688 ff.).
Such is the strength of Haemon's eyewitness account that Creon can no
longer claim universal support. Creon's "modern" view of his kingship
has been that it is based on the consent of the governed. Without that
consent now, Creon should yield and free Antigone; but he does not. Instead he abandons his "modern" view and declares that the will of the
people is irrelevant (734), and that Thebes is his alone to command (736).
Creon has now come to share the "primitive" view of Antigone, that
Thebes is the personal possession of her king (738). He has been forced by
Haemon's report to admit that, in this sense, his rule is no different from
that of the Labdacids before him.

Creon's reversal continues. The punishment for the violation of his

---

21 Haemon leaves by the exit to the left, since he will eventually go to Antigone's tomb,
which is offstage in that direction (see above, note 8).

decree was originally to have been stoning within the city (cf. 36). Now, almost as if to reassert his public posture as protector of the city as a whole, Creon changes the punishment and sentences Antigone to immurement outside the city, in order that the city might escape the pollution of her death (773 ff.). This sudden attention to piety may not be all that Creon claims it is. Stoning is a public act involving the whole community,[22] but a public which does not support Creon's policy would be unwilling to carry out the sentence. Creon avoids the potential embarrassment or worse by changing the punishment to one which can be carried out by his own servants and soldiers, and does not depend on the community as a whole. He thus saves face, but loses far more. Though he does not realize it, by this change Creon in effect surrenders his control over Antigone. The locale of her death will not be the world of the city dominated by Creon, but the outer world of the dead, and her death will be at the time and in the manner chosen by Antigone, not by Creon.

As the play progresses it becomes evident that reality is to be found in Antigone's unseen world of darkness and death, and that Creon's city of light and life is, despite the apparent reality associated with the visible stage, nothing but an illusion which Creon's own actions ultimately destroy. This had been Haemon's message when he spoke of the civil discord stirred up by Creon's punishment of Antigone. Teiresias too is a messenger from the city,[23] but his entrance and opening words suggest that, though within the city, he is part of Antigone's world, not Creon's (or, put differently, that the outer world already extends into the city through Teiresias): his blindness, which is emphasized (988–990), suggests darkness within the city, and in contrast to the city and to Creon, both oriented to the future, Teiresias refers to the past and speaks of help which he has already given to Creon in preserving the city (993–995, cf. 1058), thus giving us the first hint of any past which Creon may have had before the play began.[24] Teiresias now tells Creon of the illness the city suffers

---

[22] See E. Fraenkel, *Aeschylus: Agamemnon* (Oxford, 1950), ad 1616.

[23] Teiresias enters from his παλαιὸν θᾶκον ὀρνιθοσκόπον (999); cf. θάκους ... ἵν' οἰωνοσκοπεῖ (Eur. *Bacch.* 347), οἰωνίσματ' ὀρνίθων μαθὼν θάκοισιν ἐν ἱεροῖσιν (Eur. *Phoen.* 839 f.). The similarity of language suggests that both Sophocles and Euripides are referring to a specific well-known Theban site, which may well be the same as the οἰωνοσκοπεῖον Τειρεσίου καλούμενον located by Pausanias (9.16.1) in or near the agora within the city of Thebes.

[24] The occasion and nature of Teiresias' past assistance is not here specified, but ἐξ ἐμοῦ γὰρ τήνδ' ἔχεις σώσας πόλιν (1058) suggests some recent event: perhaps Teiresias' advice that Creon offer his son's death to save the city besieged by the Argives (cf. Eur. *Phoen.* 947–952; Megareus' death is referred to later in our play, 1303); a recent event is also suggested by 994, if we retain the present tense of the verb as in the manuscripts (see

because of him, polluted by the shreds of Polyneices' corpse which scavenger bird and beast have carried to the city and its altars (1015 ff.). Polyneices was unable to penetrate into the city while he lived, but his corpse, left unburied at Creon's command, now enters the city to befoul it after his death. In forbidding Polyneices' burial Creon had attempted to extend his control outside the city into the world of the dead; but his attempt failed, and now Polyneices and Antigone, both outside in the world of the dead, will exact Haemon's death as Creon's punishment for his mistreatment of them (1066 ff.). Creon's mistreatments of Polyneices and Antigone were political acts which denied the ties of family; but now Creon will be punished through these very family ties he had earlier denied.

It remains only to play out the inevitable. Creon leaves the stage, his world of the city, and goes into the world outside, the world of death (1114). Here obligations to the dead must override concern for those who still may live: Polyneices must be buried first.[25] In this world of dead Labdacids, Polyneices, the last dead Labdacid, must have his due from Creon, the man who has chosen to be his kin (cf. 173 f.).

Creon now goes to Antigone's tomb (1204 ff.). As we have seen, Creon surrendered his control over Antigone when he sentenced her to immurement outside the city. The outer world is Antigone's to dominate, and since Antigone now controls all, Creon must fail. Antigone must be dead by her own choice and hand (1221 f.) precisely because Creon would now rescue her (cf. 1111 f.). Haemon still lives, but in the tomb, the innermost recess of this world of death: now he truly belongs to Antigone. Creon enters the tomb (1226 f.) and beseeches Haemon to come out (1230); but it is too late. Creon had earlier forced Haemon to choose between himself and Antigone. Now that choice has been made, and Haemon will not leave Antigone. In a silence which seems deathlike in contrast to the cries of Creon (cf. 1226 f.), Haemon draws his sword and rushes at the intruder (1232 f.). For Creon is no longer his father, but the enemy[26] whom Hae-

---

A. C. Pearson, *CQ* 22 [1928], 187). H. D. Brackett, *CJ* 12 (1916–1917), 526, also sees in the αὖ of 996 (φρόνει βεβὼς αὖ νῦν ἐπὶ ξυροῦ τύχης) another possible reference to the death of Megareus.

25 It is clear from the sequence of commands at 1108–1112 that Creon recognizes the necessity of burying Polyneices first. Creon has no reason to believe that Antigone will commit suicide (or may have already done so), and so her release would not appear to require the same haste as the burial of Polyneices, the remains of whose body already pollute the city (cf. 1015 ff.); see also J. S. Margon, *CP* 65 (1970), 105–107; Brackett (preceding note), 531–534.

26 Thus Haemon "spits" at his father (1232), as earlier Creon had told him to "spit" at Antigone and treat her as an enemy (653); in both cases πτύσας is probably meta-

mon would kill. The blow misses and Haemon turns the sword upon himself (1234–1236). His rejection of Creon[27] and his union with Antigone are now complete. As Haemon falls he embraces Antigone (1236 f.),[28] corpse upon corpse as bridegroom and wife, their wedding chamber a tomb (1240 f.).

When Creon left to bury Polyneices the chorus sang an ode (1115 ff.) whose theme of deliverance for the city of Thebes, deliverance represented by the image of light, recalls the similar theme of the parodos. But while the parodos was confidently set in the light of a dawn which had already appeared (ἐφάνθης, 103) to replace the past night of danger, the present ode is set in sickness and pollution (cf. 1140–1143), from which the chorus prays to be rescued by a still future appearance of Bacchus (προφάνηθ', 1149). The nature of the rescuing light is also different in the two odes. In the parodos, the chorus sang of a new day which, by its nature as day, totally replaces the darkness of night. Bacchus, on the other hand, is a nocturnal god, and his light is a light which shines in the night but does not fully dispel its darkness.[29] By the way in which they invoke Bacchus as a bringer of light, the chorus reminds us that Thebes itself has now become a city of darkness, not the city of light promised by the parodos.

The city of darkness is also the city of death. In rapid succession Creon enters bringing Haemon's body from the tomb (1257; cf. 1258 with 1266), Eurydice's corpse is revealed within the palace (1293), and we learn of the earlier death of Creon's other son, Megareus (1303). The purpose of this accumulation of deaths is not simply to overwhelm the already humbled Creon in a sea of grief. Rather, each of these deaths has its place in the patterns we have been examining. Haemon died outside the city, and the entrance of his corpse is a visible sign of the penetration of that world of death into the heart of the *polis*. Eurydice, on the other hand, died within the city, and the appearance of her body on the stage serves

---

phorical, "expressing contempt and disgust" (see most recently P. Mazon, *RP*, 3ᵉ série, 25 [1951], 14).

[27] Haemon's suicide (like Eurydice's) is an act intended to punish Creon, and not simply a gesture of hopelessness or insanity (see M. Delcourt, "Le suicide par vengeance dans la Grèce ancienne," *Revue de l'histoire des religions* 119 [1939], 161–163).

[28] On these verses see also C. Bonner, "The Death of Haemon (*Ant.* 1236–1237)." *Classical Studies Presented to Edward Capps* (Princeton, 1936), 24–28; Bonner reads παρθένον in place of παρθένῳ at 1237, as more appropriate with προσπτύσσεται in the sense of "embraces"; see further G. Müller, *Sophokles: Antigone* (Heidelberg, 1967), ad loc.

[29] Cf. στέροψ . . . λιγνύς (1126 f., referring to the smoky torches carried by the god's devotees in their night revels; cf. Jebb [above, note 3], ad loc.); πῦρ πνειόντων χοράγ' ἄστρων, νυχίων φθεγμάτων ἐπίσκοπε (1146–1148); σε . . . πάννυχοι χορεύουσι (1151 f.).

as a visible counterpart to that of Haemon's (cf. 1298–1300). In this sense at least the world within and the world without are both seen to be the same: both are settings for death. While Haemon and Eurydice are of the present—both die in the course of the play—Megareus is of the past. Indeed, Creon's acquiescence to Megareus' death is the only thing we ever learn of Creon's past. Through most of the play that past had been completely shut out of Creon's new world; but now, as the illusion of that new world crumbles, the past penetrates into the present through Eurydice's suicide in grief for the deaths of both Haemon and Megareus (cf. 1303 ff., 1312 f.).

Amid this destruction of family the city which Creon would rule is now forgotten.[30] Creon who once seemed to control all is now seen to control nothing. Events flow under their own impetus to the final destruction of his house, and Creon is powerless to stop them. In claiming his throne on the grounds of his Labdacid connections, Creon also took upon himself that family's curse, and now this man who made himself a Labdacid must see his family perish, as all the Labdacids had perished before him. Creon who would rule κατ' ἀγχιστεῖα τῶν ὀλωλότων (174), has now become, like them, an ὀλωλότ' ἄνδρ' (1288).[31]

The new day which the chorus had proclaimed fairest of all (100–104) was an illusion. The new Thebes of light and life, the dominance of Creon, the primacy of the *polis* were all illusions too, but the illusions are gone. The old Thebes which we saw in the prologue could not be shut outside and forgotten, and now it has returned, present and real upon the stage. In this Thebes of family, darkness and death, Creon prays for the one day which will truly be fairest, the day which will be his last (1328–1333).[32]

Fairfield University

[30] From Eurydice's entrance on stage (1180), to hear of Haemon's death, until the end of the play Thebes is mentioned only once, and then in a quite unimportant way, when the messenger suggests that Eurydice may have gone into the palace to keep her grief private, and not to broadcast it to the city (1247–1249).

[31] Creon's death is metaphorical (he is an ἔμψυχος νεκρός for whom life is no longer worth living; cf. 1166 f.); but the word ὀλωλότ' does link him with Eteocles (174, 195), Polyneices (174, 1029), the whole of Antigone's family (894), and the dead Haemon (1240), all of whom were previously described by the intransitive perfect of the verb ὄλλυμι. Creon's description of himself as an ἔμψυχος νεκρός also links him with the punishment which he sought to impose on Antigone (cf. 774).

[32] I have taken some liberty in my paraphrase of 1328–1333 in order to point out more clearly the similarity between this passage and 100–104 (φανήτω . . . κάλλιστ' . . . ἀμέραν, 1329 f. ⟂ κάλλιστον . . . ἐφάνθης . . . ἀμέρας, 100–104).

3

Does Euripides Call the Gods μακάριοι?

MARIANNE McDONALD

It is likely that Euripides never applied the term μακάριος to the gods.[1] Arguments, however, must be found to show why Page and Biehl are wrong when they translate μακάριος as an epithet of the gods in *Antiope* 45 and *Orestes* 972, respectively.[2]

Lexica and etymological dictionaries regularly describe μακάριος in terms similar to those in Liddell-Scott: I, "mostly of men," and II, "of states, qualities, etc."[3] Μακάριος is never given as an epithet of the gods. Μάκαρ, on the other hand, is applied to both gods and men from the time of Homer,[4] and the lexica concur with Liddell-Scott's description of this term: "prop. epith. of the gods, as opp. mortal men."

A brief look at the history of the term μακάριος may help us understand Euripides' usage. The word is first found in the 5th century, in Pindar (*P.* 5, 46 Snell). The only other writers in the 5th century who use μακάριος are Euripides and Aristophanes. In *P.* 5, 46, Pindar calls the victorious

---

[1] This claim was first put forward in my dissertation *Terms for Happiness in Euripides* now published in *Hypomnemata* 54 (Göttingen, 1978), 231 f., 238 f., 296, 301 f.

[2] D. L. Page, *Select Papyri*, Loeb Classical Library (1941, reprint London, 1970), III, 66 f. Werner Biehl, *Euripides' Orestes erklärt* (Berlin, 1965), 106, and *Euripides Orestes* (Leipzig, Bibl. Teubneriana, 1975), 101.

[3] Cf. P. Chantraine's entry under μάκαρ: "Sens: 'bienheureux' en parlant des dieux, en ce sens souvent au pluriel (Hom., etc.), mais peut se dire d'hommes déjà chez Hom. . . . Dérivés: μακάριος 'bienheureux, favorisé des dieux' (Pi., E., prose attique), dit des hommes, . . ." *Dictionnaire étymologique de la langue grecque* (Paris, 1968), III, 659. For the -ιος suffix, see E. Schwyzer, *Griechische Grammatik* (Munich, 1953) I, 466, and A. Meillet et J. Vendryes, *Traité de grammaire comparée des langues classiques*, 4th ed. (Paris, 1968), 389: "Le suffixe a servi en effet à tirer des adjectifs de la plupart des thèmes nominaux existants."

[4] See note 3; the references in Homer given by Chantraine are: "ὦ μάκαρ Ἀτρείδη (*Il.* 3, 182), ἀνδρὸς μάκαρος pour un homme favorisé des dieux, qui est sans souci comme un dieu (*Il.* 11, 68)."

charioteer μακάριος for achieving fame after great toil. In other people's eyes he shares in a sort of divine glory. In this poem the king for whom he is driving the chariot is called μάκαρ (20), as is the king's hearth (11). A local hero, Battus, an ancestor of the king, is also called μάκαρ (94), as are the gods themselves (Κρονίδαι μάκαρες, 118). One can see the ranking: gods, hero, king (all μάκαρες, "divine"), and then the victorious driver (μακάριος, "sharing in godlike glory"). It is understandable that the driver would be on a level lower than a king, who is, of course, μάκαρ (e.g., Il. 3, 182). De Heer says that μακάριος may describe a person as "one who shares to a certain extent in the distinction of being μάκαρ."[5]

Aristophanes uses the term μακάριος in the same way as Euripides, in that it usually describes men. Aristophanes also applies it unambiguously

[5] C. de Heer, *MAKAP-EYΔAIMΩN-OΛBIOΣ-EYTYXHΣ: A Study of the Semantic Field Denoting Happiness in Ancient Greek to the End of the 5th Century B.C.* (Diss. Utrecht, Amsterdam, 1969), 31. De Heer has no example of μακάριος as applied to the gods, and when "sense components" are given for each of these four terms (p. 57), μακάριος shares seven components with μάκαρ; after component 7, de Heer states, "For μάκαρ the same numbers apply with the addition of 8: applied to the gods."

Although de Heer's work is helpful in many ways, one must use it with caution. In two tables (pp. 108–151), he says that he includes all the occurrences of the words which are the subject of his study, and then bases percentages on these occurrences (p. 58). However, he has omitted over 50% of the occurrences of these words in Euripides' fragments, and thus his percentages and statistical inferences are bound to be inaccurate. The following is a list of his omissions: *Alcestis*, εὐτυχῶν 1122, εὐτυχῶν 1158; *Medea*, εὐδαίμονας 1025, εὐδαιμονοῖτον 1073; *Hippolytus*, ὄλβον 626 (however, 625 f. are generally regarded as spurious); *Hecuba*, εὐτυχῇ 330, ὀλβίου 493; *Heraclidae*, εὐδαιμονοῖτε 582, εὐτυχεῖς 641; *Andromache*, ὄλβιον 100; *Supplices*, ὀλβίοις 5, εὐδαιμονεῖ 577; *Electra*, εὐδαιμονοίης 231, εὐτυχοῖ 1077, εὐδαιμονήσεις 1291; *Troades*, εὐτυχοῦσα 45, εὐτυχήσας 639, εὐτυχοῦντος 1162; *Helena*, εὐδαιμονίας 953 (LP reading adopted by Kannicht, rejected by Murray); *Iphigenia i.T.*, εὐτύχει 329, εὐτυχεστέροις 352 (LP reading rejected by Murray), εὐτυχοῦσα 837, εὐτυχοῖμεν 841, εὐτυχοῦμεν 850, εὐδαίμονα 1088, εὐτυχίας 1121, εὐτυχεῖν 1183; *Ion*, εὐτυχίαις 1505; *Phoenissae*, εὐδαιμονοίης 1086, εὐτυχεῖς 1163; (*Cyclops*, μάκαρ 459: read 495); *Iphigenia i.A.*, εὐδαιμονεῖν 1161; *Bacchae*, μακάριος 1243.

The following are the omissions in the fragments (Nauck): εὐδαιμονεῖ 45; εὐτυχεῖς 47.2; εὐτυχοῦντα 99; εὐτυχεῖν 142.4; εὐτυχῶ, εὐτυχῶ 143.1 f.; εὐτυχεῖ 154.2; εὐτυχῶν 262.3; εὐδαιμονεῖ 273.3; εὐτυχεῖ 285.12; ηὐτύχουν 285.20; ὄλβου 330.8; εὐτυχησάντων 362.31; εὐτυχοῦντα 402.2; εὐτυχοῦσα 409.1; εὐδαιμονεῖν 461.1; εὐτυχεῖ 463.4; εὐδαιμονούντων 536; εὐτυχεῖν 608.3; εὐτυχοῦντες 626.7; εὐδαιμονεῖ 661.1; εὐτυχεῖν 701; εὐτυχεῖ 730; εὐδαιμονίαν 745.2; εὐδαιμονίζων 778; εὐτυχοῦντας 901.5; εὐτυχοῦντα 1017; εὐτυχεῖ 1025.1; εὐτυχοῦσι 1056; εὐτυχεῖ 1056.3. Page, *Select Papyri* (1941; Loeb, vol. 3): *Antiope*, εὐτυχῇ 15; μακαρίων 45; εὐτυχῆ 102; *Hypsipyle*, ὄλβιον 79; ὄλβια 115; εὐτυχῶς 128; εὐδαιμονοίης 304; 305; εὐτυχίαισιν 324; *Melanippe*, ὄλβιος 7. *Nova Fragmenta Euripidea*, ed. C. Austin: *Archelaus*, εὐτυχήσουσ[19.11; *Erechtheus*, 65, μακάριος . . . εὐδαίμων col. II, 17; εὐτυχῇ col. II, 18; εὐτυχῇ col. V, 58. Also omitted are all the *Alexander* fragments; in addition to 45, 47.2, Snell fr. 6.8.

to the "blissful departed."[6] Again, in his works, the gods are never called μακάριοι. In Euripides, μακάριος describes men 27 times, and 17 times things rather than human beings;[7] but these things can be easily associated with human beings (such as χείρ, οἶκοι, γάμος).[8] It is never applied to the gods.

There are two late uses which may be mentioned here. (1) In Aristotle (*EN* 1178 b 9) the gods are said to be μακάριοι καὶ εὐδαίμονες because they engage in contemplative activity (ἐνέργεια θεωρητική), which is said to excel in bliss (μακαριότης).[9] This predicative usage, however, is different from an attributive one.[10] Authors previous to Aristotle do not even go this far. (2) Epicurus, in *Ep.* I, 78; I, 81; III, 123, and Κύριαι δόξαι 1, links the term μακάριος with ἄφθαρτος; in *Ep.* I the divine nature of celestial bodies is indicated, and τὸ μακάριον in Κύριαι δόξαι 1 describes the nature of the gods. Since these authors postdate Euripides, their usage does not support the interpretation of μακάριος in Euripides as an epithet of the gods.

[6] Euripides does not use μάκαρ unambiguously as an epithet for the dead, except in the phrase "isle of the blest" (μακάρων . . . νῆσον, *Hel.* 1677). Μακάριος, however, is used to describe and praise the dead hero Erechtheus (65, col. II, 17 Austin). Both terms are often used ambiguously by Euripides, in cases where the person described is dead or will be; but the person addressed takes the term as a simple one of praise. The divine departed are most likely these described in Aristophanes *Ranae* 85 (Agathon is said to have gone ἐς μακάρων εὐωχίαν). In his Ταγηνισταί the dead are called μακάριοι because they take part in a drinking feast, and a dead person is εὐδαίμων, ὅτ' οὐκ ἀνιάσεται, fr. I.6–11 in A. Meineke, *Fragmenta Comicorum Graecorum* (1857, reprint Berlin, 1970), II, 2, 1148.

[7] De Heer gives 41 occurrences of μακάριος in Euripides (p. 146), omitting *Antiope* 45 (Page), *Erechtheus* 65, and *Bacchae* 1243.

[8] The one possible exception is really no exception. In *Bacchae* 1171 θήρα is called μακάριον by Agave. Her hunting is seen as a divine thing and, ironically enough, the prize "beast" is her own son. Thus in this case too the association is all too human.

[9] Professor Peter Colaclides was kind enough to point out a passage in Plato's *Phaedrus* (247 a 4) where μακάριος and εὐδαίμων appear in close connection with the gods and μακάριος is specifically linked with θέαι (sights, a concrete form of θεωρία). He also pointed out at 250 b 6, where the vision (ὄψις τε καὶ θέα) of beauty is μακαρία, seen σὺν εὐδαίμονι χορῷ, and this is the most blest of the mysteries (μακαριωτάτη τῶν τελετῶν) and also εὐδαίμονα φάσματα. Aristotle goes much further with his image of the gods as blissful from their contemplation; but he no doubt owes much to Plato for the initial imagery of happiness linked with the gods and with a vision of beauty and goodness.

[10] See note 3. In contrast to μακάριοι, the majority of instances of μάκαρες in Homer show it modifying θεοί; e.g., *Il.* 1, 406; 4, 127; 14, 143; μάκαρες describes the gods in an absolute sense in *Od.* 10, 299. Euripides has parallel instances (e.g., fr. 453.2; *Med.* 825), and he applies this term to the gods more than to human beings (see *Terms for Happiness* [note 1], 295). In *El.* 994, *Hel.* 1348, *Ba.* 378, 1339, and fr. 912.12 μάκαρες by itself signifies the gods; in all of the other cases where it refers to the gods, some word like θεοί appears.

Page, however, translates μακα]ρίων σθένος βρόχοισι καταδεῖ [τὸν ἄδικον], at *Antiope* 45 f., as "The might of the blest gods binds down the unrighteous man in the meshes of a snare."[11] Given 5th century (particularly Euripidean) usage, μακαρίων is perhaps better translated "of the blest," referring to men, not gods. This is probably a general statement by the chorus which can be specifically applied to Lycus, an unrighteous tyrant whom Zethus and Amphion, two heroes (blest men?), have just overcome, thus enforcing divine justice (cf. *Antiope* 46 f., quoted below).[12] There are parallels in Euripides which show a tyrant meeting with just destruction. In fact, another Lycus, also a tyrant of Thebes, is slain by the hero Heracles for his evil deeds, and the comment is made by Amphitryon that Lycus is entering the net of swords (βρόχοισι δ' ἀρκύων . . . ξιφηφόροισι, *HF* 729 f.). The chorus see this as a just return for evil (734–774), and the gods (θεοί, 771) punish mortals (βροτούς, 775) for unjust deeds (ἀδίκων, 772), which is a parallel to βροτῶν δ' αὖ τέχναις [τ]ί[ς ἔφυγεν θε]όν; of *Antiope* 46 f. Both the situation and the imagery of the two passages are parallel.

On the other hand, Wilamowitz' restoration μακα]ρίων is by no means the only possibility:[13] for instance, ἀγ]ρίων might be a better reading, appropriate to the hunting imagery (cf. *HF* 1210, κατάσχεθε λέοντος ἀγρίου θυμόν). There is another possibility too: Euripides often calls a tyrant μακάριος, or if not a tyrant, someone who is powerful and wealthy.[14] Many times he comes to a bad end as a result of his evil deeds. It would seem, in Euripides, that wealth and power are corrupting agents if they are exclusive source of happiness (i.e., a reason why people are called μακάριοι).[15] Lycus was a tyrant who could be called μακάριος on account

---

11 Page follows Wilamowitz in adopting the reading μακα]ρίων here; Wilamowitz' complete reading is φονίοις μακα]ρίων.

12 The image of the net/snare is a frequent one in the *Oresteia*: Agamemnon's crimson robe becomes the net of his destruction (see Clytemnestra's speech, *Ag.* 1372 ff., and Fraenkel, Page, ad 1382). In Euripides' *Bacchae* the net image describes Dionysus' snare for Pentheus, and the term βρόχος appears again (*Ba.* 1020 ff.; cf. also 848).

13 In dealing with the word-end -ρίων, one may either interpret it as belonging to a word in close association with σθένος, or as an independent genitive, modifying or associated with something omitted. If it is linked with σθένος it may have either a positive or a negative meaning, depending on whether one regards the strength as coming from the gods/heroes or the wrongdoer. For example, the following words (all of which occur in Euripides) could belong to the positive category: ἀλεξητήριος, καίριος, κύριος, λυτήριος, σωτήριος. In the negative category appear ἄγριος, ἡμέριος, θούριος, λάθριος, ὀλέθριος. For the metrics involved, see J. Kambitsis, *L'Antiope d'Euripide* (Athens, 1972), 111, and H. J. Mette, *Lustrum* 12 (1967), 74.

14 *Terms for Happiness*, 296, sections I and III.

15 Cf. *HF* 1425 f., ὅστις δὲ πλοῦτον ἢ σθένος μᾶλλον φίλων | ἀγαθῶν πεπᾶσθαι βούλεται, κακῶς φρονεῖ.

of his wealth and power, but he abused these resources and came to a bad
end: μακα]ρίων in *Antiope* 45 might refer to a class of tyrants who took
unjust advantage of their resources and were punished. Thus one might
read something like this: ὁ θεὸς μακα]ρίων σθένος βρόχοισι καταδεῖ, "god
binds down the might of 'the blissful' in the meshes of a snare," (para-
phrasing Page).

The interpretation given μακαρίων as "of blest heroes" may have some
parallels in Euripides, too. Agave describes Cadmus as μακάριος because
of the heroic deeds accomplished by his daughters (*Ba.* 1242 f.); so also
the prize "beast" is called μακάριον (*Ba.* 1171, see note 8). Then the
"hero" Dolon will be called μακάριος if he achieves the heroic tasks which
will make him famous (*Rh.* 196).[16] In each of these cases tragic irony is
involved; Amphion and Zethus are more truly heroic than these "heroes."

Various solutions to]ρίων have just been suggested. The only solution
which is not possible, given Euripidean usage, is the one chosen by Page,
namely translating μακα]ρίων as "of the blest gods."

Now let us look at the passage *Orestes* 971–975, as interpreted by Biehl,
who seems to make the same error. The context of the passage also deals
with the downfall of a tyrant:

> βέβακε γὰρ βέβακεν, οἴχεται τέκνων
> πρόπασα γέννα Πέλοπος ὅ τ' ἐπὶ μακαρίοις
>   ζῆλος ὢν ποτ' οἶκος·
> φθόνος νιν εἷλε θεόθεν, ἅ
>   τε δυσμενὴς φοινία
> 975   ψῆφος ἐν πολίταις.

---

973 ζῆλος Musgrave: ζηλωτὸς codd.   οἴκοις Musgrave

Biehl translates μακαρίοις as "bei den seligen Göttern" (in 1965),[17]
while commenting (in 1975): "ἐπὶ ... ζῆλος: nescio an tmesis sit (i.e.
ἐπίζηλος?): ὁ ... ἐπὶ μακαρίοις ζῆλος ὢν ποτ' οἶκος ∽ ὁ (τοῖς) μακαρίοις
ἐπίζηλος ὢν ποτ' οἶκος ('domus, quae olim dis praeter omnes aemulanda erat')."
If, however, one accepts Musgrave's οἴκοις for οἶκος, the interpretation
seems to be easier: the tyrant's house is described as once μακάριος (cf.
Tr. 365, πόλιν ... μακαριωτέραν). A parallel passage may be found in
Or. 4 f., which describes the fall of Pelops' father Tantalus, a man

---

[16] One must be careful in citing this as an example of Euripidean usage, because the
Rhesus may not be by Euripides: see *Terms for Happiness in Euripides*, Appendix II, pp.
309–314. Compare, however, W. Ritchie, *The Authenticity of the Rhesus of Euripides* (Cambridge, 1964), 345 ff.

[17] In a footnote (p. 81), de Heer comments on Biehl's rendering, "this must be due to
faulty construing."

who once was μακάριος: in both cases human happiness is regarded as transient.

But with the transmitted reading οἶκος one may find a suitable meaning for ἐπὶ μακαρίοις: "the house once envied for bliss," (Wedd; ἐπί denoting the grounds of the envy, μακαρίοις being used as a neuter substantive);[18] "la maison dont la félicité était jadis un objet d'envie" (L. Méridier).[19]

One can understand why Biehl thinks Pelops' house might be a special object of envy (ζῆλος) "in the eyes of the blest gods," in view of the following line, φθόνος νιν εἷλε θεόθεν. But the image seems to become stronger if we see μακαρίοις as representing the height from which the line of Pelops fell, rather than as a simple parallel to line 973. Orestes 4 ff. describe this fall from bliss. (Compare the μακάριοι τύραννοι, El. 709 f., whom the masses come to admire and for whom disaster is imminent; once again these μακάριοι τύραννοι are from the line of Pelops. The chorus tells of the tyrants' fall from bliss because of their evil deeds, and human weakness is opposed to divine might, 727–746.)

There are other instances, too, where μακάριος (never μάκαρ) describes the powerful and wealthy in Euripides: Troades 1170 (Astyanax) and Orestes 86 (Helen and Menelaus). In the former case Hecuba's use is pathetic (Astyanax is now dead). In her dirge she speaks of the happiness which might have been his and would have come from his youth, marriage and ἰσόθεος τυραννίς, royal power which would have made him the gods' equal, thus μακάριος. However, she quickly adds, εἴ τι τῶνδε μακάριον (Tr. 1170), speculating herself on whether externals such as marriage and royal power are true sources of happiness (influenced no doubt by her present experience).[20]

In Or. 86 Electra's use of μακάριος is ironic (as it is in Electra 1006, when she calls Clytemnestra's hand μακαρία). In both cases she is vividly aware of her lowly station in contrast to these royal beings (Helen, Menelaus, and Clytemnestra), and she plots to destroy their "bliss" by murder. Murder seems to be a constant threat in Euripides to the μακάριοι, and there also seems to be a play on this word as an epithet for the dead. Thus,

18 N. Wedd, Euripides, The Orestes (Cambridge, 1926), 121.

19 Budé, 1959, translating F. Chapoutier's text: ζῆλος . . . οἶκος. The majority of the editors, however, adopt Musgrave's conjecture οἴκοις, including G. Murray (1913), A. S. Way (Loeb, 1912), V. di Benedetto (Florence, 1965).

20 See Terms for Happiness, 213 f. Ion too questions royal power as a source of happiness (Ion 621–632); if a man lacks peace and must always fear for his life, can this man be called happy? In both cases (Hecuba's and Ion's) μακάριος seems to describe a man who can be at peace and enjoy a life of ease and security, such as the gods enjoy, and a tyrant does not fit this description.

whenever Euripides uses μακάριος to describe people elevated above mankind because of their wealth and power, some sort of contrast is implied, and in most cases a fall has already occurred or is about to occur. The question is raised also about the value of this type of happiness, possibly on the grounds that it is not lasting; it is certainly not carefree. One thinks of the maxim which has haunted Greek literature since the Solon–Croesus confrontation (Herodotus 1.30–32): do not call a man happy until his death.[21]

In conclusion, μακάριος at *Orestes* 972 most probably refers to οἶκος, not to "the blest gods" (Biehl): "the house of Pelops, once an object of envy for its bliss." It is highly unlikely that Euripides was using μακάριος, in either *Antiope* 45 or *Orestes* 972, in such a strikingly novel fashion as Page and Biehl claim. If he used it as a synonym for μάκαρ as an epithet of the gods, it would be contrary to his own practice, and that of his contemporaries.

University of California, Irvine

[21] See *Terms for Happiness*, pp. 22–24.

4

The Manuscript Tradition of Aeschines' Orations

AUBREY DILLER

The manuscript tradition of Aeschines' orations has not been examined in breadth and depth.[1] The last attempts at classification and elimination[2] were before the age of microfilm. Several manuscripts of some importance (the Ambrosian especially) have not been examined at all. The mass of variant readings reported by Schultz (1865) is the available source for the tradition as a whole,[3] but it is incomplete and inaccurate for the primary mss. and overburdened with secondary mss. The latest editors (in the Budé series) collated some primary mss. in Paris and thus present most of the valid evidence for the text of the orations. The text of the prolegomena and scholia is still far from adequate.

The tradition is represented by one ms. (*f*) of the late tenth century, five (*Vakix*) of the thirteenth and fourteenth, and almost fifty of the

[1] Cf. E. Drerup, ed., *Aeschinis quae feruntur epistolae* (1904), who throws some light on the mss. of the orations. Drerup overlooked codd. Marc. gr. VIII 20; Ambros. gr. 247; Matrit. 4693.

[2] Max Heyse, *Über die Abhängigkeit einiger jüngerer Aeschineshandschriften* (Progr. Bunzlau, 1904); *idem, Die handschriftliche Überlieferung der Reden des Aeschines. Erster Teil: Die Handschriften der ersten Rede* (Progr. Ohlau, 1912). The dissertation of E. D. Goldschmidt (Berlin, 1925) has not been published; see *L'Année philologique* 2 (1927), 2; *Gnomon* 1 (1925), 52; 4 (1928), 212–217; G. Pasquali, *Storia della tradizione e critica del testo* (1934, 1952), 306. Useful meanwhile for breadth is R. Roncali, "Lista dei manoscritti di Eschine Licurgo Lisia," *Bari, Università, Facoltà di lettere e filosofia, Annali* XIV (1969), 381–399 (Aeschines 381–387).

[3] F. Schultz, ed., *Aeschinis orationes* (1865). I shall cite the text of Aeschines by the numbered variants in Schultz' text and apparatus, as Heyse has done. I follow Heyse also in the symbols for the mss.: small letters for the mss. collated before Schultz, mostly by Bekker, except *x*, added by Heyse; and capital letters for those added by Schultz (*ABFLV*) and myself (*CDMPRSWY*). The old Coislin ms. (*f* in Bekker and Heyse and here) is *F* in Schultz.

Renaissance. A Patmos codex of the early tenth century has brief excerpts from scholia on Demosthenes, Thucydides, and Aeschines,[4] and a bifolium from a fifth- or sixth-century codex from Egypt contains Aeschines or. III 178–186.[5] There are several fragments of papyrus from the first to third centuries; they are from all three orations but most from III.[6] The numerous quotations by ancient rhetoricians are often repeated by medieval authors, but there are quite a few independent medieval citations of Aeschines' orations.[7]

The standard medieval tradition, which I shall call β, carries prolegomena consisting of Αἰσχίνου ῥήτορος βίος (vita 1), Ἀπολλωνίου εἰς Αἰσχίνην ἐξήγησις (vita 2), and ὑποθέσεις (arguments) for the three orations. The three orations are accompanied by copious scholia and followed by the twelve epistles. This standard tradition β is represented by the old mss. aVx and several later independent mss. (mgL and parts of DS). The three other old mss. are outliers of β. f has all three orations and twelve epistles without the prolegomena and with only some of the scholia of β. k has only III II (sic) without arg. and with very few scholia. i has only II without arg. but with ample scholia. While β is a cluster of independent mss., fki are actually the parents of their families, as was shown by Heyse for f and is evident now for k and i also.[8]

The scholia[9] of β are preserved to the end of III only in Se and their offspring. L quits β at III 251, x at 246, V quits the scholia at III 156, g at 88, m at 18, a at II 120. The scholia in β were numbered by hundreds for reference, with corresponding numbers in the text. There are ca. 270 scholia on I, 297 on II, 440 on III. This rather fragile system is preserved

[4] Codex Patmiacus 263. See J. Sakkelion in *Bull. de corresp. hell.* 1 (1877), 1–16; 137–155; 177–194, and *Revue de philol.* 1 (1877), 182–188, esp. 154 f., 181. The scholia are from all three orations of Aeschines, in the usual order, and agree in part with the scholia of fβ.

[5] Pap. Rainer inv. 8030, Pack No. 17.

[6] R. A. Pack, *The Greek and Latin literary texts from Greco-Roman Egypt* (²1965), p. 16, 4–18. Nos. 5 and 6 belong together, see T. Lenaerts in *Chronique d'Egypte* 41 (1966), 144–159.

[7] G. Klinke, *Quaestiones Aeschineae criticae* (Leipzig, 1897) collects the testimonia earlier than the *editio princeps* (1513). It is tedious to separate the primary (independent) testimonia from the secondary (repeated). Among medieval readers of Aeschines may be mentioned Photius, the *Suda*, Tzetzes, Greg. Pardus of Corinth, Thomas Magister.

[8] The four *genera* recognized by Schultz correspond in the main to βfki with their respective offspring. Weidner, Blass, and Heyse use the symbol A for the family of k (and i), B for the standard tradition β, and M or C for the family of f. But in or. I, where k is lacking, Weidner, followed by Blass, ineptly transferred A from k to f.

[9] Sauppe (1850) and Dindorf (1852) edited the scholia from fim, Schultz (pp. 249–355) from fimgVL. Schultz later found the missing end of the scholia in e.

in *aVxm* as far as they go, but *LSi* modify it. Three scholia at the head of III are *extra seriem*, unnumbered: (a) ἡ στάσις . . ., (b) τινὲς εἶπον . . ., (c) ὅτι οὐ δεῖ . . . (Schultz pp. 151 and 315): *DWE* have (a) (b) without (c), *f* has only (a).

Some other useful marks of the main mss. may be mentioned. In or. I, which is found only in β and *f*, seven false documents are interpolated in the text of β but omitted in *f*: I 12 16 21 35 50b 66 68. Or. I has a longer ending in *f* (*expl.* ἐξετάζειν) than in β (*expl.* καταλέλειπται). The excerpt ὅτι ἠδυνήθη . . . ἀφανοῦς (Schultz pp. 5 f.) is found only in *f* and *i* (and their offspring), in *f* after the end of II, in *i* in the margin at the beginning of II. It belongs to II, but some apographs of *S* wrongly attach it to III. — In the frequent expression ὦ ἄνδρες ἀθηναῖοι the β-mss. usually omit ἄνδρες; *f* begins with ἄνδρες but soon drops it; *k* has it in III and as far as II 24; *i* has it all through II. The mss. agree in the less usual ὦ ἄνδρες without ἀθηναῖοι and ἄνδρες ἀθηναῖοι without ὦ.[10] *f* writes δ over ω, and θ or θθ over ω or α, and *k* and even β-mss. have traces of this tachygraphy, which is ancient and occurs elsewhere in the tradition of the Attic orators.[11]

The textual variation in β*fki* is frequent but mostly superficial. Few variants are from majuscule or word-division,[12] very many from slight transposition and omission or addition. In I neither β nor *f* has much advantage; their texts are equally readable, each sometimes corrupt. In II III *k* veers between *f* and β, or perhaps, as Weidner put it, *f* veers between *k* and β, but *fk* seem closer than *fβ*; there are conjunctive errors all three ways: *fk, βk, fβ*. *k* has more singular readings than *f* or β, especially in III. *i* is problematical: at first it agrees often, though not always, with *k*, but after II 40 this agreement virtually ceases and *i* goes with β; but *i* has more singular readings even than *k*, most of them transpositions, none certainly genuine.[13] From this evidence no image of a ninth-century archetype emerges. Apart from interpolations, corruptions shared by all (β*fki*) are not very frequent and are evidently ancient. The recension is open, and eclecticisim is the principle on which the modern editors have established the text. However, this does not deny the elimination of secondary mss.

The isolation of β is confused by the sporadic occurrence of *f*- or *fk*-

[10] Om. ὦ I 78 121 164, III 177 (*fβ*) 209 (*fβ*) 211 (*fkβ*); om. ἀθηναῖοι I 177 (*f*), II 4 (*f*) 7 (*fβ*) 24 (*fβ*) 69 (*fkβ*) 129 (*fβ*) 183 (*f*); δικασταί I 78 164, II 24 (*ki*) 102 (*i* bis) 129 (*i*).

[11] H. Diels and W. Schubart, eds., *Didymos Kommentar zu Demosthenes* (1904), p. 3.

[12] Majuscule variants: I 77₁₀ 101₁₁, II 8₉ 22₁₀ 49₁₀ 116₈, III 29₃ 82₉ 103₂ 167₉ 18; minuscule variants: II 15₈, III 140₈ 165₁₄ 235₃ 239₄; word-division: I 44₅, II 21₁₆ 22₁₀ 377 49₁₀ 81₈ 102₁₄ 116₈ 182₈, III 72₁₀ 126₁₃ 149₈ 179₂ 196₁ 227₅ 246₈.

[13] *i* is supported by a papyrus in two singular transpositions (II 74₇ 75₁), but I still cannot believe that *i* draws on a tradition different from β*fk*. Cf. Martin-Budé I (1927), p. ix.

readings in β-mss. We may begin with the major omissions. At I 87_9 92_{11} 196_5 omissions are shared by all the β-mss., and at I 162_2, II 32_{13} 159_{12} omissions are shared by the cognates xL. On the other hand, at II 124_{13} 160_2 omissions are shared by f^1k. But other omissions do not follow the branches of the tradition. In II 91 mxL omit in the text but supply in the margin, and a has an equivalent incipient omission, but fkiV do not omit. At II 182_6 aL^t omit and mg have an equivalent incipient omission, but again fkiVx do not omit. At III 22_3 axL omit, but fkmgV do not. Perhaps these cases may be explained as omissions supplied in the margin in the archetype of β. But there are other omissions shared by fk with some β-mss. At II 111_{12} $f^1kV^tL^t$ omit, but f^1k omit one more word (ἀλλά) than V^tL^t; iamgx do not omit. At III 20_3 $fkxL^t$ omit, while amgV and a papyrus do not; at III 86_7 f^1xL^t share an omission. Omissions of $f^tm^tL^t$ at II 154_8 and of k^aV^t at III 25_{14} may be merely coincidental.

The following list is a selection of other variant readings of f or fk occurring sporadically in β-mss.

I 29_1 εἰ fxL   ἢ amVD

39_5 ὧν εἰς τὸ σῶμα fVD   εἰς τὸ σῶμα ὢν amxL

47_{12} ἐξεργάσασθαι fxL   ἐξεργάζεσθαι amVD

51_5 μέτριον fa   μετριώτερον mVxLD

52_{22} δοκεῖ τούτω fD   τούτω δοκεῖ am(V)xL

55_9 δὲ famD   om. VxL

56_6 om. fD   οὗτος amVxL

58_1 παρὰ fa   ἀπὸ mVxLD

59_5 ἕτερά τινα f   τινα x   ἕτερα amVLD

64_{17} ἔχειν fa   ἔσχε mVxLD

78_5 αὐτοὶ fmD   αὐτὰ aVxL

79_5 ἔνοχος fm^mD ἔναγχος amVx   om. L

80_{15} ὅτ᾽ ἂν fa   ἢ ἐὰν mVxLD

90_6 ἐρημίαις fV^1x ἐρημία amLD   om. V

90_{16} ἀνήρηται fD   ἀνήρητ᾽ ἂν amVxL

95_8 τιμομάχου faxD   τιμάρχου mVL

100_7 ὑμῖν· μεταγ. fVx   μεταγ. ὑμῖν amLD

111_{15} om. fxD   ἔφη amVL

141_8 -μένως $famxL^cD$ -μένους VLS

156_5 πανταλέοντα faxL   παντολέοντα mVD

157_4 ῥαμνησίου fxL   ῥαμνουσίου amVD

157_9 παραμένοντος fmxL   παρμένοντος aVD

170_{13} τὰς οὐσίας fVxL   τὴν οὐσίαν amD

179_3 ἐκ- famL   ἐμ- VxD

II 8_9 ἐμοῖς fa   ἄλλοις kimVxL

12_5 om. fVi   περὶ kamxL

14_3 ἐγ- famxLi   ἐπι- kVL¹

15_1 ὑπὸ fkiam^m   ὑπὲρ mVxL

15_5 ἐγ- fmVxL   om. kia

15_{13} οἱ fkiam   om. VxL

21_{11} δὲ f(a)mxL   om. kiV

29_{12} καὶ μετὰ fkix   om. amVL

35_6 om. fam   ἔτι kiVxL

36_5 μόνου fa   μόνον kimVxL

39_8 αἰτίου fa°x(L)   ἐκ τοῦ ἐναντίου kimV

41_5 om. fkamV   μου xLi

49_9 οἰκ. πραγ. fkimV   πραγ. οἰκ. axL

52_9 om. fka   ἀλλὰ mVxLi

55_3 om. fka   εἶπε mVxLi

55_4 κατένειμε fka   κατανεῖμαι mVxLi

55_9 συμ- fkamLi   om. VxD

58_{11} παρὰ fkiV   ἀπὸ amV¹xL

62_{23} βουλεύεσθαι fkxL   βεβουλεῦσθαι am(V)i

64_3 μαρτ. δημ. fkx   δημ. μαρτ. amVL(i)

69_{13} om. fk(a)V   μᾶλλον mxLi

82_{17} ἀπηρκ. fkam°L   ἀπηρηκ. mV   ἀπειρηκ. xDi

93_4 ἐπιβολὴν faV   ἐπιβουλὴν kimxL

94_1 ἐν- fkxL   ἐπ- amVi

94_9 om. fkam   ἐμὲ VxLi

95_1 δήμου fkia   νόμου a°mVxL

96_1 κατηγόρεις fka   κατηγορεῖς mVxLi

98_9 ἐν- fmVi   om. kaL

109_3 ὑπ- fkiamL   ἐπ- Vx

113_2 om. fkaxL   καὶ ἀναισχυντίαν (a¹)mVi

122_{13} om. fkiamV   καὶ xL

124_{12} ἐπιδ. ἐπιστ. fkam   ἐπιστ. ἐπιδ. (V)xLi

125_7 om. fkxL   λόγους amVL¹i

125_{10} om. fkxL   πολλάκις amVx¹L¹i

140_4 ὁπλιτῶν fka   πολιτῶν mVxL

141_1 om. fkamV   τῶ φιλίππω συνιόντων xL

144_5 πορνείας fka   πονηρίας mVxLi

148_8 ἐπὶ τῶν τριάκοντα fa¹Li   om. kamVx

148_9 πολιτικῶν fkiam   πολιτῶν VxL

152_4 om. fka   δεῦρο mVxLi

154_6 εἰς fa   om. kx   ὡς VxLi°   ὡς εἰς mi

154₇ γεγενημένην *fkimVxL*¹   om. *aL*
157₁ -μενος *fkia*   -μένην *mVxL*
164₃ ἐκεῖνον *fkam*   ἐκείνω *a°m°xLi*   ἐκείνων *V*
164₁₀ om. *fkam*   αὐτοὺς *VxLi*
166₅ ἀπεστέρησας *fam*   ἐπεστέρησας *ki*   ἀποστερήσας *VxL*
173₆ om. *fka*   τοξότας *mVxLi*
175₈ om. *fkam*   καὶ *VxLi*
177₂₀ ἢ *fkam*   ἢ ἡ *VxL*   ἐξ ἧς ἡ *i*
178₇ om. *fkxL*   ὅλων *amVL*¹*i*
179₁₂ τὴν ὀργὴν *fmxL*¹(*i*)   om. *kaVL*
III 38 om. *fam*   ἤδη *kVxL*
39 εἶναι *fV*   om. *kamxL*
74 μικρὸν *fkxL*   om. *amV*
8₁₄ τῷ νόμῳ *fam*   τοῖς νόμοις *kVxL*
11₂ οὕτως *fkmVx*   om. *aL*
13₃ om. *faxL*   τινα *kmV*(*L*¹)
23₆ τοῦτο *fkxL*   τούτου *amV*
27₇ ἄλλοι *famV*   om. *kxL*
27₉ τούτων *famxL*°   τοῦτον *kVL*
27₁₉ -μελησομ. *fmVxL*   -μεληθησομ. *ka*
29₃ εἰ *famx*   οἱ *kVL*
33₂ om. *fVxL*   οὖν *kam*
39₇ om. *fam*   περὶ *kVxL*
46₁₆ om. *fka*   καὶ *mVxL*
54₄ om. *famL*   ἀπάντων (*k*)*VxL*¹
57₃ ἀπο- *fV*¹*L*   ἐπι- *kamVxL*°
57₉ om. *fam*   ἀπάντων *kVxL*
60₁₆ μετὰ *fxL*   om. *kamV*
61₃ τῶν ἑλλήνων *fkVx*¹*L*¹   om. *amxL*
62₃ τουτὶ *fVxL*   τοῦτο *kam*
63₂ πρὸς *fam*   ὡς *kVxL*
67₄ om. *faxL*   ὅτ' ἦν 2° *kmVL*¹
67₁₂ om. *fV*   ὡς *kamxL*
71₂ om. *fam*   ὑπ- *kVxL*
73₉ λέγω καθεζ. *fkV*   καθεζ. λέγω *amxL*
75₃ om. *fam*   ἦν 2° *kVxL*
76₂ αὐτοῦ *fam*   αὐτῶν *Vx*   αὐτῷ *L*   om. *k*
76₃ om. *fam*   ὦ ἀθ. (*k*)*VxL*
76₁₆ τρία *fkmV*   om. *axL*
76₁₉ καταγελ . . . ποιῶν post εἰς θήβας 2° *fkmV*   post 1° *axL*
77₇ ἑβδόμη δ' ἡμέρα *fx*   ἑβδόμην δ' ἡμέραν *kamVL*

77_{11} om. *faxL* ἀπολέσας *kmVL*¹

78_8 ποτε *fx* om. *kamVL*

81_2 τὸν *faV* om. *kmxL*

81_8 δωρ. ζηλ. *fkVxL*° ζηλ. δωρ. *amL*

82_{11} καὶ γανίδα *f(k)V* om. *amxL*

84_2 om. *f* καὶ *k* τρία *amV* καὶ τρία *xL*

84_4 μεγίστης *famV*¹*xL* θαυμαστῆς *kVx*¹*L*¹

94_8 τούτους *f(a)mxL* τούτων *kV*

98_7 om. *fam* ὑμῖν *kL* ἡμῖν *Vx*

101_{13} om. *fa* φησὶ *kmVxL*

103_7 om. *fka* πρὸς φίλιππον *f*ᵐ*mVxL*

105_1 ταῦτ' *fkx* πάντ' *amVL*

110_1 μόνον τὸν ὅρκον *faV* τὸν ὅρκον μόνον *mx* τὸν ὅρκον *L*

111_2 ἐπεύχεται *famx* ἐπεύχεσθαι *kVx*°*L*

111_3 μηδὲ *fam* μήτε *kVxL*

117_9 γε *fkaxL* om. *mV*

118_3 λέγων *fam* om. *kVxL*

120_3 om. *fam* τῶν προγόνων *kVxL*

126_5 διεγράψατο *fxL* διεπράξατο *kamV*

132_{13} ἑτέρων *fkVx*° om. *amxL*

132_{16} ἐν δελφοῖς *fam* om. *kVxL*

137_6 οὐδὲ *fkmxL* οὐ *aV*

139_1 ῥήτωρ καὶ οὗτος *fkx*¹*L*¹ om. *amVxL*

139_7 ῥήτωρ *fx*¹*L*¹ om. *kamVxL*

140_3 τῆς *faV* τῶν *kmxL*

163_5 τὸν *fxL* om. *kamV*

163_{18} θῶ *fkaxL* θεῶ *mVL*°

168_4 -βλέψητε *fV* -βλέπητε *kamxL*

170_6 om. *fam* καὶ αὐτὸν *kV* αὐτὸν *xL*

171_1 ἦν *fka* om. *mVxL*

171_6 om. *fkamVxL* ἀπόδημος *x*¹*L*¹*m*ᵐ

175_4 αὐτῷ *fV* om. *kamxL*

178_{17} -πέπλυται *fkm(V)L* -λέλυται *axL*ᵐ

181_4 περὶ *fka(m)L* om. *Vx*

181_8 τὰς τάξεις *fV* τὴν τάξιν *kamxL*

181_{11} ἐπικαλούμενος *fkxL*¹ om. *amL*

182_5 κἀκεῖνοι *fkx* κἀκεῖνο *amVL*

183_4 χρόνον *fV* πόνον *k* πόνον . χρόνον *am(x)L*

184_8 παισὶν *fkam* πᾶσιν *VxL*

202_{19} om. *fxL* κατηγόρηκα *kamV*

203_{12} ταύτας *famL* ταῦτα *kV*

205₁₂ om. *faL*   μηδ' ἀγνοεῖθ' *km(V)*
208₃ ὅτι *fkL*   om. *amV*
209₉ ἦ *fam*   om. *kVL*
212₃ φοβήσεται *fkaL*   φοβηθήσεται *Vm*
217₄ τὸ . κεφάλαιον *fka*   τὰ . κεφάλαια *mVxL*
222₁₀ -μένους *faV*   -μένος *kmxL*
228₈ οὐκ *famxL*   οὐδ' *kV*
229₁₅ τῶν αὐλῶν *fka*   τὸν αὐλὸν *mVxL*
235₆ -γενέσθαι *faL*   -γίνεσθαι *kmVx*
235₇ ὑφ' *fkmxL*ᶜ   om. *aVL*
240₄ ἐννέα δὲ *famVx*   δὲ ἐννέα *kL*
242₆ ἂν *fkVx*   om. *amL*
246₁₆ ἐνοχλ. ἐντ. *fkVx*   ἐντ. ἐνοχλ. *amL*
247₄ ἀπολογισμὸν *fkV*   ἀπολογίαν *amL*

The irrational distribution of these readings in the mss. may be attributed to various causes of deviation from simple lines of descent: (1) double readings[14] in the common archetype, including glosses and scholia; (2) contamination of β-mss. from *f*; (3) intentional intervention by scribes and correctors; (4) fortuitous coincidence. But altogether they do not seem to account for the phenomenon satisfactorily. A similar puzzling situation exists in several later mss., where contamination appears in such a form as to postulate either too many lost *Vorlagen* or else that the scribe was copying from two *Vorlagen* at once; see codices *ixSFp*, not to mention still later ones.

I shall deal now with the individual mss., in stemmatological order as far as possible, as in the following list. I have microfilm of twenty mss., as indicated; for the others I rely on published descriptions and collations. I regret I could not use watermarks for dating the mss., and that I have not recognized more of the scribes. In compensation, I have tried to find the earliest ownership of the codices. Unless stated otherwise, the mss. are of the fifteenth and sixteenth centuries and are of paper (the parchments are *fVBpce* and Ottob.). Merely for economy I shall omit references to the standard catalogues of mss. given in Richard's *Repertoire* (²1958).

β   *amgVx L*: vitae, arguments, three orat. with scholia, twelve epist.
a   Rome, Angelicus gr. 44 *s*. XIII
b   Vat. Barb. gr. 22: om. scholia epist.
m   Paris. gr. 3003

---

[14] Double readings are evident in β or β*f* (not *k*) at I 9₁₂ 7₁₅ 8₂₂ 9₆₁₁ 12₇₁₅ 168₁₂ 184₂, II 15₁₇ 3₁₆ 35₅ 44₁₃ 58₆ 73₁₇ 136₄, III 9₉ 45₁ 61₃ 84₄ 91₁₆ 17₁₉ 207₁₄.

o r	Copenhagen, regius 415: I only
v	Vind. ph. gr. 156: II only
n	Paris. gr. 3004: III only
g	Paris. gr. 2930: om. vitae arg. epist.
V	Vatic. gr. 64 mbr. *a.* 1269/70
p	Wolfenbüttel 902 mbr.: om. scholia
	Ambros. gr. 247
	Madrid 4693
x	Paris. suppl. gr. 660 *s.* XIV: om. epist.
L	Laur. 57,45: om. epist.
	Vind. ph. gr. 59: vitae arg. only
	Marc. gr. VIII 2: om. scholia
f	Paris, Coislin 249 mbr. *s.* X: three orat. twelve epist., om. vitae arg.
K	Istanbul, Panaghia Kamariotissa 158: I only
A	Laur. conv. soppr. gr. 84: I only
M	Marc. gr. 442: om. epist.
S	Ambros. gr. 455: adds vitae arg. scholia
	Leonardo Bruni *a.* 1412: Latin trans. of III
B	Vat. Barb. gr. 159 mbr.: without scholia
C	Laur. acquisto 50: without scholia
d	Marc. gr. VIII 20: III I II epist.
	Laur. 58,6: epist. II I III
	Ambros. gr. 26: III I II, om. epist.
q	Phillipps 8077: II III without scholia, epist., [I]
P	Vat. Pal. gr. 134: II III
R	Ambros. gr. 316: with scholia
	Ambros. gr. 297
E	editio princeps 1513: without scholia, om. epist.
k	Paris. gr. 2998 *s.* XIII: III II without scholia
δ	*Dle*: III II [I]
D	Ambros. gr. 409: adds vitae arg. scholia
l	Paris. gr. 3002
e	Marc. gr. VIII 4 mbr.: om. I, adds scholia
s	London, Harley 6322: II only
i	Paris. gr. 2996 *s.* XIV: II only, with scholia
F	Laur. 60,4: III II [epist.]
z	Moscow gr. 475: II III
W	Vatic. gr. 67: all of β but in disorder
v	Urbinas gr. deperd.
Υ	Vatic. gr. 72: I II III with scholia
h	Paris. gr. 2947

c   Vat. Urbin. gr. 116 mbr.: [I] III II epist.

t   Gotha 572: III [I]

I   Vat. Ottob. gr. 254 mbr.

II   Vatic. gr. 1392
    Vat. Barb. gr. 53
    Naples II E 28
    Salamanca 223
    Istanbul, μετόχιον 10
    Athens, βουλή 23 s. XVIII

III   Vatic. gr. 1585
    Vatic. gr. 2362
    Vatic. gr. 1949
    Naples II E 11
    Laur. Ashburnham 1640
    Lisbon
    Bucharest 603
    Vatopedi 736 s. XVIII

—   Oxford, Bodl. 6561: vitae arg. only
    Vat. Pal. gr. 51: scholia only
    Paris. suppl. gr. 1344 s. XIX: scholia only.

(a) Rome, Angelicus C.3.11 (gr. 44): bomb. s. XIII 318 leaves 25 × 15.5 cm. in 39 quat. and one ternion (297–302) signed α-μ. Fol. 240v 277v and parts of 237v 238v are blank, apparently because of poor paper. Fol. 3–212 Aristides,[15] 213–317 Aeschines complete β except that the scholia are incomplete and virtually cease at II 120, though blank numbers continue to II 136. A second hand begins with quire 35 (fol. 273, in II 182). The script is uncalligraphic, but the text is good. The only major omissions, apart from conjunctives, are at III 142₉ 166₁ 166₅ₐ (ὅτ' ἔφη . . . πόλιν) 214₅. An interpolation preceding III 177, ἐπεὶ ἐνταῦθα λοιπὸν ἐπιλογίζεται, matches the scholion ad loc. in Se ἐντεῦθεν λοιπὸν ἐπίλογοι. There is correction and collation by the first and later hands, usually agreeing with f and particularly with Υ (from fM),[16] which in turn has readings from a. — This codex was in the collection formed by Cards. Guido Ascanio Sforza (d. 1564) and Alessandro Sforza (d. 1581).[17] It was collated by Bekker and (in I) by Heyse. I have microfilm.

[15] B. Keil, ed., *Aelii Aristidis Smyrnaei quae supersunt omnia*, II (1898, repr. 1958), pp. XII f.

[16] Υa° I 80₁₅ 122₇ 149₃₆ 178₁₀, II 129₅. The long ending at I 196₅ is added. At I 176₇ the misreading λόγον occurs only in l^a and a° (Heyse 12), not in DΥ; it may have been in v.

[17] *Studi ital.* 6 (1898), 172. On the Biblioteca Sforziana see G. Mercati in *Studi e Testi* 164 (1952), 15–146.

(*b*) Vatic. Barber. gr. 22 (*olim* 263): 304 leaves 169 × 114 mm. Fol. 79–196 (in eleven quint. and one quat., 118 and 193–196 blank), Aeschines β without scholia and epistles, written by a non-Greek hand.[18] — This codex belonged to Lattanzio Tolomei of Sienna (d. 1543).[19] It was collated in I by Bekker and Heyse, who both recognized it as an apograph of *a*.

(*m*) Paris. gr. 3003: 222 leaves 22.3 × 14.5 cm. Fol. 1–126 Aeschines in 15 quat. and one ternion (57–62) signed ⟨β⟩-ιζ, fol. 127–222 scholia on Aristides in another hand. Aeschines is complete β except that the scholia cease at III 18. The text often agrees with *a* against *VxL*. Major omissions at I 100₆ 189₃, II 116₁₁ 154₈, III 167₈ σὺ Θετταλοὺς ἀφιστάναι (*non om.* σὺ γάρ . . . ἀποστήσαις) 168₆, are supplied by the first or later hands, and a large repetition in III 65 is deleted. Spaces for the scholia are taken out of the main column on the page. The scholia are numbered: 272 on I, 297 on II, 38 on III; sch. III abc and a few others are *extra seriem*.[20] There is correction by several hands on the epistles (Drerup) and a good deal in III, less in II and I. In I some of it is from *p*,[21] in II III it is from *fk*, from *k* alone after III 113,[22] actually from *Yh*, which are from *fM* and after III 113 from *kl*. In III the same corrections sometimes occur in *m²h²* and even *g²*,[23] and a few corrections in *m²h²* seem to be from *g*.[24] Codd. *mgh* all belonged to Janus Lascaris (d. 1534).[25] A corrector has also introduced an un-Greek feature, that is, the Italian practice in cutting lines, such as δ' transferred from the end of a line to the head of the next. There are a few conjectures and interpretations in the margin, e.g., question-marks in III 130, ἴσως λυσικλέα III 143₈ₐ (cf. Diodorus 16.88). — Codd. *mg* were collated by Taylor, Bekker, Dübner (the scholia for Dindorf), Heyse. I have microfilm of *m*.

(*o r*) Copenhagen, regius 415: 150 leaves 28 × 21 cm. Fol. 121–150 Aeschines I 1–174 (the end lost) in a different hand from the preceding parts, copied from *m* (Heyse). This codex belonged to John Locker of London (d. 1760) and to Anthony Askew (sale 1785 No. 579). Collated by Taylor for Reiske (*r*) and by Bloch for Dindorf (*o*) and by Heyse, who showed that *r* and *o* are the same.

18 G. Mercati in *Studi e Testi* 46 (1926), 149 n. 2.

19 Mercati, pp. 138–156, *Aggiunte*, pp. 5 f.

20 Corrections are mistakenly numbered as scholia at II 32₂ 154₈.

21 *pm²*: I 113 50₁₈ 66₇ 9 794 5 90₁₃ 124₁₃.

22 *fm²*: II 58₁₀ 11 12 72₃ 951 96₁, III 211 2 60₇ 82₂ 103₂, *et al.*—*km²*: III 114₃ 117₁₅ 118₇ 162₁₂ 170₇ 183₉ 186₅, *et al.*

23 *m²h²*: III 56₆ 573 9 757 931 5 101₆ 116₆ 156₇ 171₉ 185₅ (from Plutarch) 186₁₁, also I 66₇ 9, II 138₆.

24 *gm²h²*: III 49₁ 107₉ 165₁ 193₇.

25 *Mél. d'arch. et d'hist.* 6 (1886), 258, Nos. 70 (*m*), 89 (*h*), 90 (*g*).

(v) Vind. ph. gr. 196: 46 leaves 228 × 165 mm. Aeschines II copied from m (Heyse) by Constantine Mesobotes ca. 1500 (Hunger). Collated by Bremi (1824).

(n) Paris. gr. 3004: 170 leaves 203 × 146 mm. Aeschines III with arg. and Demosthenes 18, written by Georgius Hermonymus and annotated by Guillaume Budé (d. 1540).[26] Or. III is copied mostly from m, but in 227 it begins to agree with f. Collated by Bekker, inspected by Drerup for Heyse.

(g) Paris. gr. 2930: 169 leaves 28 × 21 cm. Fol. 1–117 Isocrates,[27] 118–167 Aeschines, 168–169 Dion Chrys. Aeschines begins without vitae and arg. as an apograph of A (from f), but in I 21 it switches to β, closely akin to m but independent of m; the epistles are omitted. However, both parts are contaminated (Heyse); the first has the documents and scholia of βm. The scholia cease at III 88 (at III 18 in m), but a bit of scholia is in the text at III 107$_9$, also II 119$_{12}$. There are several unique long scholia (Schultz p. 251), doubtless untraditional. Some correction in III coincides with m^2h^2.

(V) Vatic. gr. 64: mbr. 290 leaves 318 × 205 mm. in three parts by different hands, the third dated fol. 289v a. 6778 (A.D. 1269/70).[28] The second part (fol. 147–225, ten quat. α-ι lacking the last leaf) contains Aeschines and Socratic epistles, the latter in part unique. Aeschines is complete β except that the scholia[29] cease in III 156 (fol. 194, the end of quat. s). The text is rather erratic and sometimes even illiterate. I count twenty singular omissions, some of then supplied between lines by the first hand.[30] In I there are fenestrae.[31] In III variant readings of k have been entered extensively by a coarse hand. — This codex has supplements and annotations by Cardinal Isidorus Ruthenus (d. 1463) and probably belonged to him.[32] It was collated by Schultz and (in I) by Heyse. I have microfilm.

(p) Wolfenbüttel 902 (Helmstedt 806): mbr. 226 leaves 21 × 13 cm.

---

[26] H. Omont, "Notice sur Georges Hermonyme," Mémoires de la Soc. de l'hist. de Paris 12 (1885), 90.

[27] E. Drerup, ed., Isocratis opera omnia, I (1906), pp. XXIX, LV. Isocrates in g is not nearly akin to Isocrates in A.

[28] A. Turyn, Codices Graeci Vaticani saeculis XIII et XIV scripti annorumque notis instructi (1964), 46–48.

[29] Scholia III abc are at the end of II, fol. 181v. A bit of scholia in the text at I 124$_7$.

[30] Vita 2$_{27}$, or. I 64$_{15}$ 66$_3$ 149$_{14}$, II 27$_9$ 37$_4$ 111$_5$ 119$_{10}$ 156$_{18}$, III 129$_6$ 172$_5$ 255$_4$, supplied by the first hand: II 60$_{21}$ 116$_4$, III 251$_4$ 130$_6$, supplied by the second hand from k: III 62$_{10}$ 85$_5$ 103$_3$ 167$_8$.

[31] I 24$_3$ 256 7 41$_{19}$ 47$_{16}$ 48$_{10}$ 491 6 19 etc.

[32] G. Mercati in Studi e Testi 56 (1931), 522.

Fol. 1r–165r Aeschines complete β except the scholia, 165r–203r Socratic
epistles, 203r–226v Dionysius Halic. *Lysias*. The whole codex derives from
V, but with much divergence in the texts, so that the derivation has been
disputed.[33] As p does not have secondary correction, there must have been
an intermediate between V and p. In I *fenestrae* of V have been filled from
an f-text,[34] but the major omissions of V remain. However, in the documents, lacking in f, it is the reverse: the omission at I 66_3 is supplied, but the
fenestrae at $50_{13\ 24}$ remain; at 50_{18} p reads $\kappa\alpha\theta\epsilon\zeta\acute{o}\mu\epsilon\nu o\varsigma$ with a (not V). In
II p is heavily contaminated from i.[35] In III it is less heavily contaminated
from k, as is V itself, but the contamination in p is independent of that in
V.[36] — A subscription says Georgius Chrysococces wrote this codex for
Giovanni Aurispa; this was probably when Aurispa was in Constantinople
in 1421–1423. Later the codex belonged to Guarino Veronese (d. 1460).[37]
It was collated for Reiske (1771) and by Baiter and Sauppe (1840).
Heyse demonstrated its derivation from V.

Milan, Ambros. D 71 sup. (gr. 247): 152 leaves 30 × 22 cm. Fol. 1–85
Plato, 86–90 Aeschines' epistles (Drerup om.), 91–152 Aeschines I II III
without scholia, preceded by vitae and arg. The end of III (225–260) and
the epistles are by a different hand. The first hand copied from Guarino's
codex p, the second from m.[38] There is some secondary correction in I:
fenestrae and omissions of Vp are supplied from a β-ms.[39] There are also
marginal indices in Greek and Latin. — This codex and the next have not
been examined or even mentioned before for Aeschines. I have micofilm
of both.

Madrid 4693 (*olim* N 63): 135 leaves. Fol. 1–112 Aeschines, 113–135
various epistles.[40] The ms. of Aeschines is an apograph of Ambros. gr. 247
with its corrections, but the arg. are distributed to the heads of the
respective orations and the epistles are at the end (103–112). A subscription fol. 112v says Constantine Lascaris wrote this ms. in Milan; Lascaris

---

33 Drerup (1904), p. 20; (1906: see on ms. *g*), pp. LXIII f.; Heyse (1904), pp. 10–13;
K. Fuhr in *Berl. Philol. Woch.* 25 (1905), 87, J. Sykutris in *Philol. Woch.* 48 (1928),
1284–1295; P. Maas in *Byz. Zeitschr.* 28 (1928), 430.

34 *fp*: I $24_{16\ 17}$ 25_7 48_{11} 49_{18} 55_9 64_1 86_8 170_8, etc.

35 Blass (1896), p. XI. Schultz (1865) put p in his fourth class with i.

36 p shares several omissions of V, even some supplied by V^2, but does not share
unsupplied omissions of V at I 66_3, II 279 374 111_5 119_{10} 156_{18}, III 172_5 255_4.

37 A. Diller (see on ms. *S*), pp. 318 f., No. 23.

38 Readings of m or mg at III 226_4 $_{10}$ 227_4 228_{12} 229_8 231_2 235_2 236_{12} 238_5 $_8$ 239_3
$246_{16\ 17}$ 250_1. In III 234 there is an incipient omission of one line in m ($113v11$ $\epsilon\mathring{v}\tau\nu\chi o\mathring{v}\mu\epsilon\nu$
... $\phi\acute{v}\sigma\epsilon\iota\varsigma$). The ms. ignores the corrections in m.

39 Readings of β in correction at I $50_{12\ 13\ 24}$ 64_{14} 119_5 179_5.

40 These epistles, in part unique, were copied from cod. Ambros. gr. 81, see *Studi ital.*
9 (1901), 479–488.

left Milan for Messina in 1464. There is secondary correction throughout, in part at least by Lascaris himself; it is from v.[41] Fol. 1r *infra* Lascaris has written φασὶν ὅτι πρῶτος αἰσχίνης τὸ θείως λέγειν ἤκουσε διὰ τὸ σχεδιάζειν ὡς ἐνθουσιῶν (*Suda* αι 347).

(x) Paris. suppl. gr. 660 fol. 31–89 and 94–157 (*olim* 1–123, fol. 90–93 and 158 blank paper): *s.* XIV 24 × 17 cm. Fol. 31–89 Synesius,[42] 94–157 Aeschines in six quint. plus four leaves, one leaf missing after 153 (*lacuna* III 202 ὑπομνήσω [ὑμᾶς . . . 213 σφόδρα] πονηροὺς), the last leaves wormeaten. Aeschines is β, but in III 247 it switches to k and the scholia cease, and the epistles are lacking. There are some readings of k even before III 247.[43] The script is uncalligraphic but the text is good,[44] more like a than V. — This ms. was among those acquired by the Bibliothèque Nationale from the heirs of Minoides Mynas in 1864.[45] It may be the Aeschines seen by Dr. E. Zachariä in the Laura on Mt. Athos in 1838.[46] It was collated by Heyse. I have microfilm.

(L) Florence, Laur. 57,45: 312 leaves in small 4°. Fol. 2–79 Lysias I–XXXI (om. II V VI), 80–97 Lucian and Cebes, 98–245 Herodian hist. and Aeschines, 246–253 anonymous opuscula, 254–312 various epistles (including Aeschines'). Aeschines is β (vita 1 is on 173r beneath the end of Herodian) ending at III 251; a later hand has added III 252–260 without scholia (from *fS*, but not *BP*, perhaps Laur. 58,6). The ms. is messy and inaccurate, even illiterate. The text is akin to x, as Heyse found in I and I find in II III.[47] There are omissions supplied and double readings, mostly in a different script, but I do not think by a different hand or from a different exemplar.[48] — This codex was one of those purchased for Lorenzo de' Medici by Janus Lascaris in Candia (Crete) 3 April 1492.[49] It was collated by Schultz. I have microfilm.

Vind. ph. gr. 59: 254 leaves 285 × 205 mm. Fol. 1r–77r Lysias as in L,

---

[41] I 556 6215 7011 14932 46 . . . III 626 13511 16610 1679 1707 1984 20512. At vita 110, however, Lascaris supplies ἐν θήβαις from a β-ms.

[42] N. Terzahgi, ed., *Synesii hymni et opuscula*, II, 1 (1944), p. XXIV f.

[43] kx: III 2351 2397 8 2401 24310 2448 2456 2464, etc. At III 2592 x omits παρ' οὐδὲν μὲν . . . τὸ ἐκ μήδων χρυσίον because of an incipient omission in k.

[44] Unique major omissions in x: I 1178 10 1410, II 2820 21 1427a 1451, III 10313 18513 2478 2592.

[45] H. Omont, "Minoide Mynas et ses missions en Orient," *Mémoires de l'Acad. des Inscr. et Belles Lettres* 40 (1916), 337–419.

[46] E. Zachariä, *Reise in den Orient* (1840), 258.

[47] xL: II 42 273 3213 348 415 463 681 (ἐν αὐτῷ) 891 1411 15912 1825a (κάκιαν), III 21 910 244 333 1114 11614 1408 (εἰσκείτε) 1722 3.

[48] But see III 12210 αὖριον kL^1g (om. cett.).

[49] *Rivista di filologia classica* 2 (1894), 416; 422: Lisi orationes et Escinii in uno volumine. P(ap).

77v–87r Lucian *de dea Syria* (in *L*), 87r–90r vita 2 and arg. only of Aeschines as in *L* 173v–175v, 90r–120r epistles and opuscula (in *L*), 121–166 Polybius, 167–254 Herodian (in *L*). The whole codex, except Polybius, seems to be copied from *L*.

Venice, Marc. gr. VIII 2 (colloc. 1388): 297 leaves 214 × 144 mm. in four parts by different hands: (a) fol. I, 1–31 Lysias I–IX as in *L* followed by vitae and arg. of Aeschines; (b) 32–125 Aeschines I II III without scholia; (c) 126–213 Apollonius Dyscolus; (d) 214–297 epistles of Phalaris Alciphron Brutus. Parts (a) and (b) were apparently copied from *L*. — This codex came from Sts. John and Paul (see on ms. *e*). It has not been collated.

(*f*) Paris, Coislin 249: mbr. 168 leaves 252 × 177 mm. 37 lines. The script is of the second half of the tenth century; it has a good deal of tachygraphy, some of it rather unusual. Fol. 1–76 and 148–168 contain opuscula of Synesius, an oration of Lysias and one of Gorgias, and Marinus *Vita Procli* (unique). Fol. 77–147, in nine quat. (α-θ) [50] contain the three orations and twelve epistles of Aeschines ending abruptly (the last leaf is lost), without the prolegomena (vitae arg.) and with some scholia. Another hand begins quat. δ (fol. 101r at II 19); the preceding leaf has only six lines of text with a notice οὐ λείπ(ει) τι, followed by a list of the ten Attic orators with numbers of their speeches [51] (fol. 100r, 100v is blank). In I the seven documents of β are omitted, and the text has the long ending (98r, I 196 ἐξετάζειν). The excerpt ὅτι ἠδυνήθη fills 116r after the end of II. Schol. III (a) is on 116v above the heading, III (bc) are lacking. The scholia, written in small majuscule, are mostly excerpts from the more copious scholia of β; Schultz does not report them completely. There are major omissions at I 92₁₅, II 154₈, III 127₄ [52] 167₈, supplied by the first hand, and at I 149₄₃, II 111₁₂ 124₁₃ 160₂, III 86₇, supplied by later hands, and at I 152₁₂, III 20₃ 172₁₀, not supplied at all. The text is often altered by various hands, contemporary or recent; Drerup distinguished four hands. [53] In I II this alteration usually agrees with β and may be either contemporary correction (*f*ᶜ) or recent collation (*f*²); but some of it is

---

[50] Devreesse says the codex has 22 quires. It is not clear how 97 leaves form 13 quires (without fol. 77–147, α-θ). I suspect that fol. 148–168 belong at the head, so as to bring all of Synesius together and put the second hand (fol. 101–147) at the end.

[51] Edited by W. Studemund in *Hermes* 2 (1867), 434 f.

[52] The long omission in III 126–127 is supplied in the lower margin fol. 128v but interlarded with scholia so as to be unrecognizable.

[53] E. Drerup in *Bayer. Akad. der Wissensch., philos.-philol. Classe, Sitzb.*, 1902, pp. 318 f., quoted by Heyse (1912), p. 23.

unique and even arbitrary (I 5_{11} 24_{10} 47_6 62_{15} 110_8).[54] In III, where the alteration is much less, f^2 usually agrees with k, hence is mere correction of f^1, but not at III 126_3 164_7. The apographs KAM ignore much of f^2 after I 88, but S agrees with f^2 mostly throughout. — This codex seems to be one of those obtained in the East by the Greek priest Athanasius Rhetor for Pierre Séguier in 1643–1653.[55] It has been collated several times, by Bekker, Cobet, Schultz, Drerup (in the epistles), Heyse, and others. I have microfilm.

(K) Istanbul, Patriarchate, Panaghia Kamariotissa 158: 296 leaves 210 × 140 mm.[56] Fol. 267–291 Aeschines I without arg. or documents, ending abrupt 291r at I 141 τοὺς εἰρημένους ἐν; the page is full, but 291v has only irrelevant scribblings; fol. 292–296 do not belong to this ms.[57] The ms. is a manifest apograph of f, with a few of the scholia. —This collection of codices was in the island of Chalke in the last century. I have photocopy taken from microfilm in the Dumbarton Oaks Library.

(A) Florence, Laur. conventi soppressi gr. 84: 202 leaves 296 × 215 mm., "egregie scriptus." Fol. 1–178 (178 blank) Isocrates,[58] 179–202 (three quat.) Aeschines I only[59] without arg. documents or scholia, copied from f (Heyse). — This codex was in the collection formed by Antonio Corbinelli (d. 1425),[60] which was lodged in the Badia di Firenze until 1811. It was collated by Schultz.

(M) Venice, Marc. gr. 442 (colloc. 554): 199 leaves in 12°, in three parts by different hands: (a) fol. 1–86 mostly Libanius;[61] (b) 87–174 Aeschines; (c) 175–199 six monodies by one Alexius Lampenus (fourteenth century) found only here and still not printed as far as I know. Fol. 87–166, ten quat. (α-ι), have Aeschines' orations as far as III 113 τὸ πεδίον copied from f: vitae arg. and seven documents in I are lacking, I ends ἐξετάζειν, II is followed by ὅτι ἠδυνήθη. In I 39 a single line of f is omitted: εὐκλείδου . . . ἐγένετο. The scribe failed on the sign for ἐστι in f at I 9_3 22_{13} 166_5, and on the sign for πρὸς at I 4_5 $459a$ 120_0 152_4, II 1_{11a}, III 14_0.

---

[54] Heyse (1912) pp. 23–26.
[55] H. Omont, Missions archéologiques françaises en Orient aux XVIIe et XVIIIe siècles (1892), I, p. 21; II, p. 853, No. 30.
[56] R. Foerster, ed., Libanii opera, V (1909), 222 f.; IX (1927), 141.
[57] "Life of St. Mary of Egypt," Patrol. graeca 87, pp. 3697–3704.
[58] E. Drerup, ed., Isocratis opera omnia, I (1906), pp. XXIV n. 46; XLIX.
[59] Followed by an anonymous epistle de imperio, Studi ital. 1 (1893), 149; 308–313.
[60] R. Blum, La bibl. della Badia fiorentina e i codd. di Ant. Corbinelli, Studi e Testi, 155 (1951), 77, No. 28; 117; 161, No. 79.
[61] R. Foerster, ed., Libanii opera, II (1904), pp. 198 f. Fol. 83r–86r are akin to Vatic. gr. 82 fol. 192v–193v.

Most of the scholia are omitted. In II III M has collation by second hand, usually agreeing with β. This seems to be the same hand and from the same source as the continuation fol. 167–173 (174 is blank), which ends III 151 ἐπὶ δὲ τὴν παρα-. It seems to be from F.[62] — This codex was No. 300 in Bessarion's donation of 1468. It has not been collated. I have microfilm.

(S) Milan, Ambros. J 22 sup. (gr. 455): 382 leaves 222 × 143 mm. in 47 quat. and one ternion (α-μη).[63] Fol. 1–248 Themistius, 249–382 Aeschines: vitae and arg. 249r–253r (253v blank), I 254r–288v, II 289r–321r, III 322r–371v, epistles 371v–382v. The text of Aeschines is written regularly (25 lines a page) and legibly and accurately. Chapters are signalized by rubricating the first letter of the first full line, but the rubric initials are often not supplied. The text of the orations is from f in the main: I has the long ending and II is followed by ὅτι ἠδυνήθη (321v); the readings agree with f and the early and late corrections in f almost constantly. But there are important elements from β: vitae and arg. and documents in I (except 50) and complete text of omissions not supplied in f at I 152$_{12}$ and III 127$_4$, also some β-readings passim.[64] There are significant conjunctives with V,[65] and Drerup found the epistles to be from a source like V; but this agreement with V is only partial, some of the β-readings cannot be from V. Most of the scholia are added without numbers in margins and between lines by a second hand in smaller and finer script; they include scholia III abc (321v) and continue clear to the end of III as only in e elsewhere. — This codex, which is primary for Themistius,[66] was one of those bequeathed to S. Giustina in Padua by Palla Strozzi in 1462.[67] It has not been collated for Aeschines. I have microfilm.

Leonardo Bruni Aretino translated the two crown speeches, Demosthenes 18 in 1406 and Aeschines III in 1412, also Aeschines' epistle 12.[68]

---

[62] FM^2: III 81$_7$ 113$_9$ 115$_{12}$ 125$_6$ 126$_{10}$ 126$_{25}$ 128$_9$ 132$_{11}$ etc. Consequently there are k- and a-readings in M^2.

[63] Quat. λγ-λς (fol. 257–288) were first numbered κς-κθ (201–232).

[64] βS: I 34$_{11}$ 14 15 65$_5$ 9 12 13 67$_6$ 10 13 78$_{12}$ 81$_7$ 82$_4$ 84$_8$ 9 10 85$_2$ 5 7 87$_1$ 107$_{12}$ 152$_{12}$ 16, II 55$_3$ 4 56$_{12}$ 81$_8$ 92$_6$ 138$_7$ 154$_6$ 165$_4$, III 162$_{15}$ 184$_{13}$ 185$_9$ 205$_{12}$ 209$_{11}$, also corrections or interlinear variants at I 86$_8$ 109$_5$ 112$_9$ 149$_{29}$ 168$_{12}$, II 22 91 316 441$_3$ 136$_4$ 181$_3$ 184$_2$, III 81$_3$ 354 178$_{17}$ 188$_7$ 208$_8$.

[65] VS: vita 26 13 18 38, arg. III 49, I 168 10, III 26 (VS^1) 216 (V^1S^m) 86$_{16}$ 17 (kV^2S^1).

[66] H. Schenkl in *Wiener Studien* 20 (1898), 206; *Akad. der Wissensch. in Wien, phil.-hist. Klasse, Sitzb.* 192, 1 (1919), 46–49.

[67] A Diller in *Journal of the Warburg and Courtauld Institutes* 24 (1961), 315, No. 484.

[68] L. Bertalot in *Archivum Romanicum* 15 (1931), 297; 303 f. *Gesamtkatalog der Wiegendrucke*, 6750, 6751. I have microfilm of part of Vatic. lat. 5137 fol. 70r–90r and the whole of Phillipps 922 and 2621, now at Yale University, Marston ms. 10. — An anonymous translation of Aeschines II in Ambros. D. 465 inf. may have been made from the printed text; see P. O. Kristeller, *Iter italicum*, I (1963), 288b.

The translations occur in many mss. and were printed in 1485, 1488, etc. Apparently Bruni translated from codex S; he agrees with f in the main but departs from f along with S at III 21_6 (*dicet*) 1274 178_{17} (*vilescit*) 205_{12} 228_{11} (*facultatem*) 258_7 (*arthmium*). He did not use B (III 171_{10} 211_{10}).

(B) Vatic. Barber. gr. 159 (*olim* 139): mbr. 132 leaves 250 × 170 mm. (numbered 1–133 without 111) in quaternions, written regularly with 29 lines a page. Aeschines as in S, but without scholia or other marginalia and without correction or collation—a very clean ms. There are major omissions at I 39_{12} 46_7, III 171_{10} 211_{10} (one line in S), and several errors due to lack of rubric initials in S (II 69_1 76_{11} 78_1 152_2 164_4, III 8_3 16_1 75_6 203_1 227_8). On fol. 71v is an incipient omission (erased) of fol. 320v–321r in S: II 180 ποιεῖσθε [ἀναμνησθέντες ... (ὅτι ἠδυνήθη$_{12}$) τοὺς νέους] καὶ τοῖς τελειοτέροις. — This codex is probably to be identified with one in the library of San Marco in Florence,[69] which was formed in the main by Niccolò Niccoli, who had Aeschines' orations as early as 1416.[70] It was collated by Schultz. I have microfilm.

(C) Florence, Laur. acquisto 50: 180 leaves 266 × 169 mm. Aeschines as in S but without scholia and with arg. distributed to the heads of the respective orations and ὅτι ἠδυνήθη appended wronly to arg. III. The codex belonged to Francesco Castiglione of Florence (d. 1484).[71] It has not been collated in the orations.

(*d*) Venice, Marc. gr. VIII 20 (colloc. 1351): 90 leaves (numbered 1–89 with 19 *bis*) in quinternions. Aeschines as in C[72] but the order altered: III I II. "Occurrunt in marginibus textus supplementa et variae lectiones lingua graeca et latina manu ut videtur Hermolai Barbari patr. Aquileiae" (Mioni). The codex belonged to Almorò Barbaro (d. 1493).[73] It was collated by Bekker, who ignored the marginalia.

Florence, Laur. 58,6: 107 leaves in-fol. Fol. 1–32 epistles of Phalaris and

---

[69] B. L. Ullman and Ph. A. Stadter, *The Public Library of Renaissance Florence* (1972), p. 259, No. 1164: Eschinis orationes et epistolae, in membranis. No. 1165 is our codex F.

[70] *Ambr. Traversarii epistolae a P. Canneto in libros XXV tributae* (ed. L. Mehus, Flor., 1759), VI, 6: "Aeschinem quem petisti (Fr. Barbarus) mitteret (Nicolaus) si plane sciret quem velles, utrum orationem contra Ctesiphontem et Demosthenem Latinam, an magis Graecum illius orationum codicem." However, Traversari may be referring to F instead of B.

[71] See M. E. Cosenza, *Biogr. and bibliogr. dict. of the Italian humanists* 2 (1962), 1483 f.

[72] Independent of B (Heyse). ὅτι ἠδυνήθη is not mentioned, but is probably appended to arg. III as in C.

[73] This codex is supposed to have belonged to Pope Leo X (d. 1521) because of papal insignia on fol. 1r, but I do not see how this ownership combines with the other history of the codex. See E. Mioni in *Italia medioevale e umanistica* (1958), 331, and A. Diller, *ibid.*, 6 (1963), 259, No. 1601. There is a photograph of fol. 1r in *Bibliofilia* 14 (1913), 399.

Aeschines, 33–107 Aeschines II I III with respective arg., ὅτι ἠδυνήθη added to arg. III as in C, without vitae scholia epistles. Or. I has the long ending and the documents with readings of S. The headings with Aeschines' name are not supplied. There is some disorder "propter quaterniones praepostere compactos" (Bandini); from Marc. VIII 20 and Ambros. gr. 26 I would expect to find III I II here. — This codex was in the Medicean Library in 1491 and 1495 (see below). It has not been collated except by Schultz in I 1–16.

Milan, Ambros. A 99 sup. (gr. 26): 52 + 266 leaves 228 × 163 mm. Fol. 1–52 Harpocration, 1–136 Minor Attic Orators, 137–216 Lysias, 217–265 (242 bis) Aeschines III I II with respective arg. (but arg. III omitted), without vitae scholia epistles, subscribed 216v by Michael Suliardus in Florence.[74] The Minor Attic Orators were brought to Florence from Athos by Janus Lascaris in 1492.[75] This ms. of Aeschines has not been collated; it is probably an apograph of Laur. 58,6.

(q) London, Wm. H. Robinson Ltd., codex Phillipps 8077: 153 leaves 292 × 210 mm. in two parts by different hands. The first part, in ten quat., contains Aeschines II III epist. without scholia, II preceded by its arg. and followed by ὅτι ἠδυνήθη. The second part, nine quat. plus one leaf numbered separately, contains Aeschines I preceded by Liban. 18 (19) and with scholia including unique scholia of Υ, then (fol. 106v ff.) the *Golden Verses* and Hierocles, all copied from Υ. The first part also has interlinear readings from Υ.[76] This codex belonged to Richard Mead M.D. (d. 1754), Anthony Askew (sale 1785 No. 544), and Sir Thomas Phillipps (d. 1872). It is still held by Robinson, successor to Phillipps, from whom Köhler (see on Υ) obtained microfilm of Hierocles. Taylor's description, collation, and copy of scholia, were furnished to Reiske by Askew.[77]

(P) Vatic. Palat. gr. 134: 305 leaves 215 × 155 mm., composed of several parts written by different hands. Fol. 59–126 in seven quat. and one sext. (α-η, later ζ-$\iota\delta$) Aeschines II III without scholia, II preceded by its arg. and followed by ὅτι ἠδυνήθη, written regularly with 24 lines a page. The epistles are lacking. Pq agree in numerous errors and in major omissions at II 8_4 17_1 27_9 41_6 44_{14} 85_3 91_{10} 101_6 (one line in S) 123_{17}, III 4_4 5_2 20_{10} 34_9 44_{13} 45_2 65_1. They are mutually independent[78] and derive

---

74 E. Lobel, *The Greek mss. of Aristotle's Poetics* (1933), 54–56.

75 W. Wyse, ed., *The speeches of Isaeus* (1904, repr. 1967), p. vi.

76 Υq^1: II 17_4 271_4 674 68_5 71_{12} 142_{13}, III 8_{11} 90_5 170_4 205_6.

77 Taylor's description is quoted by Drerup, p. 14; compare Köhler (see on Υ), 74 f.

78 At III 57_8 P omits καὶ τοὺς φιλ . . . χρησαμένους and at 57_{10} q is said to omit τῶν δὲ . . . γεγενημένον. However, in the light of P I often doubt the reported readings of q; there is a contradiction at III 14_1 2 3.

from an apograph of *S*. — This codex was in the library of Ulrich Fugger of Augsburg in 1555, which he took to Heidelberg in 1567.[79] It has not been collated. I have microfilm.

(*R*) Milan, Ambros. E 113 sup. (gr. 316): 224 leaves 279 × 204 mm., subscribed 224r by Joannes Rhosus, Venice 1482. Fol. 1–106 Plato, 107–224 Aeschines with scholia as in *S*. It has not been collated in the orations.

Milan, Ambros. E 87 sup. (gr. 297): 134 leaves 280 × 207 mm. Fol. 1–96 (94–96 blank) Aeschines with scholia as in *S*, ὅτι ἠδυνήθη wrongly entitled ὑπόθεσις τοῦ κατὰ κτησιφῶντος. Fol. 97–134 Symeon πρὸς διαφόρους σημασίας [80] in a different hand. This codex belonged to Manuel Sophianus of Chios (16th century). It has not been collated in the orations.

(*E*) *Editio princeps* by Aldus Manutius, Venice 1513, in *Orationes horum rhetorum: Aeschinis, Lysiae,* etc. in three vols. Aeschines vol. I pp. 3–85: vitae arg., I II III without scholia, but schol. III ab after arg. II (p. 5) and ὅτι ἠδυνήθη after II (p. 52). Or. I has the seven documents of β and the long ending of *f*. The text is a conflation of *S*[81] and *m*.[82] Most of the omissions of *fS* are supplied (so the document in I 50), but not at I 26_5 107_8 178_5, II 113_2 141_1, III 76_3 120_3. At III 167_8 σὺ Θετταλοὺς ἀφιστάναι is omitted as in *amgV*, not ἀφιστάναι· οὐ γὰρ ἂν κώμην as in *f*ᵃ*S*, and at 167_9 ἀποστήσαις agrees with *amgxL* against ἀποστήσαιο *V* and ἀποστήσειας *fSk*; at $172_{2\ 3}$ ἐξ ἧς γίνονται αὐτῷ agrees with *amg* against *fS*, *k*, *V*, *xL*, all different.

(*k*) Paris. gr. 2998: *s*. XIII 389 leaves 258 × 175 mm.[83] Fol. 1–205 Demosthenes and Aeschines. Fol. 83r–117r (without 102–103, which belong at the head of the codex) Aeschines III II (*sic*) without arg. and with very few scholia. Or. II begins 101v and has a unique second title in the lower margin: αἰσχίνου ἀπολογία· There are singular major omissions at III 24_{14} 31_5 55_{12} 95_9 105_3 110_4 117_2 175_{10} $246_{7\ 10}$, II 22_5 23_{11} 41_6 71_8 79_{13} 133_4 147_{15}, incipient omissions at III 25_{14} (ἦρχον . . . ἀρχὴν), 45_5 (ἢ ἄτιμον εἶναι . . . μηδενός), and an incipient repetition at III 259_2 (ἐπιδημήσαντα . . . τὸ ἐκ μήδων χρυσίον), all three uncancelled. There are *fenestrae* towards the end: II 121_8 124_{15} $125_{5\ 9\ 12}$ $134_{2\ 13}$ $138_{1\ 16}$ etc. The text has many singular readings; they are more frequent in III than in II; sometimes they are right. — This codex belonged to Féderic Morel jr.

---

[79] Catalogues of Pal. gr. 1–352 in Pal. lat. 1925 fol. 124–135 dated 1555 and Pal. lat. 1950 fol. 182–194 before 1559; see A. Biedl in *Byz. Zeitschr.* 37 (1937), 18–22.

[80] K. Nickau, ed., *Ammonii liber* (1966), pp. IX–XII.

[81] *SE*: I $21_{2\ 4\ 8\ 10}$ 110_8 169_{15}.

[82] *mE*: I 50_{18} 154_{14} 188_4, II 15_9 21_{11} 25_2 56_4 70_8 109_3 138_6 177_1, III 76_{19}.

[83] R. Foerster in *Hermes* 9 (1875), 24–28; *idem*, ed., *Libanii opera*, VI (1911), 112–114; VIII (1915), 597.

(d. 1630) and to Etienne Baluze (d. 1718).[84] It was collated by Bekker, Heyse, and Martin-Budé. I have microfilm.

(δ) The lost parent of the closely akin but mutually independent mss. *Dle* had Aeschines III II from *k* followed by I with arg. but without scholia from β. There were major omissions at III 43₂ 140₄ 186₉, II 46₁₃ 60₁₇ (one line in *k*), I 96₁₂. The *fenestrae* of *k* in II 121–156 and the omission at II 124₁₃ were supplied from another ms. There were a few readings of *i* in the text: II 43₆ om. ἐπι-, 82₁₇ ἀπειρηκότων, 84₁₂ ἀκούοντος, 1154 ἀμφικτυόνων, 1174 χορηγήσαντας, 1494 τρίτον τουτί, 1585 ἐάσατε. Most of the readings of *l* in I cited by Heyse occur in *D* also.

(*D*) Milan, Ambros. G 69 sup. (gr. 409): 345 leaves 297 × 215 mm. Three preliminary leaves have (1rv) a *pinax* for the whole codex, (2r)vita 1, (2v–3r) vita 2, (3v) arg. II and scholia III ab, with text akin to *LW*. Fol. 4–67 are eight quat. (α-η): 4r–28v Aeschines III with *k*-scholia, 29r–46r II with β-scholia added 29rv only, 46v–65v I with arg. but without scholia, 65v Hermogenes περὶ ἰδεῶν I 11,6 (Walz III 384 f.), 66r–67v Aristides *orat. funebr.* *D* has peculiar major omissions in III 37 ὥστ᾽ ἀκύρους . . . τὴν πολιτείαν, 76 ἐμισθώσατο . . . εἰς θήβας (suppl. in marg.), 140 καὶ οἱ ἱππεῖς, 173 τίς ἐστιν . . . καταγελάστως, 202 ἐπὶ τοὺς νόμους καλεῖς, II 81 ἃ μὲν εἶδον. The scribe often corrects himself, mostly in III; usually the first writing agrees with *le*, the second with β.[85] — This codex belonged to Joannes Doceianus of Constantinople (d. after 1474), but was probably not written by him, as has been supposed.[86] It has not been collated. I have microfilm.

(*l*) Paris. gr. 3002: 112 leaves in small 4°. Fol. 1–87r Aeschines III II I without vitae arg. or scholia (except arg. I, 60v); fol. 87v–112v various epistles including Aeschines'. *l* is closely akin to *D* but independent, not

84 Montfaucon, *Bibl. bibl.* (1739), 1304aC–E, No. 9.

85 Corrections in *D*: III 179 εὖ *D*ᵃ*kl* ἐν *D*ᶜβf, 221₂ ἐν τῇ πόλει *D*ᵃ*kle* νόμων *D*ᶜβf, 2312 λόγων *D*ᵃ*l* νόμων *D*ᶜ etc., 461₂ πολίτης *D*ᵃ*le* πόλις *D*ᶜ etc., 482 ὑπο- *D*ᵃ*kle* del. *D*ᶜ, 524 αὐτῶν *D*ᵃ*kle* αὐτῷ *D*ᶜβf, 671₁ φίλιππος *D*ᵃ*kle* δῆμος *D*ᶜβf, 726 μελετήματα *D*ᵃ*le* μελ(λ)ήματα *D*ᶜ etc., 934 ἔμελλεν *D*ᵃ*ke* ἤμελλεν *D*ᶜ etc., 957 φιλίππου *D*ᵃ*e* φίλιππον *D*ᶜ etc., 1261 -λαβὼν *D*ᵃ etc. -βαλὼν *D*ᶜϒ, 1293 προειπὼν *D*ᵃ*k*ᵃ*l* προεῖπον *D*ᶜ*k*ᶜβf, 1666 -τολμήκασι *D*ᵃ*le* -τμήκασι *D*ᶜ etc., 2359 ἔξετε *D*ᵃ etc. εἴξετε *D*ᶜe, II 271₂ φιλο- *D*ᵃ*e* ἰφι- *D*ᶜ etc., 515 6 om. *D*ᵃ*k* καὶ *D*ᶜβf, 951 νόμου *D*ᵃβ δήμου *D*ᶜ*kfi*, 1623 ἐκλήθημεν *D*ᵃ*l* ἐκλήθην μὲν *D*ᶜ etc., I 340 ἀπελαύειν *D*ᵃ(*l*) ἀπελαύνειν *D*ᶜ etc., 1522₂ ἤδε *D*ᶜ*l* ἤδεται *D*ᶜ etc. — There are also some old readings in *D*ᵃ against *kle* or *l*: III 111 ἄπαγ. *D*β*f* διαγ. *kle*, 2231₀ κατασκευάσας *D*β κατεσκεύασας *fkle*, 230₂ ἀπο- *D*β*f* ἀνα- *kl*, 2441₇ διαχειρίσηται *D*β διαχρήσῃ *kl*, II 589 ἀθήνησι *D*β*fi* ἀθήναις *kle*, 601₄ τὸν νόμον *D*β*fi* τοὺς νόμους *k*, I 4712 ἐξεργάζεσθαι *DamV* ἐξεργάσασθαι *fxLl*, 1565 παντολέοντα *DVm* πανταλέοντα *faxLl*, 1574 ῥαμνουσίου *D*aᶜ*m* ῥαμνησίου *fxLl*.

86 G. Mercati in *Studi e Testi* 46 (1926), 43 f.; D. A. Zakythinos, *Le despotat grec de Morée*, II (1953), 318; P. Topping in *The Library Chronicle* (Univ. of Pennsylvania) 29 (1963), 1–16.

sharing omissions and other aberrant readings of D. It agrees with D^a against D^c. It has omissions of its own at III 159_7 168_6 175_5 222_7, I 27_5 54_{12} 66_{10} 173_6 192_8, and in general is less accurate than D. — This codex belonged to Gaspare Zacchi of Volterra before he became bishop of Osimo in 1460^{87} (it is older than Heyse thought) and later to Cardinal Domenico Grimani of Venice (d. 1523).[88] It was collated by Bekker and (in I) by Heyse.

(e) Venice, Marc. gr. VIII 4 (colloc. 1208): mbr. $1 + 209$ leaves 250×163 mm. in 21 quint. Fol. 1–144r Demosthenes 1–9 and 18–19, 144r–209v Aeschines II III without arg. but with β-scholia clear to the end as in S. At III 64_8 (fol. 180r?) "hinc altera manus". The text of the orations is from δ, but I omitted as in P and II III in the order of $f\beta$. There are major omissions at II 85_3 143_6, III 24_{14} $_{15}$ (in marg. kD) 198_3. — This codex was in the library of the convent of Sts. John and Paul in Venice, which was transferred to the Marcian Library in 1789. The text was collated by Bekker; the scholia were found by Schultz after his edition.[89]

(s) London, Harley 6322: 304 leaves 28.5×21.7 cm. in four parts, all but the first by Michael Lygizus, the same scribe as in Υ: (a) fol. 1–74 Demosthenes 1–11; (b) 75–184 Dem. 18, Aeschines II, Dem. 19, 60; (c) 185–266 Synesius; (d) 267–304 PsArist. $rhet.$ ad $Alex.$[90] Aeschines II is from k (not δ).[91] — This codex, formerly in Ripon (Yorkshire), was acquired by Harley in 1725.[92] It was collated by Taylor and for Blass and inspected by Drerup for Heyse, who showed that it is an apograph of k.

(i) Paris. gr. 2996: s. XIV 477 leaves 205×157 mm. Fol. 1–49 Demosthenes 19 abrupt at the beginning, 50–83 Aeschines II without arg. but with β-scholia, 84–418 Aristides followed (415v–418v) by an excerpt

[87] E. L. Leutsch, *Paroemiographi graeci*, II (1851, repr. 1958), pp. XXI n. 10; H. Omont in *Bibl. de l'école des chartes* 45 (1884), 333; *Revue des bibl.* 2 (1892), 15; R. Foerster, ed., *Libanii opera*, IX (1927), 147.

[88] *Index voluminum graecorum Bibliothecae D. Card. Grimani*, No. 116: Aeschinis orationes tres. — Aristotelis epistola ad Olympiadem. — Dionis epistolae quinque. — Dionysii sophistae epistolae quattuor. . . . (cod. Vatic. lat. 3960 fol. 4v). See G. Mercati in *Studi e Testi* 79 (1920, 1937), 159–162; 75 (1938), 26–34; M. Sicherl in *Byz. Zeitschr.* 67 (1974), 313–336.

[89] *Neue Jahrbücher* 97 (1868), 749–752.

[90] E. M. Thompson in *Class. Quart.* 3 (1889), 154, 441; N. Terzaghi, ed., *Synesii hymni et opuscula*, II, 1 (1944), XXIX; M. Fuhrmann in *Akad. der Wissensch. und Lit. in Mainz, Abh. der geistes- und sozialwiss. Klasse*, 1964, pp. 560, 598–601, Abb. 3; J. Wiesner and U. Victor in *Riv. di studi biz.* 8–9 (1971–1972), 60.

[91] ks: II 111_4 μεμνήσεσθε $k^t s^t$ μαθήσεσθε βƒ$k^m s^m$ 122 οἶμαι ks om. δ 211 ἦμεν βƒk οἶμαι s(?) δmg 344 δυνάμεως om. $k^t s i^t$ suppl. $k^m i^m$ hab. βƒδ 442_3 τάντι- βƒks ταυτὶ δ 611_0 ἐπιδημῆσαι βƒ$k^t s^t$ ἐπιτιμῆσαι $k^t s^t δ^t$ 164_2 ἐπεκάλουν $k^t s$ παρεκάλουν βƒ$k^m D$.

[92] C. E. Wright, ed., *The diary of Humphrey Wanley* (1966), 348, 415.

from Menander (Walz IX 287), 419–477 Aristides *pro quattuor viris pars quinta*. Fol. 54–83 are three quat. and a binion signed ιβ-ιε (74–75 are extra, see below); fol. 1–53 lacking two leaves at the beginning and one between 6 and 7 must be ε-ια, Dem. 19 beginning with ε, α–δ lost. The ms. is uncalligraphic but literate—the work of a learned scribe. There are slight changes of script at 55r and 60v. In the upper margin 50r are two titles: κατὰ τιμάρχου (*sic*) and περὶ παραπρεσβείας. In the right and lower margins 50r is the scholion ὅτι ἐδυνήθη (*sic*) . . . ἀφανοῦς found elsewhere only in *f* (and its offspring) following the end of II. The text is peculiar and problematical (see above). A bit of scholia (*VxL*) is in the text at II 39₁. Major omissions are supplied by the first hand. One very large omission must have occurred in the *Vorlage*: fol. 73v om. II 134 πρέσβεις [δεδεκότας . . . 141 ἔχθρας] φανερᾶς; this is supplied on two inserted leaves (74–75) still by the first hand; the readings show that the source was *V*, and there are a few *V*-readings elsewhere in the text.[93] — This codex was one of a number of Greek codices purchased by Francis I from Antonius Eparchus of Venice in 1538.[94] It was one source of the *scholia Bernardi* (*Scaligeri*) (Schultz pp. 249 f.). It was collated by Bekker, Dübner (for Dindorf), Heyse, and others. I have microfilm.

(*F*) Florence, Laur. 60,4: 77 leaves in large 4°. Aeschines III II without arg. or scholia followed by epistles of Aeschines (60r) and others (68r). The absence of I, the order III II, and the lack of arg. and scholia, suggest *k*, but the text is a mixture of *k*[95] and *a*[96] in III. Or. II has the unique title of *k* αἰσχίνου ἀπολογία and seems to be pure *k* in II 1–12, but from there on pure *a*. The episties are akin to *SB* (Drerup). — This codex belonged to Niccolò Niccoli of Florence (d. 1437), possibly as early as 1416 (see on codex B). It was collated by Schultz.

(*z*) Mosquensis gr. 475 (*olim* CCLIV, 267): 142 leaves 29 × 21 cm. Demosthenes 19, Aeschines II III, Dem. 18 21 20. Codex Dresden Da 11 (58 leaves: Dem. 1–17) was probably once part of this codex;[97] it is by

---

93 *Vi*: II 23₁₀ 52₆ 67₆ 16 18 94₈ 97₉ 98₉ 102₁₄ 113₂ 117₄ 126₆ 10 135₃ 7 136₅ 7 137₁₂ 141₀ (ἀρχομενίων). Fol. 74–75 have scholia also from *V*.

94 H. Omont, "Cat. des mss. grecs d'Antoine Éparche (1538)", *Bibl. de l'école chartes* 53 (1892), 103, No. 45; *idem, Cat. des mss. grecs de Fontainebleau* (1889), 53, No. 146.

95 *kFz*: III 74 10 42₅ 48₁ 8 55₅ 12 17 56₇ 9 57₁₀ 14 70₅ 79₁ 81₁₂ 82₂ 84₄ 86₁₇ 87₂ 5 92₃ 94₈, etc.

96 *aFz*: III 37 133 178 236 291 302 36₁ 397 40₅ 472 544 733 88₆, etc., but *mFz*: III 85 46₁₆ 113₉ 126₁₅, also II 60₇ 177₁.

97 O. Gebhardt in *Centralbl. für Bibliothekswesen* 15 (1898), 538 f. The Dresden codices formerly in Moscow have been returned to Moscow.

the same hand (except fol. 40–58).[98] Codex z agrees with F[99] in spite of the
order II III. It has the unique title of II in kF (Vladimir). — This codex
belonged to Giambattista Rasario (d. 1578) and Maximus Margunius (d.
1602), both of Venice.[100] It was collated by C. Hoffmann for his edition
of Aeschines III (Moscow, 1845).

(W) Vatic. gr. 67: 295 × 210 mm. Fol. 1–83r Demosthenes, 83v–142
Aeschines (142 originally blank, 1–142 are 17 quat. and one ternion),
143–256 Aristides (256abc blank), 257–276 epistles of Brutus and Phalaris.
Fol. 83v–84v vitae and arg. III I, 85r–102v I, 102v schol. III ab, 103r–121v
III, 121v arg. II, 122r–136v II, 136v–141v epistles. The orations have
scholia in red in margins and between lines. Drerup found heavy contamination in the epistles, and the same is true of the orations. The text of I
is basically V, but contaminated with f.[101] It has the short ending of βV.
Some readings of f occur as doublets with or without $\gamma\rho$. I 67 is repeated
entire after I 68, agreeing here with f. However, in the vitae arg. documents
and scholia, all lacking in f, there was another source from which defects
of V were made good; this source seems to have been like L.[102] The text
of III is still V, but contaminated with k in III 1–20. Scholia cease at III
156 as in V. There is a large *lacuna* fol. 110r: III 81 μετὰ ταῦτα [ἐβουλεύετο
... 129 ἡγεμονίαν] τῆς εὐσεβείας; this must represent a quaternion
missing in the *Vorlage*, which was not V itself. The text of II is basically i,
manifest by many unique readings of i and by ὅτι ἐδυνήθη at the head
(122r) as only in i; but it is contaminated somewhat with β and f.[103]
— This codex probably belonged with V to Cardinal Isidorus Ruthenus:
there are large additions in his hand fol. 83r and 142.[104] It has not been
examined for Aeschines before; I have microfilm.

(v) Urbinas graecus deperditus. The *Indice Vecchio* of Urbino (ca.
1485–1500)[105] has Aeschines' orations twice: *Greco 82* is certainly the

98 B. Fonkič by letter 16 December 1969, who says the hand is the one I wish to identify
as Andronicus Callistus, see *Italia medioevale e umanistica* 10 (1967), 406–408.

99 N.b. III 55₁₂ om. kz¹ suppl. z².

100 A. Turyn, *The Manuscript Tradition of the Tragedies of Aeschylus* (1943), 57 n. 59;
K. A. de Meyier in *Scriptorium* 9 (1955), 102 n. 17.

101 VW: I 50₁₃ 24 52₁₂ 83₇ 149₁₄, etc. fW: I 9₁₁ 10₇ I 11₁ 12 13₆ 17₁₃ 22₁₀ 344 41₇ 48₉ etc.

102 Not V: vita 13, doc. I 16₁₀ 66₃; WL: vita 21₄ 15 64, arg. Ia 9 17 26 Ib 9 11, arg. III
40 42 46, doc I 35₁₂ 68₃.

103 βW: II 34 11₁₃ 12₅ 23₁₃ 35₆ 58₁₁ 73₆, etc. fW: II 22 75 89 12₈ 18₇ 23₁₀ 333 434 504
52₆ 546, etc.

104 G. Mercati in *Studi e Testi* 46 (1926), *aggiunte*, pp. 1–3.

105 C. Stornajolo, *Codices Urbinates Graeci* (1895), LIX–CLXXV; L. Michelini Tocci,
"Agapito bibliotecario", *Studi e Testi* 220 (1962), 245–280, esp. 260; D. Harlfinger, *Die
Textgesch. der Pseudo-Aristotelischen Schrift* περὶ ἀτόμων γραμμῶν (1971), 235–246.

present Urb. gr. 116 (c), *Greco 164*[106] is in a section entitled *Libri Graeci in Armario* (131–168); some of these *libri* are identical with previous items in the *Indice* while others have disappeared unaccountably. *Greco 164* must be one of the latter as it cannot be our codex *c*. Now the Gotha ms. *t* has Aeschines III copied from *c* and I copied from the same *Vorlage* (*v*) as *Υ*. I venture to guess that *Greco 164* was this lost *Vorlage*. It was itself copied from *M* and *l*, which belonged to Bessarion and his secretary Gaspare Zacchi respectively; hence it was copied in Italy, probably by Michael Apostoles, who produced *Υ* from it and whose script is frequent in the present codices Urbinates. It was probably a rough ms. (to judge from *Υt*), misprized in the elegant collection of Duke Federigo.

(*Υ*) Vatic. gr. 72: 140 + 3 leaves 290 × 210 mm. in two parts by different hands, the second (fol. 81–136) by Michael Apostoles, the first by his pupil Michael Lygizus.[107] Fol. iv Libanius *hyp. Dem.* 18 (19) in a later hand; 2–47 (five quat. and a ternion, α–ϛ) Aeschines I II with scholia; 48–80 (with 80abc blank, four quat. and a binion) Aeschines III with scholia only at the beginning; 81–136 (seven quat.) *Golden Verses* of Pythagoras followed by Hierocles' commentary *et alia*.[108] The loss of the *Vorlage v* of *Υ* blurs the analysis of its sources. Aeschines in *Υ* is a hotch-potch like *W*. It is from *f* in the main: the prolegomena are lacking, I 196₅ has the long ending, ὅτι ἠδυνήθη follows II, and the text agrees mostly with *f*. But it is much contaminated with *β* in I and with *k* in II III and after III 113 agrees with *k* only. Actually the *f*-source was *M*,[109] which ends at III 113, and the *k*-source was *l*.[110] But there were other sources. Among the interlinear and marginal variants I find three unique readings of *a*: I 111₂₀ 171₁₁, II 44₂₃, also I 50₁₈; *a* also has variants from *Υ*. In the quotations from *Iliad* in I 144–150 and from Hesiod in III 135 there are big interpolations from the text of the poets. The seven documents of I are interpolated part in the text and part in the margin. The scholia, which cannot be from *Ml*, are in various scripts, red and black. A series near the beginning of I has the numbers (α–ζ) of *L* fol. 176r, where the

---

[106] Stornajolo, p. CLXXV: Aeschynis orationes, quint. XI; (S)ynesii de dono ad Paeonium, quint. 7; Cyri vita [Xen. *Anab.*], quint. 12. *Υ* has Aeschines' orations in 11 quires.

[107] On these two scribes see M. Wittek, *Album de paléographie grecque* (1967), pp. 24 f., pl. 35, 37 (Apostoles) and 36 (Lygizus), with references, also Wiesner and Victor (see on ms. *s*), pp. 53, 59.

[108] Fr. Wm. Köhler, *Textgeschichte von Hierokles' Kommentar zum Carmen Aureum des Pythagoras*, Diss. Mainz (Münster, 1965), pp. 68–72.

[109] *MΥ* vs. *f*: I 22₁₃ 29₁₂ 65₃ 70₁₁ 78₁₂ 152₄ 166₅ 174₅ 177₅ 181₅, II 86₄.

[110] *lΥ* vs. *D*: I 66₁₀, III 118₆ 159₇ 166₁₀ 168₆ 175₅ 222₇ 235₅.

scholia are numbered by the page. Codex L came from Crete, where Apostoles and Lygizus lived. At the beginning of II the first scholia are in the script of the text and have readings of L, but the long scholia on II 10 and 12 are in a different script and agree with a. There are also many unique scholia (in Schultz from q), which do not belong to the old fund of scholia. — This codex was purchased for the Vatican from Antonius Eparchus of Venice in 1551; [111] Petrus Cacus, a former owner, is unknown. It has not been examined for Aeschines before; I have microfilm.

(h) Paris. gr. 2947: 95 leaves. Aeschines I II III with Libanius 18 (19) [112] and ὅτι ἠδυνήθη as in Υ. Together with Paris. gr. 1804 (ch. 54 leaves: *Golden Verses* with Hierocles) [113] h makes a complete apograph of Υ, all written by Michael Apostoles. Scholia are not reported from h, perhaps because they were added to Υ after h was copied. There is secondary correction in III: major omissions of $l\Upsilon$ are supplied at III 117_2 1404 159_7 175_5 222_7, also I 66_{10}. h^2 agrees constantly with m and m^2, $q.v.$ — This codex belonged to Marcus Musurus (d. 1517) [114] and later (with mg) to Janus Lascaris. It was collated by Bekker and Heyse.

(c) Vatic. Urbin. gr. 116: mbr. 93 leaves 264 × 168 mm. in nine quint. plus three leaves, written regularly 28 lines a page, a clean ms. without marginalia or corrections. Aeschines I III II without scholia followed (81v) by arg. Ia, arg. III, ὅτι ἠδυνήθη, arg. II, epist., vitae. Or. I stands apart (fol. 1–24) and is from A (Heyse 1912); the rest is continuous and is from a ms. like d but contaminated from p. [115] — This codex was in the famous library of Federigo da Monte Feltro duke of Urbino (d. 1482; see on codex v). It was collated in III by Bekker. I have microfilm.

(t) Gotha, Landesbibliothek B 572: 138 leaves 221 × 158 mm. Fol. 1–3 Gorgias, 3–41 Aeschines III without scholia, 41–64 I as far as I 175 ἐκρίνετο with scholia, 66–100 Demosthenes, 101–135 Phalaris. Apparently 1–64 are eight quat. and were followed by other quat. now lost. Heyse (1904) showed that III was copied from c; but it has a good deal of correction by the first and later hands, of which he gives no account. Heyse also showed (1912) that I is closely akin to hq, that is, to Υ, but independent of Υ, which has a major omission at I 173_{12} not shared by t. In I Υ and t have similar fusions of f and β but Υ has more of β than t has. In their *Vorlage* (v) the readings of β may have been entered in such a way that t could

[111] *Studi e Testi* 244 (1965) 419 f.

[112] R. Foerster, ed., *Libanii opera*, VIII (1915), 596, Nos. 113, 116 (hq).

[113] Köhler, 72–74.

[114] M. Sicherl in *Serta Turyniana* (1974), 569, 577, 578.

[115] cd: II 10_{11} 157 164 211 12 28_{18} 22 314 336 734, etc., cp II 191_1 211_5 26_8 299 71_{18} 777 799 934 117_4 119_9 134_5 156_{13}, etc. See Heyse (1904), p. 15, for III.

ignore some of them. — This codex belonged to Barth. Walther of Pforta in 1590. It was collated by Franke [116] and Heyse. The following mss. have not been examined. They contain only single orations of Aeschines. None of them seems likely to be important.

Vatic. Ottobon. gr. 254: mbr. 57 leaves 234 × 156 mm. Fol. 1–50 Demosthenes 60 and 18, fol. 51–55 Aeschines I 1–39, the rest unfinished or lost. From Card. Gugl. Sirleto (d. 1585).[117]

Vatic. gr. 1392: 170 leaves 215 × 145 mm.[118] Fol. 108v–142v Aeschines II with arg. From Fulvio Orsini (d. 1600).

Vatic. Barber. gr. 53 (olim 127): 136 leaves 200 × 162 mm. Fol. 1–68 (eight quat. and a binion) Dem. 19, 69–104 (four quat. and a binion) Aeschines II with arg., 105–135 Dem. 20 in a different hand. From Carlo Strozzi of Florence 1636.

Neapol. II E 28: 81 leaves 282 × 204 mm. Fol. 1–75 Dem. 19, 76–80 Aeschines II 1–22.[119]

Salamanca 223 pars B: 19 leaves 262 × 192 mm. Aeschines II 1–124 (unfinished), entitled περὶ τῆς παραπρεσβείας λόγος κατὰ τίμαρχον (sic, compare ms. i). Dem. 19 (unfinished) is in ms. 71 fol. 128–143. Both mss. belonged to Fernan Nuñez de Guzman (Pintianus, d. 1552).[120]

Istanbul, Μετόχιον τοῦ Παναγίου Τάφου, No. 10: ch. 4 s. XVI, Αἰσχίνου περὶ τῆς παραπρεσβείας λόγος. This ms. listed only in a catalogue of 1845 has disappeared.[121]

Athens, Βιβλ. τῆς βουλῆς 23: 410 leaves 24 × 16 cm., s. XIX. Fol. 348-end Aeschines II.[122]

Vatic. gr. 1585: 291 leaves 222 × 161 mm. Fol. 1–229 Demosthenes, 229v–288r Aeschines III with ὅτι ἠδυνήθη, dated A.D. 1490 (288r).

Vatic. gr. 2362: 177 leaves 290 × 213 mm. Fol. 1–141 Demosthenes, 142–176 Aeschines III. The contents are the same as in Vatic. 1585.[123] From the Jesuit Collegio Romano, suppressed 1773.[124]

Vatic. gr. 1949: 217 × 147 mm. Fol. 178 179 181 Aeschines III 35–50,

---

116 Neue Jahrbücher 34 (1842), 268–273.

117 E. Miller, Cat. des mss. grecs de la bibl. de l'Escurial (1848, repr. 1966), 330 rhet. 30.

118 E. Drerup, ed., Isocratis opera omnia, I (1906), p. XVIII; R. Foerster, ed., Libanii opera, V (1909), 296 f.

119 Rivista indo-greco-italica 14 (1930), 104.

120 A. Tovar, Cat. codd. graec. universitatis Salamantinae I (Acta Salamanticensia, Filosofía y Lettras XV, 4 [1963]), 39 f., 32 f.

121 Papadopoulos-Kerameus, Ἱεροσολυμιτικὴ βιβλιοθήκη IV (1899), 437.

122 S. Lampros, Νέος Ἑλληνομνήμων 1 (1904), 363.

123 L. Canfora, Inventario dei mss. greci di Demostene (1969), 60.

124 G. Mercati in Studi e Testi 164 (1952), 28.

fol. 180r four lines only from III 58, fol. 180v 182 183 blank. The missing bifolium with III 50–58 is in Florence, Magliabech. gr. 17.[125]

Neapol. II E 11: 168 leaves 295 × 313 mm. Fol. 1–143 Demosthenes, 144–168 Aeschines III 1–192 (the rest lost).[126] The contents are not the same as in Vatic. 1585 and 2362. From the royal collection of Naples.[127]

Florence, Libri-Ashburnham 1640: 40 leaves 219 × 140 mm. Aeschines III 1–181. From Giulio Saibante of Verona 1734.[128]

Lisbon, Bibl. Nat., unnumbered ms.: 42 leaves in 4° (three quint. and a sext.). Aeschines III.[129]

Bucharest, Acad. 603: 336 leaves 21 × 15 cm. Fol. 157–294 Aeschines III with arg.

Athos, Vatopedi 736: 381 leaves 24 × 17 cm. s. XIX. Fol. 267–290 Aeschines III with commentary.

Oxford, Bodl. S.C. 6561 (Savile 14) fol. 171–180: vitae and arg. only of Aeschines. Given to the Bodleian Library by Sir Henry Savile 1620.

Vatic. Palat. gr. 51 fol. 185–224: scholia on Aeschines I II III, probably copied in Florence 1550–1560 by Arnold Arlenius, who owned the codex.[130]

Paris. suppl. gr. 1344 fol. 1–34: scholia on Aeschines prepared for an edition by Emmanuel Miller (d. 1886). Baiter and Sauppe (II [1850] p. 11) used a copy by Miller of scholia *mfi* on Aeschines II 1–71. W. Dindorf used collations of *fim* by Fr. Dübner in his edition of the scholia (1852).

Codex Mediceus deperditus. In the catalogue of the *Graeca Bibliotheca* of the *Mediceae domus insignis bibliotheca, quae nunc est apud R(everendissim)um Car(dina)lem de Medicis*, by Fabio Vigili in Rome ca. 1510,[131] codex No. 17 is as follows:

Aeschinis rhetoris orationes tres vz contra Timarchum una, περὶ παραπρεσβείας i(d est) de corrupta sive falsa legatione 2ᵃ, Contra Ctesiphontem de coronatione tertia.
Bruti epistolae ad varios.
Propositiones quaedam Geometricae Euclidis ut videtur.
M. Tullij Ciceronis Cato, sive de Senectute liber, a Theodoro in graecum sermonem conversus.

---

[125] *Studi italiani* 2 (1894), 553.

[126] R. Foerster, ed., *Libanii opera*, VIII (1915), 597.

[127] Fabricius-Harles, *Bibl. graeca*, V (1796), 783, No. 139.

[128] L. Delisle, "Notice sur des mss. du fonds Libri conservés à la Laurentienne", *Notices et extraits des mss. de la Bibl. Nat.* 32, 1 (1886), 14 n. 3, 17 n. 1.

[129] *Nouvelles archives des missions scientifiques et littéraires* 2 (1892), 304 f., repr. in *Humanitas* (Coimbra), 19–20 (1967–1968), 307 f.

[130] G. Mercati in *Studi e Testi* 79 (1927, 1937), 358–371, esp. 366.

[131] Cod. Vatic. Barber. lat. 3185 fol. 263v, unpublished; cf. M. H. Laurent in *Studi e Testi* 105 (1943), pp. XVII f.

Epistola Nicolai quinti Pontificis ad Constantinum Palaeologum Constanti-
nopolitanum imperatorem, a Theodoro in graecum sermonem conversa.
Ciceronis epistola prima ad Lentulum vz ego omni officio, ab eodem
Theodoro ut puto in graecum conversa.
Dionysij Halicarnasei De fabula et historia ac philosophia quaedam et per
consequens de poetis historicis et philosophis quibusdam ut de Homero
Hesiodo Antimacho heroicis, Panyasi Pindaro Simonide Sthesichoro
Alcaeo lyricis, Aeschylo Sophocle Eurypide tragicis, Menandro comico,
Herodoto Thucydide Philisto Xenophonte Theopompo historicis, Pythag-
oricis Xenophonte Platone Aristotele philosophis, Lysia Isocrate Lycurgo
Demosthene Aeschine Hyperide oratoribus, deque eorum intentione et
stilo.
Quaedam ad astrologica et logica pertinentia.
Isaac Argyri libellus de lingua.

Although the Medicean library is preserved as a whole in the Laurentian
Library in Florence, this codex has disappeared, unfortunately, as it was
interesting in several respects. In the register of loans for the Medicean
library [132] Aeschines' orations occur three times:

13. 1481/2 Nov. 21 to Politian: l'orationi d'Eschine e altre cose di Theodoro,
rosso, in papiro.
62. 1489 Jan. 13 to Chalcondyles: librum Aeschinis in quo sunt tres ejus
orationes.
76. 1491 Oct. 3 to Augusto Padoano: le orationi de Eschine, in un volume
nel qual sono anco le sue epistole.

No. 13 is certainly our lost codex, 62 is probably the same, 76 must be
Laur. 58, 6. In the inventory of 1495 [133] there are three mss. of Aeschines'
orations:

320. Epistole Phalaridis et Eschinis cum orationibus, in papiro contente in
quadam chartula.
329. Lysias et Herodianus, in papiro.
388. Eschines in Thimarcum et alia quedam, in papiro.

No. 320 is Laur. 58, 6; 329 is Laur. 57, 45, which came to the library only
in 1492, and 388 must be our lost codex. In Vigili's catalogue I find only
two: 17 and 54 (Laur. 57, 45). Why Laur. 58, 6 is absent I cannot say.
To return to our lost codex, the orations of Aeschines were complete
and in the traditional order, but apparently without the prolegomena and
epistles. These meagre data, which are shared by some other mss. (*MYhg*),
do not afford a clue to the classification of the ms. It was probably not

---

132 Published by E. Piccolomini in *Archivio storico italiano, serie terza*, 21 (1875), 285,
287, 288.
133 Published by E. Piccolomini, *ibid.*, 20 (1874), 51–94.

early enough to be very important. Theodore Gaza (see below) cites Aeschines' orations in his opusculum περὶ μηνῶν.[134]

The last item in the codex is problematical; no work of Argyrus de lingua is known.[135] The translation of Cicero de senectute occurs in several mss.,[136] some of which attribute it to Theodore Gaza, as here. A mistaken attribution to Maximus Planudes has gained some currency.[137] The translation of the epistle of Nicholas V to Constantine Palaeologus occurs in many mss. The epistle is dated 11 October 1451,[138] a post quem for at least this part of our codex. The translation of Cicero ad fam. I 1 is new, so far as I know. Perhaps it was an inchoate work. If so, our codex would be near to Theodore Gaza, perhaps autograph. Gaza (d. 1476) bequeathed most of his books to Demetrius Chalcondyles, then professor in Florence.[139] Perhaps this is the way our codex came to the Medicean library.

The work of Dionysius Halic. was the excerpt called ἀρχαίων κρίσις or veterum censura, now regarded as a fragment of περὶ μιμήσεως.[140] It occurs without heading and quite anonymous at the end of the famous codex Paris. gr. 1741[141] (fol. 299–301) and in a few apographs of that ms.[142] It was first edited by H. Stephanus in 1554, who attributed it de suo to Dion. Halic. because it seemed to be part of a work of his that preceded it in Stephanus' ms. This attribution, though conjectural, seems to be valid. Now we have it much earlier, apparently from Theodore Gaza. Probably Gaza had the text from Paris. gr. 1741 itself, as the apographs are mostly later and there is other evidence of his having that codex.

Francesco Filelfo says Aeschinis orationes et epistolae were among the Greek

[134] Migne, Patrologia graeca 19, pp. 1167-1218 (1173C, 1176C).

[135] On Isaac Argyrus see G. Mercati in Studi e Testi 56 (1931), passim.

[136] Laur. 58, 33; Vatic. gr. 1405; Paris. gr. 2071; Monac. gr. 289; Bodl. Barocci 165; Elbing O 2; Scorial. deperd. 733 (Miller p. 380) = 636 Andres; ed. Froben 1520.

[137] J. Irmscher, "Cicero and Byzantium", Byzantinoslavica 20 (1959), 28–39, esp. 37 f.

[138] E. Legrand, Bibliogr. hellén. des XVᵉ et XVIᵉ siècles, I (1885, repr. 1962), p. XXXIV n. 1.

[139] L. Dorez, "Un document sur la bibliothèque de Théodore Gaza", Revue des bibliothèques 3 (1893), 385–390.

[140] H. Usener and L. Radermacher, ed., Dionysii Halic. opuscula II (1929, repr. 1965), 202–214.

[141] On this codex see L. Cohn in Philologus 49 (1890), 395–399; D. Harlfinger and D. Reinsch, ibid., 114 (1970), 28–50; A. Diller in Studia codicologica, Texte und Untersuch. zur Gesch. der altchr. Lit. 124 (1977), 149 f.

[142] Cohn discusses the mss. without knowing of our lost codex. The Cambridge ms., which was Stephanus' copy, is probably the remains of a codex listed in the Index D. Card. Grimani (see on ms. l) No. 6: ... Demetrius Phalereus de interpretatione. Dionysius de compositione nominum. Idem de peccatis quae fiunt in declamationibus. Maximus de insolubilibus oppositionibus. ...

codices he brought from Constantinople in 1427. This is not enough to identify the codex, if it still exists. It might be ms. *m*. Filelfo lectured on Aeschines in Florence in 1431/2.[143]

Melanchthon says Johannes Reuchlin (d. 1522) had a ms. of Aeschines' and Demosthenes' opposing speeches,[144] which he bought from Jacob Questenberg in Rome, written by Questenberg himself in a handsome script. Other sources mention Aeschines only, without Demosthenes.[145] Reuchlin edited the crown speeches of Aeschines and Demosthenes together in 1522, but took his text of Aeschines from the *editio princeps* of 1513, to judge from the reprint of Paris, 1543, which I have examined.

Indiana University

143 A. Calderini, "Ricerche intorno alla biblioteca e alla cultura greca di Francesco Filelfo", *Studi italiani* 20 (1913), 217, 245 f.

144 Compare Paris. gr. 3004 (*n*) and Barber. gr. 53.

145 K. Christ, *Die Bibliothek Reuchlins in Pforzheim* (*Zentralblatt für Bibliothekswesen*, Beiheft 52, 1924), pp. 9, 30, 51; K. Preisendanz, "Die Bibliothek Johannes Reuchlins", *Festgabe Johannes Reuchlin* (1955), 64, 80; see Questenberg, quoted by G. Mercati in *Studi e Testi* 79 (1937), 444 f.

5

Perfect Friendship in Aristotle's *Nicomachean Ethics*

THEODORE TRACY, S.J.

We tend to think of Aristotle as the embodiment of cold, objective, and unimpassioned reason, critical, aloof and independent, self-possessed and self-sufficient, proposing contemplation of the pure intelligibles as the ultimate human happiness. It is perhaps surprising, then, to realize that two of the ten books of the *Nicomachean Ethics*, as they come to us, are devoted to *philia*, most frequently, and inadequately, translated by words full of human warmth, "love" or "friendship."[1] Aristotle sees *philia*, taken in the broadest sense of "mutual attraction and attachment," as that which ties together, along with justice, every form of natural and conventional relationship among human beings. "For in every association we find mutual rights of some sort as well as *philia*" (1159 b 26 f.).[2]

Depending upon the nature of the persons involved and the basis of their relationship, *philia* is distinguished by Aristotle into many different kinds. "*Aretê-philia*" draws together equals mutually attracted by each other's goodness; "pleasure-*philia*" unites pleasure seekers; "profit-*philia*", those who find association advantageous; "erotic *philia*" attracts the sensual lover (*erastês*) to the beloved; "marriage-*philia*" joins husband and wife; "filial *philia*" and "parental *philia*" bind children to parents and parents to children; "family-*philia*" unites brothers, sisters, and other close relations; "companion-*philia*" holds together fellow workers, shipmates, soldiers in a company; "civic *philia*" binds together fellow citizens, the

---

[1] As the commentators point out, there is no single word in modern languages that can be applied to the wide spectrum of relationships covered by the Greek *philia*. The English "love" is too strong for the relationship between business partners or fellow workers; while "friendship" is too weak for the relationship between husband and wife, or mother and child.

[2] All citations by Bekker number alone are from the *Nicomachean Ethics*.

ruler and the ruled; "hospitality-*philia*" links foreign guest-friends. For Aristotle, human beings are by nature interdependent, which implies a natural need for love or friendship. Man, he says, is first a "pairing animal" (*zôon syndyastikon*) and then a "political animal" (*zôon politikon*), a member of a *polis* with all its subsidiary associations (1162 a 16–19). To live apart from others, without love or friendship, an individual would have to be a god, or something less than human (*Politics* 1253 a 29).[3]

In Books VIII and IX of the *Nicomachean Ethics* Aristotle distinguishes the various forms of *philia* we have mentioned, grouping them into two large divisions, *philia* between equals and *philia* between unequals (1158 b 1–14). In the first group he distinguishes equals who are mutually attracted and attached by different motives—intrinsic goodness, pleasure, or usefulness (profit, advantage)—realizing of course that some relationships may be built upon more than one motive, others largely upon one of them alone. The second group, *philia* between unequals, includes such relationships as those between parents and children, the old and the young, husband and wife, ruler and ruled.

All of these types have some general characteristics implied by the term *philia*: (1) The basis of *philia* is good-will (*eunoia*), i.e., wishing the good of another, at least in some respect; (2) this feeling of good-will must be mutual, not one-sided; and (3) both parties must be aware of the other's good-will (1155 b 27—1156 a 5). (4) Moreover, the mutual good-will must be more than mere well-wishing: an operative disposition or readiness to expend effort in actively assisting the other (1167 a 7–10). Persons involved in *philia* (5) normally associate regularly (*suzên, synhêmereuein*) and (6) derive some pleasure from this association (1158 a 1–10). Finally, (7) *philia* requires the possibility of some proportionate exchange, even between persons of unequal nature or status (1159 b 1–3; 1163 a 24 ff.).

---

[3] It is true that for Aristotle one characteristic of human happiness is that the activity which constitutes its essence be, as far as possible, independent and self-sufficient (*autarkês*). But even this is qualified by man's social nature. In the first book of the *Nicomachean Ethics*, while postulating that happiness, the ultimate human good, must be self-sufficient, Aristotle warns: "We speak of self-sufficiency not as involving only oneself alone, living a life in solitude, but also parents, children, wife, and, in general, *philoi* and fellow-citizens, since man is by nature a social animal" (*zôon politikon*: 1097 b 8–11). This passage challenges the view of commentators who tend (1) to exaggerate the self-sufficiency of Aristotle's supremely happy man (e.g., A. W. H. Adkins, "Friendship and 'Self-Sufficiency' in Homer and Aristotle," *CQ* N.S. 13, 1963, 44 f.) or (2) to minimize the connection between the books on *philia* and the rest of the *Nicomachean Ethics* (e.g., W. D. Ross, in his introduction to The World's Classics edition of the *Nicomachean Ethics*, London, 1954, xx f.). The importance of *philia* to the activity of contemplation (*theôria*) will be indicated later.

Granted that the various types of *philia* share all, or most, of these common characteristics in greater or lesser degree, still for Aristotle not all are
philia in the same sense. How then are they related? In the *Nicomachean
Ethics* Aristotle conceives the various *philia*-relationships as analogous:
All may be called *philia*, but by analogy with, and resemblance to, one
perfect realtionship, which is *philia par excellence (prôtôs kai kyriôs*: 1157 a
29–32) and which alone properly deserves the name.[4] In this discussion
I shall concentrate upon the nature and characteristics of that prime
analogue or archetype, perfect *philia*, as Aristotle presents it in the *Nicomachean Ethics*.

The responses and activities of *philia*, like all human emotion and action
in Aristotle, must be evoked by some *telos*, some principle of attraction and
fulfillment, some good perceived in or connected with the person who is
the object of *philia*. Aristotle reduces all possible motives to the three we
have mentioned: (1) The intrinsic goodness or excellence (*aretê*) of that
person; (2) the person's ability to give pleasure; (3) the usefulness of that
person to the other (1155 b 17 ff.). The three are not mutually exclusive,
of course. And the last, usefulness, will in fact always be found subordinate
to the others, since a person will be useful to another in so far as he helps
the other achieve either goodness or pleasure, or both (1155 b 19–21).
Of these three motives, Aristotle believes that only the mutual possession
and recognition of *aretê*, *intrinsic excellence*, moral and intellectual, can provide the basis for perfect or complete *philia (teleia philia)*. "The perfect
form of *philia* is that between *good* persons, i.e. those who are like each
other in intrinsic *excellence*" (*kat'aretên*: 1156 b 7 f.).

For Aristotle, a person achieves intrinsic excellence, the *aretê* which
makes him a *good* human being, when he is habitually oriented, in moral
character (*êthos*), emotion, and action response, toward what is good or
noble (*to kalon*); and rejoices in the exercise of his noblest faculties, those
of the intellect (*nous*), according to their proper virtues, particularly the
activity of the virtue of wisdom in reflective study and contemplation of
the noblest realities of the universe (*theôria*). Such a person is *good*, an
excellent human being in the complete sense, possessing the moral and
intellectual virtues described by Aristotle in the first six books of the
Nichomachean Ethics.[5]

---

[4] See W. W. Fortenbaugh, "Aristotle's Analysis of Friendship: Function and Analogy,
Resemblance, and Focal Meaning," *Phronesis* 20 (1975), 51–62.

[5] It seems clear from Book IX (1169 b 3–1170 b 19) that intellectual virtues and
activities hold the same priority for Aristotle in his discussion of *philia* as in the rest of
the *Nicomachean Ethics*, so that the paradigm, perfect or complete *philia* at its fullest and
best, is assumed to be that which exists between persons of completely developed moral

When two such fully-developed human beings first come to know each other, both being habitually responsive to what is good or noble (*to kalon*), their first response may be what Aristotle calls *eunoia*, "good-will," which is the beginning of *philia* (1167 a 7 ff.; 1155 b 31—1156 a 5). True good-will must (1) be elicited by awareness of what is excellent in the other person (1167 a 19 f.), and (2) must wish the other well *for his own sake* (1155 b 31–33). "For one who wants another to do well because he hopes to gain advantage through that other, seems to have good-will not for the other but rather for himself; just as no one is a friend who cultivates another because he may be useful" (*dia tina chrêsin*: 1167 a 15–18). Friend-ships based on profit and pleasure do not arise from true good-will (1167 a 13 f.).

If perfect *philia* is to develop, both good men must feel true good-will toward one another, and both must become *aware* of their mutual regard (1155 b 31—1156 a 5). But this is not enough. To mature into *philia*, the relationship must grow beyond mutual recognition of each other's excel-lence and mutually disinterested good-will, to the point where each (1) recognizes the other's goodness, not just objectively (*haplôs*) but as relevant to himself (*pros hauton*), and (2) not only wishes the other well but wants to implement that by actively doing good to the other for the other's sake, i.e., by conferring such benefits upon the other which will preserve or increase the other's intrinsic goodness.

This transition from passive good-will to an active desire to benefit the other comes through closer association and growing familiarity between the two good men (1167 a 10–12), accompanied by an intensification of what Aristotle calls *philêsis*, "friendly feeling", the emotional attachment of *philia* which involves active desire (*orexis*: 1166 b 32–34). For both

---

and intellectual *aretê*. This is not to deny that the type of *philia* based on *aretê* can exist also between persons whose *aretai*, moral and intellectual, are imperfect or only partly developed. Aristotle asserts, for example, that *aretê-philia* can exist between a man and woman (husband and wife) of good character (1162 a 25–27), though he believes that their natural functions (*erga*) are quite different (1162 a 22 f.); and we know from else-where that he considers the female-at-best to be incapable of achieving the same standard of *aretê* as the male-at-best, being both physically and intellectually inferior to him. See *Politics* 1260 a 5–24; *De generatione animalium* 728 a 18–22; 737 a 28; 766 a 17–23; 775 a 13–22; Tracy, *Physiological Theory and the Doctrine of the Mean in Plato and Aristotle* (Chicago, 1969), 318 f., 321 f., 328 f.; and note 10, below. Hence it would not be true to say that, for Aristotle, only philosophers can be *philoi kat' aretên*, though I assume he would maintain that only philosophers enjoy human *philia* at its most perfect and best, just as they enjoy human happiness at its most perfect and best. I am grateful to Richard Kraut for pointing out this problem.

perfect *philia* and *philia* of any sort, this "friendly feeling" must of course be mutual (*antiphilêsis*: 1155 b 27 f.).

However, intense mutual friendly sentiment between good men is apparently not enough for Aristotle. He believes perfect *philia* must go deeper than feeling. In perfect *philia* the two must also be intellectually aware of each other's intrinsic goodness and accept each other as *philoi* by deliberate choice. "Friendly feeling (*philêsis*) seems to arise from emotion, but *philia* from a fixed disposition . . . Mutual *philia* is accompanied by deliberate choice (*proairesis*),[6] and choice depends upon a fixed disposition. And they want what is good for their friend for their friend's sake, not through mere feeling (*pathos*) but through a fixed disposition" (*hexis*: 1157 b 28–32).

Because each of the two is good objectively (*haplôs*), he is attractive to the other, who, as a good man, is habitually disposed toward what is noble or best. Each, in choosing the other for his intrinsic excellence to be his *philos*, identifies the other's *goodness* with his own, and desires now to preserve and increase the other's goodness *as* his own. "And in loving (*philountes*) a friend, they love that which is the good in relation to themselves (*to hautois agathon*): for the good man, in becoming beloved (*philos*) becomes the good to him by whom he is beloved. Each therefore loves (the other as) that which is good in relation to himself and so gives in return equally to the other, both in what he desires for the other and in pleasing the other" (1157 b 33–36). This is the essentially altruistic nature of true *philia*, which distinguishes it from all relationships based primarily upon the expectation of pleasure or profit. "Perfect *philia* is that between good men who are alike in their intrinsic excellence. For these desire good in the same way for each other with respect to that in which they are good; and they are good in *themselves*. But those desiring good for their friends for their *friends*' sake are most truly friends. For they feel this way because of what their friends *are* (*di' hautous*), and not because of some adventitious quality or circumstance (*kata symbebêkos*)" (1156 b 7–11).[7]

---

[6] The rational nature of *proairesis* and its connection with the person's *êthikê hexis* is assumed from earlier descriptions in the *N.E.*, e.g., 1113 a 9–14, 1139 a 31–35, 1139 b 4 f.

[7] Aristotle's insistence that true good-will and true *philia* be motivated by the intrinsic goodness of the other and desire the other's good for the other's sake, seems incompatible with Adkins' statement that in Aristotle "all three types of *philia* are equally selfish." See his article cited in note 3 above, page 39. On the other hand, it also seems incompatible with the position that finds essential altruism in all three types of *philia*. It is true that, for Aristotle, in some cases a relationship which began on the basis of pleasure or advantage may develop into a more altruistic relationship based on growing mutual recognition of the intrinsic worth of the other. He cites the case of husband and wife,

What moves two men to join deliberately in true *philia* and to work for the good of the other is ultimately their own habitual disposition to choose what is good or noble (*to kalon*). And if there is any element in their relationship that might be called "selfish," it consists in that each desires to do what is noblest and best (*ta kallista*: 1168 b 28–31). Aristotle recognizes nobility in the act of doing good for someone (1169 a 8 f.); and he compares the disinterested benefactor to the artist, who continues to love the recipient of his gifts as he does his own existence, without looking to profit or return (1167 b 31—1168 a 8). The good man will be willing to give up wealth, honors, power, and even his life for the sake of his friends, since he chooses nobility (*to kalon*) before all other goods (1169 a 16–35). A sharing association (*koinônia*) is essential to *philia* (1159 b 29 f.). In *philia* based on intrinsic goodness each partner is eager to do good for the other, and they vie with one another in this (1162 b 6–9). There is no "deal" or "contract" about mutual help, but each offers service to, or confers benefits upon, the other *for the other's sake*. Services or benefits rendered in return are not valued according to some objective measure (as in business arrangements) but according to the *intention* (*proairesis*) of the giver (1164 a 33–b 2). Among true friends it is not the value of the gift but the intention of the giver that counts.

In perfect *philia*, Aristotle explains, the good man loves his friend in the *same way* (though perhaps not to the same extent)[8] that he loves himself (1166 a 1–33). For he desires and actively promotes the good of the other for the other's sake, just as he desires his own true good and acts to achieve it for the sake of that which is most truly himself, i.e., the intellectual part of himself. Secondly, he desires to preserve the existence, the life of his

---

united first for mutual pleasure and advantage, but coming to recognize the *aretê* of the other (1162 a 24–27); and the case of an erotic relationship where one party was motivated originally by pleasure, the other by advantage, but when these motives vanish the *philia* may persist: "if as a result of their close association they have come to love each other's character" (*ta êthê*: 1157 a 7–12). It seems clear, however, that in these cases the nature of the *philia* has changed from one based merely on pleasure and/or advantage to one based on recognition of intrinsic worth, which introduces the altruistic element of loving the other for the other's sake, for what he or she is, and not merely for the (selfish) pleasure or advantage that accrues to the partners through the other.

8 Apparently Aristotle holds that the good man cannot love another *as much as* he loves himself, since even one who desires to excel in virtuous activity chooses for himself "the noblest, that is, the greatest goods" (1168 b 25–30; cf. 1159 a 8–12). On the self-love of the good man and his choosing the "best" for himself, see 1169 a 16–b 1. By equating the "best" with the "noblest" Aristotle reconciles a rational self-love with the self-privation involved in giving up wealth, position, and life itself for one's *philoi*.

friend, for his friend's sake, just as he desires to preserve his own life or existence, and particularly the life of that which is noblest in him, i.e., the intellectual part of himself. Third, he enjoys the company of his friend as he enjoys his own company, having pleasant memories of the past and hopes for the future, and a mind well stocked with matter for reflection. Fourth, he desires the same things that his friend desires, just as interiorly he is of one mind with himself, and all the powers of his soul reach out in harmony toward the same objectives. Lastly, his shared awareness of his friend's joys and sorrows matches the keen consciousness of his own. Thus a good man feels the same way toward his friend as toward himself, so that, as Aristotle remarks, in this case it is true that "a friend is another self" (1166 a 31 f.).

The personal identification of two good men in *philia* will be closest and best, of course, when they are both equally talented, fully developed in moral and intellectual excellence, and equal in status or function in society. To this effect Aristotle quotes a popular tag, *"Philotês isotês"* (1157 b 36), and later adds *"kai homoiotês"* (1159 b 3),[9] but qualifies it as applying most of all to *philia* between good men, equal and similar in excellence (*kat' aretên*). The equality and similarity of *aretê* demanded for perfect *philia* do in fact seem to lead Aristotle to deny the possibility of its existence even between persons so closely related as husband and wife, or father and son (1158 b 11 ff.). "For the *aretê* and the function of each of these is different, as is also the basis of their *philia*; therefore their emotional attachments (*philêseis*) and their *philiai* are also different. The same benefits are not exchanged in these relationships, nor should they be sought" (1158 b 17–21).[10]

On the other hand, when two men of equal status and similar *aretê* join in *philia*, the benefits exchanged between them will themselves be equally excellent, at least in intention, which contributes to the perfection of this kind of *philia* in making it most *enduring* (1156 b 33–35; cf. 1157 b 33—1158 a 1). Such *philia* is least likely to be broken up by quarrels or slander. Even when one partner succeeds in conferring objectively greater benefit upon the other, this occasions not complaint or recrimination but gratification, since he achieves what he sincerely desires, namely, the greatest

---

[9] The spirit, if not the sense, of this jingle is caught by J. A. K. Thomson in his rendition "charity is not only parity, it is also similarity" (*The Ethics of Aristotle*, Penguin Books, 1955, 243).

[10] Aristotle does not deny that true *philia*, i.e., that based on *aretê*, can exist, for example, between husband and wife (1162 a 25–27). But he sees the nature, function, and proper *aretê* of man and woman as being so different that they exclude the equality and similarity demanded for perfect *philia*. Cf. 1158 b 11–28, 1160 b 32–35, 1162 a 16–27, and note 5, above.

benefit for the other, whom he loves for the other's sake, not his own
(1162 b 6–13). And since each knows thoroughly the intrinsic goodness of
the other, neither is likely to believe slanderous reports about the other and
withdraw his *philia* on that account (1157 a 20–24; 1158 b 9 f.).

But what makes *philia* between good men especially enduring is the fact
that it is based upon what the two are essentially, i.e., upon their moral
character (*êthos*) and intellect (*nous*) perfected by mature moral and intellectual *aretê*, which, like a second nature, constitutes the most permanent
of dispositions (1156 b 11 f.). On the other hand, where profit or pleasure
is the basis of *philia*, the partners do not love each other for what they are
in themselves, but only in that some pleasure or profit comes to each from
the other (1156 a 10–14). And this basis of attachment may change easily.
As Aristotle says, "these *philiai* are based on a chance or adventitious
circumstance (*kata symbebêkos*); for the *philos* is not beloved for being the
man he is, but because one provides some benefit, another some pleasure.
Such relationships, then, are easily broken off whenever the partners themselves change. For if ever they stop being mutually useful or pleasant they
stop being *philoi*" (1156 a 16–21). Based on self-interested and changeable
motives, such relationships can, in fact, be called *philiai* only by analogy,
in so far as they resemble the usefulness and pleasure of perfect *philia*
(1157 a 25–b 5; 1158 b 1–11).

For while perfect *philia* is essentially motivated by the *aretê* of the partners, Aristotle recognizes that such *philia* is also eminently pleasurable and
useful, both objectively (*haplôs*) and with relation to the persons involved
(*allêlois*: 1156 b 12–17; 1157 a 1–3; 1157 b 25–28). The pleasure and usefulness Aristotle has in mind here is not the gross type motivating those
who associate for sensual gratification or expediency, but the pleasure that
accompanies activity of the strictly human powers (especially the intellect)
operating at their best (*met' aretês*: cf. 1175 a 20–28; 1176 a 17–19), and
the usefulness that helps to achieve what is good or noble (*eis ta kala*:
1158 a 26–34). For these are the pleasure and the usefulness offered by the
truly good man (*ho spoudaios*: 1158 a 33 f.).

The pleasure which a good man finds in association with another
equally good, the enjoyment of his company, goes as deep as that which
he derives from the consciousness of his own existence (1170 a 29–b 12;
1171 b 34 f.). For Aristotle equates existence with life activities, and
human life specifically with the conscious activities of sense and intellect
(1170 a 16–19). In a good man these faculties operate excellently (*kat'
aretên*), so that their activities are accompanied, and perfected, by the
noblest and best of pleasure, that which arises when the highest human
faculties are activated upon their highest objects according to their proper

virtues (1176 b 15 ff.). Moreover, the good man is *conscious* of these activities of sense and intellect, conscious of his own existence, conscious that it is good; and the consciousness that one possesses what is by nature good gives true pleasure, so that the good man finds true pleasure in his own existence (1170 a 19–b 5). Therefore, he also finds his own existence *desirable*, being conscious that his life activities are both good and pleasant (1170 b 3–5).

Now, as we have seen, for Aristotle the good man is disposed toward an equally good *philos* as he is toward himself, since in his case a *philos* is "another self" (1170 b 5–7). Therefore, just as he finds his own existence desirable as being good and pleasant in itself, so he desires the existence of his *philos* as good and pleasant objectively (1170 b 7–10). Presumably, the consciousness of possessing, by mutual consent, the other good man as *his philos* brings him again the pleasure of possessing somehow what is objectively good.

It is essential to perfect *philia*, moreover, that the two good men live closely together, sharing their life activities equally. But the life activities specific to human beings are, as we have seen, those of sense perception and thought, so that the partners in perfect *philia* will spend much of their time in these activities, sharing their thoughts and perceptions. This is really what living closely together means for human beings, for in this way they share the consciousness of their existence (1170 b 10–14). However, since for the good man these activities are in themselves eminently pleasurable, he will doubtless communicate his own pleasure in them to his *philos*, and enjoy also the pleasure which his "other self" finds in his own.

Furthermore, Aristotle seems to believe that sharing their conscious activities augments the pleasure of the *philoi* to a degree not possible to either of them alone. First, he asserts that "we are able to contemplate others close to us better than ourselves, and their actions better than our own" (1169 b 33–35). The good man, then, will find even keener pleasure in this contemplation, since the activities of his *philos*, being other than his own, will be more clearly observable; being activities of another good man, they will be virtuous and similar to his own; being activities of his "other self," they will in that sense be his own and shared as his own. Clear consciousness of excellence somehow communicated to oneself gives rise to pleasure, and "the good man, as good, enjoys human acts excellently done (*kat' aretên*) . . . as the skilled musician finds pleasure in beautiful melodies. . . ." (1169 b 35—1170 a 4, 8–11).

Secondly, the pleasure enjoyed by two good men in perfect *philia* will be more continuous or sustained. For the activities that give rise to that pleasure will be more sustained because they are shared. "It is not easy to keep up continuous activity by oneself; it is easier to do so with the aid of and in relation to other people. The good man's activity, therefore, which is pleasant in itself, will be more continuous if practised with friends. . . ." (1170 a 5–7, Rackham).

This also clarifies the sense in which Aristotle understands perfect *philia* to be *useful* or advantageous. It is useful, in fact *necessary*, for carrying on *best* the activities which are essential to human happiness, those of the intellectual as well as the moral life. For with the aid of *philoi* "men are better able both to think and to act" (*noêsai kai praxai*: 1155 a 14–16). Aristotle does not forget this even when, at the end of Book X, he is stressing the self-sufficiency of contemplative activity: "The wise man, even when alone, can contemplate truth, and the better the wiser he is; he can perhaps do so better if he has fellow-workers; but still he is the most self-sufficient" (1177 a 32–b 1).[11] This is what we should expect, since for Aristotle man is essentially a *zôon politikon*, born to live with others and operating best in companionship (1169 b 16–19). Finally, *philia* is useful to good men in making them better. Sharing their lives and activities is a constant training and exercise in excellence (1170 a 11–13). For "the *philia* of good men is good, growing through their association; and they appear to grow better, sharing activities and correcting each other; for from each other they take on the impress of the traits they find pleasing in one another; whence the saying 'noble deeds from noble men'" (1172 a 11–14; cf. 1159 b 2–7).

With all the qualifications he demands for the realization of this ideal of perfect *philia*, one is tempted to question whether Aristotle himself believed that instances of perfect *philia* could actually be found to exist. The answer seems to be that he did believe they existed, but only rarely. *Philia* between men of fully developed moral and intellectual excellence is rare, first of all, because such men are rare (1156 b 24 f.). "It is not possible to have many *philoi* whom we prize for their own sake because of their intrinsic goodness. One would be fortunate to find even a few such"

11 At the conclusion (page 45) of his article cited in note 3, above, A. W. H. Adkins translate the *isôs* of 1177 a 34 by an italicized "*perhaps*," apparently to imply that Aristotle really doubts the necessity of fellow-workers for carrying on better the activity of *theôria*. He goes on to suggest that "if one can practice *theôria* without *philoi*," then Aristotle believes that "behavior in accordance with *aretê* no longer requires associates, so that *aretê* and *philia* are no longer related," and philosophers operate in "splendid isolation," completely self-sufficient. A large conclusion to be supported by a single *isôs* = "perhaps." On the other hand, Rackham (Loeb, 615) translates the same *isôs* as "no doubt," and Thomson (*op. cit.*, 304) as "doubtless." The latter interpretation is supported by 1155 a 14–16, 1169 b 33–35, 1170 a 5–7, 1172 a 3–8. Adkins does not discuss these texts.

(1171 a 19 f.). Secondly, it takes long and close association to come to know another, to experience his intrinsic goodness, and learn to entrust oneself to him (1156 b 25–29; 1158 a 14 f.). Thirdly, even if there were many good men available, one could develop perfect *philia* with only a few, since one man cannot be deeply committed (*philos sphodra*) to many at the same time (1171 a 10–13); he cannot live closely together with many and share deeply the joys and sorrows of many (1170 b 33–1171 a 10). Finally, the good man's *philoi* should also be *philoi* of each other, spending their days in company with one another. But this is very difficult when many are involved (1171 a 4–6).

Did Aristotle know perfect *philia* in his own life? In a beautiful passage at the end of Book IX he seems to break away from the theoretical to the existential plane of his own experience in describing how living close to one another is for *philoi* the most desirable thing there is (1171 b 29–32): "For *philia* is a sharing (*koinônia*); and as a man is to himself, so is he to his *philos*. As the consciousness of his own existence, then, is desirable to him, so is the consciousness of the existence of his *philos*. And since this consciousness is activated in their living close to one another, it is reasonable that they desire this. Whatever constitutes existence for each group of men, whatever makes their life worth living, in this they wish to occupy themselves with their *philoi*. Accordingly, some drink or dice together, others exercise or hunt together, or engage together in pursuing wisdom (*symphilosophousin*), each group spending their days together in that which they love best of everything in life. For wishing to live closely with their *philoi*, they carry on and share those activities which constitute for them the good life" (1171 b 32—1172 a 8, reading Bekker's *eu zên* for the final *suzên* of the mss.).

In this reference to a group of *philoi* living close together and sharing the pursuit of wisdom we may perhaps detect a memory of Aristotle's years in the Academy, or a glimpse of life with his later associates. But one *philos* comes to mind above all others, Hermias of Atarneus, in whose honor Aristotle composed a hymn to *aretê*.[12]

University of Illinois at Chicago Circle

[12] I would like to express sincere thanks to John Rist, of the University of Toronto, and to Matthew Dickie and Richard Kraut, colleagues at the University of Illinois, Chicago, for reading and commenting on the substance of this paper. Fellow panelist Ladislaus Bolchazy has been most helpful with editorial suggestions. The deficiencies of the paper are solely my own.

6

Theophilus of Antioch: Fifty-five Emendations

MIROSLAV MARCOVICH

(1) Theophilus of Antioch, *Ad Autolycum* I. 2 (line 30), ed. Robert M. Grant (Oxford, 1970). Καὶ σοὶ οὖν ἅπαντα ἐπισκοτεῖ, καθάπερ ὕλης ἐπιφορὰ ἐπὰν γένηται τοῖς ὀφθαλμοῖς πρὸς τὸ μὴ δύνασθαι ἀτενίσαι τὸ φῶς τοῦ ἡλίου· οὕτως καὶ σοί, ὦ ἄνθρωπε, ἐπισκοτοῦσιν αἱ ἀσέβειαι πρὸς τὸ μὴ δύνασθαί σε ὁρᾶν τὸν θεόν. Read: Καὶ σοὶ οὖν ἅπαντα ⟨ταῦτα⟩ ἐπισκοτεῖ· καθάπερ ⟨γὰρ⟩ ὕλης ἐπιφορὰ ... τὸ φῶς τοῦ ἡλίου, οὕτως καὶ σοί, ... τὸν θεόν. "All these things bring darkness upon you too:" ἅπαντα ταῦτα are the sixteen sins quoted in lines 23–28.

(2) I. 6. 18. Οὗτος θεὸς μόνος ὁ ποιήσας ἐκ σκότους φῶς, ὁ ἐξαγαγὼν φῶς ἐκ θησαυρῶν αὐτοῦ, ταμεῖά τε νότου καὶ θησαυροὺς ἀβύσσου. ... Read: ἐκ θησαυρῶν αὐτοῦ, ⟨ὁ ποιῶν⟩ ταμεῖά τε νότου καὶ ... = *Job* 9:9.

(3) I. 8. 3. Ἢ οὐκ οἶδας ὅτι ἁπάντων πραγμάτων ἡ πίστις προηγεῖται; τίς γὰρ δύναται θερίσαι γεωργός, ἐὰν μὴ πρῶτον πιστεύσῃ τὸ σπέρμα τῇ γῇ; ἢ τίς δύναται διαπερᾶσαι τὴν θάλασσαν, ἐὰν μὴ πρῶτον ἑαυτὸν πιστεύσῃ τῷ πλοίῳ καὶ τῷ κυβερνήτῃ; τίς δὲ κάμνων δύναται θεραπευθῆναι, ἐὰν μὴ πρῶτον ἑαυτὸν πιστεύσῃ τῷ ἰατρῷ; Read: ἢ τίς ⟨πλέων⟩ δύναται διαπερᾶσαι τὴν θάλασσαν. ... Compare line 10 Εἰ οὖν γεωργὸς πιστεύει τῇ γῇ καὶ ὁ π λ έ ω ν τῷ πλοίῳ καὶ ὁ κάμνων τῷ ἰατρῷ, σὺ οὐ βούλει ἑαυτὸν πιστεῦσαι τῷ θεῷ ...; Xenophon, *Mem.* III. 3. 9 Καὶ γὰρ ἐν νόσῳ, ὃν ἂν ἡγῶνται (sc. οἱ ἄνθρωποι) ἰατρικώτατον εἶναι, τούτῳ μάλιστα πείθονται, καὶ ἐν πλοίῳ ο ἱ π λ έ ο ν τ ε ς, ὃν ἂν κυβερνητικώτατον, καὶ ἐν γεωργίᾳ, ὃν ἂν γεωργικώτατον.

(4) I. 11. 5. Θεὸς γὰρ οὐκ ἔστιν (sc. ὁ βασιλεύς), ἀλλὰ ἄνθρωπος, ὑπὸ θεοῦ τεταγμένος, οὐκ εἰς τὸ προσκυνεῖσθαι, ἀλλὰ εἰς τὸ δικαίως κρίνειν ... Οὕτως οὐδὲ προσκυνεῖσθαι ἀλλ' ἢ μόνῳ θεῷ. Read: Οὕτως οὐδὲ⟨νὶ⟩ προσκυνεῖσθαι ἀλλ' ἢ μόνῳ θεῷ.

(5) I. 13. 3. Εἶτα πιστεύεις μὲν Ἡρακλέα καύσαντα ἑαυτὸν ζῆν καὶ Ἀσκληπιὸν κεραυνωθέντα ἐγηγέρθαι. τὰ δὲ ὑπὸ τοῦ θεοῦ σοι λεγόμενα ἀπιστεῖς; ἴσως καὶ ἐπιδείξω σοι νεκρὸν ἐγερθέντα καὶ ζῶντα, καὶ τοῦτο ἀπιστήσεις; Read:

ἐγηγέρθαι, τὰ δὲ ὑπὸ τοῦ θεοῦ σοι λεγόμενα ἀπιστεῖς. ἴσως κ ἂ ν ἐπιδείξω σοι νεκρὸν ...

(6) I. 13. 15. *Ἔτι μὴν ἐνίοτε καὶ στρουθίον ἢ τῶν λοιπῶν πετεινῶν, καταπιὸν σπέρμα μηλέας ἢ συκῆς ἤ τινος ἑτέρου.* ... Read: στρουθίον ἤ ⟨τι⟩ τῶν λοιπῶν πετεινῶν ...

(7) I. 13. 22. *Εἰ δὲ καὶ θαυμασιώτερον θέαμα θέλεις θεάσασθαι γ ι ν ό μ ε ν ο ν πρὸς ἀπόδειξιν ἀναστάσεως, οὐ μόνον τῶν ἐπιγείων πραγμάτων ἀλλὰ καὶ τῶν ἐν οὐρανῷ, κατανόησον τὴν ἀνάστασιν τῆς σελήνης τὴν κατὰ μῆνα γ ε ν ο μ έ ν η ν, πῶς φθίνει, ἀποθνήσκει, ἀνίσταται πάλιν. ἔτι ἄκουσον καὶ ἐν σοὶ αὐτῷ ἔργον ἀναστάσεως γ ι ν ό μ ε ν ο ν, κἂν ἀγνοεῖς, ὦ ἄνθρωπε.* Read: τὴν κατὰ μῆνα γινομένην and compare γινόμενον twice in the context.

(8) I. 14. 7. ... *ἀλλὰ πιστεύω πειθαρχῶν θεῷ· ᾧ, εἰ βούλει, καὶ σὺ ὑποτάγηθι πιστεύων αὐτῷ, μὴ νῦν ἀπιστήσας πεισθῇς ἀνιώμενος, τότε ἐν αἰωνίοις τιμωρίαις.* Read: μὴ νῦν ἀπιστήσας ⟨αὖθις⟩ πεισθῇς ... (*isoteleuton*).

(9) II. 2. 1. *Καὶ γὰρ γέλοιόν μοι δοκεῖ λιθοξόους μὲν καὶ πλάστας ἢ ζωγράφους ἢ χωνευτὰς πλάσσειν τε καὶ γράφειν καὶ γλύφειν καὶ χωνεύειν καὶ θεοὺς κατασκευάζειν, οἳ, ἐπὰν γένωνται ὑπὸ τῶν τεχνιτῶν, οὐδὲν αὐτοὺς ἡγοῦνται.* ... Read: οὐδὲν α ὐ τ ο ῖ ς ἡγοῦνται and compare line 8 (οἱ ποιήσαντες) ἡγοῦνται θεοὺς αὐτούς.

(10) II. 3. 9 = *Oracula Sibyllina*, Fr. 2 Geffcken.

Εἰ δὲ θεοὶ γεννῶσι καὶ ἀθάνατοί γε μένουσι,
πλείονες ἀνθρώπων γεγεννημένοι ἂν θεοὶ ἦσαν,
οὐδὲ τόπος στῆναι θνητοῖς οὐκ ἂν ποθ᾽ ὑπῆρξεν.

ἂν θεοὶ Rzach: οἱ δὲ θεοὶ Venetus 496 s. XI. Read: γεγενημένοι οἱ {δὲ} θεοὶ ἦσαν with Ioannes Opsopoeus (J. Koch), Paris, 1599, and compare II. 9. 8.

(11) II. 4. 8. *Πλάτων δὲ καὶ οἱ τῆς αἱρέσεως αὐτοῦ θεὸν μὲν ὁμολογοῦσιν ἀγένητον καὶ πατέρα καὶ ποιητὴν τῶν ὅλων εἶναι· εἶτα ὑποτίθενται θεὸν καὶ ὕλην ἀγένητον καὶ ταύτην φασὶν συνηκμακέναι τῷ θεῷ. εἰ δὲ θεὸς ἀγένητος καὶ ὕλη ἀγένητος, οὐκ ἔτι ὁ θεὸς ποιητὴς τῶν ὅλων ἐστὶν κατὰ τοὺς Πλατωνικούς* ... Grant translates: " ... next they assume that uncreated matter is also God, and say that matter was coeval with God." I do not think he is right. Read instead: εἶτα ὑποτίθενται ⟨παρὰ⟩ θεὸν καὶ ὕλην ἀγένητον and compare Hippolytus, *Elenchos* I. 19. 4 (Plato) *τὴν μὲν οὖν ὕλην ἀρχὴν εἶναι καὶ σύγχρονον τῷ θεῷ.* ... (The scribe of the Venetus drops a περὶ at I. 1. 13 too.)

(12) II. 4. 25. ... *οὕτως καὶ τὸ ἐξ οὐκ ὄντων ποιεῖν* (sc. τὸν θεὸν) *καὶ πεποιηκέναι τὰ ὄντα, καὶ ὅσα βούλεται καὶ ὡς* (Otto: καθὼς Venetus) *βούλεται.* Read: καὶ ὅσα βούλεται, καθὼς βούλεται and compare Hippolytus, *Syntagma* 8 (p. 249.25 Nautin) *πάντα ποιῶν* (sc. ὁ θεὸς) *ὅσα θέλει, καθὼς θέλει, ὅτε θέλει.* 10 (p. 251.14): *τὰ γενόμενα ὅσα ἠθέλησεν, ὅτε ἠθέλησεν, καθὼς ἠθέλησεν* (and line 19): *ὅτε ἠθέλησεν, καθὼς ἠθέλησεν.*

Accordingly, *Ad Autolycum* II. 13. 5: Θεοῦ δὲ τὸ δυνατὸν ἐν τούτῳ δείκνυται, ἵνα πρῶτον μὲν ἐξ οὐκ ὄντων ποιῇ τὰ γινόμενα, καὶ ὡς (Otto) βούλεται, should read: τὰ γινόμενα, καθὼς (Venetus) βούλεται.

(13) II. 6. 14 = Hesiod, *Theogony* 129 f.

> γείνατο (sc. Γαῖα) δ᾽ οὔρεα μακρά, θεᾶν χαρίεντας ἐναύλους
> Νυμφέων, αἳ ναίουσιν ἀν᾽ οὔρεα βησσήεντα.

χαρίεντας ἐναύλους Hesiod: χαρίεσσαν ἐν αὐτοῖς Venetus. The text is good as transmitted. Read: θ έ α ν χαρίεσσαν ἐν αὐτοῖς / Νυμφέων, "the beautiful sight (or spectacle) of the Nymphs in the hills." This is the way Theophilus understood ΘΕΑΝ in his source.

(14) II. 7. 11 = *F Gr Hist* 631 (Satyrus). Ἀλλὰ καὶ Σάτυρος ἱστορῶν τοὺς δήμους Ἀλεξανδρέων, ἀρξάμενος ἀπὸ Φιλοπάτορος τοῦ καὶ Πτολεμαίου προσαγορευθέντος, τούτου μηνύει Διόνυσον ἀρχηγέτην γεγονέναι· διὸ καὶ φυλὴν ὁ Πτολεμαῖος πρώτην κατέστησεν. Read: ἀπὸ Πτολεμαίου τοῦ καὶ Φιλοπάτορος προσαγορευθέντος, τούτου μηνύει Διόνυσον ἀρχηγέτην γεγονέναι· διὸ καὶ ⟨τούτου τὴν⟩ φυλὴν ὁ Πτολεμαῖος πρώτην κατέστησεν. (Διὸ καὶ τὴν Διονυσίαν φυλὴν Bodleianus [Auct. E. I. 11, between 1541 and 1546] in margine, adopted by Meineke, Jacoby, P. M. Fraser, *Ptolemaic Alexandria*, Oxford, 1972, II, p. 120.)

(15) II. 7. 26. Ὅθεν καὶ ἐν τῇ Διονυσίᾳ φυλῇ δῆμοί εἰσιν κατακεχωρισμένοι. Ἀλθηὶς ἀπὸ τῆς γενομένης γυναικὸς Διονύσου, θυγατρὸς δὲ Θεστίου, Ἀλθαίας. Δηιανειρὶς ἀπὸ τῆς θυγατρὸς Διονύσου καὶ Ἀλθαίας, γυναικὸς δὲ Ἡρακλέους. ὅθεν καὶ τὰς προσωνυμίας ἔχουσιν οἱ κατ᾽ αὐτοὺς δῆμοι· Ἀριαδνὶς ἀπὸ τῆς θυγατρὸς Μίνω, γυναικὸς δὲ Διονύσου, παιδὸς πατροφίλης τῆς μιχθείσης Διονύσῳ ἐν μορφῇ † Πρύμνιδι †, Θεστὶς ἀπὸ Θεστίου τοῦ Ἀλθαίας πατρὸς. . . .

Read: Ὅθεν καὶ τὰς προσωνυμίας ἔχουσιν οἱ κατ᾽ αὐτοὺς δῆμοι {ὅθεν} (huc transposuerunt Meineke et Jacoby), καὶ ἐν τῇ Διονυσίᾳ φυλῇ δῆμοί εἰσιν κατακεχωρισμένοι ⟨οὗτοι·⟩ Ἀλθηὶς . . ., Δηιανειρὶς . . . γυναικὸς δὲ Ἡρακλέους, Ἀριαδνὶς ἀπὸ τῆς θυγατρὸς Μίνω, γυναικὸς δὲ Διονύσου,

> παιδὸς πατροφίλης τῆς μιχθείσης Διονύσῳ
> ἐν μορφῇ ⟨ταύρου,

Πρυμνὶς ἀπὸ⟩ Πρυμνίδος * * *, Θεστὶς ἀπὸ Θεστίου . . . and compare P. Oxy. 2465, Fr. 3, col. II, line 14; Pausanias II. 4. 4; R. M. Grant, *Vigiliae Christ.* 6 (1952), 157 f.

(16) II. 8. 25 = Sophocles, *Oedip. Rex* 978 f.

> Πρόνοια δ᾽ ἐστὶν οὐδενός,
> εἰκῇ κράτιστον ζῆν, ὅπως δύναιτό τις

and II. 8. 49 = Euripides, Fr. 391 N.²

> Σπουδάζομεν δὲ πόλλ᾽ ὑπ᾽ ἐλπίδων, μάτην
> πόνους ἔχοντες, οὐδὲν εἰδότες.

Read: πρόνοια δ᾽ ἐστὶν οὐδενὸς ⟨σαφής⟩ (= Sophocles) and πόνους ἔχοντες, οὐδὲν εἰδότες ⟨σαφές⟩ (= Orion, Floril. 5, 7).

(17) II. 8. 43. Καὶ τὰ τοιαῦτα μυρία εἰπόντες ἀσύμφωνα ἑαυτοῖς ἐξεῖπον. ὁ γοῦν Σοφοκλῆς ἀπρονοησίαν ⟨εἴρων B. Einarson⟩ ἐν ἑτέρῳ λέγει· "Θεοῦ δὲ πληγὴν οὐχ ὑπερπηδᾷ βροτός." Πλὴν καὶ πληθὺν εἰσήγαγον ἢ καὶ μοναρχίαν εἶπον. . . . Read: ἀπρονοησίαν ⟨εἰπὼν⟩ ἐν ἑτέρῳ λέγει· . . . Πλὴν καὶ πληθὺν ⟨θεῶν⟩ εἰσήγαγον and compare the phrase πληθὺν θεῶν at II. 10. 25; 28.5–7 (three times); 33.3; 38. 17.

(18) II. 10. 1. Καὶ πρῶτον μὲν συμφώνως ἐδίδαξαν ἡμᾶς ὅτι ἐξ οὐκ ὄντων τὰ πάντα ἐποίησεν. οὐ γάρ τι τῷ θεῷ συνήκμασεν. Read: ὅτι ἐξ οὐκ ὄντων τὰ πάντα ἐποίησεν ⟨ὁ θεός.⟩ οὐ γάρ τι τῷ θεῷ συνήκμασεν and compare 2 Mac. 7:28 ὅτι οὐκ ἐξ ὄντων ἐποίησεν αὐτὰ ὁ θεός.

(19) II. 10. 32. Ταῦτα ἐν πρώτοις διδάσκει ἡ θεία γραφή, τρόπῳ τινὶ ὕλην γενητήν, ὑπὸ τοῦ θεοῦ γεγονυῖαν, ἀφ᾽ ἧς πεποίηκεν καὶ δεδημιούργηκεν ὁ θεὸς τὸν κόσμον. Read: ὑπὸ τοῦ θεοῦ γεγονυῖαν ⟨ἀναφαίνουσα,⟩ ἀφ᾽ ἧς. . . .

(20) II. 12. 8. Πολλοὶ μὲν οὖν τῶν συγγραφέων ἐμιμήσαντο καὶ ἠθέλησαν περὶ τούτων διήγησιν ποιήσασθαι, καίτοι λαβόντες ἐντεῦθεν τὰς ἀφορμάς, ἤτοι περὶ κόσμου κτίσεως ἢ περὶ φύσεως ἀνθρώπου, καὶ οὐδὲ τὸ τυχὸν ἔναυσμα ἄξιόν τι τῆς ἀληθείας ἐξεῖπον. Read: Πολλοὶ μὲν οὖν τῶν συγγραφέων ⟨τὴν γραφὴν⟩ ἐμιμήσαντο καὶ ἠθέλησαν . . . ποιήσασθαι, ⟨ἀλλ᾽ ἔπταισαν,⟩ καίτοι λαβόντες ἐντεῦθεν τὰς ἀφορμάς. . . .

(21) II. 12. 25. Τὸ δὲ εἰπεῖν Ἡσίοδον τὸν ποιητὴν ἐκ Χάους γεγενῆσθαι Ἔρεβος καὶ τὴν Γῆν καὶ Ἔρωτα, κυριεύοντα τῶν κατ᾽ αὐτόν τε θεῶν καὶ ἀνθρώπων, μάταιον καὶ ψ υ χ ρ ὸ ν τὸ ῥῆμα αὐτοῦ καὶ ἀλλότριον πάσης ἀληθείας δείκνυται. Grant translates: "And as for Hesiod's statement that from Chaos were created Erebus and Earth and Eros, which rules over gods (as he considers them) and men, his discourse is futile and frigid and entirely alien to the truth." Read instead: Τὸ δὲ εἰπεῖν Ἡσίοδον . . . μάταιον (sc. ἐστί), καὶ ψ υ δ ρ ὸ ν τὸ ῥῆμα αὐτοῦ καὶ ἀλλότριον πάσης ἀληθείας δείκνυται. Compare Clement, Strom. VI. 18. 6 ψυδρὸς Theognis: ψυχρὸς Laurentianus. Hippolytus, Elenchos VI. 19. 4 ψυδρὸς Roeper: ψυχρὸς Parisinus.

(22) II. 13. 1. Ἀλλὰ καὶ τὸ ἐκ τῶν ἐπιγείων κάτωθεν ἄρξασθαι {καὶ del. Nautin} λέγειν τὴν ποίησιν τῶν γεγενημένων ἀνθρώπινον καὶ ταπεινὸν καὶ πάνυ ἀσθενὲς τὸ ἐννόημα αὐτοῦ ὡς πρὸς θεόν ἐστιν. Read: τὸ ἐκ τῶν ἐπιγείων κ α ὶ κάτωθεν ἄρξασθαι λέγειν τὴν ποίησιν . . . ἀνθρώπινον (sc. ἐστί), καὶ ταπεινὸν καὶ πάνυ ἀσθενὲς τὸ ἐννόημα αὐτοῦ. . . .

(23) II. 13. 12. Γῆν δὲ λέγει (sc. Gen. 1:1–2) δυνάμει ἔδαφος καὶ θεμέλιον,

ἄβυσσον δὲ τὴν πληθὺν τῶν ὑδάτων, καὶ σκότος διὰ τὸ τὸν οὐρανὸν γεγονότα ὑπὸ τοῦ θεοῦ ἐσκεπακέναι καθαπερεὶ πῶμα τὰ ὕδατα σὺν τῇ γῇ, πνεῦμα δὲ τὸ ἐπιφερόμενον ἐπάνω τοῦ ὕδατος ὃ ἔδωκεν ὁ θεὸς εἰς ζωογόνησιν τῇ κτίσει, καθάπερ ἀνθρώπῳ ψυχήν. . . . Read: πνεῦμα δέ, "τὸ ἐπιφερόμενον ἐπάνω τοῦ ὕδατος," ⟨φ ῶ s,⟩ ὃ ἔδωκεν ὁ θεὸς . . . and compare line 19 ἐν μὲν τὸ πνεῦμα φ ω τ ὸ ς τ ύ π ο ν ἐπέχον ἐμεσίτευεν τοῦ ὕδατος καὶ τοῦ οὐρανοῦ, ἵνα τρόπῳ τινὶ μὴ κοινωνῇ τὸ σκότος τῷ οὐρανῷ, ἐγγυτέρῳ ὄντι τοῦ θεοῦ, πρὸ τοῦ εἰπεῖν τὸν θεόν· "Γενηθήτω φῶς."

(24) II. 14. 22. Καὶ ὥσπερ αὖ νῆσοί εἰσιν ἕτεραι πετρώδεις . . . ἐν αἷς περιπείρεται τὰ πλοῖα καὶ ἐξαπόλλυνται ἐν αὐταῖς οἱ κατερχόμενοι, οὕτως εἰσὶν αἱ διδασκαλίαι τῆς πλάνης, λέγω δὲ τῶν αἱρέσεων, αἳ ἐξαπολλύουσιν τοὺς προσιόντας αὐταῖς. οὐ γὰρ ὁδηγοῦνται ὑπὸ τοῦ λόγου τῆς ἀληθείας, ἀλλὰ καθάπερ πειραταί, ἐπὰν π λ η ρ ώ σ ω σ ι ν τὰς ναῦς, ἐπὶ τοὺς προειρημένους τόπους περιπείρουσιν, ὅπως ἐξαπολέσωσιν αὐτάς, οὕτως συμβαίνει καὶ τοῖς πλανωμένοις ἀπὸ τῆς ἀληθείας ἐξαπόλλυσθαι ὑπὸ τῆς πλάνης. Grant translates: "but just as pirates, when they have filled ships, run them on the places mentioned above, in order to destroy them, so it happens that those who stray from the truth are destroyed by error." But pirates do not *fill* ships before destroying them: they incapacitate (disable, maim) them. Thus read: πηρώσωσιν for the transmitted πληρώσωσιν and compare Hippolytus, *Elenchos* VIII. 14. 6 τοῖς μὴ πεπηρωμένοις παντελῶς τὴν διάνοιαν, where Parisinus has πεπληρωμένοις.

(25) II. 17. 14. Θηρία δὲ ὠνόμασται τὰ ζῶα ἀπὸ τοῦ θ η ρ ε ύ ε σ θ α ι, οὐχ ὡς κακὰ ἀρχῆθεν γεγενημένα ἢ ἰοβόλα· οὐ γάρ τι κακὸν ἀρχῆθεν γέγονεν ἀπὸ θεοῦ ἀλλὰ τὰ πάντα καλὰ καὶ καλὰ λίαν, ἡ δέ ἁμαρτία ἡ περὶ τὸν ἄνθρωπον κεκάκωκεν αὐτά· τοῦ γὰρ ἀνθρώπου παραβάντος καὶ αὐτὰ συμπαρέβη. Ὥσπερ γὰρ δεσπότης οἰκίας ἐὰν αὐτὸς εὖ πράσσῃ, ἀναγκαίως καὶ οἱ οἰκέται εὐτάκτως ζῶσιν, ἐὰν δὲ ὁ κύριος ἁμαρτάνῃ, καὶ οἱ δοῦλοι συναμαρτάνουσιν, τῷ αὐτῷ τρόπῳ γέγονεν καὶ τὰ περὶ τὸν ἄνθρωπον κύριον ὄντα ἁμαρτῆσαι, καὶ τὰ δοῦλα συνήμαρτεν. In the first sentence read: Θηρία δὲ ὠνόμασται τὰ ζῶα ἀπὸ τοῦ θηριοῦσθαι (J. C. T. Otto) for the transmitted θηρεύεσθαι: "The animals have got the name 'beasts' from their *becoming* brutal (malignant)," and not: "Wild animals are so called from their being hunted," as Grant has it. As for the idea of *apostasy* from God by the original sin of man, compare II. 28. 28: Δαίμων δὲ καὶ δράκων καλεῖται διὰ τὸ ἀποδεδρακέναι αὐτὸν ἀπὸ τοῦ θεοῦ· ἄγγελος γὰρ ἦν ἐν πρώτοις. As for the palaeography, compare III. 5. 5 and 10 κατεσθίεσθαι J. C. Wolf: κατεσθέσθαι (both times) Venetus. In the second sentence read: τῷ αὐτῷ τρόπῳ γέγονεν καὶ τὰ ⟨ζῶα κακά, καὶ⟩ π α ρ ὰ ("through, because of," LSJ, s.v., C III 7) τὸν ἄνθρωπον, κύριον ὄντα, ἁμαρτῆσαι, καὶ τὰ δοῦλα συνήμαρτεν.

(26) II. 18. 7. Ἔτι μὴν καὶ ὡς βοηθείας χρῄζων ὁ θεὸς εὑρίσκεται λέγων·

Miroslav Marcovich 81

"Ποιήσωμεν ἄνθρωπον κατ᾽ εἰκόνα καὶ καθ᾽ ὁμοίωσιν." οὐκ ἄλλῳ δέ τινι εἴρηκεν· "Ποιήσωμεν," ἀλλ᾽ ἢ τῷ ἑαυτοῦ λόγῳ καὶ τῇ ἑαυτοῦ σοφίᾳ. ποιήσας δὲ αὐτὸν καὶ εὐλογήσας εἰς τὸ αὐξάνεσθαι καὶ πληρῶσαι τὴν γῆν, ὑπέταξεν αὐτῷ. ... In the first sentence read: Ἔτι μὴν καὶ ⟨ὅτε,⟩ ὡς βοηθείας χρῄζων, ὁ θεὸς εὑρίσκεται λέγων· "Ποιήσωμεν ... ὁμοίωσιν," οὐκ ἄλλῳ δ ή τινι εἴρηκεν ... ἀλλ᾽ ἢ τῷ ... and compare line 3 ἐν τῷ γὰρ εἰπεῖν τὸν θεὸν ..., "When God said ..." In the second sentence read: εἰς τὸ αὐξάνεσθαι ⟨καὶ πληθύνεσθαι⟩ καὶ πληρῶσαι τὴν γῆν = Gen.1:28, and Theophilus II. 11. 54; 23. 7; 32. 23.

(27) II. 19. 20. Μετὰ δὲ τὸ πλάσαι τὸν ἄνθρωπον ὁ θεὸς ἐξελέξατο αὐτῷ χωρίον ἐν τοῖς τόποις τοῖς ἀνατολικοῖς, διάφορον φωτί, διαυγὲς ἀέρι λαμπροτέρῳ, φυτοῖς παγκάλοις, ἐν ᾧ ἔθετο τὸν ἄνθρωπον. Read: διάφορον φωτί, διαυγὲς ἀέρι λαμπροτέρῳ, ⟨διέχον⟩ φυτοῖς παγκάλοις ...

(28) II. 24. 2. Ἐν γὰρ πρώτοις μόνα ἦν τὰ ἐν τῇ τρίτῃ ἡμέρᾳ γεγενημένα, φυτὰ καὶ σπέρματα καὶ χλόαι· τὰ δὲ ἐν τῷ παραδείσῳ ἐγενήθη διαφόρῳ καλλονῇ καὶ ὡραιότητι ... Καὶ τὰ μὲν λοιπὰ φυτὰ ὅμοια καὶ ὁ κόσμος ἔσχηκεν· τὰ δὲ δύο ξύλα, τὸ τῆς ζωῆς καὶ τὸ τῆς γνώσεως, οὐκ ἔσχηκεν ἑτέρα γῆ. ... Read, first: διάφορα καλλονῇ (and compare No. 27: διάφορον φωτί); second, ὅμοια καὶ ⟨ἃ⟩ ὁ κόσμος ἔσχηκεν (or ὅμοια ⟨οἷα⟩ καὶ ὁ κ. ἔσχ.).

(29) II. 24. 9. "Καὶ ἐφύτευσεν ὁ θεὸς παράδεισον ἐν Ἐδὲμ κατὰ ἀνατολάς, καὶ ἔθετο ἐκεῖ τὸν ἄνθρωπον· καὶ ἐξανέτειλεν ὁ θεὸς ἔτι ἀπὸ τῆς γῆς πᾶν ξύλον ὡραῖον εἰς ὅρασιν καὶ καλὸν εἰς βρῶσιν" (Gen. 2:8–9). τὸ οὖν ἔτι ἐκ τῆς γῆς καὶ κατὰ ἀνατολὰς σαφῶς διδάσκει ἡμᾶς ἡ θεία γραφὴ τὸν παράδεισον ὑπὸ τοῦτον τὸν οὐρανόν, ὑφ᾽ ὃν καὶ ἀνατολαὶ καὶ γῆ εἰσιν. Read: τ ῷ οὖν "ἔτι ἐκ τῆς γῆς" καὶ "κατὰ ἀνατολὰς" σαφῶς διδάσκει ἡμᾶς ἡ θεία γραφὴ τὸν παράδεισον ὑπὸ τοῦτον ⟨ὄντα⟩ τὸν οὐρανόν, ὑφ᾽ ὃν. ...

(30) II. 25. 18. Ἄλλως τε ἐπὰν νόμος κελεύσῃ ἀπέχεσθαι ἀπό τινος καὶ μὴ ὑπακούῃ τις, δῆλον ὅτι οὐχ ὁ νόμος κόλασιν παρέχει, ἀλλὰ ἡ ἀπείθεια καὶ ἡ παρακοή. καὶ γὰρ πατὴρ ἰδίῳ τέκνῳ ἐνίοτε προστάσσει ἀπέχεσθαί τινων, καὶ ἐπὰν οὐχ ὑπακούῃ τῇ πατρικῇ ἐντολῇ, δέρεται καὶ ἐπιτιμίας τυγχάνει διὰ τὴν παρακοήν· καὶ οὐκ ἤδη αὐτὰ τὰ π ρ ά γ μ α τ α πληγαί εἰσιν, ἀλλ᾽ ἡ παρακοὴ τῷ ἀπειθοῦντι ὕβρεις περιποιεῖται. Read: καὶ οὐκ ἤδη αὐτὰ τὰ πρ⟨οστ⟩άγματα πληγαί εἰσιν and compare ὁ νόμος and προστάσσει in the context; II. 15. 28 τῶν ἀφισταμένων ἀνθρώπων ἀπὸ τοῦ θεοῦ, καταλιπόντων τὸν νόμον καὶ τὰ προστάγματα αὐτοῦ.

(31) II. 26. 1. Καὶ τοῦτο δὲ ὁ θεὸς μεγάλην εὐεργεσίαν παρέσχεν τῷ ἀνθρώπῳ, τὸ μὴ διαμεῖναι αὐτὸν εἰς τὸν αἰῶνα ἐν ἁμαρτίᾳ ὄντα. ἀλλὰ τρόπῳ τινὶ ἐν ὁμοιώματι ἐξορισμοῦ ἐξέβαλεν αὐτὸν ἐκ τοῦ παραδείσου. ... Read: τὸ μὴ διαμεῖναι αὐτὸν ⟨φθαρτὸν⟩ εἰς τὸν αἰῶνα, ἐν ἁμαρτίᾳ ὄντα and ἐξέβαλεν αὐτόν. ... Compare lines 8 τὴν ἀνάστασιν, 12 ἵνα ἐν τῇ ἀναστάσει ὑγιὴς εὑρεθῇ, λέγω δὲ ἄσπιλος καὶ δίκαιος καὶ ἀθάνατος, and II. 27. 19 καὶ τῆς ἀναστάσεως τυχὼν "κληρονομῆσαι τὴν ἀφθαρσίαν" (1 Cor. 15:50).

(32) II. 28. 8. . . . μήπως οὖν ὑπολημφθῇ ὡς ὅτι ὅδε μὲν ὁ θεὸς ἐποίησεν τὸν ἄνδρα, ἕτερος δὲ τὴν γυναῖκα, διὰ τοῦτο {οὖν} ἐποίησεν τοὺς δύο ἄμφω· οὐ μὴν ἀλλὰ καὶ 〈ἔπλασεν τὸν ἄνδρα μόνον ἐκ γῆς ἵνα〉 διὰ τούτου δειχθῇ τὸ μυστήριον τῆς μοναρχίας τῆς κατὰ τὸν θεόν, ἅμα δ᾽ ἐποίησεν ὁ θεὸς τὴν γυναῖκα αὐτοῦ 〈ἐκ τῆς πλευρᾶς αὐτοῦ〉 ἵνα πλείων ᾖ ἡ εὔνοια εἰς αὐτήν. Grant adopts both supplements suggested by P. Nautin (Vigiliae Christ. 11, 1957, 218–224). But I think the first one is unwarranted. The mystery of the divine unity (μοναρχία) is demonstrated by the fact that God has created both Adam and Eve together (τοὺς δύο ἄμφω) and at the same time (ἅμα). And Adam's love for his wife is being guaranteed by the fact that she was made out of his rib. Thus read: οὐ μὴν ἀλλὰ 〈ὥ s〉 καὶ διὰ τούτου δειχθῇ τὸ μυστήριον τῆς μοναρχίας τῆς κατὰ τὸν θεόν, ἅμα δ ἡ ἐποίησεν ὁ θεὸς τὴν γυναῖκα αὐτοῦ, 〈λαβὼν τὴν πλευρὰν αὐτοῦ, = Gen. 2:21–22〉 ἵνα πλείων ᾖ ἡ εὔνοια εἰς αὐτήν. For such a δὴ see Denniston, Greek Particles,[2] p. 225.

(33) II. 30. 6. Τῷ δὲ Ἐνὼχ ἐγενήθη υἱὸς ὀνόματι Γαϊδάδ· ἐγέννησεν τὸν καλούμενον Μεήλ, καὶ Μεὴλ τὸν Μαθουσάλα, 〈καὶ Μαθουσάλα Gesner〉 τὸν Λάμεχ. Read: Γαιδάδ· 〈καὶ Γαιδὰδ = Gen. 4:18〉 ἐγέννησεν. . . .

(34) II. 30. 20. Τοῖς δὲ βουλομένοις καὶ φιλομαθέσιν καὶ περὶ πασῶν τῶν γενεῶν εὔκολόν ἐστιν ἐπιδεῖξαι διὰ τῶν ἁγίων γραφῶν. καὶ γὰρ ἐκ μέρους ἡμῖν γεγένηται ἤδη λόγος ἐν ἑτέρῳ λόγῳ, ὡς ἐπάνω προειρήκαμεν, τῆς γενεαλογίας ἡ τάξις ἐν τῇ πρώτῃ βίβλῳ τῇ περὶ ἱστοριῶν. Read: Τοῖς δὲ βουλομένοις . . . καὶ περὶ πασῶν τῶν γενεῶν 〈γνῶναι = II. 35. 45〉 εὔκολόν ἐστιν 〈ἡμῖν〉 ἐπιδεῖξαι διὰ τῶν ἁγίων γραφῶν· καὶ γὰρ ἐκ μέρους ἡμῖν γεγένηται ἤδη λόγος ἐν ἑτέρῳ {λόγῳ}, ὡς ἐπάνω προειρήκαμεν, 〈καὶ ἔστι πάσης〉 τῆς γενεαλογίας ἡ τάξις ἐν τῇ πρώτῃ βίβλῳ . . . and compare III. 3. 23 ἀκριβέστερον πεποιηκότων ἡμῶν ἐν ἑτέρῳ τὸν περὶ αὐτῶν λόγον.

(35) II. 30. 25. Ταῦτα δὲ πάντα ἡμᾶς διδάσκει τὸ πνεῦμα τὸ ἅγιον, τὸ διὰ Μωσέως καὶ τῶν λοιπῶν προφητῶν, ὥστε. . . . Read: τὸ πνεῦμα τὸ ἅγιον, τὸ διὰ Μωσέως καὶ τῶν λοιπῶν προφητῶν 〈λαλοῦν,〉 ὥστε . . . and compare II. 33. 13 οἵτινες ὑπὸ πνεύματος ἁγίου διδασκόμεθα, τοῦ λαλήσαντος ἐν τοῖς ἁγίοις προφήταις . . .; II. 10. 12 Οὗτος οὖν (sc. ὁ Λόγος), ὢν πνεῦμα θεοῦ . . ., κατήρχετο εἰς τοὺς προφήτας καὶ δι᾽ αὐτῶν ἐλάλει. . . .

(36) II. 31. 2. Πρώτη πόλις Βαβυλών, καὶ Ὀρὲχ καὶ Ἀρχὰθ καὶ Χαλάνη ἐν τῇ γῇ Σενναάρ. καὶ βασιλεὺς ἐγένετο αὐτῶν ὀνόματι Νεβρώθ. ἐκ τούτων ἐξῆλθεν ὀνόματι Ἀσσούρ· ὅθεν καὶ Ἀσσύριοι προσαγορεύονται. Read: ὀνόματι Νεβρώθ. ἐκ τούτων ἐξῆλθεν {ὀνόματι} Ἀσσούρ = Gen. 10:11.

Line 25: Σίβυλλα μὲν οὕτως σεσήμακεν . . . Oracula Sibyllina, III. 102 f. Geffcken:

> αὐτὰρ ἔπειτ᾽ ἄνεμοι μέγαν ὑψόθι πύργον
> ῥίψαν καὶ θνητοῖσιν ἐπ᾽ ἀλλήλοις ἔριν ὦρσαν.

Miroslav Marcovich 83

Read: Σίβυλλα μὲν ⟨τοῦτο⟩ οὕτως ... and ἐπ' ἀλλήλους (Rzach): cf. Or. Sib.
III. 119 and XI. 13 ἐπ' ἀλλήλους ἔριν ὦρσαν.
Line 67: ἔπειτα ἐβασίλευσεν "Εφρων καὶ ὁ Χετταῖος ἐπικληθείς. Read:
"Εφρων ὁ καὶ Χετταῖος. ...

(37) II. 33. 1. Τίς οὖν πρὸς ταῦτα ἴσχυσεν τῶν καλουμένων σοφῶν καὶ
ποιητῶν ⟨ἢ⟩ ἱστοριογράφων τὸ ἀληθὲς εἰπεῖν, πολὺ μεταγενεστέρων αὐτῶν
γεγενημένων ...; ἐχρῆν γὰρ αὐτοὺς μεμνῆσθαι πάντων καὶ τῶν πρὸ κατακλυσμοῦ
γεγονότων, περί τε κτίσεως κόσμου καὶ ποιήσεως ἀνθρώπου, τά τε ἑξῆς συμβάντα ἀκριβῶς ἐξειπεῖν τοὺς παρ' Αἰγυπτίοις προφήτας ἢ Χαλδαίους τούς τε
ἄλλους συγγραφεῖς. ... Read: Ἐχρῆν γὰρ αὐτοὺς μεμνῆσθαι πάντων (καὶ τῶν
πρὸ κατακλυσμοῦ ... τά τε ἑξῆς συμβάντα), ⟨ἢ αὐτοῖς⟩ ἀκριβῶς ἐξειπεῖν
τοὺς ... προφήτας ... and compare III. 2. 1 Ἐχρῆν γὰρ τοὺς συγγράφοντας
αὐτοὺς αὐτόπτας γεγενῆσθαι περὶ ὧν διαβεβαιοῦνται, ἢ ἀκριβῶς μεμαθηκέναι
ὑπὸ τῶν τεθεαμένων αὐτά. III. 17. 5 Ἔτι μὴν μάντεις καὶ προγνώστας γεγενῆσθαι κατὰ τοὺς συγγραφεῖς, καὶ ⟨τού⟩τους (sc. "the historians" ego: τοὺς
Venetus, "people" Grant) παρ' αὐτῶν μαθόντας ἀκριβῶς συγγεγραφέναι
φασίν.

(38) II. 36. 26 = Oracula Sibyllina, Fr. 1 Geffcken

23   Τύφῳ καὶ μανίῃ δὲ βαδίζετε, καὶ τρίβον ὀρθὴν
      εὐθεῖαν προλιπόντες ἀπήλθετε, καὶ δι' ἀκανθῶν
25   καὶ σκολόπων ἐπλανᾶσθε. βροτοὶ παύσασθε μάταιοι
      ῥεμβόμενοι σκοτίῃ καὶ ἀφεγγέι νυκτὶ μελαίνῃ,
      καὶ λίπετε σκοτίην νυκτός, φωτὸς δὲ λάβεσθε.
      ο ὗ τ ο ς ἰδοὺ πάντεσσι σαφὴς ἀπλάνητος ὑπάρχει.
      ἔλθετε, μὴ σκοτίην δὲ διώκετε καὶ γνόφον αἰεί·
30   ἠελίου γλυκυδερκὲς ἰδοὺ φάος ἔξοχα λάμπει.

What does 28 οὗτος refer to? Clement (Strom. V. 115. 5-6) understood
it as God. But God is not likely to bear the epithet ἀπλάνητος, "unerring,
not going astray." Now, since οὗτος cannot refer to the neuter 27 φῶς,
G. W. H. Lampe (Patristic Lexicon, s.v. ἀπλάνητος) referred it to 23 τρίβος.
This is unlikely, too. For, first, 23 τρίβος is too far from 28 οὗτος. And
second, τρίβος is used by Sibyl as feminine in 23 f. I think 28 οὗτος refers
to 30 ἥλιος, the line being displaced. Thus read:

27   καὶ λίπετε σκοτίην νυκτός, φ ω τ ὸ ς δὲ λάβεσθε.
29   ἔλθετε, μὴ σκοτίην δὲ διώκετε καὶ γνόφον αἰεί·
30   ἢ ε λ ί ο υ γλυκυδερκὲς ἰδοὺ φάος ἔξοχα λάμπει,
28   ο ὗ τ ο ς ἰδοὺ πάντεσσι σαφής, ἀπλάνητος ὑπάρχει.

Helios is known as "unswerving, unerring" par excellence. Sibyl may have
in mind Heraclitus Fr. 52 Marcovich (= B 94 Diels): Ἥλιος οὐχ
ὑπερβήσεται μέτρα, "Helios will never overstep his path;" and in the

Orphic hymn to Helios (8.9 Quandt) we read: κόσμου τὸν ἐναρμόνιον
δρόμον ἕλκων.
(39) II. 36. 39 = *Or. Sib.*, Fr. 3 Geffcken. Καὶ πρὸς τοὺς γενητοὺς
λεγομένους ἔφη (sc. Σίβυλλα)·

7   τῶν τ' ἐνύδρων πάλι γεννᾷ (sc. θεὸς) ἀνήριθμον πολὺ πλῆθος,
8   ἑρπετὰ δ ἐ γαίης κινούμενα ψυχοτροφεῖται . . .
28   καὶ πετεηνὰ σέβεσθε καὶ ἑρπετὰ θηρία γαίης
29   καὶ λίθινα ξόανα κ α ὶ ἀγάλματα χειροποίητα . . .

Read, first: Καὶ πρὸς τοὺς γενητοὺς λεγομένους ⟨θεοὺς⟩ ἔφη. Second:

8   ἑρπετὰ δ' ⟨αὖ⟩ γαίης κινούμενα ψυχοτροφεῖται

and compare line 28 ἑρπετὰ θηρία γαίης. δ' αὖ in the same position is to
be found at *Or. Sib.* I. 17; 173; 197; 211; 231; 297; 308; 388, et passim.
(Auratus, Rzach, Geffcken read instead: δ' [or τ'] ἐν γαίῃ, Turnebus δ' ἐκ
γαίης, Wolf δὴ γαίης). Third, read:

29   καὶ λίθινα ξόαν', εἰκαῖ' ἀγάλματα χειροποίητα

and compare *Or. Sib.* IV. 28–28ᵃ (Clem. *Protrept.* 62. 1):

καὶ βωμούς, εἰκαῖα λίθων ἀφιδρύματα κωφῶν,
{καὶ λίθινα ξόανα καὶ ἀγάλματα χειροποίητα.}

(40) II. 36. 73 = *Or. Sib.*, Fr. 3:

34   ὃς δ' ἔστι ζωή τε καὶ ἄφθιτον ἀέναον φῶς,
καὶ μέλιτος ꝏ — γλυκερώτερον ἀνδράσι χάρμα
ἐκπροχέει ꝏ — τῷ δὴ μόνῳ αὐχένα κάμπτειν,
καὶ τρίβον αἰώνεσσιν ἐν εὐσεβέεσσ' ἀνακλίνοις.

---

34 ὃς δ' Geffcken: οὐδὲ Venetus: οὗ δ' Castalio (1546)   36 δὴ Gesner (1546):
δεῖ Ven.   37 ἀνακλίνοις Rzach: ἀνακλινοῖ Ven.

Read:

34   Οὗ δ' ἐστὶν ζωή τε καὶ ἄφθιτον ἀέναον φῶς,
καὶ μέλιτος ⟨γλυκεροῦ⟩ γλυκερώτερον ἀνδράσι χάρμα
ἐκπροχέει, ⟨τού⟩τῳ ⟨δὴ⟩ δεῖ μόνῳ αὐχένα κάμπτειν
καὶ τρίβον αἰώνεσσιν ἐν εὐσεβέεσσ' ἀνακλίνει⟨ν⟩.

35 γλυκεροῦ Opsopoeus (1599) = *Or. Sib.* III. 746; *Odyssey* 20. 69; 24. 68.

(41) II. 38. 7. Τοίνυν Σίβυλλα καὶ οἱ λοιποὶ προφῆται, ἀλλὰ μὴν καὶ οἱ
ποιηταὶ καὶ φιλόσοφοι καὶ αὐτοὶ δεδηλώκασιν περὶ δικαιοσύνης καὶ κρίσεως καὶ
κολάσεως· ἔτι μὴν καὶ περὶ προνοίας, ⟨ὅτι⟩ φροντίζει ὁ θεὸς οὐ μόνον περὶ τῶν
ζώντων ἡμῶν ἀλλὰ καὶ τῶν τεθνεώτων, καίπερ ἄκοντες (Humphry, 1852:
ἅπαντες Ven.) ἔφασαν· ἠλέγχοντο γὰρ ὑπὸ τῆς ἀληθείας. Read: ἔτι μὴν καὶ περὶ

προνοίας, ⟨ὅτι⟩ φροντίζει ὁ θεὸς οὐ μόνον περὶ τῶν ζώντων {ἡμῶν} ἀλλὰ καὶ τῶν τεθνεώτων, καίπερ ⟨οὐχ⟩ ἅπαντες, ἔφασαν.

II. 38. 34. Πειράθητι οὖν πυκνότερον συμβαλεῖν, ὅπως καὶ ζώσης ἀκούσας φωνῆς ἀκριβῶς μάθης τἀληθές. Read: συμβαλεῖν ⟨ἡμῖν⟩ and compare III. 1. 6 ἡμῖν δὲ συμβαλὼν ἔτι λῆρον ἡγῇ. . . .

(42) III. 7. 5. Πυθαγόρας δέ, τοσαῦτα μοχθήσας περὶ θεῶν καὶ τὴν ἄνω κάτω πορείαν ποιησάμενος, ἔσχατοι ὁρίζει φύσιν καὶ αὐτοματισμὸν εἶναί φησιν τῶν πάντων· θεοὺς ἀνθρώπων μηδὲν φροντίζειν. Read: ἔσχατον ὁρίζει φύσιν ⟨ἀΐδιον⟩ καὶ αὐτοματισμὸν εἶναί φησιν τῶν πάντων, θεούς ⟨τε⟩ ἀνθρώπων μηδὲν φροντίζειν and compare II. 4. 3 Ἕτεροι δέ φασιν αὐτοματισμὸν τῶν πάντων εἶναι, καὶ τὸν κόσμον ἀγένητον καὶ φύσιν ἀΐδιον, καὶ τὸ σύνολον πρόνοιαν μὴ εἶναι θεοῦ ἐτόλμησαν ἐξειπεῖν. II. 8. 9 καὶ οἱ μὲν ἀγένητον αὐτὸν (sc. τὸν κόσμον) καὶ ἀΐδιον φύσιν φάσκοντες . . . III. 26. 20 Οὐδὲ ἀγένητος ὁ κόσμος ἐστὶν καὶ αὐτοματισμὸς τῶν πάντων, καθὼς Πυθαγόρας καὶ οἱ λοιποὶ πεφλυαρήκασιν, ἀλλὰ μὲν οὖν γενητὸς καὶ προνοίᾳ διοικεῖται ὑπὸ τοῦ ποιήσαντος τὰ πάντα θεοῦ. This φύσις ἀΐδιος of "Pythagoras" is his Μονάς. Compare Hippolytus, Elenchos I. 2. 2 μονάδα μὲν εἶναι ἀπεφήνατο τὸν θεόν. Aetius I. 7. 18.

(43) III. 7. 28 = A. Meineke, Fr. com. Gr., I (Berlin, 1839), pp. IX f.:

      — Θάρσει, βοηθεῖν πᾶσι ⟨μὲν⟩ τοῖς ἀξίοις
      εἴωθεν ὁ θεός, τοῖς δὲ τοιούτοις σφόδρα.
      εἰ μὴ πάρεσται προεδρία τις κειμένη
      τοῖς ζῶσιν ὡς δεῖ, τί πλέον ἐστὶν εὐσεβεῖν;
5   — Εἴη γὰρ οὕτως, ἀλλὰ καὶ λίαν ὁρῶ
      τοὺς εὐσεβῶς μὲν ἑλομένους διεξάγειν
      πράττοντας ἀτόπως, τοὺς δὲ μηδὲν ἕτερον ἢ
      τὸ λυσιτελὲς τὸ κατ' αὐτοὺς μόνον,
      ἐντιμοτέραν ἔχοντες ἡμῶν διάθεσιν.
10   — Ἐπὶ τοῦ παρόντος· ἀλλὰ δεῖ πόρρω βλέπειν
      καὶ τὴν ἁπάντων ἀναμένειν καταστροφήν.
      οὐχ ὃν τρόπον γὰρ παρ' ἐνίοις ἴσχυσέ τις
      δόξα κακοήθης τῷ βίῳ τ' ἀνωφελής,
      φορά τις ἔστ' αὐτόματος ἢ βραβεύεται
15   ὡς ἔτυχε· ταῦτα γὰρ πάντα κρίνουσιν ἔχειν
      ἐφόδια πρὸς τὸν ἴδιον οἱ φαῦλοι τρόπον.
      ἔστιν δὲ καὶ τοῖς ζῶσιν ὁσίως προεδρία,
      καὶ τοῖς πονηροῖς ὡς προσῆκ' ἐπιθυμία·
      χωρὶς προνοίας γίνεται γὰρ οὐδὲ ἕν.

Read: (1) Line 3 εἰ μὴ γὰρ ἔσται προεδρία (Meineke) and compare line 17 ἔστιν . . . προεδρία. (2) Line 8 τὸ λυσιτελὲς ⟨ὁρᾶν⟩ τὸ καθ' ⟨ἐ⟩αυτοὺς μόνον (the infinitive ὁρᾶν depends on line 6 ἑλομένους). (3) Line 9 ἔχοντας (Meineke). (4) Lines 14 f.:

      φορά τις ἔστ' αὐτόματος, ἢ βραβεύεται
      ὡς ἔτυχε πάντα· ταῦτα γὰρ κρίνουσ' ἔχειν

(Grotius). Finally (5), ἐπιθυμία, "desire," in line 18, is nonsensical. Evidently, read: ἐπιτιμία, "punishment" (Meineke).

(44) III. 7. 50. *Τὸν οὖν συνετὸν ἀκροατὴν καὶ ἀναγινώσκοντα προσέχειν ἀκριβῶς τοῖς λεγομένοις δεῖ, καθὼς καὶ ὁ Σιμύλος ἔφη·* (Meineke, *Fr. com. Gr.*, I, pp. XIV f.)

> *Κοινῶς ποιητὰς ἔθος ἐστὶν καλεῖν,*
> *καὶ τοὺς περιττοὺς τῇ φύσει καὶ τοὺς κακούς·*
> *ἔδει δὲ κρίνειν.*

καθάπερ ἐν τόπῳ τινὶ (Grant: *ἐξ οὗ τινι* Venetus) *καὶ ὁ Φιλήμων·* (Fr. 143 Kock)

> *Χαλεπὸν ἀκροατὴς ἀσύνετος καθήμενος·*
> *ὑπὸ γὰρ ἀνοίας οὐχ ἑαυτὸν μέμφεται.*

χρὴ οὖν προσέχειν καὶ νοεῖν τὰ λεγόμενα κριτικῶς ἐξετάζοντα τὰ ὑπὸ τῶν φιλοσόφων καὶ τῶν λοιπῶν ποιητῶν εἰρημένα.

First, read: *κοινῶς ποιητὰς ⟨πάντας⟩ ἔθος ἐστὶν καλεῖν* (Meineke). Second, the transmitted *ἐξ οὗ τινι* cannot yield, palaeographically, *ἐν τόπῳ τινὶ*, as Grant prints. Read instead: *καθάπερ ἐξουθενεῖ καὶ ὁ Φιλήμων ⟨λέγων·⟩*, "as Philemon too rejects it with contempt while saying." As for the confusion θ: τ (*ἐξουθενεῖ* for the transmitted *ἐξ οὗ τινι*), compare No. 43: *ἐπιτιμία* for the transmitted *ἐπιθυμία*. Finally, read the last sentence as follows: *Χρὴ οὖν ⟨τὸν συνετὸν⟩ προσέχειν καὶ νοεῖν τὰ λεγόμενα, κριτικῶς ἐξετάζοντα τὰ ὑπὸ τῶν φιλοσόφων ⟨καὶ⟩ ποιητῶν καὶ τῶν λοιπῶν εἰρημένα.* The words *συνετός* and *ἀσύνετος* appear in the context. In addition, compare III. 8. 10 *καὶ γὰρ ἱστορούμενα τοῖς συνετοῖς καταγέλωτα φέρει.* As for the transposition, compare II. 8. 2 *Ὥστε κατὰ πάντα τρόπον ἐμπαίζονται οἱ συγγραφεῖς πάντες καὶ ποιηταὶ καὶ φιλόσοφοι λεγόμενοι, ἔτι μὴν καὶ οἱ προσέχοντες αὐτοῖς.* II. 3. 36 *Ἔλθωμεν τοίνυν ἐπὶ τὰ συγγράμματα τῶν φιλοσόφων καὶ ποιητῶν.* In our passage οἱ λοιποί are the historians, οἱ συγγραφεῖς.

(45) III. 14. 1. *Καὶ τοῦ μὴ μόνον ἡμᾶς εὐνοεῖν τοῖς ὁμοφύλοις* (Clauser, 1546: *ἀλοφύλοις* Venetus), *ὡς οἴονταί τινες, Ἡσαΐας ὁ προφήτης ἔφη·* (follows *Isaiah* 66:5). Grant translates: "And concerning the good will which we exercise not only toward our own people, as some suppose, Isaiah the prophet said." But the word order of Greek is strange. Read instead: *Καὶ ⟨περὶ⟩ τοῦ μὴ μόνον ⟨ἡμῖν⟩ ἡμᾶς εὐνοεῖν, ὡς οἴονταί τινες, ⟨ἀλλὰ καὶ⟩ τοῖς ἀλ⟨λ⟩οφύλοις....* Compare line 10 *Ἔτι μὴν καὶ π ε ρ ὶ τοῦ ὑποτάσσεσθαι....*

(46) III. 15. 10. *Μακρὰν δὲ ἀπείη χριστιανοῖς ἐνθυμηθῆναί τι τοιοῦτο πρᾶξαι, παρ᾽ οἷς σωφροσύνη πάρεστιν, ἐγκράτεια ἀσκεῖται, μονογαμία τηρεῖται, ἁγνεία φυλάσσεται, ἀδικία ἐκπορθεῖται, ἁμαρτία ἐκριζοῦται, δικαιοσύνη μελετᾶται,*

Miroslav Marcovich 87

νόμος πολιτεύεται, θεοσέβεια πράσσεται, θεὸς ὁμολογεῖται, ἀλήθεια βραβεύει, χάρις συντηρεῖ, εἰρήνη περισκέπει, λόγος ἅγιος ὁδηγεῖ, σοφία διδάσκει, ζωὴ β ρ α β ε ύ ε ι, θεὸς βασιλεύει. In this elaborate rhetorical enumeration no verb is being repeated except βραβεύει ("truth controls, . . . life controls"), which is unlikely. The second βραβεύει is a dittography which had ousted the true reading: ζωὴ θρ⟨ι⟩α⟨μ⟩βεύει, "life triumphs." Life triumphs through Christ: compare Col. 2:15 θριαμβεύσας (and, of course, John 14:6).

III. 15. 18 . . . τὰ νῦν αὐτάρκως ἡγούμεθα ἐπιμεμνῆσθαι, εἰς τὸ καί σε ἐπιστῆσαι μάλιστα ἐξ ὧν ἀναγινώσκεις ἕως τοῦ δεῦρο, ἵνα ὡς φιλομαθὴς ἐγενήθης ἕως τοῦ δεῦρο οὕτως καὶ φιλομαθὴς ἔσῃ. Read: εἰς τὸ καί σε ἐπιστῆσαι μάλιστα ἐξ ὧν ἀναγινώσκειν {ἕως τοῦ δεῦρο, a dittography}, ἵνα, ὡς φιλομαθὴς ἐγενήθης ἕως τοῦ δεῦρο, οὕτως καὶ φιλομαθὴς ἔσῃ.

(47) III. 16. 10. Ἐν γὰρ ταῖς Πολιτείαις αὐτοῦ (sc. Πλάτωνος) ἐπιγραφομέναις ῥητῶς κεῖται· "Πῶς γὰρ ἄν (Otto: λέγοντος Venetus), εἴ γε ἔμενε τάδε οὕτως πάντα χρόνον . . ." Read: ῥητῶς κεῖται λέγοντος· "⟨Πῶς⟩, εἴ γε ἔμενε . . ." Compare Plato, Leg. III, 677 c 7 πῶς γὰρ ἄν, ὦ ἄριστε, εἴ γε ἔμενεν. . . .

III. 16. 16. Καὶ πολλὰ φήσας (sc. Πλάτων) περὶ πόλεων καὶ κατοικισμῶν (B. Einarson: κατακοσμῶν καὶ οἰκήσεων Venetus) καὶ ἐθνῶν, ὁμολογεῖ εἰκασμῷ ταῦτα εἰρηκέναι. Read: περὶ πόλεων ⟨καὶ⟩ κατοικισμῶν καὶ οἰκήσεων καὶ ἐθνῶν. . . . As for κατοικισμῶν, compare Plato, Leg. III, 683 a 4; as for οἰκήσεων, 681 a 7.

(48) III. 18. 12. Ὁ δὲ ἡμέτερος προφήτης καὶ θεράπων τοῦ θεοῦ Μωσῆς περὶ τῆς γενέσεως τοῦ κόσμου ἐξιστορῶν διηγήσατο τίνι τρόπῳ γεγένηται ὁ κατακλυσμὸς ἐπὶ τῆς γῆς, οὐ μὴν ἀλλὰ καὶ τὰ τοῦ κατακλυσμοῦ ᾧ τρόπῳ γέγονεν. . . . Read: τίνι τρόπῳ γεγένηται ὁ κατακλυσμὸς ἐπὶ τῆς γῆς, οὐ μὴν ἀλλὰ καὶ τὰ ⟨μ ε τ ὰ⟩ τὸν κατακλυσμὸν ᾧ τρόπῳ γέγονεν and compare II. 31. 1 Μετὰ τὸν κατακλυσμὸν ἀρχὴ πάλιν ἐγένετο πόλεων καὶ βασιλέων τὸν τρόπον τοῦτον. III. 23. 20 οὐ μόνον τὰ μετὰ κατακλυσμὸν ἱστοροῦντες, ἀλλὰ καὶ τὰ πρὸ κατακλυσμοῦ. 24. 9 Μετὰ δὲ τὸν κατακλυσμὸν. . . .

(49) III. 21. 7. Παραγενόμενοι γὰρ (sc. οἱ Ἰουδαῖοι) εἰς τὴν γῆν τὴν καλουμένην Ἰουδαίαν (Grant: Ἱεροσόλυμα Venetus), ἔνθα καὶ μεταξὺ κατῴκησαν. Read: τὴν γῆν τὴν καλουμένην Ἰσραήλ . . . ĪHΛ = Ἰσραήλ was misread by the scribe of the Venetus as ĪΛΗΜ = Ἱεροσόλυμα.

(50) III. 22. 10. Ἐν γὰρ προβλήμασιν ἀλλήλους συνεχῶς ἐγύμναζον (sc. Hieromos, king of Tyre, and Solomon)· τεκμήριον δὲ τούτου, καὶ ἀντίγραφα ἐπιστολῶν αὐτῶν φασιν μέχρι τοῦ δεῦρο παρὰ τοῖς Τυρίοις πεφυλαγμένα· γράμματά τε ἀλλήλοις διέπεμπον. Read: Ἐν γὰρ προβλήμασιν ἀλλήλους συνεχῶς ἐγύμναζον γράμματά τε ἀλλήλοις διέπεμπον· τεκμήριον δὲ τούτου καὶ ἀντίγραφα ἐπιστολῶν αὐτῶν, ⟨ὥς⟩ φασιν, μέχρι τοῦ δεῦρο παρὰ τοῖς Τυρίοις πεφυλαγμένων.

Compare Josephus, *c. Apionem* I. 111 προβλήματα γὰρ ἀλλήλοις ἀνταπέστελλον λύειν κελεύοντες . . . σώζονται δὲ μέχρι νῦν παρὰ τοῖς Τυρίοις πολλαὶ τῶν ἐπιστολῶν, ἃς ἐκεῖνοι πρὸς ἀλλήλους ἔγραψαν.

(51) III. 23. 10. Ἀλλὰ καὶ οἱ νομοθέται πάντες μεταξὺ εὑρίσκονται νομοθετοῦντες. εἰ γάρ τις εἴποι Σόλωνα τὸν Ἀθηναῖον, οὗτος γέγονεν . . . κατὰ τὸν χρόνον Ζαχαρίου τοῦ προειρημένου προφήτου, μεταξὺ γεγενημένου (sc. τοῦ Μωσέως) πάνυ πολλοῖς ἔτεσιν· ἤτοι καὶ περὶ Λυκούργου ἢ Δράκοντος ἢ Μίνω τῶν νομοθετῶν, τούτων ἀρχαιότητι (Otto: γράφων λέγει τοῖς Venetus, Bodleianus) προάγουσιν αἱ ἱεραὶ βίβλοι. . . . Read: ἤτοι καὶ περὶ Λυκούργου ἢ Δράκοντος ἢ Μίνω τῶν νομοθετῶν ⟨τῶν συγ⟩γραφέων λέγοι τις, ⟨πάλιν⟩ προάγουσιν αἱ ἱεραὶ βίβλοι. . . .

(52) III. 23. 19. Ἵνα δὲ ἀκριβεστέραν ποιήσωμεν τὴν ἀπόδειξιν τῶν καιρῶν καὶ χρόνων, θεοῦ ἡμῖν παρέχοντος οὐ μόνον τὰ μετὰ κατακλυσμὸν ἱστοροῦντες ἀλλὰ καὶ τὰ πρὸ κατακλυσμοῦ εἰς τὸ καὶ τῶν ἁπάντων κατὰ τὸ δυνατὸν εἰπεῖν ἡμῖν τὸν ἀριθμόν, νυνὶ ποιησόμεθα, ἀναδραμόντες ἐπὶ τὴν ἀνέκαθεν ἀρχὴν τῆς τοῦ κόσμου κτίσεως, ἣν ἀνέγραψεν Μωσῆς ὁ θεράπων τοῦ θεοῦ διὰ πνεύματος ἁγίου. Read: εἰς τὸ καὶ τῶν ἁπάντων ⟨ἐτῶν⟩ κατὰ τὸ δυνατὸν εἰπεῖν ἡμᾶς τὸν ἀριθμόν, ⟨τὴν ἀρχὴν⟩ νυνὶ ποιησόμεθα ἀναδραμόντες ἐπὶ τὴν ἀνέκαθεν ἀρχὴν τῆς τοῦ κόσμου κτίσεως . . . and compare line 26 ἐσήμανεν (sc. Μωσῆς) καὶ τὰ πρὸ κατακλυσμοῦ ἔ τ η γενόμενα, line 30 ἄρξομαι δὴ πρῶτον ἀπὸ τῶν ἀναγεγραμμένων γενεαλογιῶν, λέγω δὲ ἀπὸ τοῦ πρωτοπλάστου ἀνθρώπου τ ὴ ν ἀ ρ χ ὴ ν ποιησάμενος.

(53) III. 25. 1. Μετὰ δὲ τοὺς κριτὰς ἐγένοντο βασιλεῖς ἐν αὐτοῖς, πρῶτος ὀνόματι Σαούλ, ὃς ἐβασίλευσεν ἔτη κ', ἔπειτα Δαυὶδ ὁ πρόγονος ἡμῶν ἔτη μ'. γίνεται οὖν μέχρι τῆς τοῦ Δαυὶδ βασιλείας τὰ πάντα ἔτη υϟη'. Read: γίνεται οὖν ⟨ἀπὸ τῆς Μωσέως τελευτῆς⟩ μέχρι τῆς τοῦ Δαυὶδ βασιλείας . . ., "The total *from the death of Moses* to the reign of David, then, is 498 years." Compare Theophilus' *Summary*, III. 28. 5 Ἀπὸ δὲ τῆς Μωσέως τελευτῆς, ἀρχῆς Ἰησοῦ υἱοῦ Ναυῆ, μέχρι τελευτῆς Δαυὶδ τοῦ πατριάρχου ἔτη υϟη' and III. 24. 23 ᾧ καιρῷ τοῦ Μωσέως τελευτήσαντος διεδέξατο ἄρχειν Ἰησοῦς υἱὸς Ναυῆ, ὃς προέστη αὐτῶν ἔτεσιν κζ'.

(54) III. 26. 1. Ἐντεῦθεν ὁρᾶν ἔστιν πῶς ἀρχαιότερα καὶ ἀληθέστερα δείκνυται τὰ ἱερὰ γράμματα τὰ καθ' ἡμᾶς εἶναι τῶν καθ' Ἕλληνας καὶ Αἰγυπτίους, ἢ εἰ καί τινας ἑτέρους ἱστοριογράφους. ἤτοι γὰρ Ἡρόδοτος καὶ Θουκυδίδης ἢ καὶ Ξενοφῶν ἢ ὅπως οἱ ἄλλοι ἱστοριογράφοι, οἱ πλείους ἤρξαντο σχεδὸν ἀπὸ τῆς Κύρου καὶ Δαρείου βασιλείας ἀναγράφειν. . . . Read: Ξενοφῶν ἢ ε⟨ἴ⟩ πως οἱ ἄλλοι ἱστοριογράφοι and compare ἢ εἰ καί τινας ἑτέρους ἱστοριογράφους in the context.

(55) III. 27. 36. Ἀπὸ οὖν τῆς Κύρου ἀρχῆς μέχρι τελευτῆς αὐτοκράτορος Οὐήρου, οὗ προειρήκαμεν, ὁ πᾶς χρόνος συνάγεται ἔτη ψμα'. The words ἀρχῆς μέχρι τελευτῆς are Grant's emendation: the Venetus has instead: τελευτῆς

ʽΡωμαίων δὲ ἀρχῆς Ταρκυνίου Σουπέρβου μέχρι τελευτῆς. Thus read: Ἀπὸ οὖν τῆς Κύρου ⟨ἀρχῆς⟩ {τελευτῆς} ʽΡωμαίων τε ἀρχῆς Ταρκυνίου Σουπέρβου μέχρι τελευτῆς αὐτοκράτορος Οὐήρου . . ., "From the reign of Cyrus [i.e., 28 years] and the reign of Tarquin the Superbus over the Romans [i.e., 25 years] to the death of the already mentioned emperor Verus, the total is 741 years." Compare III. 27. 1–15 and 28. 9 f.

APPENDIX: *ΑΘΗΝΑ ΦΙΛΟΚΟΛΠΟΣ* (III. 3. 22)

(1) After condemning Greek gods (Cronos for devouring his own children, his son Zeus for swallowing his wife Metis, Hera for marrying her own brother, etc.), Theophilus concludes (III. 3. 21): "But why should I go on listing the stories about Poseidon and Apollo, or about Dionysus and Heracles, or about the φιλόκολπος Athena and the shameless Aphrodite, when we have already given a more precise account of them in another place?" Τί μοι λοιπὸν καταλέγειν τὰ περὶ Ποσειδῶνος καὶ Ἀπόλλωνος, ἢ Διονύσου καὶ ʽΗρακλέους, ⟨ἢ addidi⟩ Ἀθηνᾶς τῆς φιλοκόλπου καὶ Ἀφροδίτης τῆς ἀναισχύντου, ἀκριβέστερον πεποιηκότων ἡμῶν ἐν ἑτέρῳ τὸν περὶ αὐτῶν λόγον;

The other place is I. 9. There the mention is made of Cronos the consumer of his own children, and of Zeus who slew the very goat which nourished him, only to make himself a garment; who engaged in incest, adultery, and pederasty. Then Theophilus uses the same rhetorical device while asking: "But why should I go on listing the stories about his (Zeus') children: Heracles who burned himself up; Dionysus the drunkard and madman; Apollo who feared Achilles and took flight; who fell in love with Daphne, and was ignorant of the fate of Hyacinthus; or Aphrodite who was wounded, and Ares, 'the plague of men'?" (I. 9. 9). In addition, Poseidon is rebuked at II. 7. 1: "Why should I mention the Greek myths . . . Poseidon submerging under the sea, and embracing Melanippe, and begetting a cannibal son . . . ?"

Consequently, Athena ἡ φιλόκολπος and Aphrodite ἡ ἀναίσχυντος (from III. 3. 22) are mentioned nowhere else. Now, it is not difficult to see why Aphrodite could be called "shameless, impudent:" she, a married woman, was caught with Ares *in flagranti delicto* (*Odyssey* 8. 266–366; compare especially 269 f. λέχος δ᾽ ᾔσχυνε καὶ εὐνὴν | ʽΗφαίστοιο ἄνακτος). But what is the meaning of Athena's derogatory epithet—and *hapax legomenon*—φιλόκολπος?

(2) *ΦΙΛΟΚΟΛΠΟΣ.* (a) The translation *Minerva sinus amans* persists since the *editio princeps* of Theophilus (by Joannes Frisius, Zurich, 1546; Latin version by Conrad Clauser). It stands in the important edition of

J. C. Wolf (Hamburg, 1724), and J. C. T. Otto, in his critical edition (Jena, 1861) comments: "*nimirum epitheton φιλοκόλπου (sinum amantis) egregie quadrat ad impudicitiam (paullo supra:* πορνείας καὶ μοιχείας), *de qua sermo est.*" This interpretation, however, must be discarded. First, why the epithet "bosom-loving" should imply impudence or be derogatory? Second, what has "fornification and adultery" to do with the image of Athena, the παρθένος αἰδοίη (*Hymn. Hom.* 28.3), *par excellence?*

(*b*) A. Ardizzoni[1] was right when rejecting the sense "bosom" of κόλπος (LSJ, I. 1) in φιλόκολπος. But his own interpretation, built upon LSJ, s.v., II, "fold of garment," is no better. According to Ardizzoni, Theophilus has in mind the standard statue of Athena Promachos (at I. 10. 6 Phidias' Athena on the Acropolis is mentioned), with her typical dress falling in many and deep folds (cf. βαθύκολπος). Athena is then being criticized for her fashionable and elegant garment. And Ardizzoni concludes: "In fondo, per un intransigente cristiano dei primi secoli, anche la tendenza a vestire con raffinata eleganza poteva costituire una macchia" (p. 104). But, again, to be an "amante delle vesti dalle ampie pieghe" (φιλόκολπος) need not imply "moral fault," nor is it characteristic for Athena's way of dressing only.

(*c*) In his turn, A. Barigazzi[2] keeps the sense suggested by Ardizzoni but gives it a strange twist: Theophilus uses here an ironical sneer while hinting at Athena's *loss of virginity,* according to the myth of Athena as mother of Apollo by Hephaestus (Cicero *De natura deor.* 3. 55 and 59; Arnobius 4. 14; Clement *Protrept.* II. 28. 2). Barigazzi then concludes: " . . . anche Atena, che è sempre ben coperta perché gelosa del suo pudore, è vituperabile come la svergognata Afrodite; non è vero che sia rimasta vergine" (p. 381). This interpretation, too, must be dismissed, for the simple reason that φιλόκολπος, in the sense of "loving her garment's folds," cannot imply that much as ἐνταῦθα δὴ οὐκέτι παρθένος ἡ Ἀθηνᾶ (as Clement has it).

(*d*) In a more recent article, M. B. Keary[3] chooses the sense of LSJ, I. 2: *membrum muliebre,* esp. *vagina; sinus genitalis, womb* (which was mentioned but discarded by Ardizzoni, p. 100), reinterpreting Barigazzi's hint at Athena's loss of virginity. According to the myth of the birth of Erich-

---

[1] A. Ardizzoni, "Atena φιλόκολπος; un incompreso ἅπαξ λεγόμενον in Teofilo di Antiochia," *Rivista di cultura classica e medioevale* 3 (1961), 99–104.

[2] A. Barigazzi, "Atena φιλόκολπος in Teofilo di Antiochia," *La parola del passato* 16 (1961), 379–381.

[3] M. B. Keary, "Note on Ἀθηνᾶ φιλόκολπος in Theophilus of Antioch," *Revue des études grecques* 84 (1971), 94–100.

Miroslav Marcovich

91

thonius (Apollodorus *Bibl.* III. 14. 6), Athena succeeds in defending her virginity against Hephaestus' advances, and Erichthonius is born from Hephaestus' seed fallen to the ground. Hence, believes Keary, φιλόκολπος "means something like 'caring for (cherishing, holding dear, protecting) her κόλπος (sense I. 2)' and that it refers to the Athena-Hephaestus-Erichthonius myth" (p. 100).

Keary does not seem to be aware of the fact that already Tatian (*Oratio ad Graecos* 8) had used the Hephaestus myth against Athena. However, his interpretation must be rejected on the ground that φιλο- cannot yield the sense "caring for," "protecting," but only "loving, be fond of." Out of over 800 compounds with the first member φιλο-, there is no one single example of such a meaning, the basic sense being always: "*qui aliquem* (or *aliquid*) *amat*," "-süchtig, -gierig, -lustig, -freundlich, liebend, gern, geneigt, begehrend," as M. Landfester[4] has well pointed out.

(3) *ΦΙΛΟΠΟΛΕΜΟΣ*. Consequently, as φιλόκολπος cannot give a satisfactory sense it seems preferable to consider it a textual corruption. Apparently, the first to do so was J. H. Nolte,[5] who in 1856 conjectured φιλοπολέμου instead. His conjecture, however, cannot be palaeographically explained and must be dismissed. Unfortunately, it still lives in Jean Sender's *en face* translation ("Athéna la belliqueuse") to Gustave Bardy's Greek text (where, however, φιλοκόλπου is kept).[6]

(4) *ΦΙΛΟΜΟΛΠΟΣ*. M for K has been suggested first by Gb. Galliccioli, in 1804,[7] then (independently) by W. H. Roscher,[8] with reference to Nonnus *Dionys.* 24. 36 φιλόμολπος Ἀθήνην.[9] Unaware of Roscher's reference, E. Degani[10] repeated it in 1964, while supporting Galliccioli's φιλομόλπου by other references to Athena as patroness of singing, dancing and music (compare Παλλάδα τὴν φιλόχορον at Aristophanes *Thesm.* 1136).

---

[4] M. Landfester, *Das griechische Nomen 'philos' und seine Ableitungen* (Spudasmata, 11, Hildesheim, 1966), 109 ff.

[5] J. H. Nolte, "Coniecturae et emendationes ad Theophili Libros ad Autolycum," in Migne, *Patrologia Graeca* 6 (1856), col. 1168.

[6] *Théophile d' Antioche, Trois livres à Autolycus.* Texte grec et introduction de Gustave Bardy, traduction de Jean Sender (Sources Chrétiennes, 20, Paris, 1948).

[7] *Teofilo, Libri tre ad Autolico.* Trad. di Gb. Galliccioli (Venice, 1804), 183. Quoted by Enzo Degani (*infra*, note 10), 93.

[8] In O. Gross, *Die Gotteslehre des Theophilus von Antiocheia* (Chemnitz, 1896), 8. Quoted by R. M. Grant (*infra*, note 11), 158.

[9] Earlier instances of φιλόμολπος are: Stesichor. 16.10 Page; Pindar *Nem.* 7.9; Callimachus *In Delum* 197. Cf. φιλησίμολπος at Pindar *Ol.* 14.14 and Landfester (*supra*, note 4), 123 and 129–131.

[10] E. Degani, "Atena Philokolpos?," *Rheinisches Museum* 107 (1964), 92–94.

Finally, Robert M. Grant, who earlier retained φιλοκόλπου,[11] prints φιλομόλπου in his Oxford edition of Theophilus (1970), with reference to Roscher (in lieu of Galliccioli), while translating "the dance-loving Athena." Here, again, I am at a loss to see how Athena's epithet φιλόμολπος, "dance-loving," could yield a derogatory sense required by the entire context.[12]

(5) ΦΙΛΟΚΟΜΠΟΣ. That is why I would like to suggest the reading φιλοκόμπου, "boastful, vaunting, ostentatious, arrogant." The confusion of the uncial Λ and M (after some fading of the ink) seems to be likely enough (cf., e.g., Aeschylus *Eum.* 881 καμοῦμαι M: καλοῦμαι F Tri). The word φιλόκομπος is not listed in LSJ (it is missing in E. A. Barber's *Supplement* of 1968, too), but it does exist in G. W. H. Lampe's *Patristic Greek Lexicon*. It is used by Justin the Martyr (*ob. ca.* A.D. 165; Theophilus writes *post* A.D. 180) at 2 *Apol.* 3.1, then by Cyril of Alexandria (*Habacuc* 8:3, p. 523 E ed. J. Aubert). In addition, ὑπέρκομπος occurs in Aeschylus *Persae* 827 and 831; *Septem* 391 and 404; ὑψικόμπως in Sophocles *Ajax* 766; κομπός in Euripides *Phoenissae* 600, etc.

Now, why Theophilus should have censured Athena as "vaunting, arrogant"? Because the Apologists were fond of dismissing Athena on the ground of her role as *warrior*: the place of a woman is in house, not on battlefield. So Tatian (*ob. post* A.D. 172) rejects Athena as ἀνθρωποκτόνος καὶ πολεμοποιός, along with Aphrodite as γάμου πλοκαῖς ἥδεται (*Oratio ad Graecos* 8. 3). In his turn, Ps.-Justin writes (*Oratio ad Graecos* 2):[13] Ἀθηνᾶς γὰρ τὸ ἀνδρικὸν σιγῶ, καὶ Διονύσου τὸ θηλυκόν, καὶ Ἀφροδίτης τὸ πορνικόν. Ἀνάγνωτε τῷ Διί, ἄνδρες Ἕλληνες, τὸν κατὰ πατραλῳῶν νόμον, καὶ τὸ μοιχείας πρόστιμον, καὶ τὴν παιδεραστίας αἰσχρότητα. Διδάξατε Ἀθηνᾶν καὶ Ἄρτεμιν τὰ τῶν γυναικῶν ἔργα, καὶ Διόνυσον τὰ ἀνδρῶν. Τί σεμνὸν ἐπιδείκνυται γυνὴ ὅπλοις κεκοσμημένη, ἀνὴρ δὲ κυμβάλοις καὶ στέμμασι καὶ ἐσθῆτι γυναικείᾳ καλλωπιζόμενος, καὶ ὀργιῶν σὺν ἀγέλῃ γυναικῶν;

In conclusion, in calling Athena φιλόκομπος Theophilus only follows the established apologetic practice. Probably, he was inspired by such Homeric passages about the mannish "vaunting" Athena as this one (*Iliad* 21. 408–411). After smiting and felling Ares, Athena breaks into a

---

[11] R. M. Grant, "The Textual Tradition of Theophilus of Antioch," *Vigiliae Christianae* 6 (1952), 146–159, p. 158.

[12] *Contra*, e.g., Degani's reference to Tertullian *De spect.* 10.8 f.: *Quae vero voce et modis et organis et litteris transiguntur, Apollines et Musas et M i n e r v a s et Mercurios mancipes habent. Oderis, christiane, quorum auctores non potes non odisse.*

[13] P. 635.18–24 ed. A. von Harnack (*SB Berlin*, 1896). Ps.-Justin writes between A.D. 180 and 240 (Harnack, p. 646).

laugh, and vaunting and exulting over him (καί οἱ ἐπευχομένη) she says: "You fool, not even yet have you learnt how much superior to you I avow me to be, that you dare match your strength with mine!" No wonder then that Ares should complain to Zeus about Athena as "that mad and baneful maid" (ἄφρονα κούρην | οὐλομένην, *Iliad* 5. 875 f.).

University of Illinois at Urbana

7

The **v**-Recension of St. Cyril's Lexicon

† MARK NAOUMIDES

It has become an axiom of modern scholarship that a thorough investigation into the history of the transmission is a necessary prerequisite for a truly critical edition of a text. The present study will, it is hoped, illustrate this point adequately. For although A. B. Drachmann's *Überlieferung des Cyrillglossars*[1] was a pioneer work for the manuscript tradition of St. Cyril's Lexicon, it fell short of the basic goal of any such study: that of determining as closely as possible the history of the transmission and of setting forth, as clearly and indisputably as possible, the method of a future edition. Drachmann's work suffers primarily from his predilection for old manuscripts[2] and arbitrary elimination of many good witnesses of the tradition; from lack of clear and rigorous criteria in determining relationship of mss., families, and recensions; and to a lesser degree from an apparent hopelessness, shared by many others before and after him, when confronted with the almost infinite variations which the mss. present. It is hoped that the present study, a part of a general investigation into all known mss. of the Lexicon, will afford a better and more secure basis for the solution of the problem of relationship of the mss., and eventually of the extant recensions. The conclusions arrived at are based on (*a*) an exhaustive codicological study of all the witnesses of our tradition, however late; and (*b*) a minute analysis of *Stichproben* taken from three different parts of the Lexicon (θ, ξ, χ). Because of space limitations, some details have been deliberately omitted. I reserve them for my forthcoming study of the entire tradition.

[1] Det Kgl. Danske Videnskabernes Selskab. Historisk-filologiske Meddelelser. XXI.5 (Copenhagen, 1936), henceforth referred to simply as Drachmann.

[2] Drachmann also had the tendency to misdate some of his mss. Thus he assigned F to the X s. and J (dated in the year 1317) to the XI–XII s. Conversely he dated S (a ms. written ca. 1000) in the XIII s.

LIST OF THE MANUSCRIPTS OF THE RECENSION[3]

B = Vatican, Bibl. Apost. Vaticana, gr. 2130. Vellum, 276 (–280) × 216 mm., vii + 285 fols.[4] Early XII s. Contents a^r–d^v, description of contents by Jo. Pastritius[5] in 1694; f–g, two letters (dated 6 and 27 April 1688) on the sale of the ms. by a certain Antonio Bulifone to Mons. Giovanni Ciampini;[6] 1^r–154^r, St. Cyril's lexicon; 154^r–, 218^v, 236^v–256^r, minor lexica;[7] 219^r–236^v, metrologica; 256–278^v, 282^v–285^v, Theodosius Grammaticus, Commentary on canons (hymns);[8] 279^r–282^v, treatise on breathing marks. The codex

---

[3] Besides abbreviated reference to Drachmann's *Überlieferung*, the following abbreviations have been adopted: Benediktsson = J. Benediktsson, "Ein frühbyzantinisches Bibellexikon Λέξεις τῆς 'Οκτατεύχου," *Classica et Mediaevalia* 1, 1938, 243–280. Canart–Peri = P. Canart–V. Peri, *Sussidi bibliografici per i manoscritti greci della Biblioteca Vaticana*, Studi e Testi, 261, Vatican City, 1970. Latte = *Hesychii Alexandrini Lexicon* recensuit K. Latte, vol. I (Copenhagen, 1953). Naoumides, "Symmeikta" = M. Naoumides, "Σύμμεικτα Παλαιογραφικά," *EHBS* 39–40 (1972–1973), 380–383. Naoumides, *Rhet. Lex.* = M. Naoumides, 'Ρητορικαὶ Λέξεις ("Ἀθηνᾶ," Σειρὰ Διατριβῶν καὶ Μελετημάτων, 20) Athens, 1975. Pertusi, *Leonzio Pilato* = A. Pertusi, *Leonzio Pilato fra Petrarca e Boccaccio* ("Civiltà Veneziana," Studi, 16), Venice-Rome, 1964. Pertusi, "Aspetti organizzativi" = A. Pertusi, "Aspetti organizzativi e culturali dell'ambiente monacale greco dell' Italia meridionale," *L'eremitismo in Occidente nei secoli XI e XII*, Problemi e ricerche ("Atti della seconda settimana internazionale di studio: Mendola, 30 agosto–6 settembre 1962" = "Miscellanea del Centro di Studi Medioevali," IV), Milan, 1965, 382–426. Vogel–Gardthausen = M. Vogel–V. Gardthausen, *Die griechischen Schreiber des Mittelarters und der Rennaissance* ("Beiheft zum Zentralblatt für Bibliothekswesen," XXXIII), Leipzig, 1909. The authors of manuscript catalogues have been referred to by name only (in parentheses after the call-number of each ms.). For full references the reader should consult M. Richard, *Répertoire des bibliothèques et des catalogues de manuscrits grecs* ("Publications de l'Institut de Recherche et d'Histoire des Textes," I), Paris, 1958², and *Supplément I (1958–1963)*, Paris, 1964.

[4] The last seven folios (paper, XV s.) were added to replace the missing end of the volume. Two folios are missing from the main body of the ms., one after fol. 7 (the last of quire α, replaced with a seemingly blank vellum leaf), and one between 199–200 (the last of quire κέ). The last two quires have been bound in reverse order and some of their leaves are misplaced, the proper order being 261–263, 272–276, 264, 277, 278, 265–271.

[5] Giov. Pastrizio († 1708), Theology Lecturer in the Collegio Urbano de Propaganda Fide. Autobiographical notes and lists of his books have been preserved in the following mss. of the Vatican Library: Borg. lat. 62, 475, 480, 746.

[6] On G. Ciampini, cf. I. Dujčev, "Uno studio inedito di Mons. G. G. Ciampini sul Papa Formoso," *Archivio della reale deputatione romana di storia patria* 59, 1936, 137 ff., and the bibliography cited there.

[7] On these minor lexica which in our mss. commonly follow St. Cyril's Lexicon cf. Drachmann, 53–58. See also my edition of the 'Ρητορικαὶ Λέξεις (above, note 3), 26 f.

[8] On Theodosius Grammaticus and his Commentary cf. A. Kominis, *Gregorio Pardos, Metropolita di Corinto e la sua opera* ("Testi e Studi Bizantino-Neoellenici," II) Rome-Athens, 1960, 100–103.

bears numerous marginal notes in the Sicilian dialect,[9] but written in Greek characters, which together with the inclusion among the lexica minora of a lexicon to the life of St. Elias the Younger, testify to the S. Italian—Sicilian origin of this ms. Fols. 1ʳ and 285ᵛ bear the *ex-libris* of Jerónimo Zurita.[10] Schow and Schmidt refer to it as "codex Caitani Marini".[11] For pertinent bibliography cf. Canart-Peri, 687; Naoumides, "Symmeikta," 374; *Rhet. Lex.*, 9–11.

Ba = Eton College, cod. 86 (formerly Bk. 6.13; cf. James, p. 29). Paper, 270 × 197 mm., ii + 97 fols. (unnumbered). Contents: St. Cyril's lexicon. According to a note on one of the fly leaves this codex was copied in 1689 (not in 1679, as James has it), "ex codice ms.ᵗᵒ in Bibliotheca I llᵐⁱ et Revᵐⁱ D(omi)ni Joannis Ciampini Romae . . ." An even cursory comparison with B plainly confirms this. It is noteworthy that the original fol. 8 was already missing from B when the copy was made. The ms. once belonged to E. Betham who donated it to Eton College in 1775.[12]

C = Grottaferrata, ms. Z. α, XXX (Rocchi, 458–459). Vellum of very poor quality, 200 × 160 mm., 115 fols.[13] Early XII s.[14] Contents: 1ʳ–70ʳ, St. Cyril's lexicon with the beginning missing; 70ʳ–end, minor lexica and metrologica, as in B. Illumination and extensive

---

9 Specimens from fols. 4 and 5 have been published by S. Frasca, "Glosse siciliane in scrittura greca," *Bollettino del Centro di Studi Filologici e Linguistici Siciliani* 3, 1955, 314–316; and from fol. 263ʳ by S. G. Mercati, "Intorno al titolo di lessici di Suida-Suda e di Papia," *Byzantion* 25–26–27 (1955–1956–1957), 179–180 (= *Atti della Accademia Nazionale dei Lincei*, anno 357 [1960], *Classe di Scienze morali storiche e filologiche, Memorie*, ser. VIII, vol. X, fasc. 1, p. 10).

10 "Hie. Surite". On the library of the famous Spanish historian Jerónimo de Zurita y Castro, cf. Ch. Graux, *Essai sur les origines du fonds grec de l'Escurial* ("Ecole des Hautes Etudes," fasc. 46), Paris, 1880, 56–58, 331–339, 346–351 (no mention of our ms.).

11 On Gaetano Marini, First Custodian of the Vatican Library and Prefect of the Vatican Archives, cf. C. Frati, *Dizionario bio-bibliografico dei bibliotecari e bibliofili Italiani* ("Biblioteca di Bibliografia Italiana," XIII), Florence, 1933, 334; G. Mercati, *Note per la storia di alcune biblioteche Romane nei secoli* XVI–XIX ("Studi e Testi," 164) Vatican City, 1952, pp. 46; 55 n. 2; 81; 105; 111; 134 n. 3; 177 n. 4.

12 I am grateful to Mr. P. L. Strong, Keeper of the Eton College Library and Collections, for sending me a copy of the above note and for informing me that the donor's note is by the hand of Betham himself.

13 Fols. 2 and 3 have erroneously been bound there in place of some of the missing leaves of the quire, which was the second of the original volume. One folio is missing between fols. 38–39, with the beginning of the λ-section. Only one folio remains from the last preserved quire. Fols. 36–38 have been bound upside down and in reverse order.

14 Rocchi erroneously dated the ms. in the year 991. On the date of the vi archetype cf. below.

use of green and yellow ink wash over initials and titles betray
S. Italian provenance. The ms. bears corrections by a later hand.
Bibliography: A. Rocchi, *De Coenobio Cryptoferratensi eiusque biblio-
theca et codicibus praesertim Graecis commentarii* (Tusculi, 1893), 280;
O. Viedebannt, *Quaestiones Epiphanianae metrologicae et criticae*
(Leipzig, 1911), 46; S. G. Mercati, "Note critiche 9: Giambi con
quadruplice acrostico dell' imperatore Basilio," *Studi Bizantini e
Neoellenici* 3, 1931, 294–295; Drachmann, 9 f.; Benediktsson, 247;
Naoumides, "Symmeikta," 375; *Rhet. Lex.* 11.

F =   Florence, Bibl. Laurenz., plut. 57.42 (Bandini, II, 418–421). Vellum, 240 × 195 mm., 203 fols.,[15] c. 1123 (cf. Easter tables in 161ᵛ,
beg. with the year 6631 A.M.). Contents: 1ʳ–114ᵛ, St. Cyril's
lexicon with the beginning missing; 115ʳ–169ᵛ, 201ʳ–end, minor
lexica and metrologica; 169ᵛ–200ᵛ. Theodosius, Commentary on
the canons (cf. B). Bibliography: G. Vitelli, "Spicilegio Fioren-
tino," *Museo Italiano di Antichità Classica* 1, 1885, 159; P. Egenolff,
Die orthoepischen Stücke der byzantinischen Litteratur ("Wiss. Beilage
z. d. Progr. d. gr. Gymn. Mannheim"), Leipzig, 1887, 41; O.
Viedebannt, *op. cit.*, 46 f.; Drachmann, 10; G. Sola, *Studi Bizantini
e Neoellenici* 5, 1939, 318; A. Kominis, *op. cit.* (above, note 8) 100,
102 (the ms. is referred to as plut. LVI. 42, presumably a typo-
graphical error); Naoumides, "Symmeikta," 374; *Rhet. Lex.*, 11 f.

G =   Cephallenia, Μονὴ 'Αγ. Γερασίμου, No. 3 (Lambros, 389). Vellum,
230 × 188 (–190) mm., 106 fols.[16] Early XII s., by a hand closely
resembling that of F and H. Contents: 1ʳ–75ʳ, St. Cyril's lexicon
with the beginning missing; 75ʳ–end, minor lexica. In the margins
and the last two fols. there are several signatures, some of whom at
least may have been past owners or may have been affiliated with
monasteries which possessed the ms. Some of the surnames are
clearly Cephallenian. Bibliography: Drachmann, 8 f.; Benediktsson, 247; Naoumides, "Symmeikta," 374; *Rhet. Lex.*, 12.

H =   Oxford, Bodl. Libr., Holkham gr. 112 (formerly Holkham 289, cf.
de Ricci, 23, Barbour, 612 f.). Vellum, 250 × 187 mm., ii + 236

---

[15] The first and last folios of quire ᾱ are missing. Also one folio between 54–55, another
between 60–61 (the first and last of quire η̄); two between 139–140 (the last of quire ῑη̄
and the first of ῑθ̄), four between 140–141 (i.e., from the middle of quire ῑθ̄), eight between
149–150 (the last of κ̄ and the first seven of κ̄ᾱ), four between 152–153 (middle of κ̄β̄),
one between 162–163, and another between 168–169 (first and last of κ̄δ̄). The last
preserved quire (κ̄θ̄) has at present only three fols. but no visible lacuna.

[16] The first three quires and an undetermined number from the end are missing.
The last two fols. are mere fly leaves.

fols.[17] Written between 1100 and 1123,[18] possibly διὰ χειρὸς Κων(στα)ντ(ίνου) πρεσ[βυτέρου] (cf. fol. 230ʳ).[19] Contents: 1ʳ–118ᵛ, St. Cyril's lexicon; 119ʳ–183ᵛ, 184ᵛ–196ᵛ, 225ʳ–230ʳ minor lexica and metrologica; 184ʳ⁻ᵛ, Easter Tables (1355–1408); 196ᵛ–225ʳ, Theodosius, Commentary on the canons (cf. above, B); 230ᵛ–231ʳ, Interpretation of the Lord's Prayer; 232ʳ–end, Easter Tables of 1409–1492, written by a XIV s. hand. Former owners: A. E. Seidel, Thomas W. Coke, Earl of Leicester, and his heirs. Bibliography: W. Roscoe, "Some Account of the Manuscript Library at Holkham, in Norfolk . . . ," *Transactions of the Royal Society of Literature* 2, 1834, 362 f.; R. Förster, "Handschriften in Holkham," *Philologus*, 42, 1884, 161; H. Schenkl, *Bibliotheca Patrum Latinorum Britannica* ("Sitzb. Akad. Wien, Philos.–hist. Classe," 133.7), 80; C. W. James, "Some Notes Upon the Manuscript Library at Holkham," *The Library*, Fourth Series, 2, 1921–1922, 225 f.; Drachmann, 8; Benediktsson, 247; M. Naoumides, *op. cit.* (above, note 17), "Symmeikta," 374; *Rhet. Lex.*, 12 f.

I =   Mt. Athos, *M. Μεγίστης Λαύρας* 74 (Spyridon Lavriotes–Eustratiades, p. 229, No. 1361). Paper, 26 × 17 cm., 238 fols., XVII s. Contents: 1ʳ–127ᵛ, St. Cyril's lexicon; 128ʳ–180ᵛ, grammaticalia; 181ʳ–end, minor lexica.

J =   Rome, Bibl. Vallicelliana, E 37 (Martini, II, 113–116, No. 71). The volume consists of three separate parts (1–91,[20] 92–127, 128–153), of which only the first part interests us here. Paper (Western), 290 × 215 mm.[21] Written διὰ χειρός . . . πέτρου τουσκάν(ου) in 1317 (cf. fol. 91ᵛ). Contents: 1ʳ–66ʳ, St. Cyril's lexicon; 66ʳ–89ᵛ, 91ᵛ, minor lexica; 90ʳ–91ʳ dodecasyllables attributed to St. Gregory of Nazianzus, Isidore, Arsenius. For Bibliography cf. A. Turyn, *Dated Greek Manuscripts of the Thirteenth and Fourteenth Centuries in the Libraries of Italy* (Urbana, Illinois, 1972), pp. 129 f. and Pl. 101; Naoumides, *Rhet. Lex.*, 13 f.

[17] Four leaves have been cut off between fols. 183–184 containing, as it appears, Easter Tables to the year 6862 (= 1354); cf. my article "The Date, Scribe and Provenience of Cod. Holkham Gr. 112 (olim 298)", *Scriptorium* 28, 1974, 65–68.

[18] I.e., between the date of the archetype and that of F, an apograph of H (cf. below).

[19] Miss Barbour, however, considers fols. 229–230 as written by another hand. In my opinion the difference in appearance between the two "hands" is due to the poor quality of the vellum of fols. 229–230 and to the fact that they are badly wrinkled. See also my article cited above (note 17).

[20] Actually 92, since there are two folios numbered 5 (i.e., 5 and 5ᵇⁱˢ).

[21] Some leaves of quire ε̄ have been bound in wrong order, the proper order being 32, 34, 35, 33, 38, 36, 37, 39.

Mark Naoumides 99

K = Paris, Bibl. Nat., suppl. grec 1146 (Omont, III, 387; Astruc—
Concasty, 294–296). Paper, 199 × 145 mm., 189 fols.[22] Written in
Jerusalem in 1562 (cf. fol. 175^r). Contents: 1^{r-v}, didactic verses
mixed with prose in vulgar Greek, written by a XVII s. hand
(probably that of Christopher Strogia, according to Concasty);
2^r–34^r, ἑρμηνεία of three canons by St. John of Damascus; 35^r–81^v,
minor lexica; 82^r–175^r, St. Cyril's lexicon; [23] 175^v–181^v, Dionysius
Thrax, *Ars grammatica*; 182^r–187^v, lexicographical excerpts. Former
owners: Hieromonk Dionysius, hieromonk Christopher Strogia of
Corfou (cf. fol. 26^v), the deacon Daniel, son of Nicholas, also of
Corfou (fol. 188^r), hieromonk Dionysius of Crete (1782; cf. fol.
187^v). It was bought by Al. Sorlin Dorigny from the book-dealer
Rigopoulos at Constantinople in 1894 (cf. fol. 26^v). Bibliography:
Naoumides, *Rhet, Lex.*, 14.

Ka = Bucharest, Bibl. Akadem. Romane, gr. 612 (Litzica, 305). Paper,
21 × 15 cm., 225 fols. Written in the monastery of St. Anastasia
near Sozopolis (Sozopol) by the priest Gabriel[24] on 18 December,
1625 (cf. fol. 219^v). Contents: 1^{r-v}, 220^r–225^v and passim, Greek–
Rumanian lexicon; 2^r–9^v, *Disticha Catonis* translated by M.
Planudes; 10^r–18^r, Pseudo-Phocylidea; 18^v–48^v, Hesiod, *Erga* with
interlinear and marginal interpretation; 49^r–77^r, Aphthonius,
Progymnasmata; 82^r–217^r, St. Cyril's lexicon with the same beginning as in K;[25] 217^r–219^v, lexicon of plants. On some pages, left
blank by the original scribe, a later hand wrote a poem in political
verse.

L = Paris, Bibl. Nat., grec 2618 (Omont, III, 14). Paper, 265 ×
190 mm., 181 fols. Copied in the XVIII s. "e veteri codice Principis Moldaviae," according to a note written by Sevin and pasted
on the ms.[26] Contents: 1^r–91^r, St. Cyril's lexicon; 92^r–127^r, minor

---

[22] One folio is missing between 49–50 and another between 55–56. The next-to-last
quire is complete but the text clearly continued beyond. The last quire is written by a
different hand on paper with different watermarks from the rest of the volume and comes
from another ms.

[23] The Lexicon begins with the introductory note Δεῖ εἰδέναι found in Hesychius and
Par. gr. 2655 and other mss. (cf. Drachmann, 17–18, Latte, xiii). This admonition is a
feature of the p1 family of the shorter version of Pseudo-Zonaras' Lexicon; cf. my article,
cited below, on ms. Q. The interpolation is limited to the beginning of the Lexicon.

[24] The scribe's name written as a monogram in a dodecasyllabic line at the end of the
subscription: †θ(ε)οῦ τὸ δῶρον Γαβριὴλ θ(ύ)τ(ου) π(ό)ν(ος), was overlooked by Litzica.

[25] The Lexicon was apparently written independently from the rest, since the quires
containing it bear a separate numbering.

[26] This note is confirmed by a letter written by the Marquis of Villeneuve, French

lexica; 129^r–181^v, *voces hebraicae*. Bibliography: Naoumides, *Rhet. Lex.*, 14.

M = Vatican, Bibl. Apost. Vaticana, gr. 2164. Paper, 332 × 230 mm., iv + 126 fols.[27] To judge from the watermarks (Briquet 492, 13888), the ms. was written probably in Italy, in the XVI s. Contents: 1^r–73^r, St. Cyril's lexicon; 74^r–117^r, *voces hebraicae*; 119^{r-v}, metrologica. The ms. was one of the "codices Columnenses" sold in Rome in December, 1820.[28] Bibliography: Drachman, 21; Canart–Peri, 689.

N = Rome, Bibl. Apost. Vaticana, cod. Barber. gr. 39 (Capocci, 39–42). Vellum (of poor quality), 190 × 135 mm., 109 fols.[29] Written in 1294–1295 by Barnabas (cf. fol. 76^v), probably in S. Italy.[30] Contents: 1^r–76^v, St. Cyril's lexicon with the beginning missing; 78^r–end, minor lexica. For bibliography cf. A. Turyn, *Codices graeci Vaticani saeculis XIII et XIV scripti annorumque notis instructi* (Codices e Vaticanis selecti quam simillime expressi, XXVIII), in Civitate Vaticana, 1964, 88 f.; and Canart–Peri, 119, to which add the following: P. Egenolff, *Die orthographischen Stücke der byzantinischen Litteratur* ("Progr. Heidelb. 1887–88"), Leipzig 1888, 33; Sp. Lambros, *Νέος Ἑλληνομνήμων* 5, 1908, 451–453 (erroneously referring to the ms. as Barb. gr. 29. The error was repeated by Canart–Peri); Naoumides, "Symmeikta," 375.

O = Paris, Bibl. Nat., suppl. grec 659 (Omont, III, 291 f.). This ms. consists of three parts (1–150, 151–169, 170–185) of which only the first interests us here. Vellum, 142 × 110 mm., XIII s.

---

ambassador in Constantinople, to the count of Maurepas, dated October 28, 1734; cf. H. Omont, *Missions archéologiques françaises en Orient aux XVIIe et XVIIIe siècles*, II (Paris, 1902), 681–683. The Prince of Moldavia referred to is Constantine Maurokordatos, son of Nicholas Maurokordatos, Prince of Wallachia. For the attempts of the French to acquire the library of Nicholas and (after his death) Constantine M., see Omont, *op. cit.*, passim.

27 Fols. 120–126 are blank. There are two folios numbered 117 (117^a and 117^b).

28 Cf. *Index codicum graecorum Bibliothecae Columnensis* (Paris, 1820), No. 68. On the acquisition of the 93 Greek mss. of the family Colonna by the Vatican Library, cf. G. Mercati, *Byzantion* 1, 1924, 470, note 1, and C. Frati, *op. cit.* (above note 11), 178.

29 Probably a whole quire is missing from the beginning. In the midst of the δ-section (fol. 11^v) a number of glosses beginning with κ appear. They properly belong to the *Lexicon Octateuchi* (fol. 79^r), as the rubricator has rightly remarked in the margin. There was apparently a misplaced folio in N's exemplar.

30 Cf. A. Turyn, *Codices graeci Vaticani saeculis XIII et XIV scripti annorumque notis instructi* (Codices e Vaticanis selecti quam simillime expressi, vol. XXVIII), Vatican City, 1964, 88.

7 2 2 6 2

Contents: 1^r–110^r, St. Cyril's lexicon; 110^v–150^v, minor lexica.
The ms. bears the *ex-libris* of M. Mynas (fol. 1^r). It was acquired in
1841–1842, during Mynas' first mission to the Orient, possibly
from some monastery in M. Athos.[31] Bibliography: P. Egenolff,
Die orthoepischen Stücke der byzantinischen Litteratur (Progr. der Gr.
Gymn. Mannheim, 1886–1887), Leipzig 1887, 41; G. Weiss, *Studia
Anastasiana* I ("Miscellanea Byzantina Monacensia", 4), Munich,
1965, 76; Omont, *op. cit.* (above, note 31), 404.

P =   Paris, Bibl. Nat., suppl. grec 503 (Omont, III. 270 f.). Paper
(Western), 295 × 220 mm., 124 pages. XIV s. Contents: pp. 1–
122, St. Cyril's lexicon; 122–123, excerpt from St. Nicephorus'
Chronicle; 123–124, on Melchisedec; 124, Delphic oracle (from the
Life of St. Arsenius). The ms. was acquired by M. Mynas in
Thessalonica in 1841. Bibliography: H. Omont, *op. cit.*, (above,
note 31), 360, 387, 398.

Q =   Sinai, Μονὴ 'Αγίας Αἰκατερίνης gr. 1205 (Gardthausen, 249 f.).
Paper, 154 × 105 mm., i + 377 fols. XIV s. Contents: 1^r–278^v,
Ps.-Zonaras, Lexicon; 279^r–282^r, short lexicon; 282^v–301^v, St.
Cyril's lexicon (abbreviated); 301^v–302^v, brief excerpt from St.
John of Damascus; 303^r–310^v, 325^r–368^v, minor lexica; 311^r–325^r,
Commentary on canons of St. John of Damascus and Cosmas
Maiuma; 369^r–371^r, Anacreontic poem by the emperor Leo VI
with alphabetical acrostic; 371^r–end, Agapetus Diaconus, *Capita
admonitoria* (with the end missing). Bibliography: M. Naoumides,
"The Shorter Version of Pseudo-Zonaras, *Lexicon*," *Serta Turyniana*,
Studies in Greek Literature and Palaeography in honor of Alexan-
der Turyn, Urbana, U.I. Press, 1974, 487.

R =   Oxford, Bodleian Library, ms. Gr. class. f. 114. Vellum, 165 ×
137 mm., vii + 228 fols.[32] XI s. Contents: 1^r–93^v, St. Cyril's
lexicon with the beginning missing; 94^r–154^v, Homeric lexicon
similar to the one found in SU and published in part by V. de
Marco[33]; 154^v–end, minor lexica. In the lower margin of fol. 1^r,
illegible signature, apparently of a former owner. The ms. betrays

---

[31] Cf. H. Omont, "Minoide Mynas et ses missions en Orient (1840–1855)," *Mémoires
de l'Institut National de France, Académie d'Inscriptions et Belles Lettres* 40, 1916, 337–419.

[32] Fols. 215–228 are mere fly-leaves. The first two quires and the first leaf of quire γ̄
are missing. Also one leaf between fols. 6–7. The proper order of the folios from 199 to
214 is: 199, 208–213, 206, 207, 200–205, 214, i.e., the inside leaves of quires κ̄η̄, κ̄θ̄ have
been transposed mutually.

[33] *Scholia minora in Homeri Iliadem, pars prior*: Λέξεις 'Ομηρικαί codd. *Urb.* CLVII *et
Selestadiensis* CVII, Fasc. I, Vatican, 1946.

a S. Italian origin. It was acquired by the Bodleian Library from
P. Rosenthal, Oxford bookseller. Bibliography: Naoumides, "Symmeikta," 375; *Rhet. Lex.*, 14 f.

S = 　Selestat, Bibl. municipale, cod. 105 (Michelant, 593). Vellum,
170 × 135 (−140) mm., 183 fols.[34] Written ca. 1000, probably in
S. Italy. Contents: 3ᵛ–81ᵛ, St. Cyril's lexicon; 81ᵛ–96ᵛ, 134ʳ–158ᵛ
162ʳ–169ᵛ, minor lexica; 97ʳ–134ʳ, Homeric lexicon; 159ʳ–160ᵛ,
Theodosius Grammaticus, Commentary on canons (with the end
missing); 161ʳ⁻ᵛ, grammatical fragment; 170ʳ–end, Ps.-Nonnus,
Interpretatio historiarum Gregorii Nazianzeni. In the upper margin of
fol. 5ʳ the familiar *ex-libris* of Beatus Rhenanus.[35] A note written at
the end of St. Cyril's lexicon (fol. 81ᵛ) states that the ms. was
corrected by J. Conon of Nuremberg at Padua in 1501. Bibliography: Drachmann, 15; V. de Marco, *op. cit.* (above, note 33),
vii ff.; P. Adam, *op. cit.* (above, note 35), 112 f. and Plate viii;
Pertusi, *Leonzio Pilato*, 483, and note 1; *idem* "Aspetti organizzativi,"
418 and n. 3; *idem* "Leonzio Pilato e la tradizione di cultura
Italo-Greca," *Byzantino-Sicula*, Quaderni, 2, Palermo, 1966, 77;
Naoumides, *Rhet. Lex.*, 15.

T = 　Montecassino, cod. T 550 (Lambros, 344; Sajdak, 57–69, 91–92).
Vellum (except for fols. 68, 69) of poor quality, 145 × 115 mm.,
75 fols., XIII s. Contents: 1ʳ–64ᵛ, St. Cyril's lexicon; 65ʳ–end,
minor lexica. Bibliography: Naoumides, "Symmeikta," 375.

U = 　Vatican, Bibl. Apost. Vaticana, cod. Urb. gr. 157 (Stornajolo,
302–304). Vellum, 223 (−225) × 170 (−178) mm., iii + 302 fols.[36]
XI s. Contents: 1ʳ–125ʳ, St. Cyril's lexicon followed by a supple-
ment (fols. 125ʳ–145ʳ); 145ʳ–146ᵛ, *etymologia alphabeti*; 147ʳ–225ʳ,
Homeric lexicon; 225ʳ–277ᵛ, minor lexica; 278ʳ–302ʳ, Interpreta-
tion (with text and paraphrase in opposite columns) of poems by
St. Gregory of Nazianzus. For pertinent bibliography cf. Canart–
Peri, 349, to which add: Bekker, *Analecta Graeca* III, 1094 f. (note);
K. Latte, "Glossographica," *Philologus* 80, 1924, 136 f.; Naoumides,
"Symmeikta," 375; *Rhet. Lex.*, 15 f.

V = 　Milan, Bibl. Ambros., cod. B 46 sup. (formerly T 211; cf. Martini–
Bassi, I, 105–106, No. 90). Paper, 207 × 133 mm., vi + 201 + i

---

[34] Fols. 1, 2, 183 are mere fly-leaves. Fols. 157–161 should be placed after fol. 169.
Three folios are missing after 160, and at least one between 176–177.

[35] "sum Beati Rhenani nec muto dominum. Basileae MDXIII." This is therefore one
of the mss. which he inherited from J. Conon, upon the latter's death on 21 February
1513. On B. Rhenanus, his friendship with Conon, and his library, cf. P. Adam, *L'human-
isme à Sélestat* (Sélestat, 1962) and the bibliography cited there.

[36] One folio is missing between 1–2 and another between 5–6.

fols.,[37] XIV s. Contents: St. Cyril's lexicon. Former owners: Hier.
Chalcus (cf. fol. 1ʳ) and George Merula[38] (cf. fol. iʳ). A partially-
legible note written in red ink in fol. 88ʳ attests that the ms.
belonged to the monastery τῆς ὑψηλῆς πέτρας. Bibliography:
Drachmann, 19.

Va = Vatican, Bibl. Apost. Vaticana, cod. Ottob. gr. 170 (Feron–
Battaglini, 96). Paper, 215 × 145 mm., 175 fols.[39] XV s. Contents:
St. Cyril's lexicon. In the bottom margin of fol. 1ᵛ there is the
following note: "Ex codicibus Joannis Angeli Ducis ab Altaemps,
Ex Graeco manuscripto".[40] Bibliography: Drachmann, 20;
Canart–Peri, 198.

W = Florence, Bibl. Laurenz., plut. 57.50 (Bandini, II, 431–433).
Paper, 207 (–220) × 147 mm., 599 fols.,[41] year 1515 (cf. fol. 591ᵛ).
Contents: 1ʳ–456ᵛ, St. Cyril's lexicon with the title Συναγωγὴ
λέξεων συλλεγεῖσαι ἐκ διαφόρων βιβλίον παλαιᾶς τέ φημι γρα(φῆς)
καὶ τῆς νέας;[42] 457ʳ–478ʳ, minor lexica; 479ʳ–574ᵛ, commentary
on canons by St. John of Damascus and Cosmas Maiuma, with
the beginning and end missing; 575ʳ–578ʳ, iambic and anacreontic poems with alphabetic acrostic; 578ᵛ–594ᵛ, varia opuscula
astronomica et grammatica; 595ʳ–598ʳ, Funeral oration for
Catherine († 1462), wife of Thomas Palaeologus, by Charitonymus
Hermonymus.

X = Mt. Athos, M. Βατοπεδίου, cod. 418 (Eustratiades–Arcadios, 81).

---

[37] Single folios are missing between 19–20, 41–42, 116–117, 191–192. Since there is no
lacuna in the corresponding sections in Va, these fols. must have been lost after the
copying of Va or its immediate ancestor.

[38] On G. Merula (alias Γεώργιος Ἀλεξανδρῖνος, cf. cod. Ambros. E 113 sup.), cf.
F. Gobotto–A. Badini Confalonieri, "Vita di Giorgio Merula," *Rivista di storia, arte,
archeologia della provincia di Alessandria*, vols. 2 and 3 (also independently, Alessandria,
1894); Vogel–Gardthausen, 189 and n. 4; R. Sabbadini, *Le scoperte dei codici Latini e Greci
ne' secoli XIV e XV*, vol. I (Florence, 1905), 156 f. On his relations with H. Chalcus
(G. Calco) and his mss. (now in the Ambrosian Library), cf. E. Martini–D. Bassi, *Catalogus
codicum graecorum Bibliothecae Ambrosianae*, vol. I (Milan, 1906), p. xiv and n. 30.

[39] There is no fol. 41, however. Fols. 142ᵛ–143ʳ are left blank, apparently to indicate a
lacuna in the exemplar. Another hand subsequently wrote the credo in Greek on 142ᵛ.
The drawing of a bearded man with the title ὁ ταπεινὸς ἐπίσκοπος κανιν(?) καὶ αυθεν(της?)
fills the other blank page.

[40] On Altaemps cf. C. Frati, *op. cit.* (above, note 11), 16 f.

[41] With the new numbering of folios. Some folios are missing between 478–479 and
574–575. Fols. 498, 588ᵛ, 592, 593, 598ᵛ, 599 are blank. Fols. 595ʳ–598ʳ are written by
another hand.

[42] This is the title of Ps.–Zonaras' Lexicon. The ms. indeed has many marginalia
from Ps.–Zonaras. On account of its title Tittmann (*Joannis Zonorae Lexicon . . .*, Leipzig,
1808, p. xli) listed it among the mss. of Ps.–Zonaras.

Vellum, 152 × 115 mm., 63 fols.,[43] XIII s. (X s., according to Eustratiades). Contents: St. Cyril's lexicon with the beginning and end missing.

Y = Athens, Βυζ. Μουσεῖον, cod. 186 (Pallas, 77–79). The main part of the ms. (fols. 1, 44–45, 56–134, 147) was written on vellum in 1296–1297 and belongs to the g-recension. Fols. 2–43, 46–53 (containing the missing part of St. Cyril's lexicon) were copied on paper from a ms. of the v-recension in the XVII s. The same hand also copied fols. 136–146. The ms. formerly belonged to the Monastery (of the Transfiguration) τοῦ Μετεώρου (cf. fol. 2ʳ).

Z = Grottaferrata, Z. α, VI (Rocchi, 444). Vellum, 21 × 16 cm., 42 fols.,[44] XIII s. Contents: St. Cyril's Lexicon with the beginning and end missing. In the right-hand margins a contemporary hand added further explanations. This ms. was in all probability written in S. Italy. Marginal notes in fol. 16ᵛ and 32ᵛ testify that it once belonged to the Monastery of St. Mary "del Patir". Bibliography: A. Batiffol, L' Abbaye de Rossano: Contribution à l'histoire de la Vaticane (Paris, 1891), 60; A. Rocchi, op. cit., 280; Pertusi, Leonzio Pilato, 484 and n.1; idem, "Aspetti organizzativi," 419 and n.3; idem, "Leonzio Pilato," 77.

Γ = Paris, Bibl. Nat., grec 2656 (Omont, III, 19–20). Vellum, 210 (–216) × 140 (–145) mm., 128 fols. Written in early XII s., probably in S. Italy.[45] Contents: 1ʳ–103ʳ, St. Cyril's lexicon; 104ʳ–end, minor lexica. Bibliography: Drachmann, 20.

Δ = Paris, Bibl. Nat., grec 2659 (Omont, III, 20). Vellum, 175 × 125 mm., 182 fols., year 1515–1516. Contents: 1ʳ–154ᵛ, St. Cyril's lexicon; 154ᵛ–180ʳ, minor lexica; 180ʳ–end, theological treatise (sermo synodalis). In the margins there are extensive additional glosses from the Etym. Gudianum. Bibliography: H. Omont, Catalogues des manuscrits grecs de Fontainebleau sous François Iᵉʳ et Henri II (Paris, 1889), p. 115, No. 340; idem, Fac-similés des manuscrits grecs datés de la Bibliothèque Nationale du IXᵉ au XIVᵉ siècle (Paris, 1891), p. 9 and Pl. 44; R. Reitzenstein, Geschichte der griechischen Etymologika (Leipzig, 1897), 84–87; Drachmann, 20; Latte, IL.

---

43 The first five quires, the last folio of quire ιβ together with quire ιγ (between fols. 55–56), and an undetermined number of quires after fol. 63 are missing.

44 Six complete quires are missing from the beginning, two more between fols. 32–33, and an undetermined number from the end.

45 As can be inferred from the writing, quality of vellum, rubrication, and extensive use of yellow ink wash.

Θ = Munich, Bayer. Staatsbibl., gr. 298 (Hardt, III, 231). Vellum, 185 (–189) × 138 (–140) mm., ii + 138 fols. Written in the XII s.,[46] probably in S. Italy.[47] Contents: St. Cyril's lexicon with the end missing. Bibliography: Drachmann, 20; Naoumides, "Symmeikta," 376.

Λ = Mt. Athos, M. Μεγίστης Λαύρας, 20 (Spyridon Lavriotes– Eustratiades, p. 33, No. 260). Vellum, 19 × 13 cm., 224 fols.,[48] XIV s. Contents: 1ʳ–10ᵛ, fragment of a lexicon;[49] 11ʳ–179ʳ, St. Cyril's lexicon; 179ᵛ ταὐτολεξίαι; 181ʳ–end, ὅροι καὶ ὑπογραφαὶ κατὰ στοιχεῖον.

Ξ = Mt. Athos, M. Ξενοφῶντος, 83 (Lambros I, 71, No. 785). Paper, 206 × 136 mm., 170 fols.,[50] XV s. Contents: St. Cyril's lexicon with the end missing.

Π = Florence, Bibl. Laurenz., plut. 5.20 (Bandini, I, 43–44). Vellum, 236 × 165 (–169) mm., 151 fols., XIII s. (XII according to Bandini). Contents: 1ʳ–149ʳ, St. Cyril's lexicon; 149ʳ–end, minor lexica.

Σ = Munich, Bayer. Staatsbibl., gr. 230 (Hardt, II, 497; 502). Paper (oriental), 244 (–248) × 170 mm., 314 fols.[51] Written in the XIII s., in part διὰ χειρὸς Νίφωνος (μον)αχ(οῦ) (cf. fol. 291ʳ and 311ʳ).[52] Contents: 1ʳ–246ʳ, St. Cyril's lexicon; 246ʳ–286ᵛ, minor lexica; 286ᵛ–end, varia grammatica, theologica, etc. The following note appears in the margin of fol. 197ʳ: ἡ τῇδε βί | βλος πέλει | κωνσταντί | νου ἰμβρι | ώτου καὶ ὑ | πουργοῦ τοῦ | ξενῶνος | τοῦ κράλη.[53] Bibliography: Vogel-Gardthausen, 334; Drachmann, 20.

---

46 The date ͵ςψκα′ (1212–1213), which appears in fly-leaf iʳ, is by another hand and need not be the date of the ms.

47 This is inferred from the writing, illumination, and quality of the vellum. Note also the following notes by a XIII s. hand: Νός ρίβουλοι σούμους ἀφόντε μάγνα γρε (fol. iiᵛ), γεδδοὺρ κούρσον σύστημα (fol. 38ᵛ).

48 One folio is missing between 223–224 and one from the last quire of the volume (κζ̄). The first ten folios come from another ms., since the numbering of the quires begins with fol. 11.

49 The arrangement is basically alphabetical, but the order of the larger sections seems disturbed (Ν, Ξ, Ο, Μ, Ν, Λ, Μ, Ε).

50 One folio is missing between 2–3, and an undetermined number from the end.

51 Numbered 1–311, but there are two extra folios (numbered 3ᵃ, 3ᵇ), and a third unnumbered folio between 126–127.

52 To judge from the position and phrasing of the subscription, Niphon wrote fols. 1–12 and 291–311. Note that the main body of the ms. begins with a quire marked β̄, i.e., Niphon apparently supplemented the missing beginning and end of the volume.

53 On the ξενὼν τοῦ κράλη, situated near the Blachernae Palace in Constantinople, cf. A. Premerstein in the preface of the facsimile edition of the Vienna Dioscurides, *Codices*

Φ = Leyden, Univers. Bibl., cod. Voss. Gr. Q 63 (de Meyier, 180–182).
Vellum, 205 × 140 mm., iii + 176 fols., XII s., probably in
Italy.[54] Contents: 1ʳ–152ʳ, St. Cyril's lexicon; 152ᵛ–end, minor
lexica. Former owners: Paul and Alexander Petau, Queen Chris-
tine of Sweden, Isaac and Ger. Voss. Bibliography: M. Schmidt,
Hesychii Alexandrini Lexicon, vol. IV, 1 (Jenae, 1862), 366–368
(excerpts from the lexicon) and IV, 2 (Jenae, 1864), xlvi f.;
K. A. de Meyier, *Paul en Alexandre Petau* (Dissertationes inaugurales
Batavae, 5), Leyden 1947, pp. 16, 46, 50, 51, (n. 68), 200; Alberti,
Glossarium graecum in sacros Novi Foederis libros (1735), Praefatio
(pages unnumbered).

Φa = Utrecht, Univers. Bibl., cod. 14 (Omont, 209, No. 49). Paper,
212 × 165 mm., 504 pages, XVII s. Contents: St. Cyril's lexicon.
This is clearly an apograph of Φ.

Φb = Leiden, Univers. Bibl., B.P.L. 494 (Molhuysen, 131). Paper, in
quarto, 87 fols. Contents: Excerpts from Φ made by L. C. Valcke-
naer in 1739.

Ω = Vatican, Bibl. Apost. Vaticana, gr. 869. This is a composite ms.,
the first part of which (fols. 1–68) is written on oriental paper in
the XIII s. and contains the Lexicon of St. Cyril (from α to τ).
Fols. 69–82 were added in the XV s. to supplement the missing
end of the Lexicon. They also contain a small number of the
familiar minor lexica. Bibliography: cf. Canart–Peri, *Sussidi*, 505.

Three mss. which properly belong to a recension akin to what
is commonly called *Lexicon Bachmannianum* (Athens, Ἐθνικὴ
Βιβλιοθήκη 1197; Σπουδαστήριον Ἱστορικῆς Θεολογίας, 47; and
Vat. gr. 1869) contain in the θα-section a text that closely re-
sembles that of our v-mss.

AFFILIATIONS OF THE MANUSCRIPTS

BCFGH, Drachmann's best and almost exclusive representatives of the
entire recension, form a closely-knit group (vi), as can be observed both
by their readings and the arrangement of their contents. Among their
exclusive readings are not only the usual errors of text corruption, spelling,

---

Graeci et Latini photographice depicti, vol. X.i (Leyden, 1906), 10 ff.; R. Janin, *La géographie
ecclésiastique de l'empire Byzantin*, part I, vol. 3 (Paris, 1953), 572; and M. Marcovich,
"Drei Miszellen zur byzantinischen Literaturgeschichte," *Akten des XI. Internationalen
Byzantinisten-Kongresses* 1958 (Munich, 1960), 344.

54 To judge from the script, quality of vellum, and extensive use of ink wash.

and accentuation,[55] but omissions and additions of entire entries as well.[56] All but one (χ67) of the omitted glosses occur in more or less the same form in at least one recension outside **v**. On the other hand, of the eleven glosses attested by **vi** alone, only one (ξ32) seems to be a truly Cyrillean gloss found in exactly the same form in the **a**, **g**, and **n** recensions. Some are in reality but duplicates of genuine glosses (compare ξ24 with ξ28, ξ43 with ξ25, and χ6 with χ43). It is noteworthy, however, that the additional glosses in the χ-section have parallels not in the extant Cyrillean recensions but in Hesychius. In one of them (χ19) a citation from a lost Sophoclean drama (omitted by Hesychius) is preserved (a rarity for this lexicon), while χ158 is clearly a dialectal gloss of the kind found frequently in Hesychius. Such glosses are usually and almost routinely attributed to the lost lexicon of Diogenianus, the progenitor of Hesychius' Lexicon. Since, however, the hypothesis of a fuller Diogenianus seems to me to lack satisfactory proof, I am inclined to attribute them to a fuller (or pre-abridged) version of Hesychius.[57] It is significant in this connection that the home of this family seems to be in Southern Italy (cf. below), where Laurent. plut. 57.39 (= Drachmann's *S*) and the constellation of Matrit., Bibl. Univ. Z-22 No. 116, Haun. 1968, and Messan. S. Salv. 167[58] seem to have originated.[59]

Besides the internal, i.e., textual, relationship, four of the above mss. (BFGH) share a number of external features which seem to suggest that they were the product of the same scriptorium. All four mss. seem to be fine editions of the Lexicon, written in the same format, with the same color of ink and with identical purple-colored rubrication. The script is regular, formal, and impersonal, resembling print rather than handwriting. Ligatures and abbreviations are rare. Besides, the writing of FGH is very similar, as if all three were written by the same hand.[60]

---

55 Cf. θ7, 9, 12, 13, 25; ξ5, 10, 13, 18, etc.—most of the errors are confined to **vi**. In one case the word order within the entry has been changed (χ126). In another, a word has been misplaced (cf. χ110, 111). In the ξ-section two related entries have been conflated into one (ξ30, 31).

56 Omitted entries: θ20, 21, χ67, 77, 94, 95. Additional glosses: ξ8, 24, 32, 43, χ6, 19, 31, 90, 93, 157, 158. χ92 has been expanded considerably with additional matter. There are also minor additions and omissions within the entries: cf. χ62, 73, 121, 132.

57 Cf. my article "New Fragments of Ancient Greek Poetry," *Greek Roman and Byzantine Studies* 9, 1968, 267–290.

58 On the S. Italian provenance of this ms., cf. Pertusi, *Leonzio Pilato*, 484; and S. G. Mercati, *op, cit.* (above, note 9), 9.

59 Other mss. of the **v**-recension which are of S. Italian origin are S and Z. I intend to treat the question of the S. Italian copy of Hesychius more fully elsewhere.

60 Cf. my articles cited above (notes 3 and 17).

Within the family two groups can easily be distinguished: FH and BG. The special bond that ties F and H is both external (script and lay-out of the text) and internal, i.e., textual; cf. especially χ19 (ολάψει), 82 (νέος for νέας), 92 (addition of ἱμάτιον after λεπτόν), 149 (προσχῶν for προσχοῦν), and conflation of ξ43, 44. Since F is younger and shows a further deterioration of the text, it seems likely that it is a copy of H. The view of direct dependence is amply supported both by the writing and by θ24, where F seems to have misunderstood a pen correction of H in reading θατέρον for θατέρου.[61]

The special relationship of B and G is shown in a number of strikingly corrupt readings that these mss. share: cf. θ22 (θάττοντες vs. θάττον), 24 (repetition of the word θάτερον), 25 (use of the singular for the plural), etc. Since both mss. seem to be roughly contemporary, their exact relationship can be determined only from the evidence of the text. B has many separative errors and of such a nature that they could not have been corrected by the scribe of G,[62] whereas the opposite seems to be true in the case of G vs. B. Furthermore, B seems to have adopted the marginal or supralinear readings of G as well as corrections effected by the original scribe and/or the rubricator. At any rate, even if B is not a copy of G it seems to have no independent value except in the sections that are missing from G.

C stands between G and H but is generally closer to the former than to the latter. It is, however, marred with an enormous number of spelling errors. Therefore, agreement of C with either of the above mss. should indicate the reading of the family archetype (v1). This archetype was written ca. 1100, as is shown by a reference to that year incorporated in the discussion of what is περίοδος τοῦ ἄλφα and how to compute the inter-calary period κατὰ λατίνους; and it was written in all probability in S. Italy, as is shown not only from the almost-certain S. Italian provenance of BC but also from the inclusion of the λέξεις ἐκ τοῦ βίου τοῦ ἁγίου Ἡλία τοῦ Νέου, a S. Italian saint.[63] This lost ms. had a good number of errors in spelling and accentuation, omissions and other scribal errors, which were faithfully reproduced by its descendants. But to compensate for it, it was interpolated with occasional glosses from a reputable lexico-graphic source, most probably the unabridged lexicon of Hesychius.

---

[61] Similarly, in the α-section F's reading μηαρότητα (vs. μιαρότητα in H) can be explained as a failure on the part of the scribe to distinguish the *iota* from the accent of the word ἤνεγκαν just below it. Cf. also my *Rhet. Lex.*, 23.

[62] Cf. θαμμπόλος (θ7), χεδροπήν vs. χεδροπόν (χ56), μέριον vs. χιμέριον (χ92), change from the singular to the plural (χ87), omission of the article (θ7, χ62), etc.

[63] Cf. my articles cited above (notes 3 and 17); cf. also *Rhet. Lex.*

The family stemma can be drawn as follows:

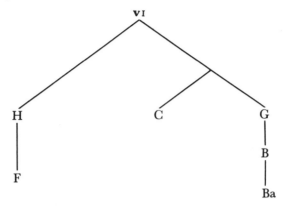

Closely related to **vi** is the **v2** family, which consists of ten mss. (IJKKaLMNOPQ), none of which is earlier than the XIII s. With the exception of J and M, these mss. have been completely ignored by both Drachmann and Latte, and no assessment of the value of this family for the recovery of the archetype of the recension has ever been made.

The origin of the family cannot be traced as easily as that of **vi**. Two of the earliest mss., J and N (both dated) come from S. Italy, while all the others, with the possible exception of M, were either written in or came from various places in the East. The difference in provenance does not coincide with the two basic groups into which they are divided (cf. below). Since, however, both branches have early representatives in S. Italy and since the family is generally close to **vi**, the possibility of a S. Italian origin should seriously be reckoned with.

Although there is greater discrepancy between the individual members of the family, the general characteristics seem clear. There are only three glosses omitted by all the mss. (in addition to those found only in **vi**), θ11, 23, and χ71; and no interpolations except those appearing in individual mss. (mostly J). The family has few exclusive readings attested by all mss., the most characteristic of which are found in the following glosses: ξ39 (addition of $\sigma\acute{v}v\theta\eta\mu\alpha$ before $\sigma\eta\mu\epsilon\widehat{\iota}ov$, omission of $\tau\iota v\acute{\iota}$), 47 ($\check{\epsilon}\xi\omega$ for $\check{\epsilon}\xi\omega\theta\epsilon v$), χ25 ($\grave{\alpha}\theta\lambda\acute{\iota}\omega\varsigma$ vs. $\grave{\alpha}\theta\rho\acute{o}\omega\varsigma$), 43 ($\chi\acute{\alpha}\rho\iota\varsigma$ vs. $\chi\acute{v}\sigma\iota v$) and the conflation of χ67, 68 into one entry. To these one may add a few more that seem to go back to the archetype, although they are not attested by all **v2** mss.[64]

---

[64] Cf. ξ21 ($\xi v\mu\beta\alpha\acute{\iota}\epsilon\iota$, but $\xi v\mu\beta\alpha\acute{\iota}v\epsilon\iota$ in Ka O), χ16 ($\check{\epsilon}\chi\omega v$, but $\check{\epsilon}\chi ov\tau\alpha$ L), 26 ($\epsilon\grave{\iota}\pi\epsilon\widehat{\iota}v$ [$\epsilon\grave{\iota}\varsigma$ $\pi\epsilon\widehat{\iota}v\alpha v$ K Ka L], but $\pi\iota\epsilon\widehat{\iota}v$ M); cf. also χ16 ($\chi\alpha\lambda\epsilon\pi\widehat{\omega}$ or $\chi\alpha\lambda\epsilon\pi\widehat{\omega}\varsigma$ for $\chi\alpha\lambda\kappa\widehat{\omega}$), and note 67 below.

The family is neatly split into two groups, the first of which is made of five mss. (JKKaLM), the other of four (NOPQ).[65] For the sake of convenience I call the first group v21, the second v22. The most characteristic reading of v21 is the change of θάλψις (θ3) to θάλπος, which subsequently (in all except M) by wrong division was transferred to the next entry (θ4), of which it became the lemma. Also in χ23 four of the five mss. (KKaLM) have extended the lemma by one syllable, χαμαιτεταιρίς.[66] The particular relationship of the v21 mss. is illustrated in the following stemma:

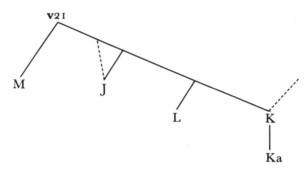

L as well as M are comparatively free from individual errors—indeed their readings are occasionally superior to those of all other v2 mss.[67] Both are corrected mss. (with different degrees of success), as one might expect from so late and possibly learned copies. This becomes evident from instances of false correction, especially in the case of L.[68] J and K (and Ka) have been interpolated, especially at the beginning of the Lexicon, but from different sources.

The second group (v22) seems to be in general more remote from the family archetype. Thus, it shows omissions of entire glosses (ξ33, 41, χ14, 85, 91), addition of an extraneous gloss (ξυνωρίδα: ζυγήν) after ξ29, reversal of the order of glosses (ξ31–32 and χ138–139), together with

65 I have no precise information about I besides a hasty examination of the ms. during my visit to Mt. Athos in the summer of 1970, but it seems to be part of the first group.

66 M actually reads χαμαιτετερίς. I consider J's reading χαμαιταιρίς as due either to emendation or haplography. The readings of the v21 mss. clearly reflect an original
supralinear correction, χαμαιτερίς or χαμαιταιρίς.

67 To the examples given above (note 64) add the following: χ69 (χήλη M: χήμη v), 148 (πεμμάτων M: πελμάτων v2); ξ42 (ξυνοδόκος L: ξυνοδοκός vi, v21), 45 (κνησμός L: κνισμός v2); χ107 (οἴστριξ L: οἴστριγξ or οἴστρυγξ v2).

68 Cf. especially χ21, where χαμεπετεῖ was mistaken for a verbal form and the explanation adjusted accordingly (ταπεινῶς ἢ χαμαὶ κεῖται), and 58, where the unintelligible τοῦ ἄδου τῆς θύρας (for τοῦ οὐδοῦ τῆς θ.) was changed to τῆς θύρας τοῦ ἄδου. Cf. also Lex. Rhet., 24 f.

spelling errors and other variants. Occasionally its readings are superior to those of virtually all **v**-mss. (cf. χοάς in χ100, χρεώμενος in χ122, and χυδαῖοι in χ145). They should be attributed to emendation. Within this group O and P form a distinct subgroup, which displays side by side corrections or improvements of corrupt readings and outright blunders. Neither seems to be dependent on the other, as is particularly shown by individual omissions. The last member of the **v2** family (Q) seems to be close to OP, but it is further abridged and interpolated.

On the whole and apart from separative errors and readings, **v2** seems to be closely related to **vI**. The two families share a number of glosses that are absent from all other **v**-mss. (ξ11, χ11, 32, 36, 125, 150, 151), whereas in some entries their explanation is "fuller" than that of the others (cf. ξ44, χ30, 46, 73, 74, 81, 120). The two families also display a few common errors and/or readings; cf. θαλησίαι (θ6), ξύνειον (ξ23), ἧλιξ (χ35), τῷ ῥωξί (χ53), χονδρίτων[68a] (χ102), πελμάτων (χ148); cf. also χωρίσατε (χ153), where **v22** is probably corrected. It is therefore quite likely that they descend from a common exemplar. The fact that J has preserved the lexicon of life of St. Elias the Younger may suggest that the common ancestor of these two families was also written in S. Italy. In this case it would be interesting to know how the family proliferated also in the East.

The third well-defined family of the **v**-recension (**v3**) consists of ten mss. (ΓΔΘΛΞΠΣΦΦaΦb), some of which are as early as the beginning of the twelfth century. The origin of the family is obscure but some claim may be made by S. Italy in view of the possible S. Italian origin of some mss. and the particular link with the Etym. Gudianum.[69]

The general characteristics of the **v3** family include: (a) addition of entire glosses. These fall into two main categories: those common to all **v3**-mss. as well as to R; and a good number of the etymological glosses attested by all **v3**-mss. except Γ and listed by Δ in the margins. (b) Omissions of entire entries or of parts thereof.[70] More often than not the shorter entries agree with the corresponding entries of the **g**-recension,

---

[68a] χονδριτόν in FHOP.

[69] On the reciprocal influence between the Gudianum and Δ, cf. Reitzenstein, *op. cit.*, 84 ff. That a ms. of the **v3** family was the source of the Cyrillean glosses of the Gudianum, is amply confirmed by such common readings as θαμίζει: πυκνάζει, συνεχῶς ἄγει (cf. *Etym. Gud.* p. 255.42 Sturz), χαμαιτυπιῶν: τῶν πολὺ μετεχόντων τῶν συνουσιῶν (cf. 962.27), and by the inclusion in the series of Cyrillean glosses listed together in the θ-section of some of the original **v3**-additamenta, e.g., θαλὴ ἡ εὐθηνία, θάλεια: ὄνομα Μούσης (255.38–39).

[70] Entries omitted: θ17; ξ14, 38; χ1, 67, 69, 71, 72, 79, 89, 145, 155, 156. Shorter entries (in addition to those found in all independent mss.): θ11, 18; ξ12, 13, 20, 37; χ14, 17, 18, 25, 33, 35, 41, 45, 60, 68, etc.

and consequently cannot be dismissed as either blunders or deliberate omissions.[71] (c) Additions and other changes within the entries.[72] Perhaps the most revealing of these are the instances of double lemmata (θ1, χ48, 56), where what seems to be a correction appears beside the original corrupt reading. (d) There is finally ample evidence of text corruption, most notably the conflation of two unrelated entries (χ115, 116) into one, and of errors in spelling and accentuation. Because of the extent of *Bearbeitung* and corruption, as shown above, the readings of this family should be admitted into the text with great caution and only if they find confirmation from the independent mss. of **v** and/or the related recensions **g** and **a**.

Within the **v3** family there is a good degree of differentiation. This appears chiefly in the number of additional entries admitted by each ms. as well as in the order of both regular and additional glosses. To take the $\theta\alpha$-section as an example, Γ lists all the **v** entries minus 6 and 17 (the latter is missing from all **v3**-mss.). The order of glosses is identical with that of **v2**, except that gloss $\theta\acute{\epsilon}\alpha$ $\gamma\acute{\alpha}\rho$ appears among the $\theta\alpha$-glosses. The additional glosses common to all **v3** mss. and R are listed together in one batch between 11 and 12; and a new addition ($\theta\acute{\alpha}\nu\alpha\tau\sigma$) appears before 18. Δ shows two more additional glosses in the main text, $\theta\alpha\lambda\epsilon\rho\acute{\sigma}$ (between 2 and 3) and $\theta\hat{\alpha}\tau\tau\sigma\nu$ (between 21 and 22); has somewhat dispersed the original *additamenta*, and has kept all the new (etymological) glosses in the margins. It has also moved 9 between 4 and 5. Θ agrees with Γ in the order of the common glosses but additional glosses $\theta\alpha\lambda\epsilon\rho\acute{\sigma}$ and $\theta\hat{\alpha}\tau\tau\sigma\nu$ are not in the same place as in Δ. The marginal glosses of Δ appear in batches in the text without much regard for the alphabetical order. Finally Θ has a number of additional glosses not found in Δ but attested in $\Xi\Pi\Sigma\Phi\Phi$a. The other mss. (referred to henceforth as **v32**) list the original, i.e., **v**-glosses in a slightly different order from the usual one, but have kept the original **v3** *additamenta* together as a batch, between 10 and 13. The other additional glosses found in Θ and in the margins of Δ have been distributed so as to fit an alphabetical order based on the first three letters of the lemmata. Gloss $\theta\alpha\lambda\epsilon\rho\acute{\sigma}$ (cf. *supra*) appears after 2 (as in Δ), but $\theta\hat{\alpha}\tau\tau\sigma\nu$ has been dropped and two new glosses added. Gloss $\theta\epsilon\iota\acute{\alpha}\zeta\omega$, which appears for the first time among the $\theta\alpha$-glosses in Θ,

---

[71] Only the following "omissions" have no parallels in the g-recension: ξ37 ($\mathring{\eta}$ $\chi\rho\acute{\eta}\mu\alpha\tau\alpha$), χ35 ($\kappa\alpha\grave{\iota}$ $\mathring{\sigma}\lambda\epsilon\theta\rho\sigma\nu$), 53 ($\tau\hat{\omega}\nu$ $\delta\alpha\kappa\tau\acute{\nu}\lambda\omega\nu$), 68 ($\kappa\alpha\grave{\iota}$ $\alpha\mathring{\iota}\gamma\acute{\sigma}$), 133 ($\pi\rho\sigma\sigma\kappa\nu\hat{\alpha}\tau\alpha\iota$).

[72] Additions: cf. θ1, 22; χ30, 48, 53, 56, 87, 103, 126, 130, 152. Transpositions: cf. θ4, 5; χ43, 60, 62, 124. Changes: cf. θ12, 16, 23; ξ17, 46; χ8, 22, 49, 56, 60, 70, 87, 114, 129, 133; some of them have parallels in R or V W.

is also found in the same place in these mss. Codex *Ξ* has added one more new gloss unattested in the other **v3** mss. The same general situation also prevails in the ξ- and χ-sections.

Despite appearances neither *Δ* nor *Θ* seem to be the direct ancestors of **v32**, but the latter group seems to have evolved from the common ancestor of *ΔΘ* through correction, possible interpolation, and a certain degree of *Bearbeitung*. This accounts not only for the absence of a few errors common to *ΓΔΘ* and hence presumably of the family archetype, but also for the conflation or elimination of similar entries.[73]

On the basis of the distribution of the additional entries as well as of their readings, the branching out of the mss. of this family can be sketched as follows:

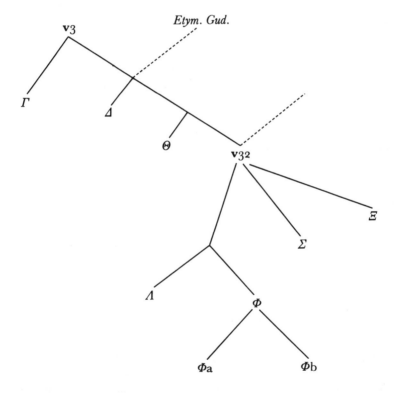

[73] Thus add. gloss χειρῶναξ has been eliminated, but its explanation has been added to that of gloss χ52. Conversely, the explanation of χ43 has been appended to that of add. gloss Χερουβίμ. The omission of χ61, 91 is clearly due to the presence of similar entries among the additamenta.

Besides the three larger families described above, there are a number of mss. which can be called independent. Some of them fall into small groups. The first such group consists of T and U. Their most striking common feature is the order in which they list the glosses. Indeed a rearrangement has been carried out with the intention of achieving stricter alphabetical order. Thus θ15 has been placed before θ1, θ25 before θ23, ξ7 before ξ6, ξ34 after 42, χ4 after χ9, χ17 before χ12, etc. However, the rearrangement is only partial. Thus θ5 and 6 still precede θ7 and 8, ξ4 is before ξ5, χ35 before ξ37, etc. The result of the rearrangement has been to effect an alphabetical order which is based on the first three or even more letters. Another by-product of the new arrangement is the occasional combination of related entries, e.g., ξ20 with 31 and (erroneously) χ61 with 85.

Besides the order of the entries, the two mss. share a number of readings that appear to be either restricted to them alone or are found only in one or more independent mss.; cf. the addition in χ76[74] and the spellings πολυκύτων (χ22), ἠλύξ (χ35), etc.

A comparison of their individual readings shows convincingly that T, although younger and in many respects inferior to U, is independent from the latter ms. Thus T lists χ107, which U entirely omits, as well as δέ in θ4, θερμᾶναι in θ5, the article in χ62 and ὡς in χ82; cf. also the following readings of U, all involving corruption of the text which attempts at emendation could not remove: ξεστῶν for ξεστόν (ξ12), συζυγῆ for ζυγή (ξ20), χάζετο: ἀναχωρεῖ for χάζεο: ἀναχώρει (χ3)[74a], and χαμαιτυπής for χαμαιτύπη (χ24). It becomes, therefore, clear that T descends not from U, but from a better and more complete ms., possibly U's exemplar. However, because of innumerable scribal errors, T is of little use for the restoration of the text of **v** beyond the evidence that it provides about the history of the transmission. U, on the other hand, occasionally offers superior readings, which must be due to emendation rather than to a better tradition (cf. θ6, ξ19, χ66). It has indeed a number of corrections by the first hand[75] and numerous additional glosses from another Cyrillean ms. at the end of the Lexicon.

The second group of closely related mss. consists of R and S. Their special relationship emerges clear from a number of common features that are restricted to these two mss. and which can hardly be considered accidental. These include the apparent conflation of θ23, 24, additions in the explanations of χ127, 139, omission of the lemma in θ20, and such

---

[74] Found also in W and originating from the g-recension.

[74a] T however omits this entry.

[75] Such corrections appear, for example, in θ18 (ἀποκτείνη [ει ex?]), χ23 (χαμαιταιρεῖς and corr. in marg. ῥιῆς).

readings as ξυνούσιον for ξυνάορον (ξ35), χιδρός (χίδρος R) for χιλός
(χ83) and βραχιόλην for βραχιόλιον (χ96). Besides these the two mss.
omit (in agreement with other independent mss. or with v3) a number of
glosses (χ69, 72, 156) and have shorter explanation in θ22, χ30, 35, 38,
60, 81, 109, 121. They also list two additional glosses in the ξ-section
(ξυμφορά, ξυνσχοῖτο). These common features are all the more remarkable,
since R seems clearly interpolated from an outside source.

Interpolation in R takes the form of additional glosses which for the
most part are identical with the original *additamenta* of the v3 family (i.e.,
essentially the additional glosses of Γ). The distribution of these new
glosses among the v-glosses varies. In the θα-section they are all listed
together as a group at the end of the v-glosses, i.e., after θ25. In the ξ- and
χ-sections, however, they appear among the regular v-glosses in approxi-
mately the same places as in v3 (especially Γ). In fact, additional gloss
ξόανον in the ξ-section has taken the place of the original v-gloss (ξ14),
while the latter appears between ξ7 and 9, out of the alphabetical order.
In the same section there are two sets of duplicate glosses: ξυνῶν-ξυνόν
and ξυνάορον-ξυνούσιον. Gloss ξυνόν is actually the corrupt counterpart of
ξυνῶν (ξ33) in v3, while ξυνούσιον is the corrupt form of ξυνάωρον (ξ35) in
S. R lists ξυνόν before and ξυνάορον after ξ34, while ξυνῶν is listed together with ξυνούσιον following gloss ξ39 and the additional gloss   ·
ξυνσχοῖτο. It is clear that here as in the case of ξ14 the v3 glosses were
given precedence over the S-glosses.

In so far as the text is concerned, R generally agrees with S, but its
text is in several instances superior, even though S may agree with T
and U. R has also adopted a number of the peculiar readings of v3; (cf.
θ1 and χ22, 30, 43, 48, 53, 56, 58, 62, 68, 100, 114, 126, 128, 129, 130,
133). Some of these involve omissions of words within the explanation,
but the majority are of such a nature as to preclude anything but direct
influence. It becomes, therefore, clear that R is a contaminated ms., i.e.,
it has combined the readings of two different strains of the tradition, one
represented by S, the other by v3. It is noteworthy that in the earlier part
of the Lexicon the scribe seems more reluctant to admit the v3 readings
and keeps the v3 glosses apart, whereas in the latter part he shows im-
partiality and even admits the shorter entries of v3 without supplementing them from S.

A third group consists of three mss., V, Va, and W. These share two
basic characteristics: a rearrangement of their entries to fit a stricter
alphabetic order, and a large amount of additional glosses not found in v.
Most of these additions are identical with glosses found in two mss. of the
g-recension to which Drachmann assigned the sigla Γ and Δ, i.e.,

Cryptensis $Z.\alpha$.V and Laurent. plut. 59.16. The new arrangement of the
glosses, based on the first three letters of the lemmata, has resulted in an
order which is not identical to that of TU.[76] This group is also distinguished for its occasional superior readings (cf. ξ40, χ1, 60, 67, 104, 147),
which however (in view of the extensive revision that it has undergone)
must not be genuine but are due either to emendation or to contamination.
Let me add that the additional glosses of V, Va, and W form a group also
found in U (as an appendix), as well as in $\mathbf{g}$1.

The dependence of Va on V is complete. Va's text, however, is considerably inferior to that of V because of omissions and errors. The number
of these blunders as well as an unexplained lacuna in the text of Va[77]
indicate that it is not a direct copy of V but is removed from it by at least
one intermediary.

The relationship of VW in the ξ- and χ-sections is unmistakable: cf.
especially ξ5, 37, χ12, 15, 22, 24, 38, 41, 45, etc. Both also have many
additional glosses. In the $\theta\alpha$-section, however, the two agree very rarely
and even then the agreement is not exclusive.[78] Besides, the additional
glosses which each of the two displays are entirely different. W's readings
as well as some of its additional glosses show a clear influence from an
outside source independent from V.[79] This source can be identified with
a distinct group within the $\mathbf{g}$-recension which consists of the following
mss.: Athens, Byz. Museum, No. 186, in its original or vellum part (see
above); Hauniensis 1970; Laurent. plut. 58.30; and Vindob. phil. gr.
319. Here are the most striking examples of the agreement: θ14 (add
$\dot{\alpha}\lambda\lambda\epsilon\pi\dot{\alpha}\lambda\lambda\eta\lambda\alpha$), additional gloss $\theta\alpha\rho\sigma\dot{\upsilon}\beta$, ξ33 (add $\kappa\omega\omega\hat{\omega}\nu$), χ54 ($\kappa\epsilon\chi\epsilon\iota\rho\iota\sigma\mu\dot{\epsilon}\nu\alpha$
for $\kappa\dot{\alpha}\kappa\iota\sigma\tau\alpha$), χ129 (add $\dot{\eta}$ $\delta\dot{\eta}\lambda\omega\sigma\iota\varsigma$) and additional gloss $\chi\rho o\dot{o}\varsigma$ $\ddot{\alpha}\delta\eta\nu$. In
many more cases the readings adopted by W independently from V are

---

[76] This is true for the ξ- and χ-sections. For the order of W in the $\theta\alpha$-section, cf. note
78 below.

[77] Va omits 70-odd entries between χ54 and 101 without apparent reason. Neither the
beginning nor the end of the lacuna coincide with the beginning or end of a page in V.
If Va was copying directly from V, the omission would not be due to a purely mechanical
error.

[78] The most striking is the reading $\dot{o}\rho\epsilon\gamma\dot{o}\mu\epsilon\nu o\varsigma$ (θ18), found also in OP. Neither ms.,
however, shows any of the striking separative errors of the other. Note also that the order
of the v-entries in this section is different in the two mss., that of W resembling closely
the order of TU.

[79] There is some external evidence to that from the cramming of some of the additional
glosses and the additions within the entries in the space between the text and the inner
margins which would otherwise be left blank. The outer margins also have numerous
additions. All these were probably due to the original scribe.

found in **g**, but they are not restricted to the above mss.: cf. θ7, 20, 23; ξ12 (om. γεγλυμμένον), 17, 36; χ30 (ἢ οἱ μικροὶ ῥύακες), 76, 94, 111, 121 (om. βήσσει οἶον), 127, 140, 143; also in listing ξ32, an entry absent from all **v**-mss. except **vi** but occurring in **g**. The manner in which W incorporates the new readings can be illustrated by the following examples. In χ96 it has adopted the **g**-reading (κόσμον περὶ τὸν βραχίωνα [sic]) and then added *supra lineam* ἢ τὸν τράχηλον, i.e., the part of the **v**-entry missing from **g**. In χ149 it introduces the **g**-reading at the end of the entry as a variant (ἀλλαχοῦ εἴωθαν προσχοῦν τὰ τείχη).[80] Because of the extent of outside influence[81] W's exact relationship to V cannot be determined.

For the convenience of reference as well as because the mss. R through W share a number of common features, I refer to them sometimes in the critical apparatus with the sign **v4**.

The remaining mss. (XYZΩ) are too fragmentary to allow (as of now) any judgement about their exact relationship to one another and to the other mss. of the recension. However, in the one section (of the three under consideration here) which they have in common,[82] they agree in omitting φόβος in θ11 and ἢ ἀποκτείνη in 18,[83] both of which are also omitted by **v3**.[84] Note also the spelling ὀρεγομένοις in θ18.

There is further agreement between YZ, shown by the omission of δέ in θ4[85] and of θαρσαλέως in θ20.[86] Furthermore, Y and Ω agree in error in reading θασσοῦ in θ25. Finally, X and Z agree in listing θ25 after θέα γάρ, the first entry of the θε-section.

Z is the best ms. of the group. It is also noteworthy for occasional interpolations from a ms. of what I call an unabridged version of Hesychius: perhaps the same ms. that provided the learned interpolations of **vi** (RS: additional gloss ξυμφορά), and of the three closely related mss. (which

---

80 The formula ἀλλαχοῦ is also found in χ147 and 136 (in the latter case ἀλλαχοῦ γρ.).

81 This is not restricted to one source only. Besides etymological additions (cf. θ7, χ5, 49, and in many marginal glosses which were clearly taken from the Lexicon of Pseudo–Zonaras), there are readings which are restricted to some **g**-mss. (especially Par. gr. 2617, which besides Cyrillus also contains Pseudo–Zonaras) but have no parallel in the four mss. listed above.

82 The χ-section is missing from three mss., while in the fourth (Ω) it has been replaced from another ms. XY also lack the ξ-section.

83 YΩ omit θ18 altogether.

84 Also by **g**, with the exception of a few mss. which have φόβος.

85 Ω omits the gloss altogether.

86 Also missing from **v3** Ω. X agrees here with RS in omitting θαρραλέως and making θαρσαλέως the lemma of the entry.

properly belong to the **g**-recension), Madrit. Bibl. Univ. Z-22 No. 116; Haun. 1968; and Messan. S. Salv. 167.[87]

X is also useful, despite omissions (θ2, 15, 21 and part of 22) and scribal errors, especially when in agreement with Z, serving as a check of the readings of the archetype, since both mss. (XZ) seem to branch out from near the top of the stemma (cf. below). Y despite its late age presents a better and fuller text than Ω, which is marred with omissions and arbitrary tampering with the text.[88]

A careful analysis of all variants of the mss. shows a consistent agreement of **v**1 and **v**2 (especially in the number and size of entries) as against **v**3, with the remaining or independent mss. splitting their allegiance between the two extremes. Indeed XYZΩ seem to side always against **v**1 **v**2, whenever the latter shows a "fuller" text as compared to that of **v**3 and **g**. This extends also to entries where **v**1 **v**2 find support for their longer entries in some of the independent mss. (cf. θ11, 18; ξ12, 13, 37). It is reasonable to assume that this agreement extended also to the χ-section (now missing from all of these four mss.), where the cases of disagreement between **v**1 **v**2, on the one hand, and **v**3, on the other, are more numerous.

The case of RSTUVVaW is more complicated. These mss. side with **v**1 **v**2 more often than not when these two groups disagree with **v**3 **g**.[89] It is not clear, however, whether these seven mss. emanated from one and the same source. RSTU have a number of common errors that may seem decisive in favor of a common exemplar, from which the progenitors of the pairs RS and TU were copied. Note especially the reading τρόφιμον (for τρίμορφον) in χ84[90] and χύδαιος (χ144), attested by all four mss. One may also add the following readings which, although confined to STU, may be considered as descending from the common source but avoided by R under the influence of its second exemplar: θαλαμίπολος (θ7), θασσοῦσαι (θ25), ξοῦθος (ξ15), χλαμύς for χλανίς (ξ25), χαλκίξ

---

[87] On the interpolation of these three mss., cf, my article (above, note 57).

[88] Thus Ω lists a number of θ-glosses before $\theta\alpha$, completely out of the alphabetical order; it often adds (in an unnecessary and often illogical manner) such trivial words as λέγει, γράφει, τίθεται, καί, simply for the sake of variation; it also joins unrelated entries into one long period; finally, it rephrases and adds outside matter in the entries.

[89] Cf. θ11, χ1, 14, 17, 18, 25, 33, 35, 41, 45, 155; cf. also ξ12, 37; χ30, 100, 107, 127, 128, 129, 133, 143, 144, where the addition is attested by all but one of the seven independent mss. (W).

[90] Other common errors are less decisive, because they are of an orthographic nature: cf. θ3 (θαλπορή), χ4 (κώμην), 35 (ῥαγδεοτέρως), etc.

(χ15), κυλώδεις (χ18), χθόϊνος (χ80). In the common traits one should also add the inclusion by RSU of the alphabetical *Homeric Lexicon*, published in part by V. de Marco,[91] which is unattested from elsewhere.

The view of a common exemplar is, however, confronted with a most serious objection: How to explain the presence in TU of some *additamenta* found also in v1 v2 but absent from RS v3 (and furthermore from **g**)?[92] Their absence from RS cannot be explained as accident,[93] because of their number and extent and because of the fact that some of these are found at the beginning or middle of the explanation. An examination of these *additamenta* shows that they originated from marginal or supralinear explanations added by the scribe or a subsequent reader of the archetype; cf. χαρίην for χαρίεσσαν (χ38), χερσὶν ἐργαζομένην for ἀπὸ χειρῶν ζῶσαν (χ60), ἄνωθεν καὶ κάτωθεν ἔμετος for ἔκκρισις διὰ στόματος καὶ γαστρός (χ109), βήσσει (actually written βίσσει) for ἦχον τῷ στόματι ἀποτελεῖ (χ121). The process of insertion of such marginal notes into the text can be seen at work in θ20, where the variant θαρσαλέως, absent from v3 YZΩ, has ousted the original reading θαρραλέως in RSX, but is listed side by side by v1 v2 TUVW; and furthermore in χ128, where the addition μαντευόμενα (omitted by v3 RW) appears before προλεγόμενα in v1 TUV but after it in v2 and S.[94] The omission of χ69 (omitted by v3 RSVW but attested by **g**), of χ72 (apparently a corrupt counterpart of χ71), and of χ156 with the unintelligible lemma χῶτα (for χρῶτα) may be deliberate. For accidental omissions cf. above, note 93.

All in all, the hypothesis of a common ancestor for RSTU is, I believe, more probable than a recourse to another split of the stemma, which would presuppose that the elimination of the common errors of RSTU further down in the stemma is due to emendation. A further comparison of the readings of VW with those of RSTU shows that they are close to TU, despite extensive correction helped by the use of a **g**-type ms. which served as a second exemplar (cf. above). For all these reasons I have assigned a special siglum (**v4**) to all these mss.

---

91 *Op. cit.* (above, note 33).

92 Cf. χ35 (καὶ χάσμα), 38 (χαρίην), 60 (χερσὶν ἐργαζομένην), 72 (entire gloss, omitted by T), 81 (τρίψημα—φρυττόμενος), 109 (ἄνωθεν—ἤτουν), 121 (βήσσει, οἷον), 156 (entire gloss).

93 Accident, however, cannot be altogether excluded; compare the omission of ἔνοπλοι in ξ14 by TU; the omission of θ18 by RS, and quite possibly of the word θαλάσσιον in χ35.

94 Cf. also χ60 (πενιχράν) and 139 (χρυσόφορα).

The final stemma of the family can therefore be drawn as follows:

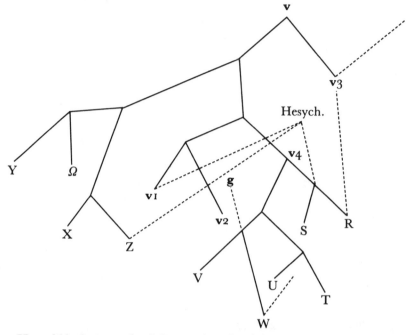

How old is the recension? On purely palaeographical grounds it must be older than 1000 A.D., since some of our mss. (especially S) can be dated around that year. I should like to suggest that the exact date is fixed by a reference to the year 876, incorporated into a treatise of how to compute the cycles of the sun and moon and preserved in the vi-mss. and in J.[95] This evidence is corroborated by the acrostic of a short epigram which refers to the reign of Basil, undoubtedly Basil I the Macedonian.[96] Both the epigram and the reference to the year 876 were transmitted to the various descendants of **v** together with the minor lexica and other material following, and in a way supplementing, the Lexicon and thus forming a corpus, as it were, which can be called the Cyrillean corpus. Since both the reference to the year 876 and that to the emperor Basil are not found among the minor lexica of the other extant recensions, we may safely, I believe, consider them as indicating the date of the formation of the **v**-recension.

---

[95] Cf. my articles cited above (notes 3, 17), and *Rhet. Lex.*, 25–27.

[96] This epigram in nine dodecasyllables with the quadruple acrostic, 'Ἐν θεοῦ νῦν | ὁ βασιλεὺς | βασιλεύει | βασίλειος, was published by G. S. Mercati in *Studi Bizantini e Neoellenici* 3, 1931, 294 f. Mercati was not sure, however, whether the epigram referred to Basil I or Basil II, but would prefer the former.

APPENDIX: THE TEXT

The text of the sections on which the present study was based is given below not in its pure form, i.e., in the form in which it presumably appeared in the lost archetype of the recension, but with all subsequent accretions as reflected in the text of vi.[97] In order to distinguish, however, the original from the extraneous matter, I have employed square brackets for the latter. Corrupt readings have been retained in the text (unless corrected in some of our mss.), whenever it was felt that this was the reading of the archetype. Some of them have parallels in **g** or other recensions. In a critical edition, however, these should be eliminated: here they merely illustrate the state of the archetype.

For similar reasons, the critical apparatus is not confined to important or true variants, but has been expanded to include all variant readings, even trivial ones, so far as they illustrate the relationship of the mss. and their families, regardless of their value for the recovery of the "original" text. Accordingly, this is not a *specimen editionis* but an appendix or supplement to the preceding discussion. Certain restrictions, however, have been set, in order to eliminate the obvious or insignificant. Thus spelling errors have not been listed for the most part, especially when occurring in secondary mss. If they are widespread but of no significance for the relationships of the mss., they have been listed with the indication *nonnulli* without further specification. All readings of Ba, Ka, Q, Va, Φa, Φb and the extravaganzas of Ω have been eliminated entirely for obvious reasons. The readings of I (and of Λ in the ξ- and χ-sections) have not been recorded for lack of collations. Parentheses have been used to indicate that the reading of a ms. is not entirely identical with the reading recorded but either presuppose it or has been derived from it.

University of Illinois at Urbana

APPENDIX

Ἀρχὴ τοῦ θ στοιχείου

1. θάκων: θρόνων, καθεδρῶν
2. θάκοις: θρόνοις

Codd.: BCFGHJKLMNOPRSTVWXYZΓΔΘΛΞΠΣΦΩ (Ba, Ka, Q, Va, Φa, Φb lectiones omisi)
1. Glossam om. Ω   θώκων O R   θάκων καὶ θώκων v3 R   καθέδρων nonnulli
2. Glossam om. X Y Ω   θώκοις O P

[97] However, all additional glosses of individual mss. or subgroups, as well as the etymological glosses of v3, have been entirely omitted.

122   Illinois Classical Studies, IV

3. θαλπωρή: χαρά, διάχυσις, θάλψις
4. θαλλός: πᾶν τὸ θάλλον· κυρίως δὲ ὁ κλάδος τῆς ἐλαίας
5. θάλψαι: περισκεπάσαι, συντηρῆσαι, θερμᾶναι
6. θαλυσίαι: αἱ τῶν καρπῶν ἀπαρχαί
7. θαλαμηπόλος: ὁ περὶ τὸν θάλαμον ἀναστρεφόμενος
8. θαλαττοπορεῖ: πλέει διὰ θαλάττης
9. θαλία: εὐωχία, τέρψις
10. θαλερόν: ἀκμαῖον, νεώτατον
11. θάμβος: [φόβος,] ἔκπληξις, θόρυβος
12. θάμνος: ξύλον ἀκανθῶδες, λέγεται δὲ βάτος
13. θαμά: συνεχῶς, πυκνῶς, διηνεκῶς
14. θαμινά: πυκνά
15. θαϊτή: θαυμαστή
16. θαμίζει: πυκνάζει, συνεχῶς ἔχει
17. θανατῶν: θανάτου ἐπιθυμῶν· λέγεται δὲ καὶ ὁ ἀποκτένων
18. θανατῶσι: θανάτου ὀρεγομένοις [ἢ ἀποκτείνει]
19. θάνοιεν: ἀποθάνοιεν
20. θαρραλέως: [θαρσαλέως,] ἀνδρείως, εὐθαρσῶς
21. θάρρος: θάρσος

3. Glossam om. Ω   θαλπορή vι (N) R S (T) U X, θαλπωροί Γ   θάλψις om. J K L
θάλπος pro θάλψις M
4. Glossam om. Ω   θαλλός O P V Y Ω: θάλλος cett.   θάλπος ante θάλλος add.
J K L   δέ om. U V Y Z   ὁ τῆς ἐλαίας κλάδος v3
5. περισκεπᾶσαι nonnulli   συντηρήσαι nonnulli, συντηρίσαι B S Γ   θερμᾶναι om. U,
θερμάναι compl.   θερμᾶναι ante περισκεπάσαι v3, ante συντηρῆσαι V
6. Gloss. om. X Γ   θαλύσιαι S Y Δ Λ Ξ Σ Ω, θαλήσιαι vι v2 T
7. θαλαμιπόλος vι R Z, θαλαμίπολος (S) (T) U   ὁ om.B   ἀνατρεφόμενος vι   καὶ
φυλάττων. εἴρηται δὲ παρὰ τὸ θάλειν ἅμα add. W
8. θαλάττεις C F H T, θαλάσσης Λ Π Σ
9. θάλια vι Z   εὐοχία vι
10. θαλαιρόν v3 (exc. Σ)   νεότατον (νεήτατον Σ) vι v3 (exc. Π)
11. Gloss. om. vι Λ   φόβος om. v3 X Y Z Ω
12. ἀκανθόδες vι N   λέγεται δὲ (καὶ add. v3) βάτος v3 V: ὁ λέγεται βάτος cett.
13. θαμᾶ v22 T W Y Ω, θάμα S U Z, θαῦμα vι   πυκνῶς ante συνεχῶς V
14. ἀλλεπάλληλα add. W
15. Gloss. om. X Λ   leg. θαητή
16. Gloss. om. Φ Ω   θαμάζει (O) P   ἄγει (λέγει Σ) pro ἔχει v3
17. Gloss. om. v3 Ω   ὁ om J T   ἀποκτενῶν M T, ἀποκταίνων S W, ἀποκτείνων L
18. Gloss. om. L R S T Y Π Φ Ω   ὀρεγομένοις X Z, ὀρεγόμενος O P V W   ἢ
ἀποκτείνει om. v3 X Z, ἀποκτείνη U V W, ἀποκτείνουσι (J) O P
19. Gloss. om. Ω
20. Gloss. om. vι   θαρράλέως om. R S X   θαρσαλέως om. v3 W V Z Ω   εὐθάρσως
nonnulli   εὐθάρσως ante ἀνδρείως W
21. Gloss. om. vι X   θαρσαλέως pro θάρσος v3

Mark Naoumides 123

22. θᾶσσον: θᾶττον, τουτέστιν ταχέως
23. θάτερον: ἑκάτερον, τὸ ἓν τῶν δύο
24. θάτερον θατέρου: ἕτερον ἑτέρου
25. θάσσουσαι: σπεύδουσαι

---

22. θᾶσσον nonnulli   θᾶττον nonnulli, θάττοντες B G   τουτέστιν om. L R S V, τουτέστι v2 X Y   ταχέως om. V   καὶ ταχύτερον add. v3
23. Gloss. om. v2   ἑκάτερον nonnulli   ἢ ἓν pro τὸ ἕν v3, τὸ ἕτερον W
24. Gloss. om. Y Ω   θάτερον bis B G   θάτερον θατέρου F   τῶν δύο τὸ ἕν add. R S
25. θασσοῦσαι S (T) U, θασσοῦ Y Ω. θαροῦσαι (-σα B G) v1   σπεύδουσα B G

Ἀρχὴ τοῦ ξ στοιχείου

1. ξαίνω: νήθω, σωρεύω
2. ξανθήν: πυρρόειδῆ
3. ξανθίζεσθαι: κοσμεῖσθαι τὰς τρίχας
4. ξενοσύνην: ξένην φιλίαν
5. ξεῖνοι: οἱ ἀπὸ ξένης φίλοι
6. ξεναγῶν: ὁ τοὺς ξένους ἄγων, ὁδηγῶν, ξενοδοχῶν
7. ξεῖνον: φίλον
[8. ξέσας: γράψας]
9. ξενίαν: καταγώγιον, κατάλυμα
10. ξενίζουσαν: ἀλλόφυλον, ἀήθη
[11. ξέοντας: μαστίζοντας]
12. ξεστόν: ὡμαλισμένον, [γεγλυμμένον]
13. ξιφήρεις: ξιφηφοροῦντες, [ἔνοπλοι]

Codd.: BCFGHJKLMNOPRSTUVWZΓΔΘΞΠΣΦΩ; XY carent (Ba, Ka, Q, Va, Λ
Φa, Φb omisi)
1. νήσω (νοήσω Σ) v3
2. πυρροειδή v1 R S Z Ω, πυροειδή v2 (T) U, πυρροηδή v31 Ξ Φ
4. ξενωσύνην L V W
5. ξεινοί v1 v2 R S T U   οἱ ἀπὸ ξένοις v1 J, οἱ ἀπὸ ξενίας V W
6. ξενάγων Ξ Π Σ Φ, ξεάγων Γ Δ Θ
7. Gloss. om. Θ   ξεῖνον B G N P S Γ, ξείνων C F H, ξεινόν U Δ   φίλων F H,
φιλόν U
8. Gloss. om. codd. exc. v1 Z
9. Gloss. om. Ω
10. ξενίζουσα Γ Π (Ω)   ἀλλόφυλλον v1, ἀλλόφιλον J (N) P W   ἀηθή F H R Δ Θ Ξ
11. Gloss. om. codd. exc. v1 v2
12. ξεστῶν U   ὁμαλισμένον (vel ὁμ.) nonnulli   γεγλυμμένον om. v3 W Z Ω
13. ξιφήροι O P   ξιφειφοροῦντες v1, ξιφηφοροῦντας v3   ἔνοπλοι om. v3 T U Z Ω

14. ξόανον: ἄγαλμα, εἴδωλον, ζώδιον, ἀνδριάς
15. ξουθός: ξανθός
16. ξουθά: ξανθά
17. ξύει: γράφει· ὅθεν καὶ ξύσματα τὰ γράμματα
18. ξυλιζομένη: ξύλα συλλέγουσα
19. ξύμμαχοι: σύμμαχοι
20. ξυνωρίς: συνωρίς, ζυγή
21. ξυμβαίνει: συμβαίνει
22. ξυνθήματος: σημείου
23. ξύνιον: ξένιον
[24. ξυνεχῶς: συνεχῶς]
25. ξύστρα: χλανίς
26. ξυνιέναι: συνιέναι, νοῆσαι
27. ξυνουσία: συνουσία, μίξις
28. ξυνεχῶς: συνεχῶς, διὰ παντός
29. ξυναρμόσας: συναρμόσας, συνάψας
30. ξυνωρίδα: ἅρμα ἐκ δύο ἵππων συνεζευγμένων
31. ξυνωρίδα: ζυγήν· κυρίως δὲ ἐπὶ τῶν ἡμιόνων. ὀρεὺς γὰρ ὁ ἡμίονος
[32. ξύνορον: κοινωνόν]

---

14. Gloss. om. v3   ζωδίον F H R S U, ζοδίον B C G N   ἀνδρίας N Oª·¹· P, ἀνδρειάς vı
S (T) V
15. Gloss. om. K L W Ω   ξοῦθος S T U Z, ξούθος O P, ξανθός pro ξουθός Kᵐ Δ
16. Gloss. om. T Ω   lemma om. Π   ξουθᾶ vı N S Γ, ξοῦθα Z, ξουσθά O P
17. Gloss. om. T   ξύφει (Ξ) (Π) Σ Φ   γράφη vı Kᵃᶜ N Z Π   ὡς παρ' Ὁμείρω post
γράφει add. W   ξύσματα γὰρ τὰ (γὰρ τὰ om. Γ) γράμματα v3
18. ξυληζομένη vı
19. Gloss. om. Ω   ξυμμαχοί: συμμαχοί vı M, ξυμμαχοῖ: συμμαχοῖ J K S T, ξυμμαχεῖ:
συμμαχεῖ v22 K L
20. Gloss. om. v32 R T U Z Ω (cum 31 iunx. T U)   ξυνορίς vı   συνωρίς om. v31,
συνορίς vı T   συζυγῇ U
21. ξυμβαίνει v2 (exc. Ka O)
22. Gloss. om. V
23. ξύνειον vı v2. ξείνιον V   ξένειον v2
24. Gloss. om. codd. exc. vı
25. ξύστρα vı V Ω: ξύτρα cett.   χλαμύς S (T) U   leg. ξυστίδα: χλανίδα
27. Gloss. om. Ω   συνουσία om. K, συνοσία B G
28. Gloss. om. Ω
29. Gloss. om. Ω   ξυναρμώσας: συναρμώσας nonnulli   συνάψας ante συναρμ. J K L Z
30. ξυνωρίς Ω   ἅρμα nonnulli   συνεζεγμένων B Cᵃᶜ G, συνεζευγμένον v2 (exc. N) v3
(exc. Σ) S
31. Gloss. om.K N, cum. praec. conf. (lemmate om.) vı V W   ἱμιόνων (vel ἱμ.) vı
ὀρεύς nonnulli   ἱμίονος (vel ἱμ.) vı
32. Gloss. om. codd. exc. vı Wᵐ

33. ξυνών: συνών
34. ξυστίδας: περιβόλαια
35. ξυνάορον: γαμετήν
36. ξυμπονῆσαι: συμπονῆσαι
37. ξύνια: κοινὰ πράγματα [ἢ χρήματα]
38. ξύνε: σύνες, ἄκουσον
39. ξυνθήματος: συνθήματος· ἔστι δὲ σημεῖον ἢ πρόσφθεγμα διδόμενον ἐπὶ
    γνωρισμῷ τῶν οἰκείων ἐν πολέμῳ ἢ ἑτέρᾳ τινὶ ἐπιβουλῇ
40. ξυνῳδά: συνῳδά
41. ξύνθακος: συγκάθεδρος
42. ξυνοδόκος: ξενοδόχος
[43. ξύστρα: ⟨χ⟩λανίς]
44. ξυστίδα: λεπτὸν ὕφασμα [ἢ περιβόλαιον]
45. ξυσμός: κνησμός
46. ξυστός: τόπος ἀνειμένος ἀθλητῶν
47. 'ξῶθεν: ἔξωθεν

33. Gloss. om. v22 Ω   ξυνῶν: συνῶν nonnulli   κυνῶν pro συνῶν v3   κοινῶν add. W
35. ξυνούσιον S T
36. Gloss. om. K T   ξυμπονῆσαι: συμπονῆσαι nonnulli   συνάρασθαι add. W
37. ξυνία V W; leg. ξυνῆϊα   ἢ χρήματα om. v3 R Z Ω
38. Gloss. om. v3
39. σύνθημα ante σημεῖον add. v2   σημείαν B C G   διδόμενος Δ Θ   ἕτερα B G Z Π
    τινί om. v2   ἐπιβουλή nonnulli, ἐπιβουλεῖ v1
40. ξυνῳδά O P V W: ξυνοδά L, ξυνώδια Z, ξύνωδα cett.   συνῳδά O P V W: σύνοδα L,
    συνώδια Z, σύνωδα (σύνοδα J S) cett.
41. Gloss. om. v22   συνκάθεδρος nonnulli
42. Gloss. om. W   ξυνοδοκός v1 J Kᵃᶜ M, ξενοδόκος V, ξυνοθόκος Wᵐ Ω
43. Gloss. om. codd. exc. v1   λανίς F H, λανής B C G
44. Gloss. cum praec. conf. lemmate omisso F H   ἢ περιβόλαιον om. codd. exc. v1 v2
45. κνισμός v2 (exc. J L) R V W, κνυσμός J   ἔξωθεν add. Γ
46. ἀνειμένον v1   ἀφορισμένος pro ἀνειμένος v3   ἀθλιτῶν C Gᵃᶜ
47. ξώθεν v1 K N Z, ξωθέν (ξενωθέν Σ) v3 V W   ἔξω v2 (exc. K) Ω

Ἀρχὴ τοῦ χ̄ στοιχείου

[1. χάδεν: ἐχώρησεν ἢ μετέσχεν]
2. χάζετο: ἀνεχώρει

Codd.: BCFGHJKLMNOPRSTUVWΓΔΠΣΦ (Ba, Ka, Q, Va, Λ, Φα, Φb omisi; non
habent XYZ(Ω)ΘΞ)
1. Gloss. om. v3   χάδεν O P V W: χαδέν cett.   ἐχώρισεν R S U
2. ἀναχωρίσειεν R

126   Illinois Classical Studies, IV

3. χάζεο: ἀναχώρει
4. χαίτην: τὴν κόμην τῶν τριχῶν
5. χάζεο τῆλε: ἀναχώρει μακράν
[6. Χαιρουβίμ: πλῆθος γνώσεως ἢ σοφίας]
7. χαζομένῳ: ἀναχωροῦντι
8. χαίρειν φράσαντες: ἀποταξάμενοι, καταγνόντες
9. χαίρετε: θαρρεῖτε
10. χαλεπήνας: ἀγανακτήσας
[11. χαλεπώτερος: δυσκολώτερος]
12. χάλεσι: τοῖς ὄνυξι
13. χαλκεομήστωρ: ἰσχυρόφωνος
14. χαλέπτει: κακίζει, [καταπονεῖ]
15. χαλκίς: ἡ γλαῦξ· εἶδος ὀρνέου
16. χαλκοκορυστήν: χαλκῷ ὁπλιζόμενον ἢ κράνος ἔχοντα χαλκοῦν
17. χαλεπῶς: δυσκόλως, [δυσχερῶς, κακῶς]
18. χαμαίζηλοι: [ταπεινόφρονες,] ταπεινοί· ἢ δίφροι κοιλώδεις [ἢ οἱ τὰ γήϊνα
       φρονοῦντες]
[19. χαμευνά: ἡ ἐπὶ γῆς κατάκλισις· καὶ τὸ ταπεινὸν κλινίδιον χαμευνή,
       Σοφοκλῆς Δόλοψι]
20. χαμαιεύνης: χαμόκοιτος
21. χαμαιπετεῖ: ταπεινῷ ἢ χαμαὶ κειμένῳ

---

3. Gloss. om. T   χάζετο U Ξ   ἀναχωρεῖ vi U
4. κώμην O P R S (T) U
5. χαζεύτηλε N R S (T) (U), χαζεοτῆλαι vi   τῆλε γὰρ τὰ μακρὰν add. W
6. Gloss. habet vi: cett. om.
7. Gloss. om. Σ   χαζωμένω C F H, χαζώμενος B G
8. καταγνῶντες vi (J) (K) N R S T U, ἀπογνόντες V, ἀπογνῶντες (ἀπογνῶναι Φ) v3 W
9. χαίρεται vi T, χαίροντες Δ   θαρρεῖται vi (N) S T
10. Gloss. om. T   χαλαιπήνας vi R Γ Δ Σ
11. Gloss. hab. vi v2: cett. om.   χαλαιπότερος vi   δυσκολότερος vi
12. χαλῆσιν V W, χαλέσι M: leg. χαλαῖσι   τοῖς om. V W Π
14. Gloss. om. v22   χαλέπτεις Δ   καταπονεῖ om. v3
15. χαλκίξ S T U, χαλκής vi   γλαύξ nonnulli, γλάξ F H, γλαῦς J K Γ   εἶδος ὀρνέου
    ante ἡ γλαῦξ V W
16. χαλκοῦ Γ Δ, χαλεπῶ Dᵃᶜ J M, χαλεπῶς v22 K L   ἔχωντα C F H Π, ἔχων v2 (exc. L)
17. χαλαιπῶς R   δυσχερῶς κακῶς om. v3
18. χαμέζηλοι vi R S   ταπεινόφρονες om. v3   διφροκοιλώδεις vi κοιλώδης N Rᶜ Wᵃᶜ Γ,
    κυλώδεις U, κυκλώδεις S, κυλῶδες T   ἢ—φρονοῦντες om. v3
19. Gloss. hab. vi: cett. om.   χαμευνά codd.   κατάκλησις codd. exc. C   κλινήδι
    codd. χαμευνῆ codd.   σοφοκλεῖς codd.   δολάψει (ὁλάψει F H) codd.
20. χαμαίευνῆς Γ, χαμεύνης v3 (exc. Γ), χαμευνῆς S T (U)   χαμόκοιτος vi, χαμαίκοιτος
    v3 (exc. Γ), χαμαικοίτης V W Γ
21. ταπεινῶν T Γ Δ, ταπεινῶς L   κειμένων K (Γ) Δ, κεῖται L

22. χαμαιτυπιῶν: τῶν πολυκοίτων συνουσιῶν
23. χαμεταιρίς: πόρνη
24. χαμαιτύπη: πόρνη ἄδοξος
25. χανδόν: [ἠνοιγμένως,] ἀπλήστως, ἀθρόως, χωρητικῶς
26. χανδὸν πιεῖν: κεχηνότως καὶ ἀθρόως πιεῖν
27. χαρακτηρίζει: διὰ τῶν αὐτῶν χαρακτήρων σημαίνει
28. χάρακες: ἄκανθαι καὶ κάλαμοι
29. χαράβδη: λύμη σίτου
30. χαράδραι: αἱ ὑδρορρόαι· [χείμαρροι, διαιρέσεις, σχίσματα, ῥήγματα γῆς·]
     οἱ μικροὶ ῥύακες
[31. χαῖος: ὃ δηλοῖ τὴν ῥάβδον]
[32. χαράδραν: τὸν χείμαρρον]
33. χάρακα: χαράκωμα, περίφραγμα, [ὑποστήριγμα]
34. χαρωπός: ἐπιχαρής, εὐόφθαλμος
35. Χάρυβδις: [θηρίον ἀναρροφοῦν τὴν θάλασσαν· καὶ] ἡ ἀναπινομένη θάλασσα
     περὶ τὰ Γάδειρα καὶ πάλιν ῥαγδαιοτέρως ἐπαναστρέφουσα· εἴρηται δὲ
     [καὶ χάσμα θαλάσσιον ἴλιγξ] καὶ πᾶν τὸ εἰς χάος καὶ ὄλεθρον κατασπῶν

22. τῶν πολὺ μετεχόντων τῶν συνουσιῶν pro τῶν πολυκ. συν. v3 R   πολυκύτων T U,
πολυκοίνων V W
23. χαμαιτερίς v22, χαμαιτερής S T, χαμαιταιρίς vi v3 J R Uᵐ Vᵃᶜ (W), χαμαιτεταιρίς
K L (M)
24. Gloss. om. v3 (exc. ΓΔ)   χαμαιτύπει C F G H, χαμαιτυπή (R) T ΓΔ, χαμαιτυπής
S U, χαμαιτυπίς V W   ἢ ἄδοξος R
25. χάνδον vi K M N S T U   ἠνοιγμένως om. v3, ἠνυγμένως vi R S T U   ἀθρῶς vi,
ἀθλίως pro ἀθρόως v2   χωριτικῶς J O R T, χωρηστικῶς B C G, χωριστικῶς F H
26. χάνδον ποιεῖν nonnulli   πολύ ante κεχηνότως add. v2 R S T U V W   κεχυνότως
F H, κεχυνότος B C G   ποιεῖν vi ΓΣ   εἰπεῖν pro πιεῖν v22 J, εἰς πεῖναν K L
27. αὐτῶν om. v22
28. ἄκανθαι v2 B Π: ἀκάνθαι cett.
29. λοίμη vi   φθορά pro λύμη R
30. χάραδραι vi N   ὑδορόαι vi J K M N, ὑδρορ(ρ)οαί R S (T) U V (W), ὑδρορίαι v3
χείμαρροι ante ὑδρ. S   καὶ τὰ κοιλώματα (κυλ.) pro χείμαρροι—γῆς v3 R W   διαιρέσεις—γῆς om. S, σχίσματα—γῆς om. T U V   ῥύγματα vi   ἢ οἱ μικροὶ ῥύακες W,
ἢ μικρὰ ῥύακια T
31. Gloss. hab. vi: cett. om.   χαιός codd.   δηλοί codd. exc. B
32. Gloss. hab. vi v2 (exc. L): cett. om.   χάραδραν vi
33. χαράκομα vi sᵃᶜ Ξ   ὑποστήριγμα om. v3
34. χαροπός vi T W   ἐπιχαρίς vi, περιχαρίς O (P)
35. Χάρυβδις L O S U: Χαρύβδης vel Χαρύβδης cett.   θηρίον—θάλασσαν καί om. v3
ἀναρ(ρ)οφῶν L O P V W, ἀναροφῶν C F H (J) (K) (M) N (T) (U), ἀναρύφων B G R (S)
γάδηρα R, γαδέρα vi   ῥαγδαιότερος (-ρον B) vi, ῥαγδεοτέρως R S T U, ῥαγδεωτέρως
V W   ἀναστρέφουσα R   καὶ χάσμα—ἴλιγξ om. v3   θαλάσσιον ἴλιγξ om. R S   ἴλιγξ
scripsi: ἴλυγξ V W, ἦλιξ vi v2, ἠλύξ T U   καὶ ὄλεθρον om. v3   κατασπῶν J K (M)

128   Illinois Classical Studies, IV

[36. χαρίεσσαν: χαριεστάτην, τερπνήν]
37. χαρία: βουνός, σωρός
38. χαρίεσσαν: [χαρίην,] χαριεστάτην, τερπνήν
39. χαρείη: τερφθείη, εὐφρανθείη
40. χαριστήρια: εὐχαὶ ἐπινίκιοι εὐχαριστίαν ἔχουσαι
41. χάσμα: σχίσμα, χάος, [στόμα ἀνεῳγμένον]
42. χαυῶνας: ἄρτους ἀναφυραθέντας κριθίνους ἢ λάγανα ὀπτά
43. Χερουβίμ: πλῆθος γνώσεως ἢ σοφίας χύσιν
44. χειρόηθες: πρᾷον, ἥμερον
45. χειρόκμητα: [χειροποίητα,] ὑπὸ χειρῶν γεγλυμμένα ἢ περιεξεσμένα ἢ κατειργασμένα
46. χειροτονία: ἐκλογὴ παντὸς δήμου [καὶ πάντων κύρωσις]
47. χειρώσασθαι: ὑποτάξαι
48. χειαί: αἱ καταδύσεις τῶν ὄφεων καὶ φωλεοί
49. χειρόμακτρον: ὃ παρὰ Ῥωμαίοις καλεῖται μανδήλιον
50. χειρόγραφον: συμβόλαιον, γραμμάτιον χρέους ὁμολογητικόν
51. χεῖρε: τὰς χεῖρας δυϊκῶς
52. χειρῶναξ: τεχνίτης
53. χείμεθλον: τὸ ἐν χειμῶνι γινόμενον ἐν ταῖς ῥωξὶ τῶν δακτύλων τῶν ποδῶν ἕλκος

---

36. Gloss. hab. vɪ v2: cett. om.   lemma om. M, χαρίεσαν Ο Ρ, χαρίεσα L, χάριες cett.
37. χάρια vɪ, χαριά Ρ V W
38. Gloss. om. L   χαρίεσαν nonnulli   χαρίην om. v3 R S, post τερπνήν hab. B C G χαρίεντα pro χαρίην V W
39. χαρίει v3 N, χαρίην Τ
40. ἐπινικίοις v3   εὐχαριστείαν vɪ (J) (Κ) S W, εὐχαριστηρίαν v3
41. χοός pro χάος V W   στόμα ἀνεωγμένον om. v3
42. χαυόνας (vel χαύονας) v3 R   ἀναφυρθέντας v3   λάχανα nonnulli
43. Glos. om. V W   Χαιρουβίμ Γ Δ Φ   ἐπὶ ἑνικοῦ δίφθογγον, ἐπὶ δὲ πληθυντικοῦ διὰ τοῦ ῑ ἔστι δέ ante πλῆθος add. v32   ἢ χύσις σοφίας v3 R   χάρις pro χύσιν v2
44. χειροηθές Γ Ξ Φ, χαροηθές Δ, χειροβοηθές Σ, χειροήθεσον Π   ἥμερον nonnulli
45. χειρότμητα V W   χειροποίητα om. v3   κατηργασμένα vɪ N Ρ W
46. χειροτονεία vɪ Μ   ἐγκλογή vɪ (exc. Β)   τοῦ δήμου R S   καὶ—κύρωσις hab. vɪ v2: cett. om.   κυρίωσις vɪ
48. χέα καὶ χειαί v3 R   ἡ κατάδυσις vɪ   καί om. v3   φωλαιοί S (Τ) U, φολεοί vɪ v3 (exc. Σ) Μ Ν, φολαιοί R
49. χειρόμακτον vɪ Τ W   ὃ ρωμαῖοι μανδείλιον λέγουσιν v3   μανδείλιον R S T, μανδίλιον B C G V, μανδήλιο(ς) U   διὰ τὸ ἐκμάσσειν τὴν ὕλην add. W
50. συμβόλεον vɪ Τ U   γραμματείον v3 R V W, γραμμάτειον Μ
51. Gloss. om. L Π   χεῖραι vɪ, (N) T (Γ) Δ Ξ   χείρας nonnulli
52. χειρώναξ vel χειρόναξ codd.   χαλκεύς add. v32
53. τῶ (τό v32) ἐν τῶ χειμῶνι v3 v22 R   γενόμενον v3 R   ἐν om. Ο Ρ   τῶ ῥωξί vɪ v2 ῥοξί vɪ Π   τῶν δακτύλων om. v3 R   τοῦ ποδός Ο Ρ   ἢ ἀποκαύματα post ἕλκος add. v3 R

54. χείριστα: δεινά, κάκιστα
55. χείριστον: χείρονα
56. χεδροπόν: ὄσπριον
57. χέλυς: κιθάρα
58. χελωνίδος: τοῦ ἄδου τῆς θύρας
59. χερμάδος: λίθου πληροῦντος τὴν χεῖρα
60. χερνῆτιν: πενιχράν, [χερσὶν ἐργαζομένην,] ἀπὸ χειρῶν ζῶσαν, [ἐριουργόν]
61. χείμαρροι: ῥύακες, ποταμοί
62. χερρονησία γῆ: ἡ εἰς θάλασσαν ἐκνεύουσα, ἡ μήτε χέρσος μήτε θάλασσα, ἀλλὰ περικλυζομένη καὶ μίαν ἔχουσα διέξοδον
63. χερσία: ἐρημία
64. χεῦμα: ῥεῦμα
65. χέρσῳ: γῆ
66. χεύματι: προχοῇ· ἡ ἐκ δεξιῶν καὶ ἀριστερῶν ἔχουσα θάλασσαν
[67. χηλή: ὁ διῃρημένος ὄνυξ τοῦ βοός]
68. χηλή: ὁπλή, ὄνυξ βοὸς καὶ προβάτου καὶ αἰγός· λέγεται δὲ καὶ τὰ τῶν θαλασσίων καρκίνων στόματα χηλαί
69. χηλή: ὄνυξ κτήνους

---

54. χείριστρα v1   χείρονα post κάκιστα add. V, κεχειρισμένα pro κάκιστα W
55. Gloss. om. V W   χείριστον F H, χειρίστρον B C G   χείρωνα v1 S Γ
56. χέδροπον S T U   χέδροπον καὶ χέδροψ (χέρδοψ R) v3 R   τὰ ὄσπρια v3
57. Gloss. om. Φ   χέλυς V: χέλις vel χελίς cett.   ἡ κιθάρα R
58. Gloss. om. Φ   χελώνιδος v1 R S, χελονίδας v3   ἄδου vel ἄδου codd.; leg. οὐδοῦ
τὰς θύρας v3 R T   τῆς θύρας τοῦ ᾄδου L
59. Gloss. om Φ   χείρα nonnulli
60. χερνῆτιν V W: χερνήτην Σ, χερνίτιν U Δ, χερνίτην cett.   πενιχράν om. R S, in finem
trans. v3   χερσὶν ἐργαζ. om. v3 R S   ἐριουργῶν N R, ἐριουργός T   χεῖραν
γερδίαν pro ἐριουργόν v3
61. Gloss. om. v32   ἢ τράγοι (cf. gl. 85) post ποταμοί add. T U, χειμέριοι post ποταμοί
add. V
62. χερονησία v1 v2 R S T U   χερονῶσία Φ, χερονωησία Ξ Π   εἰς θάλ. (om. ἡ)   v1 μήτε
χέρσος (om. ἡ) B U   μὴ ἀνέχουσα v1   διέξοδον (ἔξοδον Σ)   ἔχουσα v3 R
64. χεῦμα: ῥεύμα v1 N Γ
65. χέρσος: γῆ V W
66. χεύματι U: χεύμασι cett.   προχοῇ cum lemm. nonnulli   προχοαί Δ, προχοῆς V W
ἡ ante εἰς θ. om. P V W Γ
67. Gloss. om. v1 v3, cum sequ. conf. v2   χηλή V W: χήλη cett.
68. χηλή D Mᶜ V v32: χειλή R Γ, χήλη cett.   ὁ διῃρημένος ὄνυξ τοῦ βοός (cf. gl. 67) ἢ
ante ὁπλή add. v2   ἡ ὁπλή v1, ὁπλή nonnulli   καὶ αἰγός om. v3 R   καί ante τά
om . Γ   τά om. v22 Δ, ἢ pro τά v1   θαλαττείων v1 T   τὰ στόματα v22   χειλαί
R T Γ Δ
69. Gloss. om. v3 R S V W   χήλη M. leg. χηλή

70. χηραμοί: οἱ φωλεοὶ τῶν θηρίων, αἱ καταδύσεις τῶν ὄφεων
71. χηρώσας: χήραν ἐάσας
[72. χηρῶς: χηρείαν ἐάσας]
73. χθαμαλός: [χαμηλός,] ταπεινός, ὁμαλός, ἴσος
74. χθαμαλοῖς: [ταπεινοῖς,] χαμηλοῖς
75. χθαμαλόν: ἀσθενές
76. χθιζοί: χθεσινοί
77. χθονός: γῆς
78. χθονίοις: γηΐνοις
79. χθιζός: χθεσινός
80. χθόνιος: γήινος
81. χίδρα: [τρίψημα, σῖτος νέος φρυττόμενος,] στάχυς νεογενής· ἢ τὰ ἐξ
    ὀσπρίων ἄλευρα [ἢ καὶ αὐτὰ τὰ ὄσπρια]
82. χίδρα ἐρικτά: ἐκ κριθῆς νέας ὡς σεμίδαλις
83. χιλός: τροφὴ ἵππων
84. Χίμαιρα: τὸ τρίμορφον θηρίον ἐνταῦθα δηλοῖ, ὅπερ ἐν τῇ Λυκίᾳ ὑπῆρχεν

---

70. χήραμος: ὁ φωλεὸς τοῦ ὄφεως (tantum!) v3   φολεοί vi, φωλαιοί N R S T U V   τῶν
θηρίων, αἱ καταδύσεις om. R
71. Gloss. om. v2 v3 R   χηράσας V W
72. Gloss. om. v3 J K L R S T   χηρῶς M V, χηρώς N U W, χηρῶσα O P, χηρός vi, leg.
χηρώσας   χηρίαν vi M N U W
73. χαμηλός hab. vi v2; cett. om.   χαμιλός vi   ὁμαλός ante ταπεινός ΓΔ   ἴσος om.
vi   ἢ ἀσθενής post ἴσος add. V W
74. Gloss. om. L O   ταπεινοῖς hab. vi v2, cett. om.   χαμηλοῖς om. v22   χαμιλοῖς
vi Δ
75. Gloss. om. V W   χθαλωά pro χθαμαλόν vi
76. χθιζοί T U V: χθινοί v2 W, χθηνοί vi S, χθιζινοί v3 R   χθησινοί vi, χθισινοί V W
ἀργοὶ ἄχρηστοι post χθεσινοί add. T U (W)
77. Gloss. om vi   χθωνός T U, χθῶνος S
78. Gloss. om. J   χθοΐνοις v2 R S T U V, χθοϊνοῖς vi
79. Gloss. om. v3 R   χθηζός vi
80. χθόϊνος S T U   ἐπίγειος add. W
81. Gloss. om. v32 leg. χίδρα   τρίψημα—φρυττόμενος om. R S ΓΔ   τρίψημα
O P T: τριψίμα vi, τρίψιμα cett.   σῖτος nonnulli   φριτόμενος vi   ταχύς vi
ἢ καί—ὄσπρια hab. vi v2, cett. om.
82. Gloss. om. K   leg. χίδρα: ἐρικτά   κρίθης V W, ἐγκριθῆς vi   νέος F H   ὡς
om. U   ὁ pro ὡς vi   ὥσπερ V W   σεμιδάλις vi, σεμίδαλης S (T) U   ἡμί-
φρυκτα γενόμενα εἶτα ψυγέντα καὶ μετὰ ταῦτα πτισθέντα τουτέστι ψυγέντα. γίνονται δὲ
χίδραι καὶ ἀπὸ σίτου post σεμίδαλις add. V W
83. χίλος Γ, χίδρος R, χιδρός S   καὶ ἵππων χόρτα add. v3 (exc. Γ)
84. Χίμαιρα vi J K M N S (T) U, Χιμαίραν V (W), Χίμεραν v3   τρόφιμον (R) (S) (T) U
λικία vi N Γ

85. χίμαροι: τράγοι
86. χιονωθήσονται: λαμπρυνθήσονται
87. χίμαιρα: αἶγα ἀγρία
88. χίδρον: νέον καρπόν
89. χειά: ἡ κατάδυσις τοῦ ὄφεως
[90. χιδάλεον: τυφλόν, ἄγαμον, πεφρικώς]
91. χιτών: ἐσθής, ἱμάτιον ἀνδρικόν
92. χλαῖνα: χλαμύς, χλανίς, χειμερινὸν ἱμάτιον πορφυροῦν
[93. χλεύη: χλευασμός, γέλος]
94. χλιδῶσα: τρυφῶσα, σπαταλῶσα
95. χλιδή: τρυφή
96. χλιδῶνα: κόσμον περὶ τὸν τράχηλον ἢ βραχίονα, ὃ καλεῖται βραχιόλιον
97. χλιάζεσθαι: γαστρίζεσθαι
98. χλοάζει: βλαστάνει
99. χνοῦς: λεπτὸς κονιορτός
100. χοάς: ἐναγίσματα ἐπὶ νεκροῖς [εἰς τοὺς τάφους χεόμενα]
101. χόειον: παχὺ ἔντερον

---

85. Gloss. om. v22; cum gl. 61 conf. T U   χίμαρροι vι J K W, χείμαροι Γ, χείμαρροι S,
χ.μαρροι R   χίμαρος: τράγος v32
86. χιονοθήσονται vι (exc. B) v3 Nᶜ Rᵃᶜ S, χιωνοθήσονται S T
87. χιμαίρα (χιμαίραι B) vι   αἶγα (αἶγαι B) vι O P R   αἶξ L, αἰγίς v3   ἀγρίαι B
ἡ ἐν χειμῶνι τεχθεῖσα post ἀγρία add. v3   χίμερρα: ἀγρία αἴξ et χιμαίρα: αἰγὶς ἀγρία
περισυνή V W
88. leg. χῖδρον
89. Gloss. om. v3 V W   χειά Q P: χία M, χιά cett.
90. Gloss. hab. vι; cett. om.   πεφρικῶς codd.
91. Gloss. om. v22 v32   χιτῶν vι T Γ Δ, χιτόν S   ἐσθῆς vι T U   ἱμάτιον R T Γ
92. Gloss. om. v3   χλαίνα, χλαμὺς καὶ χλανίς: χλαίνα μὲν λέγεται τὸ παχὺ καὶ χιμέριον
(μέριον B) ἱμάτιον· χλαμὺς δὲ τὸ παρ' ἡμῶν λεγόμενον κυμάντιον· χλανὶς (χλανῆς B C G) δὲ
τὸ ἁπαλὸν καὶ λεπτὸν (ἱμάτιον add. F H) καὶ τρυφερόν vι   χλαίνα N O U V   χλαῖναν
R   πορφύρα χιμερινὸν (καὶ χειμ. R) ἱμάτιον R S
93. Gloss. hab. vι; cett. om.   χλεύει codd.   leg. γέλως
94. Gloss. om. vι   χλιδώσαις: τρυφώσαις, σπαταλώσαις W
95. Gloss. om. vι   χλίδη R Γ
96. χλιδώνα vι N, χλιδόνα (χληδόνα Γ) v3   τράχηλον ἤ om. W, sed supra lineam ἢ τὸν
τράχηλον add.   τόν om. R   βραχιόλιος Γ, βραχιόλην R S, βραχίονος Φ, βραχιόνιον L,
βραχιόνιον καὶ βραχιόλιον W
98. χλωάζει vι
99. χνούς vι M V W
100. χοάς v22 L: χόας cett.   ἐναγήσματα vι N   νεκρούς R   εἰς—χεόμενα om. v3 R   ἐν
τοῖς τάφοις S
101. χορίον O P, leg. χόριον   παχύν O P, ταχύ W

102. χονδρίτην: παχὺ σεμίδαλις γινομένη
103. χοϊκός: γηγενής, ἐκ χοός, πήλινος
104. χωόμενος: λυπούμενος, ὀργιζόμενος
105. χοιράδες: πετρῶν ὄχθοι ἢ ἐξοχαί
106. χοῖ: χώματι
107. χοιρογρύλλιος: [ἀρκόμυς,] ὕστριξ, εἶδος λαγωοῦ
108. χολέσαιμ᾽ ἄν: ὀργισθήσομαι
109. χολέρα: [ἄνωθεν καὶ κάτωθεν ἔμετος, ἤτουν] ἔκκρισις διὰ στόματος καὶ
     γαστρός
110. χολάδες: ἔντερα
111. χόνδροι ἁλῶν: θρόμβοι ἅλατος, παχὺ ἅλας
112. χορηγία: δόσις, παροχή
113. χοροστάτης: χοροῦ κατάρχων
114. χόριον: τὸ κάλυμμα τὸ συγγεννώμενον ἐν τῇ κοιλίᾳ τοῖς βρέφεσι
115. χορός: κύκλος, στέφανος
116. χοῦς: μέτρον· εἴρηται δὲ καὶ τὸ χῶμα
117. χράνας: μιάνας, ῥυπώσας
118. χραισμεῖν: βοηθεῖν
119. χραισμῆσαι: βοηθῆσαι

---

102. Gloss. om. Π   χονδρίτην Σ: χονδρίτον v3 R S (T) U, χονδρίτον V W   χονδριτών vel
     χονδριτόν vɪ v2   σεμιδάλις vɪ, σεμήδαλις R, γενομένη R S U Σ Φ, γινομένης T
103. γηγενῆς nonnulli   πήλινος ὤν v3
104. χωόμενος V W: χοόμενος cett.   ἐργαζόμενος vɪ
106. Gloss. om. Φ   χόϊ F N T U   χώματα V W
107. Gloss. om. U   ἀρκόμυς om. v3   ὕστριξ Σ: οἴστριξ vɪ L Γ Δ Φ   οἴστριξ R (T) V,
     οἴστριγξ J K M, οἴστρυγξ v22, οἴστρυξ S, οἴστρος W   λαγοῦ V W Γ Δ Φ   ἢ
     ἔχινος θηρίον post λαγ. add. V W
108. χολέσαιμεν Rᵃᵒ, χολέσαιμε v3 Rᵖᶜ   ὀργισθήσωμαι vɪ   ἄν post ὀργ. add. O P
109. χολερά L T V W, χολερὰ R S U   ἄνωθεν—ἤτουν om. v3 R S   ἔμετος v2 V W,
     αἱμετός vɪ T (U)   εἴτουν V, ἤγουν W   ἔκρισις J M N R, ἔκκρησις vɪ
110. χάλαδες vel χαλάδες vɪ   θρόμβοι post ἔντερα add. vɪ
111. χονδριαλῶν S (T) U Γ Π, χονδριάλων R   ἁλῶν nonnulli, ἁλός V W   θρόμβοι om
     vɪ (cf. gloss. praec.)   ἅλατος om. W, ἅλατος . . . ἅλας nonnulli
112. δώσις S, δῶσις R
113. χοροκαταάρχων vɪ
114. χόριον W: χορίον N T, χόρειον v3, χορεῖον (χορείον B C G) cett.   τὸ κάλυμμα τὸ
     περιέχον ἐν τῇ κοιλίᾳ τὸ ἔμβριον (τὸ ἔμβρ. ἐν τῇ κοιλ. Π Φ) v3 R   τὸ ἐκ τοῦ ἐμβρύου
     post κάλυμμα add. V W   συγγεννώμενον V: συγγενώμενον vel συγγενόμενον cett.
     βρέφεσιν v2 (exc. L) W
115. μέτρον—χῶμα (= gl. sequ.) add. v3
116. Gloss. om. V
117. ῥυπῶσας K O R T Δ
119. χραισμεῖσαι vɪ N S   βοηθῆσαι nonnulli

120. χρεμετίσαι: κράξαι ὡς ἵππος [ἢ ἀντὶ τοῦ λαλῆσαι εἴρηται]
121. χρέμπτεται: [βήσσει, οἷον] ἧχον τῷ στόματι ἀποτελεῖ, πτέρνεται
122. χρεώμενος: χρώμενος
123. χρεῶν ἀποκοπαί: ὅταν τὰ ὑπὸ τῶν πενήτων ἀφαιρεθέντα ἄφεσιν λάβωσιν
124. χρεμετισμός: ἡ τῶν ἵππων φωνή
[125. χραισμῶ, ἔχραισμον]
126. χρῆμα: πρᾶγμα, πλοῦτος, οὐσία, λῆμμα
127. χρηματίζει: ἀποκρίνεται, προλέγει, [προφητεύει ἢ πράσσει· χρῆμα γὰρ τὸ πρᾶγμα]
128. χρησμοδοτούμενα: [μαντευόμενα,] προλεγόμενα
129. χρησμόν: προφητείαν, [κληδόνα, μαντείαν]
130. χρηστοί: ἀγαθοί
131. χρήστης: ὁ δανείζων καὶ δανειζόμενος
132. χρῆσθαι: χρᾶσθαι, προσφέρεσθαι
133. χρίμπτεται: [προσκνᾶται,] πελάζει, προσεγγίζει
134. χροὸς ἀσάμην: τοῦ σώματος ἐκορέσθην
135. χρυσότευκτος: ἐκ χρυσίου κατεσκευασμένος
136. χρυσηλακάτου: χρυσοτόξου

---

120. χραιμετίσαι (J) K L M N R U, χραιμετῆσαι O P S T Σ, χρημετῆσαι vi   ἤ—εἴρηται om. v3, v4
121. Gloss. om. K   χρέμπτεται V: χραίμπτεται B C G R S U, χραίμπταιται Γ, χραίμπεται cett.   βήσσει οἷον om. v3 R S W   βήσσει V: βύσσει v2 F H, βίσσει B C G (T) Y U οἷον nonnulli   τό pro τῷ B C G O S Γ   ἢ πτέρνεται vi, πτέρεται v3
122. Gloss. om. L   χρεώμενος v22 W Σ: χρεόμενος cett.   χρόμενος R T U
123. ἀπό pro ὑπό v3 R S   λάβωσι nonnulli
124. χραιμετισμός vi v2 (T) U   ἡ φωνή τῶν ἵππων v3
125. Gloss. hab. vi v2; cett. om.   αἵχραισμον O P, ἐχραισμόν vi
126. χρῆμα vi, N   πράγμα nonnulli   πλοῦτος ante πρᾶγμα vi   ὁλκὴ χρυσίου ante οὐσία add. v3 R   οὐσία om. v32   λῆμμα nonnulli
127. χρήσματι Γ Δ, χρησματεῖ v32   προφητεύει—πρᾶγμα om. v3 W ἢ προφητεύει R S   τό om. S T U V   χρῆμα γάρ· πρᾶγμα γάρ R
128. μαντευόμενα om. v3 R W   προλεγόμενα ante μαντ. v2 S
129. χρησμός v3 R S (T) U W   προφητεία v3 R S   θεοφανεία pro κληδόνα, μαντείαν v3 R, ἢ δήλωσις W, κληδώνα vi, κλήδονα O P, κλίδονα S T V   μαντεία S
130. χρηστόν: ἀγαθόν V W   ἐπιεικεῖς ἀγαθοί v3 R   οἱ εὔχρηστοι post ἀγαθοί add. J |
131. χρηστός v3   ὁ δανιστής W   δανίζων ... δανιζόμενος nonnulli
132. χρῆσθαι om. vi   χρεῖσθαι v3 O P V   προσφέρεσθαι ante χρᾶσθαι W   προφέρεσθαι N V
133. χρίμπεται v3 O P T V W, χρήμπτεται vi, χρήπτεται N   προσκνᾶται om. v3 R   προσπελάζει T U, προσπελᾶται v3 R   ἐγγίζει ante προσκνᾶται V
134. χρωός Π Φ, χρώς R, χοός Σ, χροοσάμην vi v2, χροσάμην T U, χρωσάμην V (W)
135. χρυσώτευκτος vi, χρυσότεκτος T Φ   χρυσοῦ W   κατασκευασμένος nonnulli
136. χρυσιλακάτου C F H N Π, χρυσιλακάτω B G   ἀλλαχοῦ γρ(άφεται) χρυσηλάκτου add. W

137. χρυσάορον: χρυσόξιφον
138. χρυσάμπυκας: χρυσοχαλίνους
139. χρυσοτόρευτα: χρυσόγλυφα
140. χρυσαυγοῦντα: στίλβοντα, ἀστράπτοντα
141. χρώς: σῶμα
142. χρωτός: σώματος, ἰδέας
143. χύδην: κεχυμένως, [ὡς ἔτυχεν]
144. χυδαῖος: εὐτελής, [συρφετός]
[145. χυδαῖοι: τὸ πλῆθος δεδήλωκεν]
146. χυλός: ἐκπιασμός
147. χυμός: σίελος ἢ πῆγμα ὑγρόν
148. χυμῶν: πεμμάτων ὑγρῶν
149. χῶμα: ὕψωμα γῆς, ὅπερ οἱ πολέμιοι ἐν ταῖς πολιορκίαις εἰώθασι προσχοῦν
      τὰ τείχη
[150. χωρήσω: βαδίσω, ὑποστρέψω]
[151. χωρίον: τόπον]
152. χῶρος: τόπος
153. χωρήσατε: προσδέξασθε
154. χολωτοῖσιν: ὀργίλοις
[155. χώμασι: τοὺς ἱερεῖς τῶν ματαίων]

---

137. χρυσάωρον v22 R S
138. χρυσάμπικας vι   χρυσοχαλήνους S
139. χρυσοτόρνευτα (B) F H   χρυσόροφα post χρυσόγλυφα add. R S, pro χρυσόγλ. hab. V
140. στιλβοῦντα vι   ἀστράπτοντα ante στίλβοντα W
141. χρώς R S U V: χρῶς cett.   εἰδέα add. L
142. Gloss. om. L   ἰδέας om. V   ἰδέας O P: εἰδέας cett.
143. χύδειν R   κεχυμένος B C G Π   ὡς ἔτυχεν om. v3 W, ἔτυχον V
144. χυδαίος nonnulli, χύδαιος (R) S (T) U   εὐτελῆς vι N T Π Φ   συρφετός om. v3,
      συφερτός vι   πανπληθής pro συρφετός W
145. Gloss. om. v3 L R W   χυδαῖοι v22 V: χύδαιοι cett.
146. Gloss. om. P   ὁ ἐκπιασμός v3
147. Gloss. om. P   σίελος L O V: σιελός cett.   ἀλλαχοῦ πτῦμα ὑγρόν add. W
148. Gloss. om. W   χυμόν Δ   πελμάτων v2 (exc. M) C G, τελμάτων B F H
149. ὅπερ codd.; leg. ᾧπερ   πολεμικοί vι   πολυορκίαις nonnulli   προσχῶν F H,
      προσχοῦντα B G   τείχει B C G S   ἀλλαχοῦ εἴωθαν προσχοῦν τὰ τείχη add. W
150, 151. om. v3 v4
152. χῶρος vι N   ὁ τόπος v3
153. Gloss. om. Σ   χωρίσατε vι v21, χωρήσαται T, χωρήσασθαι Π Φ   προσδέξασθαι
      vι v3 (exc. Δ) v22 R S T W
154. Gloss. om. L   χολωτοῖσι W: χωλοτοῖσι R, χωλοτοῖσιν v2 C (S) (T) U, χωλόποισιν
      B F G H
155. Gloss. om. v3 L W

[156. χῶτα: σῶμα]
[157. χωλαβεῖ: θορυβεῖ]
[158. χῶρος: χωρίον· Κύπριοι ὅπην. δηλοῖ δὲ καὶ τὸν ἀγρόν· καὶ χωρητικόν]

---

156. Gloss. om. v3 L R S W   χῶτα vel χώτα codd.; leg. χρῶτα
157. Gloss. hab. v1; cett. om.   θορυβεῖ codd.
158. Gloss. hab. v1; cett. om.   χώρος codd.   καὶ κύπριοι F H   χωριτικόν F H,
χοριτικόν B C G

8

Method and Structure in the Satires of Persius

EDWIN S. RAMAGE

Over the last twenty years or so, Persius' satiric approach and method have attracted considerable scholarly attention, but one aspect of the satires that has not been adequately studied is Persius' use of the second person address.[1] This is a one-on-one approach in which the satirist speaks in the first person to, with, or at a variety of second persons. The device is so much a part of Persius' method that our natural reaction is to take it for granted as we read, at most ascribing it to the influence of the Cynic–Stoic diatribe. But a closer look suggests its importance for the argumentation, poetic development, and structure of the individual satires, as well as for the general impression that the poems leave.

The Method in the Satires

Persius addresses at least four different groups of second persons in his satires. First, and least important for our purposes, is a category that in-includes gods (2.39 f., 3.35–37), priests (2.69), and well-known people from the past (1.73–75, 1.87, 1.115, 6.79 f.), where the poet is aiming for vividness, variety, and emphasis. A second kind of addressee is Persius' reader or listener. He does not speak directly to his reader very often, but it should be noticed that when he does, the satirist makes him the second person subject of the verb *credo* (Prol. 14; 4.1). More important is what might be called the address to a friend—Macrinus in Satire 2, Cornutus in 5, and Bassus in 6—which the satirist inherited from the earlier satiric and epistolary traditions. We shall look at these more closely later, but two points should be made here: Persius never addresses a friend without

[1] Most of the bibliography since 1956 is gathered together in U. Knoche (transl. E. S. Ramage), *Roman Satire* (Bloomington, 1975), pp. 207 f., 224–226; see also p. 170, n. 19. At least three other studies should be added to those listed there: F. Villeneuve, *Essai sur Perse* (Paris, 1918); E. V. Marmorale, *Persio²* (Florence, 1956); J. C. Bramble, *Persius and the Programmatic Satire* (Cambridge, 1974).

naming him, and Macrinus, Cornutus, and Bassus all appear at the beginning of their satires and all quickly disappear.[2]

But the most common and most important addressee in these poems is the vague, unnamed second person to whom the poet as satirist/adviser (s/a) directs much of his criticism and advice. It predominates in the satires, occurring almost 80 percent of the time, and for this reason deserves our close attention here.

Both s/a and second person recipient remain unnamed throughout, except for an episode in Satire 4 involving Socrates and Alcibiades (1–22), which, as we shall see, is a well-motivated variation on the theme. While we do not need to be told who the s/a is, the recipient remains as vague as possible. In fact, there are two points at which the poet shows that he is consciously maintaining this vagueness. In the first satire, where the recipient is present throughout, the s/a at one point (44) prefaces a comment to him with the words, "Whoever you are whom I have just set speaking against me, . . ." The fact that the comment begins a speech and that the words neatly fill a line help to make the statement stand out. Persius is telling us here that the adversary or recipient is a vague second person "straw man" and that the poem is really not a dialogue at all.[3] The second instance occurs in Satire 6 (41 f.), when the s/a begins his address to the heir who becomes the recipient at this point: "But as for you, whoever you are who will be my heir, . . ."

There is at least one instance in which the satirist promotes this ambiguity by shifting suddenly from the second person singular to the plural and back again. This happens in the third satire (63–76), where the recipient begins as a singular (64: *videas*) and in the same line becomes a plural (*occurrite*). The plural is maintained in the imperatives *discite* and *cognoscite* (66), but the next reference, some five lines later, is singular (71: *te*), and so are those in the next two lines (72: *locatus es*; 73: *disce nec invideas*), where *invideas* recalls *videas* at the beginning. This intentional mixing of singular and plural seems intended to generalize the recipient still further. Not only is he unnamed and vague, then, but he is even singular or plural.[4]

[2] Macrinus disappears after 2.4 and Bassus is not referred to again after 6.6, so that these dedications appear almost perfunctory. We naturally contrast them with the more elaborate address to Cornutus in Satire 5 (19–64).

[3] Although he does not use this line as evidence, G. L. Hendrickson, some forty years ago, observed that this satire is not a dialogue: "The First Satire of Persius," *C.P.* 23 (1928), 103.

[4] There are other examples in Satire 1 that are not quite parallel to this one. At 1.11 a plural *ignoscite* suddenly appears; in 1.61 f. there is a shift from the singular recipient to a plural recipient, the patricians; at 1.111 f., after moving to the plural (111: *eritis*), the poet shifts back to the singular (112: *inquis*).

Generally speaking, however, the satirist simply takes full advantage of the natural vagueness of the second personal verb or pronoun when it is not related to a subject or antecedent.

What is the result of this one-on-one approach? In the first place, it helps create a strongly didactic atmosphere. It is almost a tutorial situation, with the s/a offering criticism and advice to a recipient who apparently needs it. When he wants to use examples, the s/a brings them in via the first person plural and the third person singular and plural.[5]

There are other indications of a didactic purpose in the satires. The third satire is really a statement of the need for a proper education and the right application of it. "You're just damp, soft clay," the s/a tells his recipient: "Now, right now, you have to be whirled around on the swift wheel and shaped without stopping" (3.23 f.). In the first line of the fourth satire Socrates, the s/a, is called a *magister* or "teacher." Throughout the satires vocabulary of teaching and learning is used by the s/a in addressing the recipient, much of it in the imperative.[6] And there are many jussives and imperatives that are natural components of the language of teaching.[7] All of these combine to produce the heavily didactic atmosphere that pervades the satires.

This emphasis on the one-on-one relationship between s/a and recipient also helps to produce an atmosphere of isolation in the satires. These two

[5] It is important to notice that Persius never admits directly to having faults (see also below, note 13). He does, however, include himself in the first person plural where he effectively dilutes his own shortcomings by making them part of humanity's. For want of a better designation we shall call this the collective "we." Examples: 1.13: *scribimus*, where the context has already told us that he is actually not part of this group; 2.62 and 71: *nostros, damus*, in a passage where the s/a ends up being the proper example (75); 3.3, 12, 14, and 16: *stertimus, querimur, querimur, venimus*, where, *pace* Housman (see below, note 13), Persius is at best one of a group of "sinners"; 4.42 f.: *caedimus, praebemus, novimus*, where we hardly think of the s/a as being included; 5.68: *consumpsimus*, where the criticism really involves the procrastinators, and not the s/a.

The third person examples are too easily recognized to need elaboration. They range all the way from a centurion (3.77) or centurions (5.189) to individuals putting forward the wrong prayers (2.8–14).

[6] There is a surprisingly large number of examples: 1.30, 2.31, 5.68: *ecce* ("look!" "look here!"); 2.17: *age, responde* ("come, answer me this!" a Socratic touch); 2.42, 6.52: *age* ("come now!"); 3.66: *discite ... cognoscite* ("learn!" "get to know!"); 3.73, 5.91: *disce* ("learn!"); 4.3, 6.51: *dic* ("tell me!" another Socratic touch); 4.52: *noris* ("get to know!"); 6.42: *audi* ("listen!").

[7] The satires contain many of these; a few examples will suffice: 1.5–7: *non ... accedas examenve ... castiges ... nec ... quaesiveris*; 6.25 f.: *messe tenus propria vive et granaria (fas est) | emole*; 6.65: *fuge quaerere*. Satire 4 contains no fewer than twelve imperatives and jussives. The ones involving the recipient are listed in note 6. The others with didactic overtones include 19 f.: *expecta, i, suffla* (ironic); 45: *da, decipe* (also ironic); 51 f.: *respue, tollat, habita*.

participants are constantly and consistently separated from the rest of society, except when they are included in the general or collective "we" of the Roman or Italian populace, or of humanity in general.[8] They also leave the impression of being isolated because "we," "he," and "they" that make up the rest of society provide the negative examples that the s/a chooses for his recipient.[9]

This theme of isolation runs through the satires. In fact, Persius sets the mood in the Prologue by candidly separating himself from poets and poetry of the past, and by rejecting his contemporaries.[10] This rejection is developed at length in the first satire. The satirist will have nothing to do with contemporary literature, whose depravities reflect those of contemporary society; he ostensibly cares little about a reading public (2 f., 119 f.); he professes to have no worries about the effect his satire is having (110–114); he recommends isolation to his recipient (5–7); and he even describes the important message that he has as something "hidden" (1.121: *opertum*).

Again, in Satire 5, after rejecting contemporary pretentiousness yet another time, Persius says *he* is speaking privately (5.21). Toward the beginning of Satire 6 we find that he has physically isolated himself from Rome and Romans by moving to his country estate and that he wants to make sure that we and Bassus know this. "Here I am free and safe from the mob," he says (6.12), and he repeats the adjective *securus* in the next line. The same desire for seclusion appears a little later, when the s/a overtly takes his heir to one side to make certain that he listens to what he is saying (6.42: *paulum a turba seductior audi*). Horace gets caught in the Roman Forum (*Sat.* 1.9) or bustling about Rome (*Sat.* 2.6.20–58); Juvenal stands on the street corner taking notes (*Sat.* 1.63 f.); Persius carefully takes his heir into a quiet corner to talk to him.

A third purpose that the use of the s/a and recipient accomplishes is to focus attention on the individual. In this connection, there is an important statement early in the first satire that should probably be taken as

---

[8] See above, note 5. Though the immediate situation is quite different, we can feel these isolationist tendencies in Persius' description of his friendship with Cornutus (5.19–51). What he has in effect done is to set up another one-on-one relationship with Cornutus. See the analysis of Satire 5, below.

[9] In a general article on the subject, Anderson shows that Persius rejects society and that this is a point of view quite different from that of the other satirists: W. S. Anderson, "Persius and the Rejection of Society," in *Wissenschaftl. Zeitschr. der Univ. Rostock* 15 (1966), 409–416.

[10] E. S. Ramage, D. L. Sigsbee, S. C. Fredericks, *Roman Satirists and Their Satire* (Park Ridge, N.J., 1974), p. 116.

programmatic for the satires as a whole (5–7). When the discussion of contemporary literature has barely begun, the s/a turns to his recipient and says, "If Rome in its confused state disparages something, don't run up and fix the balance that's out of kilter and don't go looking for anything that's outside yourself." There may be a rejection of society here, but it is not complete nihilism, for, negative and sententious though the statement may appear, it is Persius' way of saying that if we are going to have faith in anything, it should be the individual.

As we make our way through the satires, we find the individual to the forefront most of the time. In the first satire Persius by himself opposes popular opinion, taste, and mores. Private or individual prayers are the subject of Satire 2, where the s/a alone is represented as having the solution (75). Satire 3 deals with the education and improvement of the individual. Here the metaphor from pottery making (23 f.) quoted earlier is particularly apt, since pots are turned one at a time. The eloquent list of things to be learned that appears a little later in the poem (66–72), to a large extent involves matters of one's own worth and personal identity. There is no need to stress the emphasis on the individual that permeates the fourth satire, with its exhortation to "know thyself." The last two lines (51 f.) provide an eloquent summary: "Reject what you are not; have the mob take back its favors. Live with yourself and come to realize how sparse your furnishings are." In Satire 5 (52 f.) Persius expresses a clear recognition of the individual: "There are a thousand kinds of men and their experience differs widely. Everyone has his own desires and people don't live with a single prayer." This is an appropriate preamble to the subject of the satire, which is the nature of personal freedom. Finally, Satire 6 focuses on the proper attitude of the individual to wealth.

The one-on-one relationship between s/a and recipient reinforces this emphasis in the satires, for it is a practical example of how the education or enlightenment of the individual might take place. Actually, it is one end of the spectrum—the beginning of the educational process. The other end is represented by the relationship between Persius and Cornutus (5.19–64). This personal association has grown over a long period of time, from vague and tenuous beginnings to an ideal, clearly defined partnership for life based on mutual respect.

The one-on-one device that we have been talking about serves yet another purpose: it focuses our attention on the s/a and his criticism or advice. He is forceful, positive, and outspoken; generally he speaks with conviction. The recipient, on the other hand, is thoroughly vague, and most of the time blends into the surrounding scenery because he is simply a tacit listener. But even when he has a larger part to play, as he does in the first satire, he is little more than a straw man presenting maudlin, wrong, or at least unacceptable sentiments, which are ultimately grist for the critical mill of his opponent. And here is another reason for our focusing on the s/a. The recipient is actually a negative character who has gone wrong in his actions or thinking or who threatens to go wrong. There is no need to dwell on this; we need only think of the adversary in Satire 1, Alcibiades in 4, or the heir in 6. By contrast, the s/a is assumed to be or is represented as the positive example of what he is promoting. This clearly lies behind the argument of Satire 1, coming to a climax in the last monologue (114–134). At the end of Satire 2 we catch sight of the s/a as the one who is ideally prepared to make a proper prayer. By associating himself with Cornutus in 5 Persius shows he is the ideal *sapiens*, and we cannot forget this as we read the rest of the poem containing his account of true individual freedom. In Satire 6 he appears both as one who knows how to utter a proper prayer (22) and as a person who is fully aware of the proper use of money (12–24, 25–80, esp. 41–74).[11]

There is a final purpose that this device seems to serve. It is apparently a way of bringing in the reader and thus providing a more general application of the criticism and advice that is being put forward. Persius nowhere states that this is his purpose, but it is a natural reaction on the part of the reader or listener to take much of what is directed at a vague "you" as being directed beyond the satires to himself.

Before turning to the individual satires to see how the one-on-one method works out in practice, something must be said about origins. This is not the place to get into a long discussion of where Persius found the device and how he adapted it to his own uses. For present purposes it will be sufficient to point to the Cynic–Stoic diatribe as the most likely source. Even a glance at the reported diatribes of Epictetus suggests clear comparisons.[12]

---

11 The beginning of Satire 3 presents a problem if we take the young man who is snoring his life away as being Persius. But see note 13.

12 Cf. Villeneuve (above, note 1), pp. 119–140, 154–184. Diatribe had influenced Roman satire from the beginning. The few remaining fragments of Ennius' satires show traces of it (Knoche [above, note 1], pp. 25, 29; Ramage, Sigsbee, Fredericks [above, note 10], pp. 19, 20), and so do the more extensive remains of Lucilius (Ramage, Sigsbee, Fredericks, pp. 34, 35, 40, 43).

Horace makes use of the diatribe, but his approach is quite different from that of Persius. It appears in five satires only (1.1, 1.2, 1.3, 2.3, and 2.7). In the first three satires there is a clearer alternation between third person examples and direct address to the recipient. While the recipient is the focus of Horace's attention, the one-on-one relationship is not as tight as it is in Persius, and we do not feel the same isolation that the s/a and recipient in Persius leave. In 2.3 and 2.7 Horace is to a large extent satirizing the

THE STRUCTURE OF THE SATIRES

A detailed look at each of the poems will give a better idea of the part that the s/a and his recipient have to play in Persius' satires. For purposes of clarity the analysis of each satire, with one exception, is prefaced by an outline in which not only passages involving the s/a and recipient are taken into account, but also those in which Persius uses address to a friend, the collective "we," the third person, or an impersonal approach. Satire 1 will be left to the end, since our examination of it will benefit from looking at the other satires first.

SATIRE TWO

Lines	Method	Subject
1–4	address to friend	Macrinus' birthday
5–14	third sing.	improper prayers: examples
15–60	s/a-recip.	prayers: problem
61–70	impersonal	generalization of problem
71–75	coll. "we"; s/a alone	solution: general and personal

As has already been noted, the satire begins with a second personal address to a friend, Macrinus, who disappears immediately after Persius' observation that his friend is not in the habit of uttering improper prayers (4). This leads naturally to a series of examples of such prayers (5–14), all of them in the third person (5: *bona pars procerum*; 6: *cuivis*; 9: *illa*). The examples are an important introduction to the problem, but the passage also serves another function. The heavy emphasis on the third person singular—all the verbs but two (13: *impello, expungam*) are in this form, and these two are part of the direct quotation from a third person— provides a kind of buffer between the address to Macrinus and that to the recipient which follows. As we shall see, this occurs again in a different form in Satires 5 and 6.

Immediately after this list of prayers (15) the s/a suddenly turns to his vague, unnamed recipient and begins the discussion that takes up most

---

diatribe method as he satirizes the philosophy that spawned it. Here the one-on-one is quite different, for both s/a and recipient are named, and in both cases Horace the recipient turns the tables on the s/a at the end of the satire. The strong element of burlesque and humor in both satires should also not be overlooked.

of the rest of the satire. This falls into three parts, thus helping to avoid the tedium of a lengthy tirade. The s/a first adopts a Socratean style and puts before his recipient a series of probing questions on attitudes to the gods (17–30). He then turns to the example of the maternal aunt, using a prefacing *ecce* to draw his discussant's attention (and ours, too) to her and her prayers (31–40). Finally he returns, in a long section, to point out how wrong his adversary is to wish for a long life and great wealth, and how his materialistic outlook has affected his treatment of the gods (41–60). This arrangement not only provides the variety already mentioned, but it also enables Persius to get at the problem from a number of different angles.

The problem is now consciously generalized (61–70) with an address to souls in general (61), the use of *iuvat* (62) and the collective "we" (62: *nostros*), and the concentration on *pulpa* or "flesh" (63–68). By contrast, the solution is put in terms of the collective "we" (71: *damus*), which is actually a step on the way to the first person of the satirist or s/a who represents the right solution on a personal level (75).

Persius seems to have planned his use of the s/a-recipient in Satire 2 very carefully, since he makes it physically its centerpiece. Here as elsewhere this device is used to develop an account of the problem, and the return of the s/a in the last line of the satire serves to remind us of the method and the problem as the personal solution is presented.

Satire Three

Lines	Method	Subject
1–14	coll. "we" (s/a-recip.)— coll. "we"	improper living: example
15–62	s/a-recip.	education: problem
63–76	s/a-recip.	education: solution
77–118	third sing.—s/a-recip.	three sceptical attitudes

This is a difficult poem and its difficulties are reflected in its structure. Persius deals here with the need for a proper philosophical education and the right application of it. He begins by using what appears to be the collective "we" (3: *stertimus*) to describe an example—the person who reveals a lack of direction and purpose in his life by spending his time carousing and sleeping it off. Almost immediately one of his companions (7) addresses him in a variation of the one-on-one approach (5: *en quid agis?*). The poet then moves back to the collective first person to elaborate the problems of those who cannot get down to writing but instead spend their time inventing excuses (12, 14: *querimur*).[13]

This introduction is followed by a long passage containing a broader discussion of the problem (15–62) and a solution (63–76) in which the s/a addresses the vague second person recipient throughout. The collective "we" appears at the beginning (16: *venimus*), along with the vocative address to the recipient (15: *miser . . . miser*), to provide a bridge between the two parts. The s/a points first to the need for a proper philosophical education (15–34; esp. 23 f.), and then turns from his recipient for a moment to address Jupiter as he points out the ramifications of not having such training (35–43). There is no indication that the recipient is being spoken to as the speaker moves on to make the point that early in life a person cannot really be expected to know what is proper (44–51), but it is clear that he has been addressing the recipient, because he suddenly points a finger at him and chides him for having had the training, but still not knowing how to live (52–62). With *stertis* (58) and the rest of this line and the next, the s/a gives every indication of returning to the point at which the satire began, when he suddenly generalizes the discussion by asking the recipient whether he has any purpose in life or whether he is simply "playing it by ear" (60–62: . . . *ex tempore vivis?*).

He now turns to the solution or cure for the problem that he has outlined (63–76), with *elleborum*, the first word in the passage, metaphorically announcing the topic. These lines have already been discussed, and we need only remind ourselves of the interplay of singular and plural, and the heavy didacticism that run through them.

To this point Satire 3 has followed the pattern of the second satire:

---

[13] More than sixty years ago A. E. Housman suggested that Persius had himself in mind at the beginning of Satire 3 ("Notes on Persius," *C.Q.* 7 [1913], 16 f.). Although G. L. Hendrickson calls it "fanciful" but "by no means impossible" ("The Third Satire of Persius," *C.P.* 23 [1928], 333), the view has been widely accepted, most recently by R. Jenkinson ("Interpretations of Persius' Satires III and IV," *Latomus* 32 [1973], 534 f.). But if this is Persius in these lines, then, as has already been pointed out, it is the only place in the satires where the satirist appears in a negative light (see above, note 5). The personal account a little later (44–51) does not militate against this, since Persius points out that he was young (44: *parvus*) when he tricked his teacher and that this kind of thing was only to be expected (48: *iure*) at that age. It might also be argued that the first person plural (3: *stertimus*) softens the connection, serving as a collective "we" (see above, note 5) and so making Persius at best just one of humanity that is in the habit of sleeping away its life. Indeed, the recurrence of the first person plural (12, 14, 16) helps to leave the impression throughout these lines that Persius does not have himself in mind, but people in general. It is true that the unnamed companion does address the snorer or one of the snorers in the second person singular (5: *en quid agis?*); but this should not bother us, since it is a variation of the s/a-recipient arrangement, with the companion playing the s/a, and we would expect the recipient to be unnamed.

example(s), general discussion of the problem, and solution. But no two satires of Persius are alike, and, besides, this tripartite arrangement is more characteristic of philosophy than it is of satire. And so the satire ends with three examples of people who for one reason or another are not receptive to the advice which Persius has given. A large cross section of the population simply closes its ears to the whole idea (77–87). Another person takes the advice so long as it is expedient and then forgets about it, so that he represents the group that has the answers but refuses to use them (88–106). A third type honestly believes it does not need this kind of direction (107–118). The first two examples are in the third person and the last one promises to take this form also. But the direct quotation (107–109) is actually a transition between the previous two examples and the negative ending, where the s/a returns to speak to his recipient once again and tells him how failure to get and use this proper direction is ultimately a form of insanity. The reference to Stoicism is clear, but the satire ends on a satiric, and not a philosophic note.

SATIRE FOUR

Lines	Method	Subject
1–22	s/a-recip. (Socrates and Alcibiades)	lack of self-knowledge: example
23–50	s/a-recip.	self-knowledge: problem
51 f.	s/a-recip.	self-knowledge: solution

The whole of the fourth satire is developed by means of the s/a-recipient method, with the poet using two sets of discussants. Socrates is the s/a addressing Alcibiades, the recipient, for the first twenty-two lines, and then the unnamed s/a and vague recipient take over. In the first section, a Greek atmosphere is maintained by a careful scattering of Greek words and names: *Pericli* (3), *theta* (13), *Anticyras* (16), *Dinomaches* (20: with a Greek genitive ending), *Baucis* (21), *ocima* (22). The second section, on the other hand, is full of Roman words, things, and ideas: *Vettidi* (25), *Curibus* (26), *genio* (27), *compita* (28), *balteus* (44), *puteal* (49). This is not to say that the division of words is strictly maintained, for nothing is ever that simple in Persius.[14] The division, however, does exist.[15]

[14] Words with Roman connotations appear in the first section (*plebecula* [6], *Quirites* [8], *popello* [15]), thus keeping Rome in sight. D. Bo observes that Persius *"res ita agit ac suo more novat ut haud raro potius Romae quam Athenis esse videamur et quemdam stoicum philosophum, Seneca severiorem, audire Neronem monentem, . . ."* (*A. Persi Flacci saturarum liber* [Turin, 1969], p. 70). The most obvious examples of Greek words in the second section are *gausape* (37) and *palaestrita* (39).

[15] The general statement that suddenly appears at 23 f. signals the new section, and the rest of the satire proceeds from this. Persius does much the same thing in Satire 5,

This variation of the one-on-one approach involving Socrates and Alcibiades serves as a specific example of the problem under discussion, that is, the importance of getting to know oneself. Normally Persius would make Alcibiades the subject of a third person statement, but here he has chosen to vary his method. When we realize this, it becomes clear that this satire shows much the same development in content as the second satire and the first seventy-six lines of Satire 3. A more general discussion of the problem (23–50) is prefaced by a universal statement (23 f.) and leads eventually to a collective "we" (42 f.). The final two lines of the satire give the solution, this time in an imperative form addressed to the recipient.

SATIRE FIVE

Lines	Method	Subject
1–4	impersonal	desire for eloquence
5–18	s/a (Cornutus?)- recip. (Persius)	P. has his own eloquence
19–64	address to friend	eloquent tribute to C.
64–72	s/a-recip.	call to philosophy
73–90	third sing. (traces of s/a-recip.)	true freedom misconceived: example
91–160	s/a-recip.	true freedom: problem
161–175	s/a-recip.	true freedom: solution
176–191	s/a-recip.	examples of a lack of freedom

The fifth satire is often pointed to as the most successful of Persius' satires, and this is reflected in the methods he uses. A glance at the summary above shows a satisfying variety of approach in which content and method blend to produce a unity for the poem.

The opening statement (1–4) is mildly surprising on two counts: it is completely impersonal and might be taken as an exaggerated plea for eloquence. But when we remember what Persius has said about contemporary poets and their poetry in his Prologue and in Satire 1, the overtones of irony that are present in these lines begin to make themselves felt.

Suddenly someone begins criticizing this demand for a hundred voices, mouths, and tongues as the satirist develops a variation of the one-on-one technique (5–18). Here Persius becomes the unnamed recipient, while it

---

when he announces freedom as his subject (73: *libertate opus est*). In 6 his announcement takes the form of a metaphor (25 f.). The first line of Satire 1 falls into the same category, though it applies to all the satires.

appears that Cornutus is the s/a.[16] This substitution is thoroughly appropriate, since, as we learn a little later, the relationship between Cornutus
and Persius has been one of teacher (adviser) and student (recipient).

Now follows an address to a friend, with Persius speaking directly to
Cornutus (19–64). The poet wants his eloquence so that he can praise
Cornutus (19–29), and he proceeds to do so pointing to their close friendship (30–51) and to the fact that Cornutus' chosen profession is philosophical teaching (52–64).

At this point Persius becomes the s/a and turns smoothly to address
children and old men—in other words, everyone—as second person
recipients, telling them to seek their knowledge from Cornutus and
bridling at their procrastination (64–72). The plural (64: *petite*) effectively separates this group from Cornutus who has just been addressed in
the second person singular, but *hinc* (64) provides a connection between
teacher and potential students. Soon the s/a chooses one of this group to
set up the one-on-one method that he uses in attacking procrastination
(68: *ecce*; 70: *te*; 71: *sectabere*; 72: *curras*). It is worth noting that Cornutus
has by now disappeared entirely from the satire.

As Persius turns to discuss true freedom—presumably because this is
an important example of the kind of thing people should learn about—
he begins with a brief general statement of the need for it (73) and goes
on from there to talk about misconceptions that people have (73–90).
This passage is largely in the third person, but there are hints at an s/a-
recipient relationship in two of the verbs (79 f.: *recusas . . . tu*; . . . *palles*)
and in the Stoic who speaks to an unnamed associate (85: *colligis*; 87:
tolle). Lines 64–90 not only further the argument of the satire, but they
also serve as an effective buffer between the address to a friend (19–64)
and the long passage in which the s/a speaks to his recipient about freedom
(91–191). We have already noticed this kind of buffer in Satire 2 and we
will find it again in the sixth satire.

At this point the satire moves to the one-on-one method, and this fills
the last one-hundred lines of the poem. Within the overall s/a-recipient
arrangement there are a number of variations on the theme. For the first

---

[16] There is no way of proving conclusively that Cornutus is the speaker in these lines.
K. Reckford, "Studies in Persius," *Hermes* 90 (1962), 498; C. Dessen, *Iunctura callidus acri:
A Study of Persius' Satires, Illinois Studies in Language and Literature*, 59 (Urbana, Illinois,
1968), p. 72; and D. Bo (above, note 14), p. 82, all identify the speaker as Cornutus,
while C. Witke, *Latin Satire: The Structure of Persuasion* (Leiden, 1970), pp. 89 f., argues
against this idea, describing the passage as "the poet's device for putting words of criticism
in the reader's mouth, and for setting forth self-criticism." M. Coffey, *Roman Satire*
(London, 1976), p. 106, calls this person simply an "interrupter."

forty lines the s/a speaks directly to his second person recipient (91–131). Then, still speaking to him, he replaces himself first with *Avaritia* (132–140), and then with *Luxuria* (141–153), each of whom addresses the recipient from her own point of view. In the next few lines the s/a speaks directly to the recipient again (154–160) and after this introduces a scene from comedy to illustrate the process of achieving true freedom (161–175). We should remember that the s/a and recipient are still present, but they have been replaced "on stage" by Davus and Chaerestratus, respectively. Finally the s/a reappears speaking directly to the recipient as he provides him with more negative examples (176–191). As we look back over the satire, we see that the real subject of the poem is treated in much the same way as it had been in Satires 2, 3, and 4: specific example(s) (73–90), discussion of the problem (91–160), a solution (161–175), with the satiric ending reminding us of Satire 3.

SATIRE SIX

Lines	Method	Subject
1–11	address to a friend	Bassus and Persius away from Rome
12–24	s/a (Persius)	proper attitude to wealth: example
25–40	s/a to recip. (legator)	improper attitude to wealth: solution, example
41–80	s/a to recip. (heir)	attitude to wealth: problem

The sixth satire is more straightforward than 5 but, like it, it shows peculiarities of method not noted before. It begins, as Satire 2 does, with an address to a friend, in this case Caesius Bassus (1–11). But after the first five and one-half lines Bassus disappears, much as Macrinus did in 2 and Cornutus in 5, and Persius concentrates our attention on himself. These eleven lines show a neat balance, with Bassus the subject in the first half and Persius in the second half.

In the next section (12–24) Persius is on his way to becoming the s/a as he informs us that he is satisfied with his lot in life. Here the s/a is an example once again of the proper outlook, as he is in Satires 2, 4, 5, and also 1.

Once again, in these lines the satirist has inserted what appears to be a buffer passage between the address to the friend and the s/a-recipient device that fills the rest of the poem. We have noticed such buffers in Satires 2 and 5 in essentially the same position.

Persius' hope that he may use his wealth properly (22–24) leads to the point of the satire, which he expresses in the next two lines to begin the second section: "Live right up to your own crop and grind out your granaries" (25 f.). This is the beginning of the familiar one-on-one relationship that goes through to the end of the satire. It is fairly straightforward, except that the recipient is first the person who, like the s/a, has the money and so is a potential legator (25–40), and then he is the legatee or heir who is looking forward to inheriting the money (41–80).

The discussion in each case is fairly straightforward, but we should notice the loose dialogue that appears from time to time, especially when the heir is being addressed (esp. 51–74). The questions the heir asks and the observations he makes are typical of his selfish, self-centered outlook, and we soon realize that he is really a straw man created by the s/a for his own purposes.

The overall organization of this satire is a little different from that of the other four which we have examined. The address to the legator includes a specific example (27–33), which thus prefaces the discussion of the problem as it did in the other poems. But the solution, which is in the imperative and so resembles that at the end of 4, precedes the discussion here rather than following it (25 f.). It is repeated a little later, once again in the imperative, in the context of the example (31 f.: . . . *de caespite vivo* | *frange aliquid, largire inopi*, . . .).

SATIRE ONE

This poem does not really need a prefacing outline, since its structure is for our purposes fairly simple. It begins with an emotional but completely impersonal statement that is programmatic for Persius' satires (1), and the rest of the poem consists of the s/a speaking to an unnamed recipient. This device is signalled in the second line with a question from the s/a (*min tu istud ais?*), which at the same time warns us to look for dialogue between these two. But this question and the line as a whole indicate something else. The recipient speaks first in reaction to the programmatic statement (2: *quis leget haec?*), thus indicating that he has taken the initiative. This does not happen elsewhere in the satires, but ultimately it does not make a great deal of difference, since the s/a remains in control here as everywhere else. It is a dramatic element, however, that sets this satire off from the others, and at the same time contributes to its liveliness.

The one-on-one device which runs through the satire is firmly established in the first seven lines, not only by the question of the s/a that has already been mentioned, but also by the advice which caps this passage. Here, one cannot miss the three second person exhortations (6: *accedas*; 7: *castiges, quaesiveris*) and the second person pronoun (7: *te*). The point has already been made that this last sentence is to be taken as a programmatic statement of Persius' interest in the individual, and it also seems likely that here, at the beginning of his programmatic satire, Persius is drawing our attention to the diatribe method of s/a-recipient that he will employ consistently throughout the satires.

In these first seven lines, too, a dialogue seems to be carefully developed reinforcing the one-to-one relationship. But as the poem progresses, this dialogue becomes very loose and hazy, as words are attributed to the recipient rather than coming directly from him (40, 55, 112). Moreover, it is not clear whether some statements are to be taken as belonging to the recipient or the s/a (63–68, 76–78, 92–97, 99–102). This is as Persius wants it, and he tells us so. For when the s/a points to the fact that he has made up his adversary (44), he is in essence saying that he has made up his part of the dialogue, too. The recipient, then, is a straw man serving much the same function as the heir in Satire 6.

No matter how vague it becomes, the dialogue element does help to establish the association of s/a and recipient and carry the illusion through those parts of the poem where the relationship itself becomes hazy. If we choose only those passages in which the recipient is clearly addressed or is undoubtedly speaking, we discover an alternating pattern: lines 1–7, 15–30, 40–57, 79–91, 107–114, 120–125. This is quite different from anything else we have seen. In this version of the s/a-recipient device the recipient keeps fading and returning. When he fades the first time (8–14), the s/a uses a collective "we" to generalize about Rome (9: *nostrum*; 10: *facimus*; 11: *sapimus*; 13: *scribimus*), but he keeps the recipient in sight with *ignoscite* (11), and by having him "recite" the kind of thing the s/a has been talking about in these lines (15–17: *haec . . . leges*). As the recipient fades again a few lines later (30–40), the s/a keeps him in the dramatic picture by prefacing *ecce* to the third person examples (30), as we have seen him do elsewhere. In the next passage where the recipient seems not to be present (58–78), the s/a begins by addressing a new plural recipient (61–68) and then suddenly draws attention to the presence of the singular recipient with *ecce* strategically located at the approximate center of the scene (69). There is no such sign-post in the next passage (92–106), but the recipient's comment immediately following it (107–110) shows that he has been present and has heard it.[17] The next passage where

---

[17] Most editors see dialogue here: 92–97 = recip.; 98 = s/a; 99–102 = recip.; 103–106 = s/a. But Persius leaves things vague, probably on purpose.

the recipient is at least blurred (114–120) is actually a direct answer to the query put forward by the adversary a few lines earlier (107 f.) and so presupposes his presence. The recipient does not appear in the final lines of the satire (126–134), but the dramatic momentum and the fact that the s/a has returned to the issue that he and the recipient were discussing at the beginning of this poem allow us to presuppose the latter's presence.

Indiana University

9

Nero's Retinue in Greece, A.D. 66/67

K. R. BRADLEY

The full significance of Nero's visit to Greece in A.D. 66/67 will probably never be known because a complete account of the episode has not survived among the ancient literary sources.[1] Quite clearly, however, Nero's behaviour as aesthete and sportsman did nothing to halt the deterioration of relations between emperor and senate that went back to the early sixties, not to mention the political removal of Cn. Domitius Corbulo and the Sulpicii Scribonii.[2] But one subject on which there is a relatively plentiful supply of information is the composition of the imperial retinue which accompanied Nero on the tour. The purpose of this paper is to draw that information together and to offer the suggestion that the location of Nero's court and the political importance of its members contributed to and aggravated the decline of Nero's stock with the senate in Rome.

Most of the material on the identities of the individuals who accompanied Nero to Greece comes from the epitomated account of the tour of Dio Cassius, whose jaundiced view of the whole expedition is made very clear from the start (63.8.3). It is not always certain from this that everyone mentioned was a member of the imperial entourage, but most cases can probably be assumed so. Thus, the first names to appear are those of Terpnus, Diodorus and Pammenes (Dio 63.8.4), musicians who were defeated by Nero in Greece; there follow the imperial freedman Phoebus

---

[1] On the Hellenic tour generally see B. W. Henderson, *The Life and Principate of the Emperor Nero* (London, 1903), 382 ff.; A. Garzetti, *From Tiberius to the Antonines* (London, 1974), 181 ff.

[2] An absolutely fixed date for a breach between Nero and the senate is not likely, but for the various possibilities see M. T. Griffin, *Seneca: A Philosopher in Politics* (Oxford, 1976), 423 ff. On the political side of Nero's aestheticism see C. E. Manning, "Acting and Nero's Conception of the Principate," *G&R* 22 (1975), 164 ff.; for the deaths, Dio 63.17.2–6.

(63.10.1ᵃ), who is shown influencing access to the emperor; Calvia Crispinilla (63.12.3–4), who is described as wardrobe mistress and chaperone of
the eunuch, and Nero's homosexual partner, Sporus; Sporus himself;
Pythagoras (63.13.2), another homosexual partner of Nero; the imperial
herald Cluvius Rufus (63.14.3); the praetorian prefect Ofonius Tigellinus
(63.12.3–4); and from a later portion of Dio's history (66.11.2) the future
emperor Vespasian is named as a member of the retinue. Vespasian's
presence is also attested by Josephus (*BJ* 3.1.3) and by Suetonius, who
describes him as being *inter comites Neronis* (*Vesp.* 4.4; cf. 5.4). Phoebus'
name might also be confirmed if the story of Tac. *Ann.* 16.5.5 belongs to
Greece, which it might (cf. Suet. *Vesp.* 4.4; Dio 66.11.2). Philostratus
(*VA* 5.7) gives the name of Terpnus and that of another apparent musician, Amoebeus (though the source is not especially reliable), while the
presence with Nero of his wife Statilia Messalina is made clear from
inscriptional sources.[3]

This list of personnel is not likely to have composed the full retinue, for
Suetonius' text at *Vesp.* 4.4 (above) implies the presence of others like
Vespasian, Cluvius Rufus and Tigellinus among the *comites*, men, that is,
of senatorial or equestrian status; but other names are not available. As it
is, freedmen seem to predominate in the list and this may not be altogether
fortuitous;[4] indeed, other freedmen are likely to have been with Nero, for
one would expect the presence of the *a libellis*, Epaphroditus, and the *ab
epistulis*, whose name however is not known at this point in time.[5] In any
case, the identifiable members of the entourage were supplemented by
Nero's crowd of cheerleaders, the Augustiani (said to number five thousand), members of the praetorian guard and, perhaps, the German imperial bodyguard.[6] The full entourage was thus enormous, and in the
tradition as worthy of contempt as the emperor himself.[7] But a closer look
at some of the individuals whose names have been listed reveals a greater
collective importance than at first appears from the hostile tradition.

In spite of Dio's description of her duties Calvia Crispinilla cannot have
been a woman of no consequence: she was well born and in the later
crisis of 68 was sufficiently trusted by Nero to be sent on a mission of some
political importance, an attempt to deal with the rebellious Clodius Macer
in Africa.[8] Dio's story of her rapacity in Greece (63.12.3), even if

---

[3] See further below. Amoebeus may be the person mentioned at Ath. 14.623 d.

[4] For the predominance of freedmen late in Nero's reign see Griffin, *op. cit.*, 108.

[5] Epaphroditus, *PIR²* E 69; on the attendance of secretaries, Fergus Millar, *The
Emperor in the Roman World* (London, 1977), 69 ff.

[6] Dio 63.8.3; Suet. *Nero* 20.3; 19.2; Millar, *op. cit.*, 62 f.   [7] Dio 63.8.3–4.

[8] *PIR²* C 363; *AJP* 93 (1972), 451 ff.

exaggerated, is surely an indication that the emperor was well disposed towards her and suggests that she had influence with him. His wife, Statilia Messalina, must also have had influence. Her presence on the tour has sometimes been doubted,[9] but she was probably included in the sacrifices of the Arval Brethren made for Nero's return and departure in 66,[10] while the people of Acraephia honoured both Nero and Augusta Messalina after the liberation of Greece in 67.[11] This can only mean that she was with Nero, as indeed one would expect under immediate circumstances: Nero had married Messalina in 66, shortly before the Hellenic tour began, but a liaison between them extended back in time; a proposed alliance with Claudius' daughter Antonia, the probable basis of which had been concern for the succession, had not proved viable,[12] and this made Statilia's presence in Greece compelling, because it was impossible that all thought of a successor be neglected by Nero. His homosexual relationships should not of course be thought to preclude this.

By 66, when the tour of Greece began, Vespasian had a considerable record of achievement behind him despite insignificant prospects at the outset of his senatorial career: before the consulship of 51 he had established a military reputation in Germany and Britain; and although the enmity of Agrippina had delayed further progress during the early years of Nero's reign, the proconsulate of Africa which was held in the early sixties marks his return to imperial favour.[13] Later propaganda made Vespasian's attendance on Nero in Greece appear ridiculous;[14] but there must have been more to Vespasian's selection as *comes*, as the propaganda itself and his subsequent treatment of Neronian favourites show (below). One should remember that the Hellenic tour was originally intended as part of a more extensive expedition in the eastern Mediterranean and that plans of conquest were in the air.[15] Under these circumstances it is hard to believe that Vespasian was a purely random choice for the retinue; and of course he was very conveniently available when the Jewish problem required an extraordinary appointment.[16] It is thus beyond doubt that Vespasian was closely connected to Nero in 66/67.

The same is probably true for Cluvius Rufus, also a consular by 66.[17] The position of imperial herald was not usually held by a senator, but

[9] A. Momigliano, *CAH* X (1934), 735 n. 1; cf. Garzetti, *op. cit.*, 181.

[10] E. M. Smallwood, *Documents Illustrating the Principates of Gaius, Claudius and Nero* (Cambridge, 1967), 26.

[11] *SIG*3 814.   [12] See "Nero and Claudia Antonia," *SO* 52 (1977), 79 ff.

[13] *PIR*2 F 398; Griffin, *op. cit.*, 241 f.; 452 f.

[14] Tac. *Ann.* 16.5; Suet. *Vesp.* 4.4; Dio 66.11.2.

[15] Cf. Garzetti, *op. cit.*, 181 f.   [16] See further below.   [17] *PIR*2 C 1206.

rather than reflecting adversely on him this should be put down to Rufus' credit. He had a reputation for eloquence,[18] which could easily lead to influence with the emperor; and his proximity to Nero is signified by the claim in a later age that he had not used his influence to cause anyone harm.[19] One wonders though about his blamelessness; Dio hints[20] at Nero's susceptibility to informers while in Greece, and there was surely more to the removal of Corbulo and the Scribonii than imperial whim. Rufus may have figured here, as may Tigellinus, whose political status with and military importance to Nero hardly calls for emphasis; it is enough to note Dio's comment (63.12.3) that he was constantly in the emperor's presence all through the tour of Greece.[21]

There is not a great deal of information on the freedmen present with Nero, but there are nevertheless some intimations of the power their closeness to the emperor could produce. L. Domitius Paris was apparently put to death in Greece, but the motive of jealousy ascribed to Nero for this by Dio and Suetonius is suspicious.[22] Tacitus makes it clear that Paris owed his position with Nero to his talents as an actor, and the relationship was of longstanding.[23] Early in the reign Paris had been involved in an accusation against Agrippina contrived by Junia Silana;[24] the freedman had been convincing in his role as denunciator, and this combination of artistic interests and palace intrigue was not to be taken lightly. Pammenes is known from Dio simply as an aged citharoedus not liked by Nero, though this should not exclude him from the retinue. It is tempting, in fact, to identify him with the astrologer known from Tacitus,[25] and if correct this makes Pammenes also a figure tied to court politics; for in 66 the exiled Antistius Sosianus drew on the astrologer's knowledge in order to bring charges against those responsible for his own relegation.[26] In the troubled atmosphere of the mid-sixties it is not impossible that Nero wished to have close to him a man who could produce imperial horoscopes, at least as a precautionary measure; Pammenes' association with Sosianus would make much better sense of Nero's distaste for him than aesthetic rivalry alone. Diodorus was another citharoedus defeated by Nero in Greece, but he did not lose favour as a result; he accompanied the emperor upon the entry to Italy and Rome in 68 and, remarkably, was later given financial rewards by Vespasian when emperor.[27] So too was

---

[18] Tac. *Hist.* 4.43.   [19] *Ibid.*   [20] Dio 63.17.3–4.
[21] On Tigellinus cf. Griffin, *op. cit.*, 90.   [22] Dio 63.18.1; Suet. *Nero* 54.
[23] Tac. *Ann.* 13.20.1; 22.3.   [24] Tac. *Ann.* 13.19–22.
[25] Tac. *Ann.* 16.14.1; cf. *PIR*[1] P 56; 55.   [26] Tac. *Ann.* 16.14.
[27] Dio 63.20.3; Suet. *Vesp.* 19.1.

the third defeated citharoedus, Terpnus, also a longtime favourite of
Nero.[28] Phoebus was also well treated by Vespasian, though in a different
way; he had been powerful enough under Nero to reproach the future
emperor for indiscretion, though Vespasian did not take any later action
against him for this.[29]

Nero's entourage was a diverse body. But the common features which
united people of different social status and function were the important
ones of having immediate access to the emperor and the capacity to exert
influence upon him. Routine and serious business still had to be conducted
in Greece by Nero, and although the sources do not show a lot of interest
in this, there are signs that decisions were being made. When the governor-
ships of Upper and Lower Germany were left vacant by the deaths of the
Scribonii, they were filled by the new appointments of C. Verginius Rufus
and Fonteius Capito.[30] The latter was probably one of the *consules ordinarii*
of 67, but he had left office by 20 June of that year,[31] presumably to take
up the German command. Likewise, C. Cestius Gallus is not on record in
his province of Syria after the autumn of 67, and he was probably replaced
late in the same year by C. Licinius Mucianus.[32] The appointment of
Vespasian to the Jewish war, moreover, was made early in 67.[33] Military
appointments such as these had to continue to be made, but what is significant is that only the emperor could make them. In the province itself,
when news of an uncomfortable situation in Rome reached Nero from
Helius, Suetonius' quotation of an imperial rescript in reply indicates that
the emperor was receiving correspondence as normal;[34] and at least one
embassy, of Jews, appeared before him in Greece.[35] Further, the project
to cut a canal through the isthmus at Corinth had a serious side to it and
is suggestive of previous careful consideration.[36] And it is similarly in-
structive that when Nero died in 68, it was known that arrangements for
the holding of the consulship had been made by him for some time
ahead;[37] this procedure, and the planning involved, must have been
applied retrospectively too.

---

[28] Suet. *Vesp.* 19.1; *Nero* 20.1; cf. Philostr. *VA* 5.7.   [29] See n. 14.

[30] Cf. E. Ritterling, *Fasti des röm. Deutschland unter dem Prinzipat* (Vienna, 1932), 17 ff.;
51 ff.

[31] *PIR²* F 468; cf. A 1580 (L. Aurelius Priscus).

[32] *PIR²* C 691; L 216; cf. K. Wellesley, *Cornelius Tacitus: The Histories III* (Sydney,
1972), 232; G. E. F. Chilver, *JRS* 47 (1957), 32.

[33] E. Schürer, *The History of the Jewish People in the Age of Jesus Christ*, revised and
edited by G. Vermes and F. Millar (Edinburgh, 1973), 491.

[34] Suet. *Nero* 23.1.   [35] Jos. *BJ* 2.556.

[36] Suet. *Nero* 19.2; B. Gerster, *BCH* 8 (1884), 225 ff.   [37] Tac. *Hist.* 1.77.

If business such as this simply could not be neglected, the only advisers available to Nero on whom he could draw for opinions (whether or not they were followed) were the people present in the retinue, who, in effect, came to form the government of the Empire. The entourage, however, was an exclusive body, composed of individuals who have a collective history of involvement in court politics, and it had the capacity to block all access to the emperor.[38] Now the mobility of the court throughout imperial history has been shown to be something characteristic of the way in which government functioned;[39] but this broad view tends to underestimate the element of time for immediate political contexts. What is unusual in this case is that, from a narrower viewpoint, Nero's tour of Greece was the first occasion on which the emperor and his court had been out of Italy since Claudius' expedition to Britain, more than twenty years before. From the senate's vantage point in Rome, the situation must have recalled the earlier experience with Tiberius on that emperor's withdrawal to Capri; for there was no way of telling how long Nero would be away from Rome and Italy: when he did return, it was clearly a sudden move on his part.[40] Nothing in actuality could demonstrate the powerlessness of the senate as a bloc more than the display of power by the emperor from the provinces and the display of influence, real or imagined, by those with him, particularly freedmen. On this basis it seems plausible that Nero's eventual loss of support among the upper sections of Roman society while he was in Greece was due, not to the actions of Helius and Polyclitus in the capital alone, nor just to the execution of prominent members of the senate and his own "unimperial" behaviour, but also to the resentment against the emperor and his retinue felt by those who found themselves in no position to make recommendations or overtly influence what decisions were being made while Nero was in Greece. It is worth the final observation that no emperor after Nero again left Italy before Domitian went on campaign, almost twenty years later.[41]

Stanford University

38 Cf. Dio 63.17.4.   39 Millar, *op. cit.*, 59 ff.   40 Cf. Dio 63.19.1.
41 For which cf. Garzetti, *op. cit.*, 286 ff.

10

Amicitia and the Unity of Juvenal's First Book

RICHARD A. LaFLEUR

The theme of treacherous friendship recurs throughout all sixteen of Juvenal's Satires.[1] *Amicitia* and the adjective *amicus* are in every instance used by the satirist ironically; and only in a very few of as many as thirty-nine occurrences does the noun *amicus* bear an interpretation of honest camaraderie. Among the "friends" of Books Two through Five there are niggardly patrons, avaricious, self-serving clients, sexual degenerates and eunuchs, thieves, and others we might call at best fair-weather friends. The alliance depicted is nearly always in fact an unfriendly bond between men somehow unequal. Most often Juvenal has in mind the miserably eroded state of the patronage system; he employs the term *amicus* for both *cliens* and *patronus*, but he always underscores the paradox of applying this traditional label to the frequently impersonal and sometimes overtly antagonistic patron-client relationship. Through all the later books Juvenal's picture of friendship in general, and of patronage in particular, is consistently dismal.

The unhappy idea is first introduced, however, and most thoroughly developed in the five satires of Book One, where friend/friendship words are more numerous than in the other four books combined.[2] "It's difficult

---

[1] For a briefer, more general treatment of the friendship theme in Juvenal's five books, see my "*Amicus* and *Amicitia* in Juvenal," *CB* 51 (1975), 54–58; a useful discussion of *amicitia* as it applies to the patron-client relationship appears in Peter Green's introduction to his Penguin translation, *Juvenal: The Sixteen Satires* (Baltimore, 1967), 30–32, and passim.

[2] *Amicus* (noun) appears twenty times in Book One, at 1.33 and 146; 2.134; 3.1, 57, 87, 101, 107, 112, 116, 121, and 279; 4.88; 5.32, 108, 113, 134, 140 (regarded by some editors as an interpolation), 146, and 173; *amicitia* occurs at 4.75 and 5.14; *amica* (noun) at 1.62, 3.12, and 4.20; and *amicos* (adjective) should be read for *acutos* in 5.41, as I have argued in "Juvenal's 'Friendly Fingernails'," *WS* 88 (1975), 230–235. In Books Two through Five the words are far less frequent; *amicus* (noun) appears eighteen times, in a fairly even distribution.

not to write satire," Juvenal insists in his program poem, and to prove his point he parades before us a scurrilous band of knaves and villains certain to rouse any audience's indignation. Following the betrothed eunuch, the bare-breasted, pig-sticking huntress, Crispinus and the other millionaire parvenus, there menacingly appears the *magni delator amici* (1.33–36):

> . . . magni delator amici
> et cito rapturus de nobilitate comesa
> quod superest, quem Massa timet, quem munere palpat   35
> Carus et a trepido Thymele summissa Latino.

Although the *delator* cannot be certainly identified,[3] it is clear that the *magnus amicus* against whom he informed was no very dear comrade. Here, as often, *magnus* is equivalent to *potens*: the "great friend" is some powerful associate, doubtless the informer's *patronus*, like the other *magni amici* of Book One. This reference to dangerous friendships, and the introduction of Crispinus, Massa, Carus, and several other Domitianic figures in this section of the poem (verses 22–50) are intentionally programmatic, designed by Juvenal to foreshadow themes, characters, and situations that will be more attentively explored later on, particularly in Satire Four.[4]

The audience is permitted a second glimpse at Roman amicability in this opening poem, when the satirist describes the frustrations of a group of clients at their patron's less than generous treatment (132–146):

> vestibulis abeunt veteres lassique clientes
> votaque deponunt, quamquam longissima cenae
> spes homini; caulis miseris atque ignis emendus.
> optima silvarum interea pelagique vorabit   135

---

[3] There is little to recommend the recent suggestion that Juvenal refers to Publicius Certus' role in the prosecution of Helvidius Priscus, made by Léon Herrmann, "Cluviaenus," *Latomus* 25 (1966), 258–264. The context seems to demand a Domitianic figure who could have been involved with the other characters in 35 f. Several commentators have favored M. Aquilius Regulus (*PIR*[2] A1005): see, e.g., J. E. B. Mayor (ed., London, 1886), *ad loc.* See below, n. 11.

[4] As can be seen from a glance at the commentaries, the several identifiable figures in 22–50 are associated with the reign of Domitian. Juvenal's purpose here is, not only to justify his interest in satire, as he says he will do in 19–21, but also to give a specimen of his objects and his techniques. He will name names, but only of those who are dead (like Massa and Carus) or otherwise politically impotent (like the exile Marius: 49): thus the satirist demonstrates by example what he will explicitly announce later, in 150–171, where he discusses the dangers of *onomasti komodein*. He will in this book attack characters drawn primarily from the Domitianic period: thus he anticipates Satires Two and in particular Four, which are most critical of the *ultimus Flavius* and his regime. On the naming techniques employed in 1.22–80 and their programmatic function, see John G. Griffith, "Juvenal, Statius and the Flavian Establishment," *G&R*, 2nd ser., 16 (1969), 147 f., and my "Juvenal 1.80: *Cluvianus?*," *RPh* 50 (1976), 79–84.

rex horum vacuisque toris tantum ipse iacebit.
nam de tot pulchris et latis orbibus et tam
antiquis una comedunt patrimonia mensa.
nullus iam parasitus erit. sed quis ferat istas
luxuriae sordes? quanta est gula quae sibi totos   140
ponit apros, animal propter convivia natum!
poena tamen praesens, cum tu deponis amictus
turgidus et crudum pavonem in balnea portas.
hinc subitae mortes atque intestata senectus.
it nova nec tristis per cunctas fabula cenas;   145
ducitur iratis plaudendum funus amicis.

The gluttonous patron is called *ipse* and *rex*, like Virro, the stingy *patronus* of Satires Five and Nine, and like his lordship Domitian in Four. The personified *gula* of verse 140 anticipates *gula saevit* and *plorante gula* in 5.94 and 158, while *comedunt patrimonia* (138) recalls the *nobilitas comesa* metaphor of line 34 in the earlier *amicus* passage.[5] The patron's hungry friends are, again like Virro's, his aging, tired dependents. After years of grudging abuse, the *clientes* are now dealt one final disappointment—the old man has died intestate! It is with this scene that the satirist aptly completes his re-creation of a typical day in the city (the topic of 127–146). The afternoon closes with a funeral, an event to be applauded by the deceased's angry retainers. Here, too, concludes the satirist's diatribe on the corrupting effects of avarice, a major theme of 87–146 (Juvenal's epilogue on the perils of *onomasti komodein* follows with the transition at 147–150). *Amicis* is the satirist's last word; and it is delayed, like *amici* in verse 33 and *amicus* throughout Book One, to final position in the line, where the *para prosdokian* is specially accentuated.[6] As William Anderson has remarked, the "epigrammatic statement [of 146] punctuates this section decisively."[7]

It can hardly be construed as accidental that this dramatic closing scene of the program poem neatly prefigures the closing poem of the book, with its description of Virro's demeaning dinner for his client-friends and its sardonic portrayal of *amicitia* (Satire Five, like the *cena* passage in One, ends abruptly with a form of the word *amicus*). But, like the earlier allusion

---

5 If the *comedere* echo is intentional, Juvenal looks forward to the association of gluttony and other vices which he establishes later in Satire Four. For *ipse* and *rex* in Four and Five, see below. *Gula* does not occur again until the Fourth Book, though compare the related *gluttisse* in 4.28 (of Domitian).

6 Throughout the sixteen satires *amicus* occupies final position (the single exception is in 6.510). The deliberate positioning seems to reflect, not merely considerations of metrical convenience, but also Juvenal's wish to emphasize the word's nearly always ironic sense.

7 Page 41 of his "Studies in Book I of Juvenal," *YCS* 15 (1957), 33–90. Cf. E. Courtney, "Some thought-patterns in Juvenal," *Hermathena* 98 (1974), 15–21, esp. 20; Courtney detects the use of ring-composition in 87–149.

to a "great friendship" (line 33), the patron's feast in 1.132–146 also foreshadows Satire Four, where both Crispinus and Domitian are, as we shall see, a nearly perfect match for this cormorant who, excluding his *amici*, "devours the choicest foods of the sea" (135) and gorges alone on a huge creature "born for a banquet" (141).

In Satire Two we meet a single *amicus*; he, as might be expected in this poem, is a pervert (134 f.):

> quae causa officii? "quid quaeris? nubit amicus
> nec multos adhibet."   135

"Why so busy?" says one. "You ask?" quips the other, "It's a special friend—he's going to be a bride—and only a few are invited!" In this one exchange may be seen the essence of the satire: business has become buggery, man has become woman, friendship has become farce.

Up to this point Juvenal's *amici* fall a trifle short of the Ciceronian ideal. But the next friend in the book is none other than Satire Three's Umbricius, fugitive from the slings and arrows of a corrupt and thankless Rome. Most students of Umbricius take him to be a purposely sympathetic figure, an actual friend of the poet or perhaps a Juvenalian alter-ego.[8] The satirist himself, however, is admittedly *confusus* (3.1–3):

> quamvis digressu veteris confusus amici
> laudo tamen, vacuis quod sedem figere Cumis
> destinet atque unum civem donare Sibyllae.

A curious, enigmatic preface. *Confusus*, usually rendered "upset" or "saddened," can suggest intellectual rather than emotional confusion, and hence might be translated "puzzled." Indeed, though Umbricius' sentiments are frequently close to those which Juvenal expresses elsewhere, there is much in his program that seems paradoxical and un-Juvenalian, not least of all the proposed exile to the not so idyllic *umbra* of Cumae. No longer *quieta* (as Statius had called her: *Silvae* 4.3.65) since completion, more than a decade earlier, of the *via Domitiana*, which passed directly through her forum, and oldest of the Greek cities in Italy, Cumae was a doubly peculiar retreat for the xenophobic pastoralist Umbricius, who should have preferred the rustic simplicity of Gabii or some sleepier Latin

---

[8] Barry Baldwin's recent discussion of Umbricius, if it can be said to take a position, is traditionalist ("There is nothing un-Juvenalian about Umbricius' diatribe...."): "Three Characters in Juvenal," *CW* 66 (1972), 101. My own view of the character's intended function, suggested below, is more fully defended in "Umbricius and Juvenal Three," *ŽAnt* 26 (1976), 383–431.

town.[9] Juvenal himself would hardly have considered permanent withdrawal from the city that provided the *farrago* for his satire; indeed he seems almost certainly to have remained in Rome throughout his literary career.[10]

We should take a clue to Juvenal's real intention for the Umbricius character from the meaning of *amicus* and *amicitia* elsewhere in the Satires, especially in Book One. In the Third Satire itself *amicus* appears eight more times. The first friend after Umbricius is another *magnus amicus*, a rich patron whose guilt makes him the timorous victim of an amicable blackmailer (*a magno semper timearis amico*: 57); the obvious irony recalls the "great friend" of 1.33. In the space of thirty-five lines (87–121: part of the invective *in Graeculos*) the word occurs six times, always for uncaring patrons like the one who has rejected Umbricius. The Greek parasites who have succeeded in wooing these *patroni* are, Umbricius protests, flatterers, debauchees, faithless villains. At worst, repeating the crime of Egnatius against his patron Barea Soranus, they will even murder their "friends": *occidit . . . delator amicum* (116, at line's end) is unquestionably meant to echo *magni delator amici* in the program poem (1.33, also at line's end).[11]

---

9 Umbricius complains, "*Non possum ferre, Quirites,* | *Graecam urbem*" (60 f.), and late speaks nostalgically of Praeneste, Volsinii, Gabii, Tibur (190–192), Sora, Fabrateria, Frusino (223 f.), and Juvenal's own Aquinum (319), all (except Volsinii) in Latium. If Umbricius is to be narrowly identified with Juvenal, why does he not retire to Aquinum or one of those other towns nearby? Why Cumae of all places, a city so Greek in its associations? Not, certainly, to escape crime and vice: as the *ianua Baiarum* (4), Cumae was gateway to the Roman Sodom, and, by Umbricius' own admission, the neighborhood was infested with brigands (305–308). Nor for solitude, since the new coastal highway had brought visitors, money, and a flurry of new construction: see J. Rufus Fears, "Cumae in the Roman Imperial Age," *Vergilius* 21 (1975), 1–21.

10 Even if the uncertain tradition of Juvenal's exile to Egypt is accepted, Umbricius' flight from Rome is no parallel. The Egyptian exile was by all accounts involuntary, and would likely have antedated Juvenal's literary career in any case, as Gilbert Highet contends in *Juvenal the Satirist* (Oxford, 1954), 26 f. The poems furnish no evidence of any violent disruption in his lifestyle; in the later satires Juvenal seldom retreats farther than into the comfort of his own urban apartment.

11 The scholiast on 1.33 sees the *delator amici* reference as an allusion to the same incident touched upon here in 3.116, Egnatius Celer's appearance as a witness against his friend and patron Marcius Barea Soranus in A.D. 66 (Tac. *Ann.* 16.32). Against this identification is the fact that the context of 1.33–35 is Domitianic (above, n. 3), while Celer's activities date to Nero's reign (he was exiled in 69). Still, the undoubtedly intentional echo links the two poems thematically through the similar depiction of comparable events. Soranus (who is mentioned again favorably in 7.91) and his daughter were condemned to death for their anti-Neronian sympathies along with Thrasea Paetus (for Thrasea in Juvenal 5.36, see below and n. 39).

Amicus, even at its final appearance later in the poem (278–280), becomes ironic through the satirist's incongruous analogy:

> ebrius ac petulans, qui nullum forte cecidit,
> dat poenas, noctem patitur lugentis amicum
> Pelidae, cubat in faciem, mox deinde supinus. 280

The drunken bully has no friend, Juvenal implies; nor is such epic friendship as that of Achilles for Patroclus to be found in the seething cosmopolis.

Umbricius' place in all of this is that of the *exclusus amicus* at his patron's threshold, resenting the orientals who have displaced him, not so much for their alleged treachery toward the patron-friend as because they refuse to share him. Umbricius' last complaint is the most revealing (121–125):

> . . . numquam partitur amicum,
> solus habet. nam cum facilem stillavit in aurem
> exiguum de naturae patriaeque veneno,
> limine summoveor, perierunt tempora longi
> servitii; nusquam minor est iactura clientis. 125

When Juvenal labels this frustrated client *vetus amicus* in line 1, he may only mean to recall the *veteres lassique clientes* of the program satire: like them Umbricius is old (3.26–28), tired (25: he likens himself to Daedalus, who put off his *fatigatas . . . alas* at Cumae), and disappointed at his patron's door (3.124, 1.132 f.). Umbricius is also close to the mistreated *amicus* of Five, Virro's client Trebius (5.64: *veteri . . . clienti*), and especially to Naevolus, the parasite discarded by Virro in Juvenal's only other dialogue, Satire Nine.[12] A more patently unsympathetic figure, Naevolus, aging, tattered and torn, like Umbricius, and rejected by his patron, even considers abandoning Rome and settling at Cumae.[13] The correspondences are too striking not to have been intended.

Both characters function very like Catius and Horace's other interlocutors in *Sermones* Two: each represents the *doctor ineptus* type, to use Anderson's expression, the "teacher who fails to grasp the implications

---

[12] H. A. Mason has noticed the kinship of Three and Nine, pp. 100 f. of his study, "Is Juvenal a Classic?," in J. P. Sullivan, ed., *Satire: Critical Essays on Roman Literature* (Bloomington, 1968), 93–176; like most readers, however, Mason takes Umbricius too seriously and fails to notice the numerous similarities between him and Naevolus. In an article not available to me when I wrote "Umbricius and Juvenal Three" (above, n. 8), Franco Bellandi has drawn attention to many of the characteristics shared by Umbricius, Trebius, and Naevolus: see "Naevolus cliens," *Maia* 26 (1974), 279–299.

[13] Cf. 3.24 f. with 9.21 (their *proposita*); 3.22 with 9.27 f. (their labors unrewarded); 3.26–28 with 9.9, 129 (their age); 3.125 with 9.59 f., 71 f. (the two as rejected clients); 3.148–151 with 9.28–31 (tattered clothing as evidence of their *paupertas*); 3.2, 24 f. with 9.56–60 (their interest in Cumae).

of his own precepts and thus ends as a figure of fun."[14] Catius, "Mr. Shrewd," lectures Horace and his audience on *delicatessen* in *Sermones* 2.4.[15] The piece concludes with some good-natured humor at the expense of the Epicureans and with Horace's swearing, sarcastically of course, by Catius' friendship (88 f.):

> docte Cati, per amicitiam divosque rogatus,
> ducere me auditum, perges quocumque, memento.

Introduced by the satirist near the beginning of the poem, given the pulpit and allowed to dominate the satiric dialogue,[16] friend Catius proceeds to expose himself and his *praecepta vitae beatae* to ridicule, not so much on account of his basic principles (his culinary advice is essentially sound, as Anderson remarks) as for the absurd, un-Roman extremes to which he would carry them, and the grandiose tone in which he offers his expert advice. Umbricius may be just such a "friendly advisor," meant more to provoke than to persuade. Certainly Juvenal meant to draw attention to the problems of life in Rome, a topic that was commonplace, but he also expected his audience to question Umbricius' motives and his irrational, unproductive solution to those problems.[17]

---

[14] William S. Anderson, "The Roman Socrates: Horace and his Satires," in Sullivan, *Satire*, 34, and see also 29–37.

[15] *Catius* I take to be a significant name, a device common in satire. For other etymologically appropriate names in Horace, see Niall Rudd's "The Names in Horace's Satires," *CQ*, n.s., 10 (1960), 168–170. *Umbricius* may also have been chosen for its etymology. Anna Lydia Motto and John R. Clark suggest an intended connection with *umbra*, in the sense of "ghost," and view Umbricius as a kind of Spirit of Rome Past, withdrawing from the corrupt reality of the present to the supernatural world of Cumae and Avernus: *"Per iter tenebricosum*: The Mythos of Juvenal 3," TAPA 96 (1965), 267–276; cf. Baldwin, 101, and pp. 147 f. of S. C. Fredericks' chapter, "Juvenal: A Return to Invective," in E. S. Ramage, D. L. Sigsbee, and Fredericks, *Roman Satirists and Their Satire* (Park Ridge, New Jersey, 1974). Perhaps more likely is the possibility that *Umbricius* was meant to suggest the adjectives *umbraticus* and the sometimes pejorative *umbratilis*, "fond of the shade," (*umbra* in the sense of leisure and retirement: cf. Juvenal 7.8 and 173), in which case the name would be quite appropriate to the character's *propositum* of abandoning Rome for the idyllic seclusion of Cumae. For other pastoral elements in Satire Three, see Charles Witke, pp. 128–151 of his *Latin Satire: The Structure of Persuasion* (Leiden, 1970), esp. 133 f. Similarly Naevolus' name, "Master Wart" (perhaps borrowed from Martial 3.71 and 95), suits his ugly disposition.

[16] Catius is given about 86 percent of the lines in Horace's satire, while Umbricius has 94 percent; Damasippus, in *Serm.* 2.3, controls 96 percent of the conversation.

[17] Thus the satire cuts in two directions, like many of Juvenal's later poems; cf. David S. Wiesen on Satire Seven, p. 482 of his "Juvenal and the Intellectuals," *Hermes* 101 (1973), 464–483: "This counterpoint of two opposite and conflicting themes, one of which

The Third Satire is in scope the most comprehensive poem of Book One, and the longest. With its 322 lines, in fact, the piece is nearly identical in length to Satires One and Two combined (341 lines), and to Four and Five combined (327 lines). Probably later in composition than both Two and Four (which are more concerned with Domitian), Satire Three is given the position that befits both its own importance and the structural balance of the book as a whole.[18] Viewed in this way, the two poems that follow constitute an equivalent third part of the volume. And indeed there is reason to believe that Juvenal intended his readers to perceive Satires Four and Five as a cohesive unit, an inseparable, because complementary, pair. It is the prominence of the *amicitia* theme that, beside establishing a link with the preceding satires and responding to the program poem in particular, provides the remarkable parallelism between Four and Five themselves.

On the surface the two satires appear unalike: one burlesques an imperial *concilium*, while the other describes an ungenerous patron's dinner party for his miserable *clientes*. Four begins with a prologue that reintroduces the Domitianic rogue Crispinus (1–27).[19] Juvenal touches first on the man's foppishness (hinted at in the program, 1.26–29) and his gross sexual vices, and then concentrates on a more trivial aspect of his general degradation, his gluttony. There is a single illustration: Crispinus, once a fishmonger himself in his native Egypt, had recently purchased an enormous mullet for 6,000 sesterces. "The fisherman himself could have been

---

questions the validity of the other, is an essential but little noticed characteristic of Juvenalian satire." Similarly, in the mock consolation of Thirteen, Juvenal "satirizes the genre itself [*consolatio*] and Calvinus [his addressee]": so Mark Morford, "Juvenal's Thirteenth Satire," *AJP* 94 (1973), 26–36. Only a few scholars have detected the anti-Umbrician aspect of Juvenal Three, and none have sufficiently discussed the matter: see Mason, 126, 135; Anderson, "*Lascivia* vs. *ira*: Martial and Juvenal," *CSCA* 3 (1970), 29; and S. C. Fredericks, "Daedalus in Juvenal's Third Satire," *CB* 49 (1972), 11–13, esp. 13: "Umbricius' personal solution to the evils he sees around him is merely to escape and to leave the city behind him no better for his departure. Like the disgruntled members of our own society who flee the Inner City for a more pleasant life in the suburban fringes, Umbricius has merely contributed to the problem, not to the solution." Fredericks takes a more traditional stand in his chapter for *Roman Satirists*, but even there comments on the similarity of Umbricius to the unsympathetic Trebius.

[18] Cf. Highet, 89: "Satire Three, long and finely constructed, is placed in the middle for the maximum effect." See further p. 366 of W. Heilmann's valuable study, "Zur Komposition der vierten Satire und des ersten Satirenbuches Juvenals," *RhM* 110 (1967), 358–370.

[19] For Crispinus, who is otherwise known only from Martial 7.99 and 8.48, see Peter White, "*Ecce Iterum Crispinus*," *AJP* 95 (1974), 377–382.

bought for less," the satirist complains. But far worse than the extravagant price was the fact that Crispinus had acquired the fish, not as a gift for some childless old man aimed at securing a place in his will, nor for some "powerful woman-friend" in order to win her favor, but solely for his own palate (18–22):

> consilium laudo artificis, si munere tanto
> praecipuam in tabulis ceram senis abstulit orbi;
> est ratio ulterior, magnae si misit amicae,   20
> quae vehitur cluso latis specularibus antro.
> nil tale expectes: emit sibi.

Crispinus' gluttony recalls the *cena* of 1.132–146, while *munere* and *magnae . . . amicae* echo *magni . . . amici* and *munere* in 1.33–35. The hypothetical great lady is the third "powerful friend" of the Satires: the first is betrayed (1.33), the second is intimidated (3.57), the last is the prospective victim of *ratio ulterior*.

In a transitional passage of nine lines (28–36) Juvenal shifts our attention toward Domitian. When a scoundrel like Crispinus can rise to such luxury in the imperial palace, belching up thousands at a single course, what should we expect of his model, the emperor himself? Vice loves vice—this is Juvenal's point here and throughout the satire. A man of influence, whether an emperor, a bureaucrat, or a wealthy patron, will surround himself with associates who are his moral equals from the start or who will rise or (more easily) descend to his level.

The major division of the poem (37–149) is a seriocomic burlesque, mock epic in tone, of an emergency meeting of Domitian's council. A fisherman from Picenum has taken a huge turbot in his nets. Fearful that Domitian's agents would confiscate the fish, claiming it as imperial property, the *piscator* determined to profit in grace at least, by delivering his catch personally to the emperor. While Domitian's *amici* look on from the doorway, fish and fisher are admitted to the royal chambers (*exclusi spectant admissa obsonia patres*: 64), and the gift is ceremoniously presented: "Rejoice, accept and consume this fish, too great for a private oven. Preserved by the gods until your generation, it insisted on being caught . . . for thee!" No one loved flattery more than Domitian, and so he accepted all the fisherman offered. But then an unnerving discovery was made— the palace cupboard lacked a platter large enough to hold the emperor's new fish. Straightaway the *amici principis* were summoned into special session.

Verses 72–149 caricature the councillors, eleven men closely associated with the Flavian regime, most of them known to us from other sources.[20] Although the satire contains little in the way of direct criticism of Domitian himself, we are nonetheless, as Highet observes (page 82), "conscious of his power, and of his brooding incalculable dangerous character, silent and unpredictable like a snake." The emperor is seen most clearly as a reflection of those men who come under his influence. Earlier in the poem intimations of Domitian's character were to be gleaned from the behavior of Crispinus and the fisherman; but the most damning insight is provided in the depiction of the advisors as they hasten into the meeting-room (72–75):

> vocantur
> ergo in consilium proceres, quos oderat ille,
> in quorum facie miserae magnaeque sedebat
> pallor amicitiae.   75

Once more we are reminded of the "great friendships" of One and Three; and we may even recall the *magna amica* of 4.20, and thus see the theme of perverted *amicitia* as yet another link between the prologue and the narrative of this poem, whose structure has been so frequently criticized.[21] In the lines that follow, the behavior of the councillors ranges from timorous reticence to gross adulation. The group, in which Crispinus makes his final appearance, includes adulterers, informers, murderers, and others, like Crispus and Acilius, whose worst crime was submissiveness. The relationship with Domitian shared by all of them, Juvenal suggests, was quite literally appalling. It parallels almost exactly the dread friendships of the earlier satires: here the emperor is the ultimate patron, while the

[20] See Griffith (above, n. 4); Ronald Syme, *Tacitus* (Oxford, 1958), 5 f., 636; John Crook, *Consilium Principis* (Cambridge, 1955), 49–51.

[21] Green has remarked (pp. 46 f.) that Four "is a broken-backed affair which has defied even the most ingenious attempts to unify its parts"; and Michael Coffey concludes that the poem "remains obstinately in two parts," in his "Juvenal Report for the Years 1941–1961," *Lustrum* 8 (1963), 206; cf. E. J. Kenney, "The First Satire of Juvenal," *PCPhS* 8 (1962), 30 f. The work of Stegemann, Helmbold and O'Neil, and Anderson should have saved the poem from this criticism. The first cogent defense of the satire's unity was offered by W. Stegemann, who pointed to the essentially chiastic structure (Crispinus' *scelera*, 1–10; his *facta leviora*, 11–27; Domitian's *nugae*, 37–150; his *scelera*, 150–154): *De Juvenalis dispositione* (Weyda, 1913), 30–34, esp. 33. W. C. Helmbold and E. N. O'Neil build upon Stegemann's work in "The Structure of Juvenal IV," *AJP* 77 (1956), 68–73; William Anderson has contributed other important insights, "Studies," 68–80; cf. Heilmann, 359–365; Ross S. Kilpatrick, "Juvenal's 'Patchwork' Satires: 4 and 7," *YCS* 23 (1973), 230–235.

frightened and frightening advisors are his gloomy *clientes*.[22] Their terror is wholly justified, for, as the satirist remarks (86–88):

> . . . quid violentius aure tyranni,
> cum quo de pluviis aut aestibus aut nimboso
> vere locuturi fatum pendebat amici?

Friendship, Juvenal repeats, can be fatal.

In the end the counsel of mountainous Montanus prevails (his culinary expertise was apparent from the fact that his belly had arrived at the meeting before him: 107). The fish would not be carved into plate-size portions, but rather, with suitably epic flair, a mammoth platter would be fashioned for it, and royal potters would be appointed to meet similar crises in the future. The *amici principis* are abruptly dismissed, like the client-friends of 1.132; and Domitian, as Helmbold and O'Neil rightly suppose (page 72), prepares to glut himself alone on the monstrous scaly beast.

If the fish is a symbol "of the Empire and what Domitian has done to it," as Professor Anderson has argued,[23] then the emperor is more ghoul than glutton. Although Anderson does not make the point, this is precisely the image Juvenal wished to convey in his epilogue (150–154):

> atque utinam his potius nugis tota illa dedisset   150
> tempora saevitiae, claras quibus abstulit urbi
> inlustresque animas inpune et vindice nullo.
> sed periit postquam Cerdonibus esse timendus
> coeperat: hoc nocuit Lamiarum caede madenti.

Cerdonibus in 153, rightly construed by Mayor and Knoche as a cognomen (rather than a common noun), is used as a generic plural.[24] Through his

---

[22] Green's observation is apropos (p. 30): Juvenal "saw the feudal relationship everywhere: between master and slave, between patron and client, between the jobber of army commissions and the hopeful military careerist. Roman society formed a vast pyramid, with the Emperor—the most powerful patron of all—at the top, and the rabble roaring for bread and circuses at the bottom; in between came an interlinked series of lesser pyramids, where one man might play both roles, patronizing his inferiors and toadying to those above him."

[23] Anderson, "Studies," 78: "The physical enormity of the *rhombus* . . . ideally symbolizes the sensual and moral enormity of the court, for both suffer the violence of Domitian, and the court is a microcosm of the Empire."

[24] The word is capitalized by both Mayor (see his note, *ad loc.*) and Ulrich Knoche (ed., Munich, 1950); both likewise capitalize in 8.181 f., *quae | turpia Cerdoni Volesos Brutumque decebunt*, with which cf. 4.13 f., *nam, quod turpe bonis Titio Seiioque, decebat | Crispinum*. In both Four and Eight *Cerdo* is a type-name (like *Titius* and *Seiius*) for the lower classes, in contrast to the Lamiae, the Volesi, and the Bruti, despite those who persist in reading *cerdo* as a common noun (including Highet, 82; the *OLD*; W. V. Clausen, ed.,

selection of this Greek name ("Mr. Craft"), common in Italy only among slaves and freedmen, Juvenal is reminding us that Domitian was assassinated, partly at the instigation of his wife Domitia Longina, by a gang of palace menials and *libertini* who felt themselves threatened by the emperor (hence *timendus*).[25] *Cerdonibus* is neatly balanced by the plural cognomen *Lamiarum*, which occurs in the same metrical position in the following line. The allusion in 154 illustrates by example the general statement of 151 f., for the Aelii Lamiae, a family praised by Horace and Tacitus, were among the innocent victims of Domitian's scourge. As commentators have generally noted, Juvenal's audience would think in particular of L. Aelius Lamia Plautius Aelianus, consul suffect in A.D. 80: Domitian first stole his wife Domitia (who would subsequently participate in the plot against the emperor's life) and then had him murdered about twelve years later.[26] But *Lamiarum*, like so many of Juvenal's personal names, contains a double meaning. Besides alluding specifically to Aelius Lamia and to the failure of the senatorial class in general, however severely abused, to remove Domitian from power, the name conveys a final intimation of the emperor's bestiality. The last two words of the poem, *caede madenti*, the careful juxtaposition *Lamiarum caede madenti*, would conjure up for the ancient audience a vision of the Lamiae of myth and Märchen, the carnivorous, bloodsucking death-demons who victimized poor innocents asleep in their

---

Oxford, 1959). The name is related to Greek κέρδος, and thus connotes profiteering and cunning; for its use as a cognomen, esp. for slaves, see *RE* Suppl. 1 and 3, s.v., the *Onomastica* in *TLL* and Forcellini, and the indexes to F. Preisigke, *Namenbuch* (Heidelberg, 1922) and D. Foraboschi, *Onomasticon Alterum* (Milan, 1971). Cf. Martial's *sutor* (*PIR²* C662), 3.16.1; 3.59.1; 3.99.1; the merchant in Apul. *Met.* 2.13 f. (*PIR²* C663); Petr. 60.8: *aiebat autem unum Cerdonem, alterum Felicionem, tertium Lucrionem vocari.*

25 Suet. *Dom.* 17 numbers among the actual assassins Stephanus *Domitillae procurator*, Clodianus *cornicularius*, Maximus *Partheni libertus*, Satur *decurio cubiculariorum*, and an unnamed man *e gladiatorio ludo*; Juvenal's *timendus* may be explained either by the fact that Stephanus had recently been charged with embezzlement (a crime possibly hinted at in the name *Cerdo*: cf. K. H. Waters, "Juvenal and the Reign of Trajan," *Antichthon* 4 [1970], 70 and n. 33), or by Dio's testimony (67.15) that the conspirators included chiefly men whom Domitian held suspect and had designated for execution, a fact of which they were apprised by Domitia. Cf. Dio 67.16–18.

26 The cognomen *Lamia* is common only to the *gens Aelia*; for the family, see Hor. *Carm.* 1.26.8; 1.36.7, and esp. 3.17; and Tac. *Ann.* 6.27 (where the Aelii Lamiae are described as a *genus decorum*). For Domitian's abuse of Lamia Aelianus (*PIR²* A205), see Suet. *Dom.* 1 and 10, where the man's death is connected with the executions of Thrasea Paetus and Acilius Glabrio (the councillor of Juvenal 4.95), and with the exile of Helvidius Priscus (on Paetus and Priscus, see below, n. 39).

beds.[27] If Domitian does not actually devour his prodigious turbot before our eyes, Juvenal nonetheless leaves us with the ghastly spectre of Rome's most literally monstrous emperor *Lamiarum caede madenti,* "dripping wet with vampires' gore," fresh from feasting upon the state's nobility—once more an image foreshadowed in the program poem by the *nobilitas comesa* of 1.34.

This grisly fusion of gluttony and murder, besides recalling the cannibalism metaphor of Satire One, glances back at the opening lines of Four itself.[28] In fact, the entire epilogue serves a dual purpose. First, it enhances the satire's unity: the closing vision of Domitian's monstrous bloodfeast brings to mind the prologue's depiction of Crispinus, his gluttonous consumption of an enormous fish (as in Domitian's case, implied, not described), and his characterization as an irredeemably vicious monster (*monstrum*: a word conspicuously repeated throughout the poem).[29] As readers have seen with increasing clarity, Crispinus and Domitian reflect one another;[30] their actions here, which, it is emphasized, comprise every kind and degree of vice, are mirrored in the poem's opening and conclusion. And the behavior of both men, it is equally important to realize, is intentionally prefigured by the poet in the two *amicus* passages of Satire One. Secondly, while focusing most sharply on the emperor, the epilogue affords the satirist one last gibe at those men who are equally his target, the *amici principis* like Crispinus and Acilius, and others of the *nobilitas comesa,* like the Lamiae, who were either too terrified or too corrupt themselves to exorcise Rome of her demonic possessor: men "on whose faces had settled the pallor of a great and miserable friendship."

---

[27] Though I was independently attracted to this interpretation, the double sense of *Lamiarum* has already been noticed by R. J. Rowland, Jr., in "Juvenal's *Lamiae*: Note on *Sat.* 4.154," *CB* 40 (1964), 75; Rowland's suggestion appears to have been ignored in all subsequent studies of the poem. The double entendre develops from the possibility of reading *Lamiarum* as both objective and subjective genitive.

[28] See above, on *nobilitas comesa* and *comedunt patrimonia,* 1.34 and 138. In the prologue to Four gluttony is emphasized as just one aspect of a more general degradation. Murder and gluttony coalesce in cannibalism, subject of the metaphor at 1.34 and the vampire image it foreshadows in 4.154. Juvenal's interest in a more literal cannibalism surfaces in Satire Fifteen.

[29] *Monstrum* is applied to Crispinus (2), to the turbot (45), and (in 115) to Catullus, not, as Anderson supposes ("Studies," 78), to Veiiento (the relative clause and all of 114–122 describe Catullus). This Catullus, the *grande monstrum* (the *quoque* of 115 is meant to recall Juvenal's similar labelling of Crispinus and the fish) and *caecus adulator* (116), is to be identified with L. Valerius Catullus Messalinus (*PIR*[1] V41), consul with Domitian in 73. For his actual blindness see Pliny *Ep.* 4.22.5 f.; but *basia* (118) and *qui numquam visae flagrabat amore puellae* (114) are designed to evoke the *caecus amator,* Messalinus' relative and namesake, the republican poet Catullus: see my "Catullus and Catulla in Juvenal," *RPh* 48 (1974), 71–74.

[30] Esp. Helmbold and O'Neil, 70; 73; Anderson, "Studies," 70.

The principal theme of Juvenal Five is likewise *magna amicitia*. As Peter Green has commented in comparing this poem to the Fourth Satire, "it is the same story, but the props have been changed."[31] Again the relationship is an unfriendly one, between the sadistic Virro and his grovelling client Trebius; again, whatever "greatness" may exist in the partnership derives merely from the patron's wealth and status. The noun *amicus* appears seven times in this satire, more frequently than in any other, and always in the emphatic final position; significantly, *amico* is the last word of the poem (and of the book).[32] In each case the term is equivalent to either *cliens* or *patronus*: the union between patron and client has become, Juvenal once more suggests, venal, contemptuous, even hostile.

Like Satire Four, the poem opens with a brief prologue and a transitional section (1–11, 12–23), in which theme and context are established, the client-friend introduced, and the posture of the satirist indicated. Trebius is here a fitting counterpart to Crispinus in the prologue to Four. Both *amici* are of undistinguished origin; both have become shameless dependents; the two differ more in degree than in quality.[33] Crispinus is ridiculed as Domitian's court dandy (*deliciae*: 4.4), while Trebius (5.3 f.) is scornfully compared to Augustus' palace jesters, Gabba and Sarmentus (whom Plutarch similarly labels δηλίκια).[34] The kinship between Five and the preceding poem is most clearly revealed, however, by the echo of *magna amicitia* from 4.74 f. which we hear in the cynical pronoucement of verse 14: *fructus amicitiae magnae cibus.*[35] "The only profit from this great

---

[31] Page 32; Green further compares Four, Five, and Nine as treatments of "Juvenal's favourite theme, the corruption of personal relationships," (48) and comments on the double-edged attack in each of these three poems (32 f.). What he does not point out is that the double-edge slices at all the "friends" of Satires One, Two, and Three as well.

[32] Line references are given above, n. 2.

[33] Juvenal alludes to Crispinus' base origin; see also White (n. 19, above). Neither Trebius nor his wife Mygale (or Mycale) bears a distinguished name; they and their host are likely fictitious, though for some attempts at identification see my "Umbricius," 384 f. n. 5.

[34] Sarmentus (*PIR*[1] S144) is almost certainly the *scurra* named in Hor. *Serm.* 1.5.51–70; once the property of Maecenas, Plutarch says of him, ὁ δὲ Σάρμεντος ἦν τῶν Καίσαρος παιγνίων παιδάριον, ἃ δηλίκια Ῥωμαῖοι καλοῦσιν (*Ant.* 59: 32 B.C.). Quintilian mentions both Sarmentus and Gabba (*PIR*[2] G1) as wits (6.3.58; 62). The two Augustan buffoons are a proper match for Trebius, who provides the *comoedia* (157) for his unpleasant host.

[35] The phrase, in the genitive case at both 4.74 f. and 5.14, appears nowhere else in the Satires (though cf. 6.558 f.); we are meant, of course, to recall the *magni amici* of One and Three. We may here cite a valuable study of the structural and thematic interrelations of Horace's Satires (which so profoundly influenced Juvenal), C. A. van Rooy's "Arrangement and Structure of Satires in Horace, *Sermones*, Book I, with More Special Reference to Satires 1–4," *AClass* 11 (1968), 38–72. Commenting on Horace's pairing of intentionally complementary poems, van Rooy affirms the principle that, beyond the

friendship is . . . food": the sort of parasite typified by Trebius will do anything for a free meal, and so, quite appropriately, this is all he will get. But even dinner invitations are rare, continues the satirist-advisor, and they are always carefully recorded by the grudging patron in his account of services rendered (15–23).

The following 146 lines (24–169) illustrate in detail the inferior drink, food, and service that Trebius will endure at Virro's board while his lordship, looking on with a cruel haughtiness, dines in the grandest style. Even this division of the poem bears striking resemblances to the narrative in Satire Four. In both the context is culinary. In both the imperious patron and his submissive *amici* are gathered about a table (somewhat like the friends of the program poem who cheered the funeral of their niggardly *patronus*).[36]

Whereas the *concilium* in Four dealt with the matter of how to serve the emperor's marvelous fish, the longest section of Five (80–106, at the poem's center) describes the seafood actually served at Virro's *cena*. Trebius gets an eel that looks like a snake, or a pike fat from the sewers, and a single prawn. The biggest fish, as in Satire Four, goes to the host: Virro dines on a richly garnished lobster, a huge lamprey (*muraena . . . maxima*: 99), and, most significantly, an expensive mullet, just like Crispinus' in the prologue to the earlier poem. Compare in particular 5.92; 97 f.,

> mullus erit domini . . .
> . . . .
> instruit ergo focum provincia, sumitur illinc
> quod captator emat Laenas, Aurelia vendat[37]

---

mere repetition of a theme, "repeated use of a particular word, or name, or of a special phrase, will be found to be even more significant in proving that the author, usually in a most subtle manner, deliberately wrote or edited two satires to form a pair" (p. 41).

36 In One, the patron actually dines alone (136; 138: *mensa*), but we later find his *irati amici* at table (145); cf. 5.4, 145. In Four, the "host" and his councillors are seated (76: *sedit*; 144: *surgitur*), and the topic of conversation recalls the traditional symposium; foremost among the "guests" is the plump gourmand Montanus (130–143). The word *cena* recurs through all three poems: 1.133, 145; 4.30; 5.9, 24, 85, 117. Heilmann (367) rightly compares *longissima cenae | spes* (1.133 f.) with *votorum summa* (5.18) and *spes bene cenandi* (5.166): the client-friends of the program and Trebius are alike in having as their highest aspiration the hope for a meal. Witke's reaction to the *irati amici* in this regard is just what Juvenal must have intended: "Here Juvenal by a brief touch puts these wretches into proportion: they have sunk so low that their most far-reaching expectation is free dinner. He states it aphoristically, with no overt condemnation" (p. 122).

37 Laenas is unknown (though see Highet, 293); Aurelia is meant for a woman of position, perhaps to be identified with the victim of Regulus' *captatio* known from Plin. *Ep.* 2.20.10 f. Heilmann (368) also compares the two mullet passages.

with 4.15; 18–21,

mullum sex milibus emit   15

. . . .
consilium laudo artificis, si munere tanto
praecipuam in tabulis ceram senis abstulit orbi;
est ratio ulterior, magnae si misit amicae,   20
quae vehitur cluso latis specularibus antro.

Thus Juvenal deliberately employs in both passages the example of a costly fish, a mullet in either instance, whose value is ironically computed in terms of its worth to a *captator* as a present for some influential woman. Trebius' "great friend," like Domitian and Crispinus and the nameless patron in One, will devour the extravagant treat without sharing it. Moreover, just as the patron of Satire One is served—besides seafood (135)—an entire boar, so is Virro (5.116); Trebius, on the other hand, eats cabbage (5.87), and so do the *irati amici* of the program poem (1.134).

When he first mentions Virro's mullet, Juvenal calls it the "master's" fish (*mullus . . . domini*: 92). The epithet *dominus* had been a favorite of Domitian's, of course, and the satirist applies it to him twice in Satire Four, once in a comment about his fish (*piscem | . . . elapsum veterem ad dominum debere reverti*: 50–52), and again in describing the emperor's savage abuse of his *amici* (*mors tam saeva . . . | et domini gladiis tam festinata*: 95 f.). Virro likewise is master to both fish and friends: Juvenal titles him *dominus* again at 71, 81, 137, and 147. And, like the gluttonous Domitian of 4.28 f. (*qualis tunc epulas ipsum glutisse putamus | induperatorem*) and the selfish patron of 1.136 (*vacuis . . . toris tantum ipse iacebit*), Virro is five times referred to with the lordly *ipse* (30, 37, 56, 86, 114). When Virro is dubbed *rex* (14, 130, 137, 161), we are once more reminded both of the greedy patron-king of the program (*optima silvarum interea pelagique vorabit | rex horum*: 1.135 f.) and of Domitian, whom Juvenal had compared with Tarquinius Superbus (4.103) and sardonically labeled *induperator* (29), *Caesar* (51, 135), *Atrides* (65), and *dux magnus* (145). The intent of these several correspondences should be obvious: Virro (like Crispinus) is a reflection of *der Führer*. Both *patroni* are cruel, voracious tyrants who take sadistic pleasure in sneering at and intimidating their "friends." And all three men, Virro, Domitian, and Crispinus, are prefigured by the vile potentate of Satire One, whose malicious perversion of friendship was specifically designed to foreshadow the *magna amicitia* of Four and Five.

What could otherwise have been a wholly apolitical satire, is intentionally politicized—and thus brought nearer to Four—through the parallelism of theme and setting, and this association of Virro with Domitian. Political comment is interjected in other ways. At the outset Trebius is compared with abused palace clowns, a slur at the imperial wit (3 f.). When Juvenal describes the wine served Virro (which he refuses to share with a friend: 32), it is said to be of the vintage that Thrasea and Helvidius used to quaff when toasting the birthdays of the republican heroes, Cassius and the Bruti (32–37):[38] Thrasea Paetus, a friend of Juvenal's predecessor Persius, had been executed by Nero for his republican sympathies; his son-in-law Helvidius Priscus, exiled by Nero, had been executed by Vespasian; and Domitian himself had ordered the deaths of Junius Rusticus, biographer of the two men, and Helvidius' son, the younger Priscus (a satirist of sorts, possibly alluded to in Satire One).[39] Virro's luxuriousness is likened to the opulence of Rome's kings (56–59); and when Juvenal contrasts his stinginess toward his clients with the generosity of kinder patrons, he again selects the names of men condemned for their antimonarchical activities, Piso and Seneca (108–111).[40] In a last taunt at Roman royalty, the mushrooms offered Trebius and his fellow clients are compared to those served Claudius by Agrippina (146–148):

> vilibus ancipites fungi ponentur amicis,
> boletus domino, sed quales Claudius edit
> ante illum uxoris, post quem nihil amplius edit.

A political undercurrent flows throughout the satire, linking the degeneracy of Rome's social institutions, the patronage system in particular, with the degeneracy of her emperors.

The epilogues of Four and Five are also similar. While in the concluding line of each poem there is a final thrust at the odious lord (*Lamiarum caede madenti*, 4.154; *tali ... amico*, 5.173), his compliant friends are rebuked as well. In Four, as we have seen, Juvenal condemns Domitian's councillors and the aristocracy in general for submitting to his reign of terror. Here

---

[38] Audiences might think not only of the conspirators M. and D. Junius Brutus, but also of L. Brutus, Tarquin's nemesis, to whom Juvenal had earlier alluded in a gibe at Domitian (4.102 f.).

[39] For Thrasea, see *PIR*[2] C1187; for the Helvidii, *PIR*[2] H59–60; our principal sources are Tac. *Ann.* 16.21–35 and Suet. *Dom.* 10. The Helvidii were from the Samnite town of Cluviae, and it has been suggested that the younger Priscus is the *Cluvienus* (or *Cluvianus*) of Satire One: see L. A. MacKay, "Notes on Juvenal," *CPh* 53 (1958), 236–240, and my 'Juvenal 1.80." Cossutianus Capito had compared Thrasea to Cassius and the Bruti in an accusatory speech to Nero; Juvenal may have this speech, or Tacitus' account of it (*Ann.* 16.22), in mind here.

[40] The two Neronian suicides appear together again as men of unexampled generosity in Mart. 12.36.8. With them Juvenal also names a Cotta, probably the same as the patron of 7.95, and perhaps to be identified with M. Aurelius Cotta Maximus, son of Messala Corvinus and younger friend of Ovid (*Pont.* 1.5 and 9, 2.3 and 8).

in Five the satirist reproaches Trebius for shamelessly enduring Virro's
tyranny (170–173):

> ille sapit, qui te sic utitur. omnia ferre   170
> si potes, et debes. pulsandum vertice raso
> praebebis quandoque caput nec dura timebis
> flagra pati, his epulis et tali dignus amico.

Just as Rome herself was envisioned in the earlier poem as a slave to the
"bald Nero" (*calvo serviret Roma Neroni*: 4.38), so here Trebius plays the
willing *servus* to Virro's *dominus*. The *amici* in both poems, because of their
servility, are no less guilty than their masters. The two epilogues even
perform a comparable structural function. In the same way that Domitian's bloody feast, at the end of Four, evokes the more literal gluttony of
the *monstrum* Crispinus at the beginning, Juvenal's cold stricture against
Trebius, in the closing lines of Five, is carefully designed to recall his opening criticism: in both prologue and epilogue Trebius is pictured as a slave,
and the emphatic condition *omnia ferre* | *si potes* in 170 f. (with *pati*, 173)
is a shrill echo of *si potes illa pati*, in verse 3.[41]

   Thus in their form, characterizations, and setting Satires Four and Five
are markedly alike; in both *magna amicitia* is the dominant theme. Virro,
with Trebius and the other *amici* gathered at his dinner table, are intended
to mirror Domitian, with Crispinus and his fellow *amici* gathered about
the conference table. The correspondences constitute far more than artistic
nicety. Juvenal unquestionably meant to suggest that corruption had in-
sinuated itself into every stratum of Roman society. In modelling Virro
after Domitian he may further have wished to imply that a leader sets the
moral tone, not only for his own close associates, but for the citizenry at
large, ultimately influencing, for better or for worse, men of every station.

   There can be little doubt that Juvenal published his sixteen satires, not
individually, but in five separate volumes.[42] Moreover, as modern
scholarship has become increasingly aware, the poet was quite naturally

---

41 Juvenal underscores the reproof in both 3 and 171 through his use of short, choppy
words, the repeated dentals and labials, and through the clash of ictus and accent in 171,
with the caesura at full stop in the center of three spondees. Cf. Highet, 263 n. 4, who also
observes that "*quis enim tam nudus?* (163) recalls lines 6–11." Thus the arrangement of the
opening eleven lines and the closing eleven lines is to an extent chiastic, another feature
of the poem's structure paralleling Four. For comparable structural parallelism in the
Sermones, see van Rooy, esp. 41–56, and David Armstrong, "Horace, Satires I, 1–3: A
Structural Study," *Arion* 3 (1964), 86–96.

42 Note Juvenal's own words, *nostri farrago libelli* (1.86); the five books as we have
them from about 500 mss. are certainly arranged in chronological order (cf. Highet, 10–
16, 45); early references to the Satires include book numbers (Highet, 192; J. D. Duff, ed.
[Cambridge, 1925], xv).

concerned with the formal and thematic integrity of each volume as a published unit. Each of Juvenal's books open with a program poem, written or at least revised last, which looks forward to material that will be developed in the following satires.[43] This is especially true of Book One, a carefully organized, finely balanced whole, whose construction reveals the author's extensive rhetorical training. The first satire is broadly, sometimes minutely programmatic, introducing not only themes, but even techniques, and some of the specific characters and situations to be employed later in the book. The remaining four poems have been edited and arranged, not chronologically, but in accordance with thematic and structural aims.

While there are important ancillary topics, such as avarice and hypocrisy, it is the predominant theme of corrupted *amicitia* and the general disintegration of personal relationships that contributes most to the book's unity. "Juvenal's programme-satire hinges round the caricature of a patron-client relationship," as Green has remarked (page 30), and indeed most of the *amici* of Book One are clients and patrons. The friendship theme was first introduced early in Satire One with the appearance of the treacherous *magni delator amici*, and then brought up again toward the end of the same poem, in the more detailed scenario of the greedy *patronus* and his angry dependents. The Second Satire, concerned primarily with sexual degeneracy, touches upon another perversion of *amicitia*.

In Satire Three the character who so bitterly denounces Rome is himself a rejected dependent. Is Umbricius the lone true friend of Book One, Juvenal's "old comrade"? Or, when interpreted in light of the book's other four poems, should this *vetus amicus* be seen only as another aging client, prefigured by the anonymous *veteres lassique clientes* of the program satire, and himself anticipating Trebius, the more openly criticized *vetus cliens* of Five? It may not be, as Highet supposes, that the client-friends of this book, sympathetic in the earlier satires, become suddenly "disgusting" in the closing poem, but rather that Juvenal's own position, through a favorite device of Roman satire, is only very gradually revealed.[44] As the

---

[43] The exception is Book Two, with its single, long Satire Six. See William S. Anderson, "The Programs of Juvenal's Later Books," *CPh* 57 (1962), 145–160, esp. 145: "the initial satire in *every* book, while less obviously than Satire 1, serves a programmatic purpose in its particular book." Regarding the unity of each volume, Highet comments (45), "when Juvenal published a book of them he designed it as a group, knowing what was in it and what collective effect it would produce."

[44] Highet (85) is "sorry" for the "middle-class parasites" of Satire One and shares "their wry humiliations" in Three. But Juvenal certainly did not mean us to sympathize with the *magni delator amici* of 1.33 nor his counterpart in 3.116 (*occidit . . . delator amicum*),

poet's "friend" in a satiric dialogue, Umbricius calls to mind methods employed in *Sermones* Two, and in particular the ironic friendship of Horace and Catius; and while, as an abused client, Umbricius invites comparison with Trebius, he is not coincidentally a close match for Virro's other dependent, Naevolus, the discarded homosexual companion in Juvenal's later, more Horatian dialogue, Satire Nine. Whether or not we are to feel as little sympathy for Umbricius as we do for Naevolus, Satire Three's other *amici* all continue the pessimism of the preceding poems.

Set at the end of the *libellus*, equal in length to Satires One and Two, and following the central, more comprehensive Third Satire, Four and Five together neatly balance the collection. In juxtaposing the two poems he had made so alike structurally and thematically, Juvenal intended to draw attention to their affinity, and thus develop to completion an idea that had been introduced in the program poem and given increasingly sharper focus. Both poems respond directly, and at times in detail, to the *amicitia* passages of Satire One. Four takes up especially the theme of dangerous friendships and extends the *nobilitas comesa* metaphor. Five not only mirrors the preceding poem, but—most appropriately, since it concludes the book—it develops notions implicit in the patron-client scene at the conclusion of the program satire. Perverts and princes, the old nobility and the nouveaux riches, and even—the Fifth Satire would emphasize—the poor and the dependent, all are equally to blame for the social corruption in Rome and the dissolution of traditionally sacred bonds. Gilbert Highet calls Satire Five "the climax of the entire book."[45] It is indeed, both in the sense that Highet proposes, and in the fact that it at once fully clarifies and confirms the book's dominant theme. *Magna amicitia*, in every sense and at every level of society, is extinct.

University of Georgia

---

both of whom are client-friends; and, once we consider the book as a whole, we need to reassess our sympathy for the dinner-grubbing *irati amici*, and all the other *veteres clientes* and *amici* of One and Three.

[45] Highet (85) sees the Fifth Satire as climactic in its final revelation of the character of the Roman upper class; but it is equally true that Juvenal's attitude toward the client class, increasingly direct, is here most completely revealed.

11

Irony of Overstatement in the Satires of Juvenal

S. C. FREDERICKS

In *The Satirist*, Leonard Feinberg offers a suggestive definition of satiric technique as a *"playfully critical distortion of the familiar."*[1] This tactical approach to satire thus involves four interrelated parameters: by "play-fulness" Feinberg means that wit and humor are essential to satiric discourse; "criticism" presupposes that the satirist rejects an established set of values in favor of another set which is not yet established, or (if he is a conservative) no longer in force, or perhaps only implicit in his thinking; "distortion" suggests that the fictions created by the satirist are bound to be unrealistic to some extent since it is the satirist's purpose to induce a new sense of the real in his readers; finally, "the familiar" informs us that satire requires norms, at least as a point of departure. It is this fourth parameter, "the familiar," which has often limited our understanding of individual satirists and satiric literature as a whole. We may regard as typical Gilbert Highet's assertion that the subject matter of satire should be topical: that is, it should be directed toward the realia of contemporary life and name specific people, places, and actual events.[2] Though satire

---

[1] Ames, Iowa, 1963, 7 (the italics are his). I recognize a general debt to W. C. Booth, *A Rhetoric of Irony* (Chicago, 1974), whose analysis of irony—as complex and elusive a quality in literature as it is a difficult critical concept—is now the most sophisticated known to me; to T. Wymer, "The Swiftian Satire of Kurt Vonnegut, Jr.," in T. E. Clareson, *Voices for the Future* (Bowling Green University Popular Press, 1976), 238–262, for a model analysis of another "ironic exaggerator;" and to W. R. Irwin, *The Game of the Impossible* (Urbana, 1976), for a model analysis of "unreality" as a structural principle in literature. My critical views of parody are derived from G. D. Kiremidjian, "The Aesthetics of Parody," *Journal of Aesthetics and Art Criticism* 28 (1970), 231–242.

[2] *The Anatomy of Satire* (Princeton, 1962), 16 f. For recent attempts to view Juvenal specifically as topical in this sense, see B. Baldwin, "Cover-Names and Dead Victims in Juvenal," *Atheneum* 45 (1967), 304–312; U. Knoche, "Juvenals Maßstäbe der Gesell-

certainly can be topical and realistic in this direct way, I believe that "the familiar" against which a satirist reacts comprehends a much broader and more imaginative range of possibilities than this.

By now it should be axiomatic that Juvenal is one great satirist whose effectiveness cannot be ascribed to topicality or contemporaneity in Highet's sense. K. H. Waters and G. B. Townend are two important scholars who recently have insisted that the center-focus of Juvenal's imagination is late Flavian society, and that it is this era, already part of Roman history, which provides the satirist with his major characters and events.[3] We simply do not learn many facts, if any, about Trajanic or Hadrianic society from reading Juvenal, yet the poems seem to have been published under two later Emperors, if we may trust the reconstructions of our best scholars.[4]

This recent trend in scholarship is valuable mainly for directing our attention to areas other than immediate topicality in order to discover the sources of Juvenal's satiric power and vitality. Like other satirists, Juvenal is dependent on the conventions and institutions of his culture as a point of departure for his peculiar kind of communication, but this basis in "the familiar" goes far beyond those topical considerations which have too often been the sole domain of critical investigation. First, there is earlier literature: Roman satiric traditions, the epic genre in general, and Vergil, Ovid, and Martial in particular are all fundamental to Juvenal's imagination and the verbal means of expressing that imagination.[5] Second, there is moral philosophy, the younger Seneca's in particular, though Juvenal

---

schaftskritik," in W. Hering (ed.), *Römische Satire* (*Wissenschaftliche Zeitschrift der Universität Rostock* 15, 1966), 453–462; P. Green, "Juvenal and His Age," in *The Shadows of the Parthenon* (Berkeley and Los Angeles, 1972), 216–267. Of course, G. Highet, *Juvenal the Satirist* (Oxford, 1954), remains the paradigmatic reading of Juvenal's works for possible topicality, though Highet's many contributions to Juvenalian scholarship cannot be reduced to this alone.

[3] K. H. Waters, "Juvenal and the Reign of Trajan," *Antichthon* 4 (1970), 62–77; G. B. Townend, "The Literary Substrata to Juvenal's Satires," *JRS* 63 (1973), 148–160. For an important background study, cf. K. H. Waters, "Traianus Domitiani Continuator," *AJP* 90 (1969), 385–405.

[4] For the standard view see Highet, *Juvenal* (above, note 2), 10–17, and cf. M. Coffey, "Juvenal 1941–1961," *Lustrum* 8 (1964), 165–170, and, more recently, Waters, "Juvenal" (above, note 3).

[5] In addition to Townend (above, note 3), see R. E. Colton, *Juvenal and Martial* (Diss., Columbia Univ., 1959); W. S. Anderson, "Roman Satirists and Their Tradition," *Satire Newsletter* 1 (1963), 1–5, and "*Lascivia* vs. *Ira*: Martial and Juvenal," *CSCA* 3 (1970), 1–34; G. Highet, "Juvenal's Bookcase," *AJP* 72 (1957), 369–394; E. Thomas, "Some Aspects of Ovidian Influence on Juvenal," *Orpheus* 7 (1960), 35–44.

really reacts to the entire system of intellectual and moral clichés that underlie contemporary moral philosophy.[6] Third, there is also the old Greek mythology, which is supposedly rejected in the satirist's apology in the First Satire, but which is fundamental to his imagination throughout the satires.[7] Fourth, there is the all-encompassing field of rhetoric, which has long been a major focus of scholarly research, with basic studies by Josué De Decker and Inez Scott-Ryberg.[8]

What is significant in Juvenal's technique is that he simultaneously exploits and satirizes each of these cultural forms just mentioned. Or, rather, we would do better to refer to them not merely as cultural forms nor merely as modes of discourse, but—in terms of their functions in Juvenal's works—as the essential forms of imagination available to contemporary society. Juvenal succeeds, not by avoiding these various sterile forms which were to become even more ossified in the second century, but by working through them to provide such outrageously exaggerated pictures that we cannot take the forms seriously any longer. We must call into question the nature and limits of intellectual forms whose potential Juvenal elaborates to the point of making their unreality obvious and explicit. However, we cannot embark on such speculations about Juvenal's art unless we are willing to look at him from a perspective which is the opposite of the conventional one. That is, we have to recognize from the outset of our investigation that *the satirist is no believer.*

In the area of rhetoric, the scholarship has long been led astray by the manuscript *vitae*, which assert that until middle age Juvenal practiced declamation as a personal interest, and by the one reference in the First Satire (15) that the satirist had experienced the regular school training in rhetoric. Yet there are more telling expressions of Juvenal's real attitude toward the suffocating effect of rhetoric on contemporary culture: his ridicule of the famous Quintilian in the Sixth (75 and 280) and Seventh Satires (186–198), his deflation of the reputation of Hannibal in Satire 10 (166 f.) by remarking that the whole majestic career of the great general is reducible to a schoolboy's declamation, and the joke in the Fifteenth

---

[6] W. S. Anderson, "Anger in Juvenal and Seneca," *UCPCPh* 19 (1964), 127–196; B. F. Dick, "Seneca and Juvenal 10," *HSCP* (1969), 237–246; C. Lutz, "Democritus and Heraclitus," *CJ* 49 (1953–1954), 309–314.

[7] J. C. Bramble, *Persius and the Programmatic Satire* (Cambridge, 1974), 12 f.

[8] J. De Decker, *Juvenalis Declamans* (Ghent, 1913), and I. G. Scott [-Ryberg], *The Grand Style in the Satires of Juvenal* (Smith College Classical Studies 8, 1927). Cf. E. J. Kenney, "Juvenal: Satirist or Rhetorician?," *Latomus* 22 (1963), 704–720, and W. S. Anderson, "Juvenal and Quintilian," *YCS* 17 (1961), 3–93.

Satire (112) that the world has become so corrupt that even the fanciful land of Thule now has its own schoolmaster of rhetoric.

We must also approach mythology with a similar awareness. Ovid had already demystified mythical narrative in the *Metamorphoses*, revealing that myths were the creative universe of the story-teller and his art.[9] Juvenal definitely shows a preference for the *Metamorphoses*, not only for the substance of his mythological allusions throughout every satire, but also for the spirit in which he treats myth. Thus in the longer myths of Satires 1 (Deucalion and Pyrrha), 3 (which assumes the overall, "archetypal" structure of the myth of degeneration from the Golden Age),[10] and 6 and 13 (Golden Age), Juvenal establishes a contrast between contemporary reality and the mythical, divine, and heroic past, which is doubly ironic because neither present nor past is idealized.[11]

We know, for example, that Juvenal is not being serious about the myth of *Saturnia regna* in Satire 13 (38–52) when he says Juno was just "a little maid" and Jupiter was still only a "private citizen." But the satirist goes further than this when he embarks on a remarkable series of *negative exempla*: "There was no banquet of heaven-dwellers up in the clouds, no boy from Ilium, nor Hercules' lovely wife by the cups, nor Vulcan, after slurping down the nectar, scrubbing his arms black from his Liparian smithy (*taberna*, 45, here a comic anachronism); each god dined by himself, and there wasn't a crowd of deities as there is today; and the stars, happy with a few divinities, crushed poor Atlas with a lesser weight; not yet had fierce Pluto and his Sicilian wife been allotted the gloomy empire of the lowest abyss, nor was there the wheel [of Ixion], nor Furies, nor the rock [of Sisyphus], nor the punishment of the black vulture [for Tityus] (42–51)." Ironically, what made the Golden Age golden was the very fact that there weren't so many gods! Yet this passage must also be juxtaposed with an analogous catalogue, later in the same poem (75–85): men will take an oath by just about every religious relic (and many in this list are incredibly exotic), and even by the whole "arsenal of heaven," because

---

[9] C. Altieri, "Ovid and the New Mythologists," *Novel* 7 (1973), 31–40; G. K. Galinsky, *Ovid's Metamorphoses: An Introduction to the Basic Aspects* (Berkeley and Los Angeles, 1975), 28 f. and 235.

[10] A. L. Motto and J. R. Clark, *"Per iter tenebricosum*: The Mythos of Juvenal 3," *TAPA* 96 (1965), 267–276. Cf. S. C. Fredericks, "Daedalus in Juvenal's Third Satire," *CB* 49 (1972), 11–13.

[11] This point has been raised often enough. See S. C. Fredericks, "Juvenal's Fifteenth Satire," *ICS* 1 (1976), 189 and note 32 (for cross-references to the work of M. Morford and D. Wiesen), and, earlier, "Calvinus in Juvenal's Thirteenth Satire," *Arethusa* 4 (1971), 219 f. and 229, notes 7 and 8.

they know they cannot be held accountable unless there are *human* witnesses. There is a serious message to be gained from the satirist's comic exaggerations: men who are willing to worship anything, as Juvenal says his contemporaries do, really hold nothing sacred. But this is just one of his many studied overstatements in the satires to the effect that quantity has displaced quality in Roman society.

Juvenal manifests the same scepticism toward the other two imaginative forms mentioned earlier. Thus in Satire 2, Juvenal can ridicule Stoicism, not for its intrinsic worthlessness as a moral philosophy, but because it is just another massive deception in a society already mired in pretense and artificiality. Perhaps we expect Juvenal to treat the sacred cow of literature more gently, but that is not what he does in either the First or Seventh Satires, whose attacks against the sterility of contemporary literary art are obvious and elaborate. What could be more explicit than this sarcastic image in the Seventh Satire: "Nevertheless, we still keep at this (poetry); we keep turning our plows in the meager dust, and keep overturning the shoreline with sterile plowshares (48 f.)."[12] The reference to a *poetica tempestas* in the Twelfth Satire (23 f.) is another recognition by Juvenal of the unreality of much poetic discourse, especially epic.

We therefore must now approach Juvenalian satire with a much expanded awareness of what constitutes the object of his attacks. Even when he appears to deal most directly with contemporary social givens, actually he is often providing exaggerated counter-structures to current Roman cultural "myths," especially those related to literary conventions and traditions. In Satire 2, to counter the Roman mythology of virility and manliness and martial virtue, particularly elaborated in Silver Age epic, Juvenal gives us a contrived epic travesty about the total effeminacy of an entire culture's males. To correspond to the overly pious and traditional view of Roman woman, paraded in Statius' *Silvae* and elsewhere,[13] Juvenal gives us an equally exaggerated portrait of female *impudicitia* and *luxuria* in Satire 6. Satire 5 (based on the conventional *cena*-theme) exposes the complete impossibility of the traditional patron-client relationship, a social structure hopelessly perverted by a mean, vicious patron like Virro, but also perverted by a decadent, servile client like Trebius.[14]

---

[12] Ironically, "plowing the shoreline" as a metaphor for the pursuit of a useless task is still another literary commonplace exploited by Juvenal opportunistically. For a list of occurrences, see J. D. Duff's commentary (ed. M. Coffey, Cambridge, 1970), ad 1.157.

[13] See D. W. T. C. Vessey, "Statius to His Wife: *Silvae* III.5," *CJ* 72 (1976–1977), 134–140.

[14] For the views expressed in this paragraph, I admit my debt to W. S. Anderson, "Studies in Book I of Juvenal," *YCS* 15 (1957), 33–90, and "Juvenal 6: A Problem in Structure," *CP* 51 (1956), 73–94.

Satire 4 is an analogous case. Highet has argued persuasively that Juvenal is parodying a court epic by Statius,[15] but even without relying on his special way of looking at the poem we still have the effusive praise of Domitian in Statius' *Silvae* and in several epigrams of Martial.[16] The demonic portrait of the emperor sketched by the satirist is therefore an inversion—of equal degree in the opposite direction—of his image as "dominus et deus" in literature (e.g., Martial 5.8.1) while alive. The satire is therefore just as much an indirect attack against the perversion of literature and thought as it is direct satire against the deceased Princeps. In other words, what actually constitutes "the familiar" in this poem is the world of Imperial poetic propaganda, whose pretentiousness and artificiality, masking murderous viciousness, are properly deflated by Juvenal's inflated and travestied portrayal of a solemn meeting of the ministers of state on the matter of a large fish caught recently in the Adriatic.

Hence, we should now consider that Juvenal's art can be "contemporary" or "topical" in an extended sense because it so often reacts to the contemporary Roman *imagination*—its modes of expression, its norms and conventions, in particular those which reflect a long and obvious tradition (and might therefore seem even the more inadequate for contemporary needs). In Juvenal's first two books, satire against this intellectual framework of conventional and traditional ideas is mostly indirect. In these six poems Juvenal presents his arguments against contemporary life through vivid and indignant attacks couched in his own voice—this mode of presentation commonly being referred to as a "persona" in satire scholarship[17]—or in barely disguised versions of that indignant voice, like Laronia in Satire 2, or Umbricius in 3. However, what is exposed in addition in these poems is the futility of reactionary Romanism, insofar as the desire for the "old ways"—for all of its emotional satisfaction—is *irrational* and impossible in a contemporary context. Perhaps this much indicates only that the traditional Roman system of values has become senile; yet there is further evidence that, beneath his apparent nostalgia for a lost age of idealism, there is a deeper self-awareness on the part of the satirist that his fiery vehemence is acutely decadent. I refer specifically

---

15 *Juvenal* (above, note 2), 256, note 1.

16 In addition to the very full listing of passages in Highet, *Juvenal* (above, note 2), 256–262, see the discussion in K. Scott, *The Imperial Cult Under the Flavians* (Stuttgart, 1936), 88–125.

17 On this concept in satire criticism—in addition to the works of W. S. Anderson and S. C. Fredericks cited throughout these notes—see "The Concept of Persona in Satire, A Symposium," *Satire Newsletter* 3 (1966), 89–153. G. Highet, "Masks and Faces in Satire," *Hermes* 102 (1974), 321–337, remains the most outspoken opponent of the *persona*-theory.

to the highly stylized, polished, and self-conscious rhetorical cast of the first six poems. This is certainly no mark against Juvenal's wit or creativity, but it does suggest another dimension by which the *laudator temporis acti* exposes his own artifice.[18] We share with the satirist the realization that what we have before us achieves its ultimately serious purposes only through the indirect route of artful play.

The prologue to the Third Satire provides one of the most obvious and effective examples of the kind of wit generated by playful, self-effacing overstatement. Here the satirist emphasizes his horror of Rome in a crescendo of terrors, from fires to "constant" (*adsiduos*, 8) collapses of buildings, to the "thousand perils of the savage city (8 f.)," only to cap his series with a deflationary anti-climax, "and poets reciting in the month August." We know that this item has been included in the wrong kind of list, that Juvenal is not being serious at this specific point (though we cannot generalize from this that he is not being serious elsewhere in the poem, nor that his wit cannot have a serious function), that fear of sitting through a hot, stuffy recitation should not be included in a list with real terrifying catastrophes. The inclusivity is momentarily appealing through sheer perverseness, through its following out of the logic of overstatement already begun in the list of real terrors (as in the emotionally charged words *horrere* and *saevae*), but it finally ends up by pointing to its own unreality. Though catalogues and lists are often evidence of a satirist at work, and are one of the typical satiric techniques for the distortions mentioned by Feinberg, they are particularly well suited to Juvenal's technique of creating vivid overstatements to violate our sense of the familiar.

Such sophisticated "showpieces" as this indicate that Juvenal is no simple conservative moralist, as if he naively and nostalgically fantasizes that his society could ever return to the glory, freedom, and creativity supposedly the possession of the great days of the Roman Republic. Like Petronius before him and like his great contemporary, Tacitus, Juvenal sees that contemporary reality involves a two-fold hypocrisy. On the one side, the facts of recent Roman history were unmistakable: this world was indeed dominated by the highly artificial pursuit of money and the power represented by it. Direct satire against this parvenu culture (e.g., wealthy Greeks and freedmen in Satire 3) is an obvious feature of Juvenalian satire. On the other, possibly under the continued influence of the Augustan *renovatio*—which constituted a peculiar Roman cultural myth dominant in the early Principate—there was a second and conservative intellectual layer by means of which contemporary Romans could believe they were

---

[18] See Anderson, "Anger" (above, note 6), 127 and 131–135.

still part of the great traditions of the Republic and its ancient institutions.[19] It is Juvenal's indirect satire against this anachronistic moral code that W. S. Anderson and other exponents of the *persona*-theory have brought to our fuller awareness in recent years. Indeed, among the "familiar" givens of Juvenal's world we must also include *mos maiorum* and the *laudator temporis acti*, whose futility is implicitly explored in Books 1 and 2. Overall, therefore, Juvenal is a satirist of the "double irony" in these first six poems:[20] he would have us reject both contemporary decadence and archaic pseudo-morality.

Since Gilbert Highet's study, scholarship has generally recognized that Book 3 begins a new phase for the satirist, since he no longer emphasizes an angry *persona* whose overstated beliefs and excessive indignation are a means of critical self-exposure (as, e.g., paradoxically, the enraged Umbricius of Satire 3 seeks to escape Greek-ridden Rome by migrating to Greek Cumae). Instead, many of these later poems involve various forms of imaginative (especially literary) decadence and sterility as the primary object of satiric attack. I believe, however, that Juvenal's most explicit and self-conscious statement that his poetry deals with the failure of the human imagination comes in his Tenth Satire, the classic on "The Vanity of Human Wishes," which we have too long read with an emphasis on vanity and without enough attention to *wishes*.

The first detailed elaboration of men's misconceptions about what is good for them is the Sejanus-episode (56–81). There is no question that the Emperor Tiberius' infamous praetorian prefect serves Juvenal's portrayal of the first vicious desire explored in the poem, which is ambition for political power at any cost. This theme is announced at once by the word *potentia* (56). But what is more remarkable is that Juvenal does not describe Sejanus himself until line 67. It is the *public image* of Sejanus that he ridicules: first in an outrageous description of the destruction of the erstwhile master politician's statue of himself done up in a triumphal chariot (58–60), which ends with Juvenal ludicrously expressing sympathy only for the "innocent horses," whose legs are shattered by the hammer.

---

[19] In addition to Ronald Syme's classic *The Roman Revolution* (Oxford, 1939), the most valuable background study is H. W. Litchfield, "National *Exempla Virtutis* in Roman Literature," *HSCP* 25 (1914), 1–77.

[20] For the expression, "double irony," a common satiric technique by means of which "two equally invalid points of view cancel each other out," see Booth (above, note 1), 62 Wymer (above, note 1), 239 f., refers to this phenomenon as "the problem of secondary irony," and distinguishes these direct and indirect levels of satire as "thesis" and "antithesis" layers, respectively. R. C. Elliott, *The Power of Satire* (Princeton, 1960), provides an analogous approach with his idea of "the satirist satirized."

The pretentiousness of Sejanus' "public relations" image is justifiably deflated by the colloquial word for horses, *caballis*, "nags." Then we get a picture of metal statues being melted down in the forge, and what were once grand and fine displays of one's own power have now been turned into "water jars, basins, a skillet, and piss pots (64)." But at last we do see Sejanus—being led by the hook to the Gemonian steps. Now is when he will be seen (*spectandus*, 67), in the real flesh of a corpse, not in the artificial "public relations" forms of marble and bronze; Juvenal lets us know those are gone before the *corpus delecti* is.

The incredible swiftness of Sejanus' fall is reinforced by one of Juvenal's more memorable epigrams, which tells how it happened: *verbosa et grandis epistula venit | a Capreis* (71 f.). From the inflated expression "wordy and pretentious" we descend to the realization that it was only a letter which brought seemingly so great a man so low, so quickly. This is what justifies Juvenal turning in subsequent lines to the fickleness of the mob, disposed to believe in the power of the goddess Fortuna: for if events had by chance gone the other way, they would have been ready to accept Sejanus, just as slavishly, as their emperor. Hence, Juvenal's sarcastic expression, *turba Remi* (73), "Remus' crowd," is certainly justified to emphasize the cowardly (*anxius*, 80) loser-mentality of the Roman *populus*—quick to cringe or condemn, depending on shifting political winds in the imperial court, yet slavishly worshipping these same power-figures (in their ultimate daydreams for like powers), before settling for the dole of their "bread and circuses."

Later in the same poem Juvenal turns to famous generals and conquerors in world history, and certainly there is explicit, direct satire against the *reputations* of men like Xerxes, Alexander, and Hannibal (133–187). There are, however, two suggestions in this passage that Juvenal is doing something more than this. His Hannibal is described like some overpowering natural force: ". . . he leaps across the Pyrenees; nature sets the snowy Alps in his path, but he tears the cliffs apart and shatters the mountains with vinegar (153)." Although Juvenal borrows this detail about Hannibal's use of vinegar to break up blocked mountain passages from Livy's description (21.37.2), he exaggerates it by the use of overly graphic verbs, *diducit* and *rumpit*. After the chiastic word order of *diducit scopulos et montem rumpit* the final word in the hexameter, *aceto*, which goes with both preceding clauses, must come both as a surprise and as a deflation of the epic grandeur of the previous words.

Juvenal makes the feats of conquerors even more incredible—and more explicitly so—in a later reference, to Xerxes: "men believe that once upon a time ships sailed through Mount Athos [*velificatus*, 174, an instance of overly pompous diction] and whatever else that lying nation of Greece is bold enough to tell in history, that the sea was paved with those same Persian ships and set as a solid track beneath chariot wheels; we believe that deep rivers went dry and streams were drunk away by the foraging Mede, and all the rest of what Sostratus sings with drenched wings (173–178)." The satirist continues for some time in this same vein, even naming the sea "Ennosigaeus," "Earthshaker," a far-fetched application of Poseidon's Homeric epithet as a metonymy for the sea, and finally, Xerxes, too, is deflated by the ignominious realities of his defeat by the Greeks. However, what is perhaps just as important in this *exemplum* is that Juvenal's exaggeration of Herodotus (to be sure, mediated through the otherwise unattested epic poetaster, Sostratus) corresponds to his earlier exaggeration of Livy's words on Hannibal. The satirist's emphasis on the verbs *creditur* (173) and *credimus* (176) is intended to develop a larger dimension to his satire, to deliberately render the general's successes incredible and unrealistic, and consequently to deflate the power-fantasies and wish-fulfillments of his contemporaries. Juvenal thus ridicules people who believe in the Hannibals and Xerxes of this world.

Another illustration of this same function of exaggeration is one of the most brilliantly sustained exercises in irreverence in ancient literature. I refer to the repulsive description of old age in this same Tenth Satire (188–239). Juvenal starts with physical deformity, and after a blunt insistence on its sheer bodily ugliness, the opening lines are capped by a hilariously overlong and pretentious simile of two verses, which describes wrinkles on the elderly as like those which "a mother ape scratches on her ancient cheek where Numidian Thabraca extends shade-bearing glades (194 f.)." Then we turn to a list of specific physical infirmities (198–200, 203 f.), capped here by a vivid, obscene description of sexual impotence (204–207). From here the argument takes an abrupt turn to describe all the pleasures the elderly are incapable of feeling—starting from the sexual (208–212), then portraying the hopeless limits imposed on the hard of hearing (213–216). Next Juvenal leaps to still another semantic order—claiming that the elderly are plagued by such a race of illnesses that he could sooner count the adulterous lovers of the infamous Oppia, the number of victims accounted for in just one season by the doctor Themison, the number of business partners cheated by one man, wards cheated by still another, the number of sexual victims exhausted by a famous prostitute, and finally—with an obscene capping—the number of pupils seduced by a teacher (219–224). And we are surely on safe ground in spotting in Juvenal's comparison between illnesses on the one side and classes of vices on the other a non-serious mode of exaggeration through incongruity.

After this one inverted and ironic departure from the physical effects of old age (let us call it a catalogue within a catalogue), Juvenal returns again to listing physical infirmities: of shoulder, loins, hips (227). Then second childhood is described, culminating in another grotesque simile, parallel to the earlier one on the Numidian ape (229–232), comparing the old man's helplessness in acquiring food to the actions of a swallow's chick. Finally, in rapid order come true senility, lapses in memory, total forgetfullness, terminating in a will which ends up in the possession of a mistress (an ex-prostitute besides!) who was acquired late in life.

Except for the ironic comparison between numbers of illnesses and numbers of vices as a way of overstating them both non-seriously, the passage is an accumulation of physical defects. The emphasis is on the natural and the physical, and any *single* incident is reasonable in the elderly: it is only the total portrait, working through strained epic diction, which seems so overdone as to be distorted. This is why Juvenal emphasizes lists and catalogues of infirmities which are physical and natural—to point out the quantity of things that can go wrong as a shocking counter-structure to those who would again substitute quantity of life (*spatium vitae*, 188) for quality of life. These grotesque, sensual, physical deformities are therefore accumulated into one intensely exaggerated list, in order to deflate empty wish-fulfillments. As a composite or unified conception judged for atmosphere, the description of the horrors of old age is clearly unrealistic, an exaggeration, but its *function* is certainly realistic: to jolt men out of unrealistic wishes that old age will somehow prove an attainable ideal—old age is attainable all right, Juvenal says, but it is no ideal.

Juvenal maintains this same emphasis on the physical and natural in the attack on "beauty" or *forma* (289–345), which here bears a reductive meaning of sexual attractiveness. To counter this wish-fulfillment, at one point Juvenal brings his reader back to reality with the threat of castration—a permanent and absolute impairment of the natural human capacity for sex—because of the large market for sexually attractive eunuch lovers. Juvenal here thus shows more than a flair for exaggeration; he has a way of deflating extravagance with an appropriate tactic. Castration is introduced into the argument not so that Juvenal can just be obscene or titillating, but to raise a disturbing counter-fantasy to the over-commitment by Juvenal's contemporaries to unrealistic wishes for sexual powers.

The preceding observations about exaggeration apply more generally than to one poem. The Twelfth Satire, for instance, shares many features with the Tenth, but until recently it has been so universally condemned as a failure that its meaning and structure could not expect much except to be misunderstood. It is not to my purpose in this paper to reinstate the poem as a work of art,[21] but only to make the local observation that with Juvenal's elaborate description of *captatio* or "legacy-hunting" (83–130) we are certainly entering an atmosphere of overstatement. A climactic order is presupposed.

First, legacy hunters would sacrifice a whole hecatomb of elephants (hence, an exaggerated number of beasts of exaggerated proportions for a sacrifice), except that the only herd belongs to Caesar. Another feature of overstatement is the list of famous generals who were borne by the elephants into battle: Hannibal, Pyrrhus (who is identified by an epic periphrasis, 108), and Roman generals; and finally we see the elephant carrying whole cohorts on its back (with this we are sure the exaggeration is ironic). The elephant is also called "a tower going into battle" (*turrem*, 110, here an amphibology, since *turris* is the normal Latin word for the howdah on the back of an elephant). Hence, individual details only heighten our awareness of the general idea of exaggeration, inherent in sacrificing a whole hecatomb of something as large, rare, and expensive as an elephant.

But this particular climactic arrangement starts out high and gets higher progressively, for after elephants we are told that legacy hunters would even turn to human sacrifice, first a "herd" of slaves (sarcastic use of *grex*, 116), then even one's own daughter, if necessary, as Agamemnon did with Iphigenia. Once again, Juvenal has chosen for his most overstated and unrealistic *exemplum* to cap the series with a *literary* one (I assume that *tragicae* in 120 directs us to think of tragedy specifically, and not myth or epic in general).

Again, this tremendously unrealistic series of exaggerations is not intended to give us a realistic portrayal of *captatio*, but to expose the increasing falseness and sterility which such artificial social institutions were producing to the detriment of true feelings between friends. *Captatio* is even worse than the pretense that one is after another's money through the illusion of friendship, because it also involves a ridiculous and fantastic overevaluation of the rewards involved ("Nor do I compare a thousand ships to an inheritance," 121 f., as Juvenal ironically puts it). In other words, *captatio* is not simply a moral vice for Juvenal, since his portrayal of its effect on the human *imagination* shows its true outrageous colors. It is the total perversion of the simple human capacity to evaluate what is

---

[21] My colleague E. S. Ramage accomplishes that purpose in "Juvenal, Satire 12: On Friendship True and False," *Illinois Classical Studies* 3 (1978), 221–237, to whom I owe a debt for several of my ideas about this poem.

worth doing that Juvenal is exploring in this passage and, in general, in this fourth book of satires. In the Twelfth, as in the Tenth Satire, his exaggerations point out that contemporary men are wasting their time and effort on the wrong goals.

But it is now appropriate to turn back from these analyses of the satirist's violent overstatements which contain ironic layers of meaning to Satire 1, his first statement of the purpose of his art. I refer specifically to the satirist's self-stated program of replacing the cliché-ridden epics and dramas prevalent in his own age with satire on the grand scale: a satire whose excesses are to mirror the extravagant excesses and perversions of contemporary life, and will for that reason be a "realistic" literature, since in its vices, and only in its vices, can contemporary Rome match the heroic scale of legendary epic. But at the end of his poem (147–171), Juvenal seemingly turns aside from this program, responds to an imaginary *adversarius*,[22] and admits that a satirist cannot really write about actual contemporary life, since punishment is sure to be meted out by those in power.

It has troubled critics that Juvenal not only concedes his adversarius' point, but caps his poem with the specific concession that he will direct his satire against those "whose ashes are covered by the Flaminian and Latin Ways (171)." Duff assumed this reference to the tombs of the wealthy and influential was a way for Juvenal to say his satire was directed against the aristocracy. But in addition this admission describes the actual historical (at least, "Domitianic") environment of his poems.

Further, there is some implication that Juvenal's insistence on the futility of literature in this and the Seventh Satire involved him in an ironic attitude toward his own artistic products. This is something more than the view that literature was a failure in his age. It is also the satirist's self-critical awareness that his own satire was also doomed to inadequacy. Satire would not reform an age simultaneously decadent in ideas, literature, and politics; an age decadent in two dimensions—in its busy creation of sham new values, and in its arteriosclerotic maintenance of time-worn old ones. Thus, to explore the full impact of the last line of Satire 1, we should understand it as a metaphor for Juvenal's art. The "ghosts" which are assailed in his poems are more than the dead of history; the list must also include haunting nostalgic memories of virtues and ideals which had really not had authentic life for well over a century.

The range and variety of Juvenal's exaggerations are truly impressive.

---

[22] Apparently this passage is modelled on Lucilius' Book 30. See J. G. Griffith, "The Ending of Juvenal's First Satire and Lucilius, Book XXX," *Hermes* 98 (1970), 56–72.

They cut across literary, rhetorical, philosophical, and mythological modes of expression, and thus it is unlikely that Juvenal's artistry can be reduced to any single one of them without doing violence to the total fabric of his poems' meaning. His exaggerations are best regarded as a special kind of satiric cognition, as one distinctive way of looking at the world in the satirist's distorted way. Exaggerations are a way of focusing attention on reality by seemingly removing us clearly from it. Thus, after expanding to a great length on certain ideas and obsessions, Juvenal reaches a point of self-evident unreality, which pops the whole illusion. By breaking through intellectual illusions, we may be led back to a dis-illusioned sense of reality. It is this satirical structure of two alternating moments which I have called the "Irony of Overstatement."

Indiana University

12

Satira and Satiricus in Late Latin

KENNETH M. ABBOTT

The title of this paper involves some kind of answer to the question whether the Latin satura as a literary type influenced satirical writing in general; or in short when, if ever, or at least before Sidonius Apollinaris,[1] in whose work the lexicons recognize what becomes the usual Medieval Latin sense of "satire, satirical," the shift occurred which has left its mark on all modern languages in contact with the Latin tradition.

That Latin *satura* is not quite "satire" in the sense or senses which the vernacular languages inherit from Medieval Latin, no one, I think, really doubts. Dr. Johnson, to be sure, could still speak of satire as "a poem in which wickedness or folly is censured,"[2] but this is both too narrow and too broad for Latin *satura*, and irrelevant to most modern satire. Latin satirical writing covers much more ground than *satura*; not all *satura* is satirical in tone, and I should hope that no Latinist would classify, say, *The Tale of a Tub* as *satura*. In whatever way it has been proposed to misunderstand Quintilian's *satura tota nostra est* (10,1,93), no one, I think, has ever thought he credited the Romans with the invention of satire but only *satura*. Important as it may be, however, for the history of Latin literature not to confuse *satura* and "satire," once the question of a distinction arises, difficulties or at least complexities immediately follow.

If defining *satura* would suggest St. Jerome's figure of trying to get a firm grip on an eel,[3] defining vernacular *satire* might well suggest what I

---

[1] That a new sense, i.e., departure from the *form* of satura, does indeed occur in Sidonius, is by no means clear; where in *Ep.* 1,11 he speaks of *satirographus* and *satira*, a *poema* is under discussion; while *satirice* in Donatus on *Eun.* 232, if genuine, which is not beyond question, seems to mean "in the fashion of a writer of *satura*."

[2] Problems of definition and characteristics of satire are succinctly covered by Robert Elliott in *Encyclopedia of Poetry and Poetics*, ed. Alex Preminger, Princeton University Press, 1965, 738–740.

[3] *Praef. in Librum Job: ut si velis anguillam aut muraenulam strictis tenere manibus, quanto fortius presseris tanto citius elabitur.*

have been told is an old country expression, "trying to nail a custard pie to a wall." *Satura* at least is a major literary type in Latin, which arose at one time and place, and has, technically speaking, a limited history from the time of Lucilius to Juvenal; while "satire" has existed from time immemorial or since first men recognized that the opinions, habits or features of others were inferior to their own and consequently not conducive to the public good. The grammatical tradition of *satura* as a Latin literary type is clear enough, as succinctly stated in Diomedes: *Satira dicitur carmen apud Romanos nunc quidem maledicum et ad carpenda hominum vitia archaeae comoediae charactere conpositum, quale scripserunt Lucilius et Horatius et Persius.*[4] Granted that the *nunc quidem* does little to assure a date for what is likely to be a traditional statement, it does clearly, with its contrast accent, indicate a realization that *satura* was not always satirical in tone, but that nowadays, i.e., at almost any time after Persius's work was in circulation, the satirical tone is a distinguishing mark of what is still a *carmen*. When the term becomes extended to prose as well, what we may have is a shift from *satura* as a genre to the spirit and tone and perhaps the intent to tell the truth, whether with laughter as in Horace or with derision as in Persius and Juvenal, in the interest of some however vaguely envisaged public good. And if we may regard vernacular satire as a literary form, it may profitably be considered with the rhetorical background of persuasion as its goal—persuasion from a course of conduct or a set of views likely (whether or not designed) to darken public counsel.

If then we are looking for a point at which *satura* could be transferred from a form or literary type to writing in the satiric spirit no longer restricted to inheritance of a poetic tradition, it is with St. Jerome that it can be suspected as occurring. This indeed is the argument of David Wiesen in his full study of St. Jerome as a satirist, with which Hritzu[5], concurs yet without reference specifically to *satura*. This, then, is the question which lies before us.

That there is a vast amount of satire in all its aspects in Jerome's work, no one could doubt. Cavallera, in his comprehensive biography of St. Jerome,[6] had already gathered numerous samples in his *Index*, under the

---

[4] 1.485,30 Keil. Diomedes does allow for *satura* in other senses, but dramatic *satura*, if it ever existed (which I doubt), has no relevance here, nor does the so-called Menippean satire or *Cynica* (Aul. Gell. 2,18,6).

[5] David S. Wiesen, *St. Jerome as a Satirist*. Cornell University Press, 1964. St. Jerome, *Dogmatic and Polemical Works*, translated by John N. Hritzu (*The Fathers of the Church*, Vol. 53), Catholic University of America Press, 1965, note 42, pp. xvii–xix.

[6] Ferdinand Cavallera, *Saint Jérôme, sa vie et son oeuvre* (*Spicilegium Sacrum Lovaniense*), 2 vols. Louvain and Paris, 1922.

head *Satirique* (*esprit*) *de Jérôme*, and no one could read far in any of his works without having it forcibly brought to his attention. So much is true even if, as I should insist on doing, one excludes from this satiric spirit mere invective and abuse. Of this there is much to be found without searching. But where we are regarding satire as a literary form or device with the rhetorical background of persuasion in written form, invective and abuse are hardly to be regarded as belonging. In any case, invective, as he said, came to him from the influence of Cicero's and Demosthenes' Philippics,[7] and hardly shows the influence of Latin composers of *satura*. In fact, if one were to deny any considerable debt of Jerome to the Latin satirists, one could certainly subtract much on the ground of his temperament (which was hardly saintly in any modern sense), his hasty temper, a constant tendency to dramatize and exaggerate, which was hardly tempered by his admirable rhetorical education, and, by no means least, the hostilities and disappointments he encountered.

Much that might account for his becoming embittered, for those who wish to argue that he did become so, certainly sprang from a temperament that past ages would have called perfervid. His response to criticism or dissent was rapid and violent to a degree which not only made him enemies but sometimes pained his friends. His support of virginity and the ascetic life in his *Adversus Jovinianum* aroused so much opposition in Rome through the apparent denigration of marriage and the normal Christian life, that his school friend, the senator Pammachius, was alarmed by the public reaction and attempted in vain to buy up and suppress the version in circulation. Cavallera, in fact, in his Appendix (Note P, pp. 103–115) devotes 13 pages to a digest of what he calls the Tribulations of St. Jerome; and J. Brochet's older book on the enemies of St. Jerome[8] does not suffer from a want of material.

After his education at Rome and experience with religious communities at Aquileia and Emona (Ljubljana), whose devotion to religion very nearly matched his own, he had written,[9] "my native country [Stridon in Dalmatia], where rusticity is at home, has the belly as its god. There they live from day to day; the richest is the most saintly. 'The pot,' according

---

7 The influence of Demosthenes here may be more decorative than historical, but of Cicero there is no doubt.

8 J. Brochet, *Saint Jérôme et ses ennemis*. Paris, 1905.

9 *Letter* 7,5 (A.D. 375–376), from the desert at Calchis, in about his 27th year: *In mea enim patria rusticitatis vernacula deus venter est et de die vivitur: sanctior est ille qui ditior est. Accessit huic patellae iuxta tritum populi sermone proverbium dignum operculum, Lupicinus sacerdos— secundum illud quoque, de quo semel in vita Crassum ait risisse Lucilius: "similem habent labra lactucam asino cardus comedente . . ."*

to a proverbial expression, 'has a lid worthy of itself,' the bishop Lupicinus." It is perhaps no marvel that sinister stories emanating from an "Iberian viper" at Stridon, as Jerome called him, had driven Jerome into exile. He had also quarreled with his aunt Castorina (*Letter* 13, A.D. 375–376), to whom he wrote demanding rather than seeking a reconciliation. He complains of hearing no news from Stridon, suggesting estrangement from his entire family. Nor did he find things much better in his retirement to the desert of Chalcis. There he not only found the monks barbarous, but their theological disputes harried him to such an extent that he had to leave and return to Antioch. When his life of Paul of Thebes, the earliest, in his view, of the desert saints, first began to circulate, his opponents, not without reason, maintained that that saint had never existed. Jerome responded, in his life of Hilarion, ten or more years later (ca. 389–392), with his customary heat, that he would pass by these dogs of Scylla with his ears stopped up.[10] This confounding of the story of the Sirens with the monster Scylla would arouse little interest in the crowded history of mythological garbling, but what is noteworthy is that Jerome did indeed know better, yet indulged his anger at the expense of his knowledge. As a very generous critic very gently put it, "he did not intend to leave his opponents a monopoly of invective,"[11] and rarely in his prefaces, in the years that followed, did he fail to refer to his literary enemies, as here, as reptiles, birds and beasts whose habits and character were to be deplored. A fair sample perhaps is in Preface to *Hebr. Quaest. in Genesim* (*PL* 23, 983K), "those filthy sows who grunt against me, *parvum homunculum.*"[12]

When a council was convened at Rome in 382, he gladly returned there and became the friend, adviser and protégé of Pope Damasus. But risen to prominence and having perhaps some hopes of succeeding to the papacy (who hoped so is not clear), he had accumulated enemies numerous and powerful enough to force him once more to choose to go to Bethlehem (from 385 on), never to return to Rome. Thus from the age of about 40 for the next thirty years he lived the ascetic life of a monk, the life he had so ardently promoted from his early years and so vigorously, if not violently, demanded of others as the true Christian life. Still from his retreat poured forth not only works of scholarship but also of controversy, which

---

[10] *Vita Sancti Hilarionis* 1: . . . *maledicorum voces contemnimus, qui olim detrahentes Paulo meo, nunc forsitan detrahent et Hilarioni, illum solitudinis calumniati, huic obicientes frequentiam: ut qui semper latuit, non fuisse: qui a multis visus est, vilis existimetur. Fecerunt hoc et maiores eorum quondam Pharisaei, quibus nec Iohannis heremus atque ieiunium, nec Domini Salvatoris turbae, cibi, potusque placuerunt. Verum destinato operi imponam manum, et Scylleos canes obturata aure transibo.*

[11] Cavallera I, 133.

[12] *Non mirum ergo si contra me parvum homunculum immundae sues grunniant.*

inflamed more hostility in those with whom he disagreed or whom he held up to ridicule. He found few to commend but many and much to condemn, and in response to criticism he pointed out (*Hebr. Quaest. in Gen.*) that Terence, Vergil, Cicero had all been criticized too, in spite of their eminence. In his life of Malchus, written shortly after his final withdrawal from Rome, in a preface full of bitterness, he described this narrative as a practice run in preparation for a history of the Church, "from the coming of the Saviour to our times, that is," he says, "from the apostles to the dregs of our time—by whom the Church was born and grew, increased by persecutions, was crowned with martyrdoms, and after it came to the Christian emperors became greater in power and wealth, but less in virtue."[13]

This projected history he never finished, but certainly his numerous and vigorous strictures left the impression that the clergy of his time was in many cases corrupt, ignorant, debauched and greedy, as well as quarrelsome.[14] The exaggeration is obvious enough; although at least some of the clergy strongly opposed Jerome's propaganda for monasticism and asceticism, their objections were serious enough, and the charges he makes against some smack of fiction, as in his accusation of those who get up early to start potations and continue to drink until evening.[15] Furthermore, the whole list of these vices, drunkenness and gluttony among the rich and powerful in particular, repeat the traditional themes of *satura* and suggest adaptations from literature. In particular, his attacks on women, from which it has been argued that pagan antifeminism became part of medieval tradition,[16] raise a question as to how far his zeal for reform in the Church and mankind as a whole has not drawn him into intensification of literary themes. How much observation can really lie behind these scandalous charges? In any case, his response to criticism, more in anger than in sorrow, did (even when he was clearly in the right, as in the attacks made on his biblical translations) result in bitter quarrels, rupture of old friendships, and even, towards the end of his life, grave personal danger. His vigorous attacks on Pelagianism, in fact, aroused the Palestinian monks of that persuasion to attack his monasteries, and Jerome, as well as his monks and nuns, barely escaped being murdered.

---

13 *Vita Malchi Captivi* 1: *Scribere enim disposui (si tamen vitam Dominus dederit, et si vituperatores mei saltim fugientem me et clausum persequi desierint) ab adventu Salvatoris usque ad nostram aetatem, id est ab apostolis usque ad huius temporis fecem, quomodo et per quos Christi ecclesia nata sit et adulta, persecutionibus creverit, martyriis coronata sit; et postquam ad Christianos principes venerit, potentia et divitiis maior, sed virtutibus minor facta sit.*

14 Wiesen, Chapter III, "The Church and the Clergy," deals fully with the subject.

15 Wiesen, p. 108. *Commentary on Isaiah, PL* 24, 83C.

16 E.g., P. Delhaye, in *Mediaeval Studies* 13 (1951) 65–86.

In circumstances such as these and in the midst of such enmities, it might suffice to ascribe Jerome's satire to the bitterness of disappointed hopes and to his natural resentment at unjustified criticism, as manifested in the constant carping at his biblical translations, reaching a crescendo with his Old Testament translations from the Hebrew rather than from the Septuagint. But this would account only for the invective, and not for the obvious literary character of much of his satire. For instance, if his attacks on the clergy of his own day may be said to be something new and based on observation, yet it is the princes of the church in the main that he attacks, and attacks on the same grounds (such as drunkenness, lechery and particularly gluttony) that the rich and powerful are ridiculed for in the earlier literature. The very traditional character of these charges suggests that their sources are in part literary, exaggerated in turn by his very genuine zeal for reform of society in general and the Church in particular. Most specifically, what is hard not to call the antifeminism, so rampant in his writing, can hardly have been an accurate representation of those women who were his closest friends and stoutest supporters. It might be well to remember that he had, after all, passed most of his life away from Rome, and the latter part of it in semi-retirement, far from the bustle and perhaps the corruptions of city life. In fact, a dissertation on St. Jerome's observations on daily life by Sr. M. Jamesetta Kelley [17] finds very little to collect. Jerome was, as was natural in his circumstances, an intensely bookish man, and to such an extent that Cavallera could demonstrate that what he professed to be a confession of his youthful sins, had in fact been lifted from his translation of a work of Origen. [18] Is it fantastic to suggest that a man who can plagiarize his sins might not be the best guide to his own biography?

Jerome's devotion to classical literature might appear, of course, to have been interrupted (if hardly forever, at least for a considerable period, perhaps for as much as fifteen years) by his celebrated dream, recorded in *Ep.* 22,30. Yet I think no one after Arthur Stanley Pease's demonstration of 1919 [19] has maintained that he long kept the vow he there records; i.e., that from a tribunal on high he was judged, "*Ciceronianus es, non Christianus. Ubi thesaurus tuus, ibi et cor tuum,*" and in his terror and pain at the beating he was receiving as punishment, swore more than was required, "*Domine, si umquam habuero codices saeculares, si legero, te negavi.*" Famous as this dream

[17] *Life and Times as Revealed in the Writings of St. Jerome Exclusive of the Letters* (Catholic University of America Patristic Studies, 70), Washington, 1944.
[18] Cavallera II, 72–75.
[19] "The Attitude of Jerome towards Pagan Literature," *TAPA* 50 (1919), 150–167.

is, in the innumerable discussions it is often forgotten what this punishment was to correct: not so much the reading of classical authors, as to count these as his treasures while rejecting religious texts as uncouth because of their *sermo . . . incultus*.[20] The significance of the dream, then, is not so much a rejection of Cicero, Vergil and other pagan authors, as a turning to Christian scholarship, in which his censor had found him wanting. Letter 22 probably dates from 384, and the dream some ten years earlier. During these years and for sometime following, Jerome had to perfect himself in Greek and acquire a grasp of Hebrew for his translations and commentaries. This work would certainly leave him little time for reading for pleasure, and he writes with regret of what the neglect of the Latin classics had done to his style, in his commentary on *Galatians* (*PL* 26, 399C): "all *elegantia* of speech and *venustas* of Latin eloquence had been defiled by the *stridor* (hissing) of Hebrew reading." And gives one reason:[21] "For you know," he says to the noble ladies Marcella, Paula and Eustochium, to whom he addresses his work, "that it has been more than fifteen years since Cicero, Vergil or any pagan author has come into my hands. And if it happens that, when we are speaking, anything of that sort creeps in, it is as if we remember an ancient dream through a cloud."

In any case, the most thorough study of St. Jerome's references by Harald Hagendahl has shown, more fully than previous work, the great extent of Jerome's indebtedness to classical Latin authors. As for the satirists, Hagendahl is certainly correct in observing of Jerome's treatise against Jovinian, and its reminiscences of Persius, "I think we may safely conclude that Jerome at that time [i.e., in 393, nine years after *Ep.* 22] intentionally renewed his acquaintance with the Stoic poet."[22] Jerome has in common with the satirists not only the traditional themes but also, very frequently, the use of historical or fictitious names to designate his opponents, in order to give the impression that it is the sin and not the sinner he is aiming at: for instance, Luscius Lanuvinus (Lavinius?) as a pseudo-

---

[20] *Bibliotheca . . . carere non poteram* [at Jerusalem]. *Itaque miser ego lecturus Tullium ieiunabam. Post noctium crebras vigilias, post lacrimas, quas mihi praeteritorum recordatio peccatorum ex imis visceribus eruebat, Plautus sumebatur in manibus. Si quando in memet reversus prophetam legere coepissem, sermo horrebat incultus et, quia lumen caecis oculis non videbam, non oculorum putabam culpam esse, sed solis.*

[21] *Sed omnem sermonis elegantiam et Latini eloquii venustatem stridor lectionis Hebraicae sordidavit. Nostis enim et ipsae quod plus quam quindecim anni sunt ex quo in manus meas nunquam Tullius, nunquam Maro, nunquam gentilium litterarum quilibet auctor ascendit: et si quid forte inde dum loquimur obrepit, quasi antiqui per nebulam somnii recordamur. Quod autem profecerim ex linguae illius infatigabili studio, aliorum iudicio derelinquo: ego quid in mea amiserim scio.*

[22] Harald Hagendahl, *Latin Fathers and the Classics* (*Studia Graeca et Latina Gothoburgensia,* VI). Göteborg, 1948, 145.

nym for an opponent.[23] More than that: if the range of subject, sharpness of tone and, what is perhaps even more striking, the wide range in levels of style and language suggest *satura* as in some way offering models, with these the diffuse unity of the *sermo* would fit. That his connection of his satire with *satura* is conscious is, I think, indicated in two passages, which Wiesen also discusses. The first of these is contained in the famous *Letter* 22,32, telling of a rich hypocritical woman and her vicious treatment of an old hag trying to collect alms twice; to which he adds, *nomina taceo, ne saturam putes*, as if it fit otherwise the requirements of the genre. And in *Letter* 40,1, addressed to a certain Onasus (clearly a pseudonym), he says, "You claim that you are the one I am pointing out in my comments, and you call me into court and foolishly charge me with being a writer of satire (*satiricum scriptorem*) in prose." Interpretations of these somewhat ambiguous remarks differ; but clearly, in the first case, all that distinguishes some of Jerome's work from historical Latin *satura* in his eyes is that he does not dramatize by introducing a cast of names, which *satura* normally does. In the second case, "you foolishly charge" seems clear enough, because a charge of slander or libel will not lie when the plaintiff is not clearly identified.

Thus, on what scanty material is left us, it would appear that Jerome consciously chose what he felt was the spirit, tone and dramatic vivacity of *satura* in Horace and Persius, at least, and interpreted *satura* as now meaning the manner and the matter but not the form, thus giving impetus to new movements to come. That the *carmen*-aspect was overlooked, may still seem strange; but it is noteworthy that the one comedy surviving from this period is in prose, even though a kind of rhythmical prose. And I have argued elsewhere[24] that the so-called verse of Commodian is not verse, quantitative or accentual, but prose poetry. I do not know whether there is any connection to be found here; but the whole problem of novelty versus tradition in the Late Latin period awaits an answer.

The Ohio State University

[23] *Liber Hebr. Quaest. in Genesim, Praefatio, PL* 23, 955A.
[24] "Commodian and His Verse," in *Classical Studies Presented to Ben Edwin Perry*, University of Illinois Press, 1969, 272–283.

13

Disiecta Membra: On the Arrangement of Claudian's *Carmina minora*

In our manuscripts and editions the order of Claudian's *Carmina minora* varies considerably, and the arrangement adopted by Th. Birt (*Monumenta Germaniae historica: Auctores antiquissimi*, vol. 10, 1892) and M. Platnauer (*Loeb Classical Library*, 2 vols., 1922, reprinted 1963) has no more authority, I think, than that of J. M. Gesner (1759). But since Birt, in his long *Praefatio*, claims to have discovered the arrangement closest to that of the archetype, we shall examine its merits first. It is based on the Mediceus, a fifteenth century codex which derives from an "antiquus codex" and is found, with minor variations, in the Ambrosianus, also fifteenth century, and about twenty other witnesses. Before reaching any conclusions we must survey the poems from the point of view of their content and their literary form. This paper will be partly a catalogue of the extant poems, but since they are hardly read nowadays except perhaps by a few specialists, such a survey is necessary. I realize how sketchy my contribution is, but a great deal of work is needed. For one thing, the text is corrupt in many places. Birt's text is far too conservative, his own conjectures are often rash and implausible.

The first group of poems in Birt's edition includes eight pieces, mainly of the descriptive genre. The very first piece repeats verbatim one of the four *Fescennina* which form a sort of varied prelude to the Epithalamium of Honorius and Maria. Was it lifted out of that context and placed here because it is the shortest of the four? But any of the others might have qualified as a "short poem." It is certainly an ingenious compliment to Stilicho, and his name is only mentioned here. Whoever put this piece at the head of the *Carmina minora* must have understood it as a tribute to Stilicho, perhaps the shortest in Claudian's oeuvre.

Number 2 is the description of a harbor. Why it should be the harbor of Smyrna (according to the lemma in some manuscripts) or Sarona (according to the lemma in the "vetus Cuiacii") is not clear. In some cases (see below, on No. 12) a lemma seems to have information which is not found in the poem itself; but this may be guesswork. These few lines could be a *topos* to be inserted into a longer poem where needed. There must be some connection between this and No. 5 (see below).

Number 3 is altogether different: four lines addressed to Aeternalis, the proconsul of Asia of A.D. 396 and apparently a patron of Claudian's, for the poet calls him *meus . . . Apollo* (v. 4; cf. Birt, *Praefatio*, p. XIV). The text of v. 3, as given in Birt and Platnauer, is unsatisfactory. The point of the poem is that Claudian can only speak in verse (cf. Ovid, *Tristia* 4,10,23–26), because he is inspired by his Apollo, Aeternalis, just as the oracle at Delphi, inspired by Apollo, is given in verse. Read: *carmina sunt, nam verba negant communia Musae* (*non* Heinsius ex codd.: *sed* vulgo). Claudian contrasts poetry (*carmina*) and prose (*verba communia*). The vulgate *sed* makes sense but lacks point, and *non*, found by Heinsius in some manuscripts, clashes with the beginning of the next lines: *carmina sola loquor*. The poem looks like the dedication of a collection of Claudian's poems to Aeternalis, but what texts would have been included? All the *Carmina minora*? Or just the ones dealing with ordinary subjects—subjects that someone else would write about in prose, such as No. 10, *De birro castoreo*? Number 4 is the description of a handsome bull: the lemma *Descriptio armenti* or *armentorum* is clearly misleading and probably read out of the last word of v. 1, *armentorum*.[1]

Number 5 presents the same kind of problem as No. 2. In the "Excerpta Florentina" (15th cent.) it has the lemma *Est in conspectu longe locus*, probably a hint that these four lines are a variation on a Virgilian theme (*Aeneid* 1,159–168), but Virgil wrote *est in secessu longo locus*. A scribe or editor perhaps recognized the parallel but quoted from memory. It is also possible that this piece originally was connected with No. 2, which begins with the words *Urbs in conspectu*. But the beginning of No. 2 is almost certainly corrupt, and probably should be restored as Pricaeus and Heinsius had suggested: *Urbis conspectum montana cacumina vallant | tranquillo praetenta mari*. Perhaps Nos. 2 and 5 are fragments torn from the same contest—a safe harbor and the city which it serves—or else they are variations on a passage in the *Aeneid*, to be inserted into a longer poem. Poets must have kept such patches for future use, just as Cicero had his collection of *praefationes*. Number 6 is similar: a variation on Virgilian themes (*Aeneid* 1,148–150 and 7,503–508). The lemma in some

---

[1] In v. 12 read *praestassent* (*praestarent* "vetus Cuiacii" : *portassent* vulgo).

manuscripts reads *rimanti telum ira facit*, an exact quotation of Virgil, *Aeneid* 7,508. Did the poet himself supply this piece of information? Or did a reader note the reminiscence in the margin (see above, No. 2)?

Number 7 is separated by Birt into two poems of four lines each. Both of them celebrate a marble sculpture: a chariot with four horses and the driver, all made from one block. This is the typical *ecphrasis* of a work of art, perhaps a well-known monument in Rome. Birt compares *Anth. Pal.* 9,759 (Ἀδέσποτον) and 760 (Ἄλλο), both consisting of one line only, both almost identical, with minor variations. Number 8, *De Polycaste et Perdicca*, is about the incestuous love of a mother for her son. There are different variations of this story in other sources,[2] but the lemma is questionable: nothing indicates that Claudian refers to the young hunter Perdiccas and his mother Polycaste (or Polycarpe). The text is corrupt: in v. 1 read *flammatum* (Heinsius) for *flammarum*; in v. 2 read *sanguinis, heu, fetum . . . timens* for *sanguinis effetum . . . timet*; and in v. 6 read *consule iam Veneri* for *c.i. Venerem*.

Number 9, *De hystrice*, could be part of a series on animals (cf. Nos. 18; 27; 42; 49; *Appendix*, No. 9, etc.). Claudian was clearly fascinated by the strange variety in the animal world. Number 10, *De birro castoreo*, a satiric epigram in the style of Martial, describes a shabby old overcoat made of beaver's fur. The coat was never worth much (*sex solidi* was apparently very cheap for such a garment at this time), but now it is only a shadow of its former self: *nominis umbra manet veteris* (mock-heroic after Lucan 1,135, *stat magni nominis umbra*, of Pompeius Magnus).

Number 11, *In sepulchrum speciosae*, could be inspired by a funeral monument, perhaps a statue that Claudian saw somewhere along a highway. It could also have been intended as the epitaph itself; though the name of the woman is missing, it could have been inscribed somewhere else on the monument. But the epigram might be purely literary; cf. Iulianus Aegyptius, *Anth. Pal.* 7,599. Number 12, *De balneis Quintianis quae in via posita erant*. The name of Quintius is not mentioned in the poem; hence the lemma either preserves independent information or is based on guesswork (see above, on No. 2). Again, it is not impossible that Claudian was asked to compose an inscription for this bath-house along the highway; the name of the benefactor might have been found on another part of the building.

Number 13 attacks a critic who claimed that Claudian's verse did not scan properly: "*claudicat hic versus; haec*," inquit, "*syllaba nutat*." Hence, he concluded, *totum carmen non stat*. These must be technical terms used by ancient metricians, and from that point of view the poem is quite important. Claudian replies that the critic is unable to read verse; he is

---

[2] Cf. Fr. Vollmer, *RE* 5 (1905), 1644.

therefore *podager*. This does not mean, of course, that the critic actually suffers from gout; it means that something is wrong with his "feet," i.e., the meter of Claudian's verses as he reads them. He actually "butchers" them, Claudian says (at the end of v. 2 read *lacerans* for *laceras*, following the edition of P. Burman the Younger, 1760). Number 14 is a brief poetic thank-you note for some honey which Maximus had sent him. Numbers 15 and 16 are two Latin versions of the anonymous epigram *Anth. Pal.* 5,50, which is attributed by some critics to Claudian himself. These are literary exercises.

Number 17 celebrates the statues of the two brothers who carried their parents to safety from a burning house. Claudian apparently saw these statues in or near Catina (Catania) on Sicily, and he praises the work of art no less than the act of *pietas* which it commemorates. During an eruption of Mt. Aetna, a miracle happened: the masses of hot lava stopped at this very monument, as if in awe of such devotion. The story is told elsewhere in different versions, e.g., in Ps.–Aristotle, *De mundo* 400 a 34–b 6: here the lava stream separates to spare the two living brothers and their burden. Henceforth the place was called εὐσεβῶν χῶρος, *piorum locus*. The text is greatly in need of restoration: read, e.g., in v. 35 *patri* for *pater* (with A), and in v. 42 *dicabit* for *dicavit* (with R and Heinsius).

Number 18, on a team of Gallic mules and their trainer, describes some kind of a circus act. Claudian is astonished at the skill and obedience of the animals. He notes that the trainer gives his commands in his native tongue, a Celto–Roman dialect (*barbarici . . . soni*, v. 8 = *Gallica verba*, v. 20). This could have been written anywhere, not necessarily on a trip through Gaul.

Number 19 is a short epistle in verse to Gennadius, the prefect of Egypt in 396 who seems to have lived in Ravenna after his retirement. Gennadius had asked for some of Claudian's poems, and is now told that none are left at home:

> *Nam mihi mox nidum pennis confisa relinquunt*
> *et lare contempto non reditura volant.*

Claudian compares his poems to young birds who have learned to fly and are eager to leave their nest, i.e., to reach the person who has commissioned them or to whom they are dedicated. Claudian's poetry is, to a large extent, *poésie d'occasion*, written to celebrate a certain event or a person, composed for a special καιρός. Even if Claudian kept—as he must have— a copy of his "official" poems, this was hardly the kind of thing Gennadius wanted: he probably was hoping for a more personal kind of poem, and this is what he gets, though it is quite short. Birt concludes from this poem that Claudian did not make a collection of his own works. This may be true, but the poem itself does not support it. Number 20 is a charming piece, often quoted, on an old man of Verona who—unlike Claudian—had never left his home.

Number 21 attacks two high officials of opposite tempers, Flavius Mallius Theodorus and Rufius Synesius Hadrianus: one is too lazy, the other hyper-active. Theodorus was consul in 399, but before that time, it would appear, had dedicated himself for years to philosophy and agriculture (Claudian 17,138; 174 ff.).[3] Hadrianus held the office of *praefectus praetorio* of Italy in 401–405 and apparently used his power to enrich himself.[4] Claudian managed, in one short epigram, to offend two influential men at the same time, but Mallius seems to have forgiven him, while Hadrian, furious, demanded an apology (No. 22, immediately following), which turned out more than ten times as long as the offending poem. One cannot help wondering what the occasion may have been. Perhaps both men were candidates for a political office, and Claudian made it clear that he thought them both unfit, for different reasons. Number 22 is the *deprecatio* for the preceding attack on Hadrianus, a piece so humble and abject in tone that—like so many ancient poems of flattery—it seems almost ironical. And yet, I suppose, that was the required attitude, and Claudian may have been forced to write it under pressure from Stilicho; at least that is what the title in M (the catalogue) suggests: *excusatio pro se ad Stilichonem*. Number 23 is also a *deprecatio*, also addressed to a political figure, the quaestor Alethius,[5] but without political character. Claudian had been critical of Alethius' poetry; Alethius was hurt, and Claudian, appearing very remorseful and contrite, promises from now on to praise everything Alethius writes. The way in which Alethius is compared to Homer and Virgil (vv. 15 f.) would indicate that the whole poem is not meant seriously. There is a thread connecting poems 21–23: an attack on two political figures; the apology addressed to one of them; an apology addressed to a third politician, but the attack itself is missing. This short series, however, is separated from related poems (attacks on Claudian, or Claudian's attacks on others: Nos. 13; 50).

Number 24 is a brief (fragmentary?) description of a lobster, probably not a living one but a cooked specimen on the table. It may be compared with *Appendix*, No. 3 (see below), with which it is connected in the Vaticanus 2809 (12th cent.). Number 25 is a long Epithalamium for Palladius and Celerina, similar to the *Laus Serenae* (No. 30) and the Epithalamium

---

[3] Cf. A. H. M. Jones, J. R. Martindale, and J. Morris, *The Prosopography of the Later Roman Empire*, I (Cambridge, 1971), 900 ff.; W. Ensslin, *RE* 5A (1934), 1897 ff.

[4] *Prosopography* (above, n. 3), I, 406; O. Seeck, *RE* 7 (1912), 2178.

[5] *Prosopography*, I, 39.

for Honorius (among the "official" poems). Both epithalamia have an elegiac *praefatio* followed by hexameters. One might ask, why this was not included among the "official" poems (see below, on No. 30). Perhaps because it is relatively short, although it is one of the longest texts in the *Carmina minora*. Could it be unfinished?

Four poems dealing with scientific lore follow. Number 26 praises the hot mineral springs of Aponos (Abano, near Padua). Obviously the poet had visited the place; perhaps he had even taken the waters there. He saw the many *graffiti* and other inscriptions of grateful patients, some in crude verse. This must be the meaning of v. 4, *cum tibi plebeius carmina dictet honos*, not "seeing . . . that a people's love bids poets to honour thee in song," as Platnauer translates. Number 27, on the Phoenix, follows Herodotus 2,73, and is partly mythological, partly epideictic or allegorical: the fabulous bird stands for immortality. Number 28 celebrates the Nile, and seems to be incomplete (J. J. Scaliger, F. Buecheler). Though Claudian was born in Egypt he follows literary models, such as Herodotus 2,20 ff.; Seneca, *Nat. quaest.* 4,1 ff.; Lucan 10,194–331. Number 29, on the magnet, blends science and mythology.

Laus Serenae (No. 30) should be added to Claudian's "official" poems (as should No. 25), and one is surprised to find it here. Again, it may be unfinished. Serena is Theodosius' niece and adoptive daughter, and Stilicho's wife (ca. 384–408).[6] In the charming passage vv. 132–139 there is a textual problem:

> *Ambas* (sc. *sorores*) *ille quidem patrio complexus amore,*
> *sed merito pietas in te proclivior ibat;*
> *et quotiens, rerum moles ut publica cogit,*
> 135 *tristior aut ira tumidus flagrante redibat,*
> *cum patrem nati fugerent atque ipsa timeret*
> *commotum Flaccilla virum, tu sola frementem*
> *frangere, tu blando poteras sermone mederi.*
> *Alloquiis haerere tuis, secreta fideli.*[7]

Theodosius loves both Serena and her sister Thermantia; but Serena is his favorite. Even when he is depressed or angry, even when his two sons, Arcadius and Honorius, and his wife Flaccilla are afraid to talk to him, he will listen to Serena. She alone can put him in good mood; and he tells her state secrets. That much is clear. But the transition from 138 to 139 is difficult, and it seems possible that one or two lines had fallen out, as Heinsius suggested. Or else v. 139 is the beginning of a period which Claudian left unfinished. Apparently there is something missing also at

---

6 *Prosopography* I, 824; O. Seeck, *RE* 2A (1923), 1672 f.
7 *fideli* codd. : *fateri* Birt.

the end of the poem, for the "Excerpta Gyraldina" note: *In exemplari antiquo scriptum est in fine "hic deest," quod est verisimile.* There are some unusual corruptions in the text, too: perhaps it was preserved in a not easily legible autograph. We have asked the question, why were Nos. 25 and 30 not included among Claudian's "official" poems? The answer may be: because both were unfinished. This, of course, would affect their chronology. The place of the *Epistula ad Serenam* (No. 31), immediately after the *Laus*, is logical (though they are separated from each other in some manuscripts, and some preserve the *Epistula* without the *Laus*). The *Epistula* is more personal. We hear that Claudian, though painfully aware of his poverty (45 f.), was encouraged by Serena to propose to a young woman in North Africa. The letter seems to have been written immediately before the poet's marriage, to which, because of the distance, he cannot invite Serena. Vollmer[8] and Seeck[9] think the poem was written during Claudian's honeymoon and that he died soon afterward.

Number 32, *De Salvatore*, is a poetic paraphrase of the beginning of the Gospel according to St. John. It is comparable to the *Laus Christi, Appendix*, No. 20. Numbers 33–39 are seven epigrams on a crystal enclosing a drop of water. To those may be added two Greek epigrams by Claudian on the same subject (*Anth. Pal.* 9,753 and 754). This crystal obviously fascinated him and gave him an ideal opportunity to show his talent of deriving ever new ideas from the same theme. Numbers 40 and 41, the letters to Olybrius and his younger brother Probinus, resemble each other: both urge a friend to write soon (cf. Ovid, *Tristia* 4,7 and 5,13). The two brothers are also connected in Claudian's *Panegyricus dictus Probino et Olybrio consulibus*. The two letters stand next to each other in all manuscripts. Number 42, *De apro et leone*, appears to be unfinished; one would expect to hear about the outcome of the fight. Numbers 43 and 44 are invectives against Curetius. In 43 Curetius is introduced as the whoring son of a fraudulent astrologer (whose name, Uranius, is as fanciful as is the family tree of the astrologer in Propertius 4,1), and in 44 his vices are explained in terms of his father's art, i.e., through an interpretation of his own horoscope. Number 45: On the shell in which Serena used to wash her face. We learn that she wrote poetry.

The following poems are all connected with Honorius and his favorite horse. Number 46 is ostensibly written to accompany a cloak and a bridle given to Honorius by Serena: the cloak was her own work. Number 48 celebrates a strap for the horse embroidered by Serena. And No. 47, addressed to the horse, makes clear what valuable gifts the bridle, the

[8] *RE* 3 (1899), 2655 (s.v. *Claudianus*).
[9] *Op. cit.* (above, n. 6), 1673.

collar, the strap, and the blanket woven of gold and purple are (the strap must be the same strap as the one in No. 48). In this series we are not told specifically about the collar and the blanket (the *chlamys* of No. 46 must be for the horseman rather than the horse), but we can assume that they too were the gifts of Serena. The order of these poems, the same in all manuscripts (though 48 is missing in some witnesses) is misleading and could not possibly, I believe, have been planned by the poet. The address to the horse (No. 47) anticipates the gift of the strap which is introduced more elaborately in the following poem (No. 48). There is another problem: it is by no means certain that 46 and 47 are separate poems; Mommsen, for instance, thought them to form one piece. In this case the most natural order would be: 48, 46, 47. The lemma of No. 48, *De zona equi regii missa Honorio Augusto a Serena*, is more specific than those of 46, *De chlamyde et frenis*, and 47, *De equo dono dato* (a bizarre way of saying *de donis equo datis*). But the lemmata vary in the manuscripts: some do introduce the name of Honorius *ad* 46. The problem is complicated by the fact that another poem belonging here appears detached from the series in most witnesses (it follows 48 in the Veronensis), and was put into the *Appendix* by Birt (No. 4, see below). We can see that this short series of poems which are obviously related presented difficulties to the ancient editors.

Number 49, *De torpedine* (the electric ray), could be associated with Nos. 9, 18, etc. (see above). Number 50, often discussed because of its references to Christianity, attacks a certain Iacobus, commander of the cavalry, who had criticized Claudian's poetry. Claudian hits back as hard as he can, and denounces Iacobus as a coward and drunkard (cf. the methods of denigration in Nos. 13, 43, and 44). Whether a poem of this kind was ever published, is doubtful. Such poems are written to let off steam and to be shown to a few intimate friends. Number 51 is on the planetarium of Archimedes. Number 52, *De lanario*, a miniature cento, is missing in four important manuscripts (omitted in Platnauer's edition)· Perhaps it is a torso as well as a cento. Neither the title nor the text have been explained so far. Could it be an improvisation, or some kind of a riddle? Number 53 (52 in Platnauer), the *Gigantomachia*, is clearly unfinished.

Birt has not included the poems of the so-called *Appendix carminum minorum* in the scheme which he proposes. The very existence of this *Appendix*, as indicated above, makes the problem with which we are concerned, almost insoluble. The poems of the *Appendix* are similar in character to the *Carmina minora* discussed above, but they are missing in some of the main manuscripts; therefore, their authenticity has been doubted, and they have received even less attention than the *Carmina minora*. A few of the poems are in the Veronensis (9th cent.; R), some are in the

Vaticanus 2809 (12th cent.; V), but some are known only from early editions. Almost all of them, however, show Claudian's elegance in style and versification.

Appendix, No. 1, *In Sirenas*, stands in R after *Carmina minora* 49, *De torpedine*. A series of oxymora makes it a remarkable *tour de force*: the Sirens are *dulcia monstra*, | *blanda pericla maris, terror . . . gratus in undis* (vv. 3 f.), and the death they bring is sweet for their victims: *nec dolor ullus erat: mortem dabat ipsa voluptas* (9). Number 2, *Laus Herculis*, follows the *Gigantomachia* (*C.min.* 53) in R. With its 137 lines it is the longest poem of the *Appendix*. But it is incomplete: only three out of Heracles' twelve (or twenty) labours are told. Like the *Gigantomachia* it is the torso of a rather ambitious project. The style is reminiscent of Callimachus' hymns. Number 3, *De dulcio*, consists of just one line: *Nectareo muro dulces cinguntur harenae*. This must be a kind of dessert, described in mock-heroic style: a sweet powdery substance surrounded by ripe grapes. In V it comes after *C.min.* 24, *De lucusta*. Are these pieces from a catalogue-poem describing the menu of a memorable banquet, from the hors d'oeuvre to the sweet? Number 4, *De zona missa ab eadem* (sc. *Serena*) *Arcadio Augusto*: If Serena, as we have seen above, had embroidered a strap for Honorius' horse, it is quite probable that she also made one for his brother's horse. In V the poem comes after *C.min.* 48. It is also preserved in M (Ambrosianus M 9, 13th cent.). Why is it missing in other manuscripts? Perhaps because they have the character of anthologies and do not attempt to collect the whole work of the poet.

Number 5, *Epithalamium Laurentii*, is rejected in the strongest terms by Birt (Praefatio, p. CLXVI), along with Nos. 6–8. A Laurentius is attested as *comes rerum privatarum* in the Eastern part of the Empire on 24 April 396.[10] Whether the poem is genuine or not, it seems a very fine work of art, not just a conventional wedding-poem. Aldhelm knew and admired it. The description of a late Roman orchestra, as it performed at the wedding (vv. 60–63), will be of interest, not only to musicologists:

> 60 *Tympana, chorda simul symphonia, tibia, buxus,*
>   *cymbala, bambylium[11] cornus, aes,[12] fistula, sistrum,*
>   *quaeque per aeratas inspirant carmina fauces,[13]*
>   *humida folligenis exclament[14] organa ventis.[15]*

[10] O. Seeck, *RE* 12 (1925), 1015.

[11] *bambylium* is Buecheler's conjecture for *bambilium* VM. Birt proposed *bombylium*, and this may well be right; but other forms, such as *bamborium* (*Gramm. Lat.* Keil 4,532.2), are attested too. It must have been a wood instrument with a deep humming sound, similar to the bassoon.

[12] *aes* Birt : *et* VM.   [13] *fauces* M. Haupt : *voces* VM.

[14] *exclamant* VM, corr. G. Wernsdorf.   [15] *ventis* L. Mueller : *vocis* V[1] M.

The number of different wind instruments is impressive. Another passage (vv. 68–78) deserves to be mentioned: When the young couple has finally entered the bridal chamber, it is the duty of the *pronuba* to take away the bride's jewelry, her pins, etc., as a measure of precaution; during the customary *luctamen Veneris* the girl might get carried away, play become earnest, and the man might get scratched or even seriously wounded.

Numbers 6, 7, and 8 are prayers for safe return from a trip abroad, one addressed to Bacchus, the other to Mars, the third (which is incomplete) to Juno. The lemmata (*De Liberalibus; Laus Martis; De Iunonalibus*) are entirely fanciful, and the whole evidence is presented in a misleading way by Birt. If the poems are given any title at all, it should be something like *De reditu ad Liberum; D. r. ad Martem; D.r. ad Iunonem.* The composition is the same in all three poems: first an ἀρεταλογία of the divinity, then the prayer (*da reditum nobis,* or *da nobis reditum,* for variety's sake, 7,11), and then, introduced by *sic,* the wish that something pleasing to the divinity may come true. Numbers 6 and 7 are preserved in V and three other sources; No. 8 is found in V only (perhaps it was incomplete in the common source of these witnesses).

Number 9, *De hippopotamo et crocodilo,* is similar to the animal poems among the *Carmina minora.* It is almost certainly incomplete, as the *Schedae Peirescianae* of Vaticanus 9135 note. Number 10, *De aquila quae in mensa de sardonyche lapide erat,* is on a precious table, and can be compared to the *ecphraseis* of works of art (e.g., *C.min.* 7). Number 11, *De Isidis navigio,* is a prayer to Isis not to leave the country. Claudian was familiar with the cult of Isis (cf. Claudian 8, 570 ff.). The author of the poem calls her *nostra dea* (3). Number 12, *De lavacro,* is on a luxurious bathing establishment on the Black Sea (the poem is incomplete). Someone called Florens is invited to use these baths on a holiday. An Alexander and his mother are mentioned: this could be Alexander Severus and his mother Iulia Mammaea, as Birt observes. If so, then the poem could hardly be by Claudian, although it is most accomplished (the pleasures of a scented shower are described very gracefully, 6 ff.). Number 13, *De Vinalibus,* is on the Roman wine festival, which was celebrated on 22 April and 19 August (cf. No. 15 below, on the *Floralia*). The poem is probably incomplete. Number 14, *De Cytherea*: There are several textual difficulties, and the piece ends rather abruptly, but it seems to describe an epiphany of Venus, who visits the poet early one morning. Number 15, *De cereo,* is on the candles that were lit on the eve of the *Floralia* (on 28 April) and carried in a procession.[16] Numbers 16–19: Only the titles are preserved in the catalogue of M. The scribe

16 Cf. G. Wissowa, *RE* 6 (1909), 2752.

may have seen them in his *exemplar*, but he just copied the titles. They all dealt with animals (cf., e.g., *C.min.* 9). Number 20, *Laus Christi*, appears first in Camers' edition (Vienna, 1510) along with No. 21. Birt deals with this and the following poem No. 21, *Miracula Christi*, at length in his *Praefatio*, pp. CLXX ff. Number 20 is incomplete (Scaliger), probably No. 21 as well (Gesner). Finally, No. 22, an epigram from Claude Binet's codex Cuiacianus, first published in his edition of Petronius, is on a pederast who introduces a *puer delicatus* as his son. The text as printed by Birt is unsatisfactory: lines 9 f., separated from lines 1–8 by the editor, should be inserted between 4 and 5. Read *puer* for *pater* in v. 9 (with W. Meyer), and *hic* for *huic* in the same line (with Patisson).

Before drawing any conclusions from this survey we should look briefly at the textual tradition of Claudian, because it affects our problem in various ways. For unknown reasons, Claudian's unfinished epic *De raptu Proserpinae*, as well as his panegyric on Probinus and Olybrius, became detached from the rest of his opus. For several centuries these two works had their own textual history. What we have of Claudian's Latin poems seems to have been handed down in several lines: (1) *Claudianus maior* (or *magnus*), including his longer poems (without the Panegyricus on Probinus and Olybrius) and the *Carmina minora*, probably along with some of the poems in the *Appendix*. But the Veronensis 163 (R) represents a separate tradition of the *Carmina minora*.[17] (2) *Claudianus minor* (or *parvus*), containing *De raptu Proserpinae*. (3) The Panegyricus on Probinus and Olybrius, separated from (1) probably because it did not concern Stilicho, but joined to *Claudianus maior* in the twelfth century, as it seems. The distinction between (1) and (2) is simply based on the size of the codices: a volume containing only *De raptu* was of course much smaller than the volume with the rest of the works. This distinction is current in incipits and explicits of the manuscripts from the thirteenth and fourteenth centuries; it is also found in Vincent of Beauvais (Birt, p. LXXVII, n. 4).

Within (1), as we have seen, the order of the *Carmina minora* varies greatly. The Veronensis 163 (R), an important eighth century witness (though *akephalos*, it probably never included the long "official" poems), has them in the following order: *C.min.* 29 (starting with v. 34); 9; 17; 18; 20; 22; 23; 50; 49; *App.* 1; *C.min.* 51; 19; 40; 41; 32; 27; Lactantius' *Phoenix* (same theme as the preceding piece); 3; 6; 10–16; 21; 31; 53; *App.* 2; *C.min.* 46–48; 45. This is about half the number of poems included in Birt's edition; this, and the fact that at least one piece by another author

---

[17] Cf. M. Fuhrmann, *Der kleine Pauly*, 1 (1964), 1203 (s.v. *Claudianus*).

is included, would characterize R as an anthology rather than part of a complete edition. Though the arrangement is quite different, the series *C.min.* 9–23 and 45–51 are represented in both collections: R and V (Vaticanus 2809). This seems to indicate that the scribe of V made a selection from a larger corpus. He went through it more than once, adding poems that he had left out previously.[18]

According to Birt's survey (p. CXXXV), there seem to be at least five different types of arrangement of *Carmina minora* found in various manuscripts and groups of manuscripts. None of them can be considered authentic, but not for the reasons given by Birt (pp. LXXVI f.; CXXXIV ff.). He seems to think that poems of considerable length—such as the Epithalamium for Palladius (*C.min.* 25, 145 lines long), the *Laus Serenae* (*C.min.* 30, 236 lines, perhaps planned to be even longer), the torso of a *Gigantomachia* (*C.min.* 53, 128 lines)—could not have been placed next to epigrams of eight and ten lines. Birt claims that Latin poets tended to place poems of similar length next to each other; he compares the *Priapea*, on the one hand, Statius' *Silvae*, on the other (p. LXXVI). But there is no rule which can be applied to all poets: analogies are not always helpful. One might compare the *Corpus bucolicorum*, i.e., a collection of bucolic and non-bucolic poems by Theocritus and other poets. Some manuscripts include more poems than others, and the order of poems varies. Many seem to have the character of anthologies, but we know (from Artemidorus, *Anth. Pal.* 9,205) that in the late Hellenistic period an effort was made to collect all the bucolic texts. The desire for completeness may have led ancient editors to include more and more poems that were not bucolic, and not by Theocritus.

Catullus' *liber* is not a good analogy either. It includes relatively short poems at the beginning and end, and a number of long ones in the middle. Birt (p. LXXVI) is forced by his theory to assume that Catullus' book was shortened and rearranged by an editor (*Neque Catullus suam syllogen talem qualem habemus promulgavit, sed inferior aetas et decurtavit et ordinavit*). But Wendell Clausen[19] has shown convincingly, I think, that what we have is not one *liber* but three *libelli*, and that an "editor, more concerned to preserve than to present," (p. 40) placed some unfinished or otherwise unsatisfactory poems at the end of the first *libellus* (cc. 1–60). Not much is to be gained from the textual tradition of Ausonius. Birt believes (p. CXXXVI and n. 2) that the order found in the Vossianus Latinus 111

---

[18] The scribes of the cod. Palatinus of the *Greek Anthology* seem to have followed the same procedure, especially in Book Seven.

[19] *Classical Philology* 71 (1976), 37–43.

(9th cent.) is due to an editor, not the poet himself. But the possibility of a double *recensio* in Ausonius remains. Finally, the codex Salmasianus (Birt, *loc. cit.*), probably compiled in the 6th century, is an anthology. Even though some of the Claudian manuscripts, as we have seen, are anthologies, the tradition as a whole reflects the wish of many readers to have a complete edition, including everything the great poet wrote, *even* fragments, improvisations, and pieces whose authenticity was not above dispute.

We have seen that the problem of order and arrangement in Claudian's *Carmina minora* is closely connected with the textual tradition of the poet's works. The fact that certain poems are missing in some of the main manuscripts has led modern editors to relegate them into an appendix. Under such circumstances no manuscript can be a reliable guide. None of the different arrangements seems to reveal a principle, even though related poems are sometimes grouped together. Incidentally, there seems to be some evidence that none of our editions of Claudian is complete: a fragment quoted by a grammarian (*G.L.* Keil, 5,589,3), *rus istud pretio constat vili*, cannot be found in any of the extant poems. The grammarian, however, may have made a mistake: he also quotes four short passages from Ausonius which do not occur anywhere in the direct tradition.

But there is another argument overlooked so far. We have seen how many poems among the *Carmina minora* and in the *Appendix* are unfinished, mere fragments or possibly first drafts: Nos. 2; 5; 6; 24 (?); 28 (?); 30 (?); 43 (?); 52; 53; *App.*, Nos. 2; 9; 13; 20; 21. There is a difference between these pieces and the finished poems (short or long) which appear in both collections, but no attempt was made in ancient times to sort them out. Some unfinished poems appear in the series *C.min.* 1–25, which, as Birt claims, occurs in all the main witnesses, and must therefore be, in his opinion, the order of the archetype.

In conclusion, it is better to resign oneself than to indulge in fruitless speculation. *Magna pars scientiae est quaedam nescire*, as Grotius said. What we seem to have in Claudian's *Carmina minora* are pieces of all kinds and sizes, genres and styles from the poet's workshop, some finished, some fragmentary. One admires the versatility, craftsmanship, and fine literary style of the poet. Even a torso, left by a great artist, can be impressive. After his death, everything must have seemed important to an admiring public, and within a short time, I suspect, not one but several editions were made. The published material was soon rearranged and excerpted for different purposes, perhaps for use in schools, for anthologies, etc. The preserved manuscripts reflect many centuries of this editorial process, fluctuating between two extremes: a *Gesamtausgabe*, on the one side; an

Anthology, on the other. Our conclusion may seem disappointing, but it helps us to understand what could have happened when a prolific author suddenly died. Many unfinished projects were found among his papers. What we have is valuable, I think, just because some of it represents "work in progress" at various stages.

ADDENDUM

When I wrote this article, during a sabbatical leave of absence, I had no access to Alan Cameron's book on Claudian (Oxford U.P., 1970), nor had I read Christian Gnilka's review in *Gnomon* 49 (1977), 34–51. I am glad to see now that Cameron's views concerning the publication of the *Carmina minora* are consistent with my own. Cameron is convinced that the *Carmina minora* were published soon after the poet's death, at the order of Stilicho (pp. 416 ff.). Following Platnauer (Loeb edition, vol. I, 1928, p. xviii, n. 2) he believes that some pieces are mere jottings from Claudian's notebooks, fragments to be worked into a longer poem some day; he sums up: "Brief epigrams, epithalamia, half-finished epics and panegyrics all jumbled together in no apparent order, with a number of hexameter poems of 50–100 lines." (p. 418).

There are many valuable comments on the *Carmina minora* in Cameron's book: compare especially pp. 406 ff. on Nos. 30 and 31. He must be right when he says that No. 52 was unfinished at Claudian's death. In his opinion, Nos. 4, 9 and 10 of the *Appendix* are probably genuine (pp. 203; 407 f.). I think he has misunderstood No. 18 of the *Carmina minora* (pp. 391 f., "it describes with some admiration and astonishment how the farmers of Gaul control their oxen"). Gnilka's comments on Nos. 23 (*Studien zur Literatur der Spätantike*, Bonn, 1975, pp. 70 ff.) and 32 (*Gnomon*, loc. cit., pp. 50 f.) deserve to be read carefully.

I am very grateful to Miroslav Marcovich for editorial suggestions.

The Johns Hopkins University

14

Interpreting Second Declension Singular
Forms in -*u*

PAUL A. GAENG

With the fall of final -*m* in spoken, i.e., so-called Vulgar Latin, and the merger of /ō/ and /ŭ/ in the unstressed final syllable, the accusative is said to have been assimilated to the ablative, thus giving rise to what was to become, in the second declension singular, the general oblique case in -*o*.[1] Thus, an originally phonological phenomenon eventually turned into a morphological one.[2] However, the orthographic change from -*u* to -*o* in the final syllable, reflecting the emergence of this new case form (a change that is clearly reflected in studies of Late Latin documents like those of Pei, Sas, B. Löfstedt, Politzer, Cooper, Jennings, my own on Christian Inscriptions, and, more recently, Charles Carlton's study on documents from Ravenna)[3] is far from characteristic of the earlier Vulgar Latin period (say, up to the fourth–fifth centuries). Indeed, the phenomenon is *extremely* rare in Diehl's seminal study on final -*m* in epigraphic material,[4] where instances of an -*u* ending in what appears to be the classical accusa-

---

[1] Cf. Mario Pei, *The Language of the Eighth-Century Texts in Northern France* (New York, 1932), 106 ff. and 141 ff., with additional bibliographical references.

[2] Henri F. Muller and Pauline Taylor, *A Chrestomathy of Vulgar Latin* (New York, 1932), 54.

[3] Pei, *op. cit.*, 141 ff.; Louis Furman Sas, *The Noun Declension System in Merovingian Latin* (Paris, 1937), 124 ff.; Bengt Löfstedt, *Studien über die Sprache der langobardischen Gesetze* (Stockholm, 1961), 226 ff.; Robert L. Politzer, *A Study of the Language of Eighth-Century Lombardic Documents* (New York, 1949), 73; Paul J. Cooper, *The Language of the Forum Judicum*. Unpublished Ph.D. dissertation (Columbia University, 1952), 51 ff.; Augustus Campbell Jennings, *A Linguistic Study of the Cartulario de San Vicente de Oviedo* (New York, 1940), 95 ff.; Paul A. Gaeng, *An Inquiry Into Local Variations in Vulgar Latin As Reflected in the Vocalism of Christian Inscriptions* (Chapel Hill, 1968), 221 ff.; Charles Merritt Carlton, *A Linguistic Analysis of a Collection of Late Latin Documents Composed in Ravenna Between A.D. 445–700* (The Hague, 1973), 81 ff.

[4] Ernst Diehl, *De m finali epigraphica* (Leipzig, 1899), 268 ff.

tive case abound, e.g., *deus magnu oclu habet, filias titulu posuerunt, Petrus cum suis votu solvet, vixit annu et dies L, post ovitu meu,* and passim.

It must be pointed out, however, that the apparent omission of final *-m* in the classical accusative, even on inscriptions of a later date, such as Christian inscriptions of the fifth and sixth centuries, is far from overwhelming, let alone universal. While there are many examples of the omission of this final consonant in the accusative, in both dated and undated inscriptions, there are also a great number of correct occurrences. To illustrate this phenomenon and to get some idea of a possible ratio of omission versus retention of final *-m,* I have selected a sampling taken from Chapter XXVI of Diehl's collection of *Inscriptiones Latinae Christianae Veteres* (ILCV) (Vol. II, 279 ff.),[5] which includes 55 epitaphs from the area of *Rome* concerned with the purchase of burial places and sarcophagi for two or more persons, so-called *loci bisomi, trisomi,* and even *quadrisomi.* Out of a total of 74 occurrences of the direct object—the usual formula being *emit* or *fecit* (*fecerunt*) *sibi locum bisomum* (*trisomum, quadrisomum*), or simply *locum* or *bisomum,* etc.—I found 36 occurrences spelled with *-u* and 38 with *-um.* On six inscriptions, furthermore, I noted the concurrent use of classical accusatives in *-um* and forms in *-u* in the same function, as in *emit sibi et Maxentiae locum bisomu* (3810A).[6] It is also interesting to observe that in five out of seven cases where the expected accusative appears with an *-u* ending, the ablative preceded by the preposition *a(b)* is also spelled with *-u,* as in *locu bisomu emptu ab Ursu fossore* (3811A, a. 403). (This group of inscriptions, incidentally, seems to come from the first half of the fifth century, seeing that some of them are precisely dated.)

A sampling such as this nevertheless seems to suggest a considerable hesitation between forms in *-um* and *-u* to signal direct object function, even in formulaic expressions involving high frequency words, in which the retention of final *-m* as a written device may not reflect the true state of the spoken language at all.[7] In fact, such a hesitation on the written level must surely reflect new spoken language habits. Without wishing to embark upon a discussion of the chronology of the loss of final *-m* in Latin speech—scholars do not seem to be in agreement on this point anyway[8]—

[5] Second edition, revised. Berlin, 1961.

[6] The number in brackets refers to the reference number in Diehl's collection, from which these and all subsequent examples are taken.

[7] Cf. in this connection Emil Seelmann, *Die Aussprache des Lateins nach physiologisch-historischen Grundsätzen* (Heilbronn, 1885), wherein the author states: "Die Vulgärsprache hat . . . jedwedes M dem Schwunde preisgegeben" (p. 357 f.).

[8] On this subject cf. Robert K. Higgins, "Research Into the Phenomenon Involving Latin Final M." Unpublished Master's Essay, Columbia University, 1951.

I hope to show in my subsequent line of argument that written -*m* at this point in time (late fourth–early fifth centuries) no longer reflects a spoken /m/ accusative marker, but merely represents an orthographic tradition which some stonecutters continue to observe, in accordance with their training in Latin grammar.

But what about a form like *annu* in such expressions as *qui vixit annu et meses IIII* (3299)? Could this form, which we might assume to be an accusative without final -*m*, not also stand for a classical ablative? Singular ablative forms spelled with -*u* for the expected -*o* are attested in inscriptions from all over the Roman Empire. And although the form *annu* has generally been interpreted as an equivalent of *annum* whenever it is followed in these time expressions by the accusative plural forms *menses* and *dies*,[9] the interchangeability and practical identity of accusative and ablative in expressions of time duration—as further evidenced by the frequently concurrent use of both cases in the same inscription—would lend support to the ablative interpretation of *annu* also.[10] After all, *vixit anno* (also found on inscriptions) is perfectly acceptable to Latin grammarians,[11] even though *vixit annum* is the more usual formula in expressions indicating length of time a deceased person had lived. Thus, we are really left in the dark as to whether *annu* is to be interpreted as a classical accusative without final -*m* or an ablative in -*u* for the expected -*o*.[12]

The difficulty of deciding whether forms in -*u* represent accusatives or

[9] Otto Prinz, *De O et U vocalibus inter se mutatis in lingua latina* (Halle, 1932), 122.

[10] On the interchangeability of accusative and ablative "ad spatium temporis designandum," cf. Guilelmus Konjetzny, "De idiotismis syntacticis in titulis latinis urbanis conspicuis," *Archiv für lateinische Lexikographie und Grammatik*, 15 (1908), 297–351. Cf. also Jules Pirson, *La langue des inscriptions latines de la Gaule* (Brussels, 1901), where he states: "Dans les inscriptions de la Gaule, à quelque époque qu'elles appartiennent, l'ablatif a été complètement assimilé à l'accusatif pour exprimer la durée" (p. 183). In a similar vein, and with specific reference to inscriptions from Spain, Henry Martin makes the statement that "it is not at all rare to find the Accusative and Ablative side by side in the same expression of time, thus confirming their practical identity to express duration of time." *Notes on the Syntax of the Latin Inscriptions Found in Spain* (Baltimore, 1909), 23.

[11] Allen & Greenough's *New Latin Grammar*. Revised edition (New York, 1903), 266.

[12] Albert Carnoy suggested in his *Le latin d'Espagne d'après les inscriptions* (Louvain, 1906) that these apparent ablatives in -*u* may be due to hypercorrections of a semi-literate stonecutter who is vaguely conscious of the difference in the ablative endings of second and fourth declension nouns but no longer remembers which noun belongs to which class. Cf. also the studies by Pirson (*op. cit.*, 20) and B. Löfstedt (*op. cit.*, 116) for similar views. Since, however, more often than not fourth declension ablatives are spelled with -*o* rather than -*u*, as in the frequent occurrence of *spirito* for *spiritu* (cf. Diehl, *ILCV*, Vol. III, p. 409), one wonders whether fourth declension ablatives in -*u* were either frequent enough or exerted enough of a pressure on second declension ablatives to create such a confusion in the stonecutter's mind.

ablatives is further compounded by the fact that in some instances, as in *contra votu et dolo suo* (4181, a. 400) (for the expected *dolum suum*), forms in *-u* and *-o* occur concurrently in the same syntactic function. Are such cases to be taken as *prima facie* evidence that the form in *-u* reflects an accusative? This is, in essence, what Prinz[13] suggests when he claims that the frequent forms spelled with *-u* occurring side by side with classical ablatives in *-o* are to be interpreted as final *m*-less accusative forms. On the strength of forms like *tertiu idus, se vivu, vixit annu*, and many others, the German scholar sets out to show that in inscriptions from *Gaul* and *Italy* the *-u* spelling reflects a classical accusative case, the final *-m* having been omitted by the stonecutter for reasons of contraction, haplology (when the following word begins with *m-*), and lack of space (*margine urgente*), while in the *Iberian Peninsula* and in *Africa* the *-u* seems to stand for the classical ablative. His line of reasoning runs something like this: whenever the *-o* spelling occurs in the ablative almost to the exclusion of forms in *-u* and *-um* (the latter being an inverse spelling, also attested here and there, particularly after prepositions, as in *fecit cum maritum annos III* [4219B, a. 392]), the occasional orthographic *-u* is to be interpreted as representing the ablative case. Conversely, where frequent *-u* and *-um* spellings occur in an ablative function beside the normal ablative form in *-o* (particularly when found in the same inscription side by side), the orthographic *-u* would rather reflect a classical accusative form with the final *-m* omitted, i.e., a syntactic confusion. It is perfectly true that in many instances forms in *-u* and *-o* (and also forms in *-um*) occur on one and the same inscription in what appears to be the ablative case; by the same token, there are just as many instances, and in some cases even more (e.g., in *Rome*), where the ablative is represented by a form in *-u* exclusively. The fact that Prinz himself seems to throw up his hands in desperation when he admits "difficillimum est iudicare, utrum in U terminatione accusativus an ablativus subsit"[14] would suggest that there is hardly any point in trying to decide when the *-u* spelling stands for final Lat. /ō/ in the classical ablative, and when for a final *m*-less accusative form. Under the circumstances, Bengt Löfstedt is quite right when he states, in connection with later inscriptions (and surely he must have Christian inscriptions in mind), that it is in principle wrong to try to decide in every instance which form in *-u* stands for an accusative, and which one for an ablative; the stonecutters often did not know it themselves.[15]

The problem of the *-u* spelling for an expected accusative in *-um* or an ablative in *-o* must be considered in the light of an overall comparison of

13 *Op. cit.*, 121 ff.   14 *Ibid.*, 130.   15 *Op. cit.*, 116.

these two cases, that is, an analysis of the way accusative and ablative are orthographically represented in our documentary material. Thus, in addition to the replacement of the expected accusative in -*um* by a form in -*u* (i.e., the apparent omission of final -*m*), this case also appears spelled with -*o*, as in the already mentioned phrase *contra dolo suo*. Similar examples occur in *deo temens* (1340, a. 486), *pater titolo posuit* (3584D, AD), *tumulavit marito* (362), and passim. This spelling occurs both in direct object function and after prepositions that traditionally take the accusative case, and the phenomenon is by no means limited to a particular area. The earliest example of a direct object in -*o* is found on a Roman epitaph, which is believed to have been composed no later than the early third century: *ne quis titulo molestet* (3972). It is significant, I believe, that forms in -*o* for the expected -*um* also occur in highly formulaic expressions, such as *titulo posuit* for *titulum*, which a stonecutter would be least likely to misspell. Also, both the classical accusative in -*um* and its substitute form in -*o* occasionally appear on the same epitaph, as in *contra votum suo* (756) or *gesisti sacrum officio* (1075, a. 630), suggesting a purely formal rather than grammatical opposition between the accusative in -*um* and the ablative in -*o*.

Although the ablative is generally speaking signalled by the -*o* ending in our inscriptional material, an occasional replacement by -*u* and even -*um* is attested here and there, again without any particular restriction as to region. (*Baetica* and *Lusitania*, however, seem to show greater orthographic conservatism than any other regions of Western Romania.) The replacement of the -*o* by what would appear to be a morpho-syntactic substitution of the classical accusative for the ablative occurs particularly after prepositions, as in *de donum dei* (121), *in hoc tumulum* (3550, a. 511), *positi sunt in cimiterium* (2000, 7th cent.), *cum virginium suum* (1263a), and passim. This latter example is of some interest. The inscription on which it is found commemorates a deceased wife. On the same stone we also find another epitaph (1263b) which is dedicated to the woman's deceased daughter. Each epitaph appears to have been written by the respective husband; one of them writes: *vixit cum virginium suum*, while the other uses the correct ablative *cum virginio suo*. Does it seem likely that the hypercorrect form in -*um* should have sounded any different from that in -*o*? Sittl[16] claimed, more than half a century ago, that the form *oblatum* on an

16 Karl Sittl, "Zur Beurteilung des sog. Mittellatein," *Archiv für lateinische Lexikographie und Grammatik*, 2 (1885), 550–580. This [o] pronunciation also seems to be reflected in the *so* spelling of the verb form *sum* in *Iulia vocata so* (Diehl, 1537), found on a Roman epitaph. Cf. also W. D. Elcock, *The Romance Languages* (London, 1960), p. 28, who cites *hic so et non so* from a pagan inscription found at Naples.

inscription from *Neretum* (*Calabria*) (CIL IX 10) dated A.D. 341 was pronounced /oblato/. I am most inclined to agree with him.

Within the framework of such an analysis of these two cases—an analysis for which I used about 5,000 inscriptions, from all areas of the Western Roman Empire, to the exclusion of Africa and the eastern territories, for which a comparable study still remains to be done—and in view of the likely collapse of their opposition on the level of content, it is indeed futile to attempt to determine whether orthographic -*u* represents a classical accusative form with final -*m* omitted, or an ablative. With the fall of final -*m*, forms like *titulu* (acc.) and *titulo* (abl.) fell together in pronunciation as /titulo/, bringing about a collapse of accusative/ablative distinction, although, in terms of flexional elements, still being observed in traditional orthography, in accordance with the writer's level of instruction. It may well be, as Hugo Schuchardt[17] once suggested, that the final spoken /o/, represented in writing now by -*u* (or -*um*) now by -*o*, at first sounded like an [u]-colored [o] or an [o]-colored [u]—a "Mittellaut," to use his term; most Western Romance languages in which the final vowel survived have eventually developed an /o/, except for those dialects in which a stronger [u] coloring finally resulted in /u/, as in the general area south of Rome.[18] Thus, we see emerging a single *oblique* case form on the level of content in which semantic relationship is no longer bound to morphological distinction, the same form—innovative -*o* and residual -*u* (-*um*)—serving to express both classical accusative and ablative functions.

In this context, then, it seems reasonable to conclude that forms in -*u* are neither accusatives nor ablatives, but rather represent a "transitional" spelling in the overall process of restructuring the system of *casus obliqui* in the singular, as a result of eliminating the formal category of the accusative in -*um* from the language.

University of Illinois at Urbana

17 *Der Vokalismus des Vulgärlateins* (Paris, 1866–1888), II, 94 f.
18 Schuchardt, *loc. cit.*

15

Aspects of Roman Poetic Technique in a Carolingian Latin Satiric Text

CHARLES WITKE

E. R. Curtius has averred that "it was through Charlemagne that the historical entity which I call 'the Latin Middle Ages' was first fully constituted. . . . I use the term to designate the share of Rome, of the Roman idea of the state, of the Roman church and of Roman culture, in the physiognomy of the Middle Ages in general—a far more inclusive phenomenon, then, than the mere survival of the Latin language and literature."[1] Hence significant aspects of Carolingian Latin literature must be studied not merely in relationship to influence from classical Latin works, or in terms of imitation.[2] Yet the very term "Carolingian Latin satiric text" implies, first, the existence of a literary genre in Latin called *satura*, and second, a continuity of that genre to at least the age of Charlemagne. The term implies, in addition to such generic incitements to write and to comprehend satire, an awareness of the form *qua* form or genre. To use the formal possibilities of a literary form one must be aware of the form first; "Carolingian Latin satire" implies such an awareness.

Even in antiquity the *satura* was an elastic literary genre, accompanied by problems of definition for audience and poet alike. Elsewhere I have suggested that the Carolingian age was aware of the satiric tradition of

---

[1] E. R. Curtius, *European Literature and the Latin Middle Ages*, tr. W. Trask (New York, 1953), 27. One should also bear in mind that Charlemagne's people paid a high price for his imposing on the Franks and other peoples a language, beliefs and institutions that were basically incompatible with their own culture. For an assessment of the literary and linguistic implications of the classicism of Charlemagne's hegemony, see E. Auerbach, *Literary Language and its Public in Late Latin Antiquity and in the Middle Ages*, tr. R. Manheim (New York, 1965), 119 ff.

[2] Auerbach, *op. cit.* (*supra*, n. 1), 112 ff., and my review of the German edition of 1958, in *Speculum* 34 (1959), 440 ff.

Horace, Persius and Juvenal.[3] Further, the writer of the text under review, Theodulph of Orléans, had a good model for writing mordant invective in elegiac distichs, in the denunciation of Calvitor by an anonymous poet in the Latin Anthology, 902 Riese. Although it takes more to make a satire than such invective, I hope to demonstrate here that the verses in question are properly regarded as satire as well as satiric, even though they are an address on the theme *quo indoctior nemo*, and have no named recipient (though the addressee is very probably a specific person).

To turn briefly to the other term in this essay's title, "Roman poetic technique" means Roman norm, not Roman influence, though this latter subject could easily be analysed along historical lines. "Influence" has often been used, especially since the nineteenth century, to signify the transfer and rearrangement of literary forms and themes from one work to another. There are drawbacks to such a narrow definition of influence, especially in light of neoformalist, or structuralist, approaches to literature, according to which a form cannot be de-formed and still persist or subsist as the same form. Theme is best taken as pre-poetic outline, like a topos. The theme *per se* cannot be transferred from one work of literature to another.[4]

The metamorphic implications of "influence" (from *fluere* onward) imply that influence is an objective, tangible and measurable connection. Further, this view of influence equates it to textual parallelism or textual similarity. Actually, according to modern criticism, influence pertains only to the writer's internal intellectual or psychic experience, the world of his experience in reading and otherwise exposing himself to literature, whilst textual parallelism pertains to the world of literature itself. I propose to avoid influence and textual parallelism in favor of "norm."[5]

Many students of the continuing development of Latin literature in the post-Augustan world tend to emphasize too heavily one end of the spectrum of creativity in literature, just as the student of the more rigorously classical tends to inhabit, instinctively perhaps, the other end. I refer to a continuum running from viewing the composition of literature as a pure process of transfer and reorganization of received materials, to another extreme, that of absolutely *ex novo* creation. The one is based too closely on biological analogy, rampant in the nineteenth century, when theories

[3] For further details on Theodulph's awareness of Latin satire as a genre, see Ch. Witke, *Latin Satire* (Leiden, 1970), 168 ff.

[4] For the working definition of influence in this and the following paragraphs, see C. Guillen, *Literature as System* (Princeton, 1971), 17 ff.

[5] Cf. E. D. Hirsch, *Validity in Interpretation* (New Haven, 1967), 69 ff.

of influence and means for assessing influence were codified, especially in
the theory and practice of classical philology; the other is based illegiti-
mately on a religious analogy.[6]

The mediaevalist runs a hazard of thinking of early mediaeval Latin
texts especially in terms of how they deviate from classical practice; he runs
the risk of unconsciously measuring negative influence. What is reputed
to be valuable and interesting in such texts is what has been transferred
thither from classical literature and what has been reorganized out of a
kit of classical parts, as it were. This view thwarts a mature and insightful
critical understanding of how and why mediaeval texts are mediaeval, and
also subverts the idea of a norm, a canon of expectations on the part of
the audience and an environment of formal possibilities[7] on the part of
the poet or writer.

My task is to show how a Carolingian Latin text, written before 780 by
Theodulph of Orléans, who died around 821, and printed in the *Monumenta Germaniae Historica, Poetae Latini Aevi Carolini*, I (ed. E. Duemmler,
Berlin, 1881), pp. 464 f., is a special kind of Latin satire. I should like to
demonstrate how this text is written out of different formal possibilities
than those informing a classical text; that it is nevertheless a satire; and
that the Roman norm of poetic composition, of composing satire specifically, can be easily discerned behind stylistic, syntactic and grammatical
elements which are definitely post-classical, that is, Carolingian in this
text.

> Illum non sal, non istum sapientia condit,
>   hunc doctrina nequit vincere, sal nec eum.
> doctrinam cuius vanum est adhibere medullis,
>   quoque magis doceas, stultior inde fiet.
> sic crudum studeat laterem dum quisque lavare,   5
>   quo magis eluerit, plus facit inde luti.
> quid bona verba iuvant, ubi nil habet alma voluntas,
>   aut quid in urticis semina iacta iuvent?
> flava quid horrendis prosunt data mella lacunis,
>   quid litor aut olei stercore mixtus aget?   10
> quid iuvat aurito lyra si persultet asello,
>   cornigero aut lituus si strepat arte bovi?
> sole oriente viget quantum tua visio, caece,
>   tantum eius sensus post bona verba solet.
> carmina plura queunt, nequeunt tamen omnia, quamvis 15
>   littera gentilis, hoc quoque sancta canit.

---

[6] On originality and influence, see also R. Wellek and A. Warren, *Theory of Literature*[3]
(New York, 1956), 257 ff.

[7] Cf. K. Vietor, *Geist und Form* (Bern, 1952), 300.

dicitur et Circe socios insignis Ulyssis
 mutasse in varias carminis arte feras.
plurima cum possint, scabiem sanare nequibunt,
 tinea nec horum murmure sana fiet.   20
ut tamen illa nihil cui manserit hernia prosunt,
 cumque fiunt, totum perditur illud opus:
sic deperdet opus tibi qui, simulator inique,
 quiddam nisus erit insinuare boni.
denique rex sapiens cum plurima dixerit istinc,   25
 hoc unum exempli ponere sorte libet.
si contusus erit pilae in vertigine stultus
 ut far, segnities non sua linquet eum.
verba ducis posui, ponam quid rustica plebes
 re bene de tali dicere saepe solet: 30
non facere hoc usu, non verbere quibis, ut unquam
 bubo sit accipiter, qui petat ungue grues,
utque tuum officium, cape, vultur possit habere,
 est quia tardus, edax, inque vehendo gravis.
discere nulla cupit bona, sed mala discere cuncta,   35
 vis cur hoc faciat discere? stultus inest.
hic Iuda peior, melior te, Petre, videri
 vult, mala multa tegit sors simulante peplo.
hic bona parva putat magna, et mala plurima nulla:
 se, cum vult alios fallere, fallit inops.   40

The text before us is Latin. The *langue* of which this is a *parole* is a system, not merely the sum of all extant Latin words, phrases or indeed sentences.[8] Rather it is a system which can generate new phrases and sentences by means of its grammar, and hence can generate new poems by means of the grammar of literature. The *parole* itself, namely this text beginning with *illum* and ending with *inops*, is likewise a system of signifiers and of signifieds. Classical Latin satire is not coterminous with all extant works of Horace, Persius and Juvenal. It too is a system, a network of formal opportunities or possibilities, of incitations to commit or to understand *satura*.[9] This text's signifiers and significations, locked into arbitrary and conventional relationships first on the merely semantic level (the poem is in Latin, not Greek or Japanese), reflect this arbitrary associativeness on

[8] The terms are borrowed, of course, from F. de Saussure, *Cours de linguistique générale*[3] (Paris, 1967), passim. See also J. Culler, *Structuralist Poetics* (Ithaca, 1975), 8 ff. My adaptation of certain structuralist frames of reference for situating the problems of Theodulph's text implies nothing about the efficacy of structuralism (or of post-structuralism) as a means of critically approaching classical or mediaeval works of literature.

[9] Cf. C. A. van Rooy, *Studies in Classical Satire and Related Literary Theory* (Leiden, 1965), 30 ff.

another level: the text is not an epic fragment or a romance, but a satire.

How is this known? The first two lines provide an answer. The *ego*, the "I" speaking the poem, the first-person singular of the verb system, is asserting the inoperability of intellectual activity on *illum*. Even though no first-person singular verb appears until line 29, we must understand that the speaker is speaking *in propria persona*, and that the whole poem is a pronouncement, a speech act, in the first person singular. In poems in Latin where the speaker goes on at some length to characterize in negative terms the shortcomings of another, speaking from a judgmental perspective that is rarely tested and sometimes cleverly concealed, we have either a comic excerpt or *satura*, including satiric invective. The former possibility can be ruled out by the absence from this text of other arbitrary systems of the comic, viz., dialogue between characters, reversal of expectations, surprise, and other familiar elements. It can also be demonstrated on an *a priori* basis that Carolingian Latin court poetry did not develop extra-classical genres, and that this poem is not a modern forgery.

If, as I believe, this *parole* or speech act is in the *langue* of satire, what do its signifiers and significations do that is different from other examples of an earlier, or classical, stage of the development of this *langue*? What systems does the relationship between signifier and signified constitute—systems that are like other ones, yet unlike? Another way of asking this question is, how does the writer make this writing something that his audience and he himself can decode without being an antiquarian or indulging in pre-artistic archaeology? Alternatively, how does the writer make a speaking voice, the first-person singular, which is intelligible not only on the level of Latin (e.g., these are well-formed grammatical sentences) but simultaneously on the level of code or the generic level?[10] Further, how does the "I," first-person singular, show that he has naturalized both *langue* and *parole*, and is not fashioning or re-fashioning an antique artifact? In a word, what is traditional and what is Carolingian?

I shall invert the order of this query and deal first, and primarily, with what is Carolingian; because one may assume that readers are already familiar with the larger hallmarks of the classical exercise of satire, such as direct address of the reader, as we see in line 36 of Theodulph's text; abrupt beginnings, as in line 1; the proverb, as in lines 5 ff., and again in 27 f.; and the whole practical everyday tone of the piece, with its exempla drawn equally from life and from literature; and also the discrepancy

---

10 "Writing" here subsumes a view of the post-structuralist J. Derrida, *Of Grammatology*, tr. G. C. Spivak (Baltimore, 1976), 6 ff. However, I do not intend my term "writing" to be only so narrowly construed.

between outer appearance and inner reality of moral status, as in lines 37 f.[11] Whilst these formal features assist in identifying this poem as satire, they do not alone constitute what I would call the Roman norm.

What is Carolingian in this text could be divided into what is non-Roman as well as what is reworking or reshaping of what is Roman. However, there would be no advantage in pursuing such a dichotomy, which might induce our methodology merely to discover what is Latin, and to call this simple heuristic exercise by a grandiose name, perhaps "structuralist approach." I prefer to isolate what is Carolingian the way one would isolate the idiolects of any given text, without bias concerning good, i.e., classical practice, and bad, i.e., mediaeval distortion, to mention cryptic prejudices all too often met with in classical scholarship that extends itself to post-classical concerns.

First of all, we may note that each couplet is end-stopped, that is, it finishes a sentence; this situation is rarely met with in twenty continuous couplets of Roman elegy, and ostensibly is an aesthetic blemish. Such repetition violates a sense of expectation for *variatio*. Second, the poem seems to have no coherent thematic structure. That is, its poetic texture seems to be meagerly derived not from metaphor or even metonymy but principally from the regular recurring units of the meter, which some would say recurs all too regularly indeed, as well as ending monotonously in sentences coinciding with the end of each couplet.

Another post-classical feature in this text is the use of the pronouns *illum, istum, hunc,* and *eum* at the opening; if by these pronouns only one person is signified their use is illogical and improper. However, one might see in this series of pronouns a sort of *priamel* wherein various evidences of stupidity are catalogued. Then the text goes on to concentrate on the kind of *stultus* who merely becomes *stultior* the more he is instructed. This obliging the reader or audience to sort out *en route* these two possibilities is obviously a feature of post-antique rather than of classical poetry. Texts from the classical period rarely are ambiguous in this non-creative way, and some would say that the text before us is therefore of a low grade for reasons apart from the quality of Latinity displayed. To this one can only observe that mediaeval art is not classical art. Some would see in the attack on a variety of *stulti* that veers off into a series of illustrations on the observation that innately depraved character cannot be changed for the good by teaching or discipline, and that culminates in an identification of

---

[11] Witke, *op. cit.* (*supra,* n. 3), passim and 271 ff. For a view that Latin satire did not continue beyond Juvenal, see M. Coffey, *Roman Satire* (London–New York, 1976; I have not had access to this book).

the *stultus* with one who is morally defective, not so much disjointed thinking as evidence of the Christian axiom that the interior life is a continuum, and that failing to heed instruction puts one in the camp of scoundrels, hypocrites and Judas himself. What would in classical poetry have been a human type is in this mediaeval text confined to an unnamed individual whom the poet detests. But he detests him for his evil, which brings us to the somewhat more general conclusion about moral evil, lines 37 ff. This view is consonant with Carolingian concerns to upgrade the quality of moral life and to do it by didactic means: a basic premise of Christianity itself as well.

Further, this text is Carolingian in that there is a relative absence of reiterative patterns, such as those formed in classical poetry by tense, person, grammar itself in other ways; by theme, image or lexical choice.[12] Meter and the voice of the narrator alone unify and poeticize this text, it would appear. However, the relatively low frequency of such features should not lead us to conclude that the text is not poetically functional or that it is merely phatic. Two basic modes of arrangement are used in behavior that is verbal: selection and combination. Selection of words in a speech chain is based on equivalence, similarity and dissimilarity, synonymity and antonymity; the combination of words, the syntactical build-up or sequence, is based on contiguity. If the poetic function of language projects from the axis of such selection along the lines of contiguity into the axis of combination, as in Roman Jakobson's famous aphorism, then equivalence is made to become the organizing principle, the constructive device of poetry.[13]

It is because such a principle of equivalence can be demonstrated in the poem of Theodulph under review that it is undeniably poetic. Further, the principle of equivalence is projected into the axis of selection in a special way. The equivalents themselves, the syllables as units of measure (all shorts are equally short, all longs equally long), the reiterative figures of sense and hence of sound in this text, are Roman, or more precisely, are selected in accord with a Roman norm. This norm is, grossly, the elegiac meter. More finely, it can be seen in respect for word-boundaries at the diaeresis, in chiastic arrangements such as *illum non sal | sal nec eum*, lines 1 and 2, i.e., pronoun-negative conjunction-noun, where noun equivalence is also semantic and lexical identity. Examples may also be found in the

---

12 See, e.g., J. P. Elder, "The 'Figure of Grammar' in Catullus 51," *The Classical Tradition: Literary and Historical Studies in Honor of Harry Caplan*, ed. L. Wallach (Ithaca, 1966), 202 ff.

13 R. Jakobson, "Linguistics and Poetics," *Style in Language*, ed. T. A. Sebeok (Cambridge, Massachusetts, 1960).

alteration of finite verb indicative present active / finite verb subjunctive present active in lines 7 and 8, and again in lines 9 and 10, 11 and 12, framed by an inversion of this pattern in lines 5 and 6, *studeat/facit* and a variation, indicative / indicative in lines 13 and 14. Such patternings can be found in many continuous passages of Vergil or Ovid, and are akin to the organizing principles one comes upon in Merovingian Latin poetry, such as organization of strophes by means of the physical senses of sight, smell, etc., in Fortunatus' *Vexilla regis*.[14]

But if the empirical linguistic data are constituted on a Roman basis, out of the resources of the Latin poetical language, and selected in accord with the, or a, Roman norm, the referential function of the text and its cumulative aesthetic impact are not Roman but mediaeval: specifically, early mediaeval style associated with the court of Charlemagne, its widespread veneration of the Augustan poets, and its wholesale, even uncritical, adoption of their poetic techniques, to use them to compose unroman, unaugustan poetic texts.[15] The tension between the Roman norm and the mediaeval reference and aesthetic can be seen to a greater extent in other forms, particularly panegyric and epic, and need not detain us here.

Once agreement is reached that this text is poetic use of language, we must press on with another question: are its poetical qualities mere versification along Roman canonical lines, normative in that sense, following techniques dead and gone with the rest of Romanitas? Has Roman metaphor left behind only the empty shell of mediaeval metonymy? Does the absence of metaphor, that poetic trope *par excellence*, leave us with a prosaic variety of metrical art?[16] Mediaeval Latin literary theory shares with Old Indic a clear dichotomization of two poles of verbal art, *ornatus difficilis* and *ornatus facilis*. The latter is much harder to analyse, both linguistically and from a literary critical point of view, since the language has few verbal devices and is close to everyday referential language. Yet I submit that the prolonged grammatical trope noticed above in reference to the verbs in lines 5 through 14 would alone lift this text from the realm of metrical prose. Further figures and tropes concealed in the morphological and syntactical choices of these lines can readily be found by the attentive reader. The poet has exploited the poetic resources adhering in both the *langue*, Latin, and the *parole*, the genre of satire. A dearth of lexical tropes

---

[14] This poem will be discussed in a forthcoming paper.

[15] See Auerbach, *op. cit.* (*supra*, n. 1), 117 ff.

[16] Culler, *op. cit.* (*supra*, n. 8), 179 ff.; for the subsequent statement on *ornatus*, see Jakobson, *loc. cit.* (*supra*, n. 13).

beyond the proverbs in lines 5–6 and 27–28 should not dull our response to the poetic texture of this metonymical composition.

Latin satire is not a genre relying heavily on the arsenal of poetic techniques familiar in, say, Roman lyric or mediaeval hymn. Absence of much poetic density in a satiric piece of writing or in formal satire should not cause alarm or provoke opinions about mediaeval incompetency to compose satire. Classical satire's meter is not elegy, but hexameter. Theodulph, however, is using *the* didactic meter for his age. His elegiacs are functionally the hexameters of the Augustans. Here again Ovid's example in the *Ars Amatoria* can be adduced. But further, generic deviance can easily be seen in this case as one of those literary mutations which uphold a conservative tradition whilst seemingly slighting it. Genre and metre are inextricably twined together in both the classical and the mediaeval practice of Latin poetry. Yet even in the classical age, experimentation was carried forth, as can be seen from a close examination of Ovid, whose elegiacs (apart from the *Ars Amatoria*) yielded motifs and poetic principles of organization also to his epic *Metamorphoses*.

Let us now examine Theodulph's text for more local effects. What sets it off from the Roman practice of the genre of satire? Intense observation yields relatively little, apart from too great regularity of diaeresis, absense of caesura, certain traps of syntax (in lines 39 f., for instance), that would presumably have not been imposed on a Roman audience for such a poem; and, of course, relatively minor cultural shifts, such as *littera sancta*, line 16, *rex sapiens*, i.e., Solomon, line 25, Judas and Peter, line 37. Apart from these, the *ingenium* of the poem's *parole* is Roman, just as the ethos or grammaticality of the *langue* is Latin.

What, then, gives it a Carolingian aesthetic, as I have several times asserted it has? It would seem to subsist in the *rate* of selection of elements of equivalency, and the lack of variety with which they are projected into combination. See, for instance, *discere/discere/discere*, lines 35 f.; *nulla/cuncta*, line 35; *peior/melior*, line 37; *fallere/fallit*, and *se/alios*, line 40, to confine observation solely to those visible on the level of lexical choice, from the poem's locale where parallelisms dramatically increase toward the closure of the poem. A more Roman norm for such combinations can also be seen in this text, such as the bracketing of such topical units as lines 4 and 20, *fiet/fiet*; or 15 and 25, *plura/plurima*, with *plurima* also in line 19, in the middle as it were; see also lines 15 and 19, *nequeunt/nequibunt*, on a smaller scale of separation. But even here, such dense lexical repetition is unroman, or worse, a feature of bad Roman poetry, such as the repetition of morphological units in a touchstone of bad Roman verse, Cicero's "o fortunatam natam me consule Romam!"

None can deny that the principles of selection and of combination on the linguistic, lexical, semantic and generic levels are principles of Roman poetic composition, specifically of satire, that is, are elements of the Roman norm. The out-of-scale usage, dense frequency and lack of inflectional variation of the choices, however, are Carolingian. Poetic texture is achieved through repetition and density; the scale of the reactive units or locales of the text is relatively small, although larger units (such as lines 4 and 20, as mentioned above) do occur, and seem to offer our best evidence of the Roman norm.

Roman too is the reliance on exempla drawn from vivid scenes of everyday life, such as the man who in vain washes a brick,[17] or the proverb from the *Old Testament*, *Proverbs* 27:22, in the Vulgate "si contuderis stultum in pila quasi ptisanas feriente desuper pilo, non auferetur ab eo stultitia eius" (5 f.; 27 f.). Further, the Roman norm is at work in selecting the wisdom of the *rustica plebes*, closer to nature and hence to timeless truths (lines 29 ff.), here exemplified in the comparison of rates of velocity of birds of prey, such as owl and hawk, vulture and falcon. The comparison is merely incidental to the inability to change the innate nature and capacities of the birds mentioned, and, by implication, the inability of art or training to alter any living being's innate nature: a point not to be confused with the Christian doctrine of salvation for all who heed the teachings of the church. Theodulph's victim is being satirized (a classical literary activity), not relegated to damnation (a Christian pastoral function). It is precisely at this juncture of ancient poetic practice—viz. the genre of satire with its overdrawn denunciation, and Christian doctrine and convention of salvation for the transgressor—that the classical-Carolingian frontier is most uneasy. However, one may say that Christian institutions have been so thoroughly internalized (e.g., Judas and Peter, line 37) that they disappear behind the artistic fabric, the literary artifact, the text itself. Probably the original audience saw no discrepancy between asserting the impossibility of growth or development or alteration of habit, and the doctrine of accessibility for all to God's grace, once the second idea had deeply sunk into the culture, and was perhaps as removed from daily Carolingian social and hortatory concerns as it is now.

The compartmentalization of the birds, their classification and incipient grouping as noble (hawk, falcon) and ignoble (vulture, owl) is also Carolingian, or at least in the spirit of an Isidore, who provides a useful if dubious etymology in this connection: "capus Italica lingua dicitur a

---

[17] A. Otto, *Die Sprichwörter der Römer* (Leipzig, 1890), s.v. *later*, has seven citations, of course not including Theodulph.

capiendo. hunc nostri falconem vocant."[18] The observation of the world of nature, to return later in Walahfrid Strabo, is here nevertheless Roman in spirit and akin to, say, Horace *Satires* 2.6. It is thoroughly Augustan.

One may also with confidence assert a Roman value expressed in the words "poetry can do many things, but not all," line 15. Some persons, the poet admits, can never be reached and taught; all the art and wisdom cannot dissuade the fool from his folly, the dissimulator from his deception. This insight proceeds more from an awareness of human nature than of theology or even practical pastoral experience. That same human nature was well studied in the Roman comedians, as well as in Ovid, who at *Fasti* 6.469 uses the locution *auritis . . . asellis*, should one seek for a classical parallel for the well-known and obvious zoological feature of the ass-ears in line 11 of Theodulph's text.[19] Ovid likewise asked in *Metamorphoses* 7.167, "quid enim non carmina possint?", with *carmina* in the sense of spells. The more mundane or realistic Carolingian court poet limits himself to qualifying poetry's capacity to effect change. Even the exemplum from the *Odyssey* (17 f.), via Vergil, *Eclogues* 8.70, "carminibus Circe socios mutavit Ulixi," with *carminibus* again meaning spells, puts everyday and very mediaeval limits on what verbal art of any kind can do to or for a closed mind. The day for incantations was past.

We find in these borrowings from Ovid and from Vergil classical influence of a mechanical sort, mere transferred verbal signals, mentioned at the outset of this discussion. It would, however, be rash and narrow in outlook for the critic, on the basis of such textual parallels, to say that this poem is classically influenced. If we can see the Roman norm at work, shaping this poem, it is in the areas I have drawn attention to, and it is not limited to mere verbal parallelisms, interesting and important in their own right though they be. The Roman norm can be seen best in such features as the purely operational terms in which *ille*, the stupid man, is characterized up to lines 23 f., where the depiction turns assertive or descriptive.

What is post-Augustan, post-antique, is best characterized by the end-stopped lines, a doublet pattern signalled at the outset by *sal* repeated in two lines of parallel grammar and syntax recurring in narrow space (1 f.) and reinforced by *variatio* in lines 4 and 6. This locus and other similar ones in the poem suggest that a binary code pervades this text; an algorithm is demanded by such poetic parallelism as *nulla/cuncta*, line 35,

---

[18] Isidore, *Etym.* XII.7.57. Cf. Du Cange, s.v. *capus*; the bird might also be a hunting hawk.

[19] The proverb ὄνος λύρας in Latin has also a long career; see Otto, *op. cit.* (*supra*, n. 17), s.v. *asinus*. Cf. Boethius, *Cons. Phil.* I.4.

peior/melior, line 37, and many other locations. Such parallelisms are not to be explained by adducing poverty of intellect or of poetic technique. The procedure of the two-line units both strengthens the dichotomy of binary opposition and draws attention to the problem of juxtaposition of king and peasant, noble and ignoble bird, sighted and blind, honey and dank caves, cleansing agent[20] and filth, music and the brute animal world, strength and inefficiency, and all of the other contrasting, antonymic equivalencies with which this text abounds, and which form its principle of poetic organization. These juxtapositions, in turn, underlie the major confrontation of the text, its major contrast, that of *sapiens* or the I-narrator, and *stultus*. The line-formation in two-line units does not permit qualification, run over, shading, nuance or perspective: only confrontation.

Elsewhere I have tried to show that Theodulph of Orléans is different from a Roman satirist, in having in his Christian culture a calculus of values dichotomized along clear-cut, even binary lines.[21] We are not far in the Middle Ages from those great static balancings in visual art of virtues and vices in dichotomized adversary relationships. There are four manuscripts of the ninth century that present such arrangements of the virtues and vices: Bern, Burgerbibl. Cod. 264; Leyden, Cod. Bur. Q3; Brussels, Bibl. Roy. ms 974; and Paris, B.N. lat. 8085. The first is probably from St. Gallen. All are considered of the second half of the ninth century. Theodulph is conceiving of his balancings along lines that may have had their origins in a fifth century archetype for Prudentius' *Psychomachia*.[22] At any rate, the literary pairing is not Roman, but Carolingian.

It should come as no surprise to the careful student of post-classical Latin literature to see how a Latin satirist of the Carolingian court, though working from entirely different cultural premises, uses the Roman norm of satire to fashion a message of counsel and of insight into abiding human characteristics, though the message be unmistakably Carolingian in aesthetic impact.*

University of Michigan

20 Line 10, *litor*, var. *lutor*, "washer," "fuller."
21 See above, n. 3.
22 A. E. M. Katzenellenbogen, *Allegories of the Virtues and Vices in Mediaeval Art from the Early Christian Times to the Thirteenth Century* (London, Warburg Institute, 1939), passim. I am indebted to my colleague Professor Ilene Forsyth for aid in assessing the manuscript evidence.
* [Theodulph, 1 *sal* . . . 2 *sal* : Read 1 *sal* . . . 2 *sol*. For, 2 *doctrina* = *sol* ∽ 13 f. *bona verba* = *sol*. Cf. Cicero *De fin.* 1.71 *ea quae dixi sole ipso illustriora et clariora sunt.*—Line 10 *litor* . . . *olei* : Read *liquor* . . . *olei*: Unguent is applied to a clean, not to a dirty body.— *Editor.*]